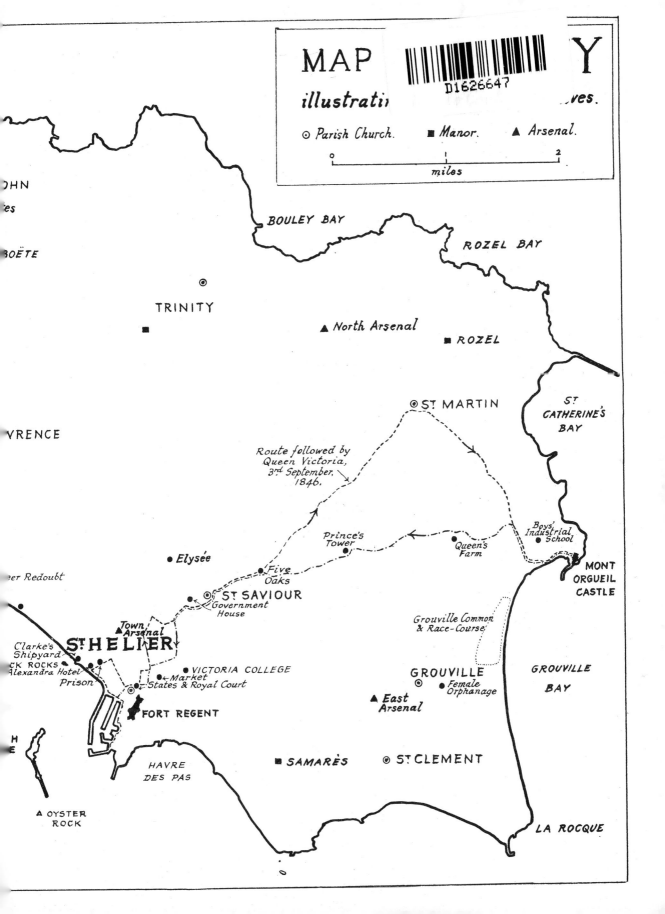

In memory of Roma!
Thank you for everything;
Adam

VICTORIAN VOICES

VICTORIAN VOICES

An introduction to the papers of

SIR JOHN LE COUTEUR, Q.A.D.C., F.R.S.

by

JOAN STEVENS

Drawings by
CHARLES STEVENS

"Oh! This is Le Couteur".

His Majesty
King **WILLIAM IV**, in London
27th October, 1830

By the same Author:

Old Jersey Houses, 1965
Second Edition, 1966

DEDICATED TO

the descendants of Sir John Le Couteur,
who have faithfully preserved these
papers, to the great benefit of posterity.

Published by La Société Jersiaise,
Pier Road, St. Helier, Jersey,
Channel Isles.

Printed by Litho-Print & Ashelford, Jersey.

1969

FOREWORD

Diaries are a fascinating form of literature because they give a far greater insight into the writer's life and character than does either an autobiography or a biography. This is even true to some extent when the diarist has an eye, as did Pepys, on future publication. A man is frank with himself if with no one else, and when he keeps a diary he commits to paper many things which he would be unwilling to disclose to others. It is this frankness which makes the published diary so popular.

Jersey has long boasted of Jean Chevalier, a contemporary of Pepys, who in his own way rivals that king of diarists. His diary has left us an unparalleled picture of the Island during the troublous times of the Civil War. Other Islanders, such as Daniel Messervy, have made their contribution to this particular form of literature. Both Chevalier's and Messervy's diaries have been published by the Société Jersiaise, which is now publishing "Victorian Voices", a work principally based on the diaries of that eminent Jerseyman, Sir John Le Couteur.

There is a notable difference between Chevalier and Messervy on the one hand and Le Couteur on the other; the former were Islanders whose world was Jersey; the latter was a man whose world was the world.

The Société is indebted to the Sumner family for access to Le Couteur's diaries and other papers and to Mrs. Joan Stevens for undertaking the considerable task of presenting them in what is so acceptable a form, as well as for making their publication financially possible. Those who have read the same author's "Old Jersey Houses" will have expected her to have carried out the task—which has been more in the nature of a labour of love—in an exemplary manner and in this they will not be disappointed.

Mrs. Stevens has skilfully conjured from the diaries and other papers the real Sir John Le Couteur—a man of many parts—a great son of Jersey, who achieved much both inside and outside his native Island; and she has also conjured up the Jersey which he served so well.

Each person who reads this book will have his favourite chapter. Mine is undoubtedly that which gives an account of Queen Victoria's visit to Jersey in 1846. However, it is not only from the text, but also from the many excellent illustrations, that pleasure is to be derived.

As with all books which trace a person's life from birth to death, the reader is sad when the last words have been read and the story told. So it is with "Victorian Voices" and one feels a sense of loss when one reads of "Grampy's" death at his beloved Belle Vue and lays aside the book.

RAOUL LEMPRIERE
President of the Société Jersiaise.

PREFACE

In these chapters I have tried to convey the extent and purport of the voluminous manuscripts preserved by the Le Couteur family of Belle Vue in Jersey. They fill over one hundred closely written books, and many unbound documents as well. They have taken eighteen months to read and index. For the most part, they are from the pen of Sir John Le Couteur, though some are written by members of his family. It is a miracle that they have survived the vicissitudes of the century which has elapsed since his death and have now, through the generosity of Sir John's descendants, been placed at the disposal of La Société Jersiaise, in whose name I have the honour to offer this book to the public.

We owe a substantial debt of gratitude to successive generations of the family for preserving these archives, and in particular to the late Mr. Cyril Sumner who, a fortnight after the Liberation of Jersey in 1945, wrote: "I have all Sir John's diaries safe, and of course the Bible and telescope". There are, in fact, gaps in the diary series and one cannot tell whether those missing have been lost, or were for some reason never written. Unfortunately one of the gaps is for the years 1831-39, the period of his greatest activity, but the letter-books and other papers to some extent compensate for this loss.

This is not quite the first attempt to share the Le Couteur archives with the reading public. About a quarter of a century ago Mrs. Gould, née Sumner, great-granddaughter of Sir John, began to compose a manuscript based on some of the more interesting episodes in his life. But the war intervened, and she was not able to complete the task in her lifetime.

The archives are nearly all in English, though Sir John could write fluent French when occasion arose, and spoke Jersey-French as well. They fall into four groups, of which the most important is the diaries. The second group is Sir John's letter-books, in which he kept meticulous copies of important letters he wrote, though he rarely kept any he received. The third group is a miscellany of account books, notes on Jersey history, poems, pedigrees, and some of the diaries of his parents and grand-father. The fourth group includes the family's drawings, paintings and sketch-books. Sir John's mother painted some lively water-colours in the West Indies, and his wife's album of paintings of fruit is spectacular. His son showed similar talent with pencil and brush, and Sir John himself contributed a number of sketches and paintings. They all enjoyed drawing the vessels they saw in Island waters and further afield, and the archives contain dozens of little ships of every shape and size.

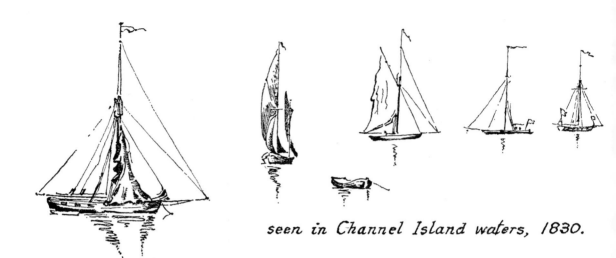

seen in Channel Island waters, 1830.

A comprehensive and detailed index of the archives has been prepared and has been lodged with them in the Library of La Société Jersiaise, where I hope it will be of assistance to any researcher on social conditions in Jersey and elsewhere during the period, or on any other fact or facet of these documents.

There is material here to cater for every taste. Conversations with important men, and eye-witness accounts of great events could by themselves fill a volume: agricultural matters another: military subjects a third. The contents are so rich that only the cream has been taken, though, to be sure, it is Jersey cream and therefore a good proportion of the whole. Readers may sometimes be disappointed at not being told the sequel to some episode, but in order to avoid a book of excessive length I have confined myself as a rule to the information given in the archives. I have also refrained from giving biographical details of individuals, if such are accessible elsewhere, and here the Dictionary of National Biography and Balleine's Biographical Dictionary of Jersey usually provide the information sought.

The first diary in the collection begins in 1786 and the last is for the year 1890; and as we turn their pages we perceive the robust ways of the Georgian era giving place to the serene attitudes of full Victorianism. But there were even more dramatic changes taking place during this period. In the early diaries we are travelling by sailing-ship and post-chaise: at the end, in steamers and express-trains. Things undreamed of when we began reading are commonplace as we close. The gas, electric light, telescopes, railway tunnels and letter-boxes which the first diarist never knew are taken for granted by the last. Inventions and novelties crowd their way into these years at speed, more slowly, it is true, than in the twentieth century, but a great deal faster than ever yet seemed possible.

Born in 1794, Sir John Le Couteur died in 1875, shortly after being knighted, an honour which his "beloved Harriet" did not live to know, and enjoyed by him for only a small fraction of his life. Nevertheless I have called him Sir John, once he was grown up, to distinguish him from his father and his son, both named John Le Couteur, and from his grandfather and son-in-law, both John likewise. Of Sir John himself we gain the impression of a man of unbounded vitality and an unusually wide variety of interests: who could approach a technical problem with the mind of a scientist, an aesthetic matter with the eye of an artist: who could design a gun, befriend a stray kitten, plead in Court, judge a cow, plant dahlias, dine with monarchs, and sit for hours at the bedside of an invalid employee. He had an unconcealed affection for his family. His home, Belle Vue, was the centre of a gay social life, with parties occurring at breathless pace: and here, as time went on, children, grandchildren and great-grandchildren came to enjoy its happy atmosphere and liberal hospitality. Profoundly religious, and of great moral rectitude, he had a keen sense of humour, and though generous in word and in kind to those who deserved it, his criticism of those who fell below his own high standards could be scathing. He had his faults. Who has not? But after reading through this great mass of literature I, for one, am left with the impression of a great and lovable man.

La Grange,
St. Mary,
Jersey.
1969.   JOAN STEVENS.

CONTENTS

xv

B

PHOTOGRAPHS

xvii

DRAWINGS

ACKNOWLEDGEMENTS

The author of a survey of this kind is inevitably indebted to many fellow-workers and friends who have assisted in it. Foremost, of course, are Mrs. Cyril Sumner and her children, John, Nancy and David, who so generously passed over the whole collection to La Société Jersiaise, permitted many photographs to be taken, and also caused to be restored and then presented to La Société Boaden's splendid portrait of Sir John.

I have, for the past two years, pestered many friends for help in specialised subjects and sought information from many Government departments, both in Jersey and in England, and to them all I am most grateful. Amongst those who have been so kind I should like to mention: Mr. P. Ahier, Mr. J. Appleby, Miss J. Arthur, Dr. J. Bell (of the Plant Breeding Institute, Cambridge), Mr. P. Bisson, Mr. S. W. Bisson, Dr. J. R. Blench, Major Boyne, Mr. P. Collins, Miss R. de Saumarez, Mr. G. Drew, Dr. W. Mortimer Evans, Mr. J. Faiers, Miss P. Le Feuvre, Brigadier R. Lemprière-Robin, Mr. A. Le Sueur, Mrs. F. Le Sueur, Mr. R. Long, Mrs. W. Macready, Sir Robert Marett, Mr. R. Mayne, Dr. A. E. Mourant, Mr. A. Podger, Mr. H. Porter, Colonel J. Pallot, Mr. L. Sinel, Mr. G. Speer, Field Marshal Sir Gerald Templer, Mr. J. C. Vincent, Dr. F. Wakelam and Miss P. Webb. And also my daughter Collette, who gave many hours on two successive annual holidays to help me with the typing, and with expert advice on horsemanship. And most of all, of course, my husband, without whose ever constructive criticism and generous encouragement I could not have faced this important and rewarding task. He also transcribed many of the letters from the Crimea, no easy task, and prepared all the maps and drawings which, with very few exceptions, have been taken from sketches by Sir John, his mother, his wife and his son. The drawings of Queen Victoria's carriage and of Government House are adapted from the Ouless engravings.

Over photographic illustrations I have been especially fortunate. These, aside from a few snapshots of my own, are the work of experts in this field, who were often set well-nigh impossible tasks. I particularly mention:

Professor H. A. Nieboer	(13, 14, 17, 34, 37).
Mr. R. Le Vaillant	(I, III, IV, V, 8, 11, 23, 24, 25, 26, 27, 29, 33, 38, 39, 40, 42, 43, 44, 50, 51, 52).
Mr. A. Davey	(30).
Mr. E. F. Guiton	(22).
Lady McKie	(1).
Mr. R. C. Querée	(4, 10, 16, 41, 45, 47).
Mr. S. Senett	(31).
Mr. E. A. Sollars	(36, 46, 53, 55, 56).
Mr. G. R. R. Stevens	(5, 12, 15, 18, 19, 20, 54, 57).

No. 7 was supplied by the courtesy of Mr. L. Hymer of Montreal: no. 15 by that of Mrs. M. Godfrey of Le Bocage: and no. 32 by that of Mr. R. Mayne. Also:—

The National Portrait Gallery	(28).
The National Maritime Museum, Greenwich	(9).
The Jersey Department of Education	(50, 51).
The Jersey Department of Public Works	(V, 43).
La Société Jersiaise	(II, VI, VII, VIII, 6, 7, 22, 24, 25, 30).

CHRONOLOGY OF THE LIFE OF SIR JOHN LE COUTEUR, IN THE CONTEXT OF WORLD EVENTS (the latter being shown in Italics.)

1781. The Battle of Jersey.
1794. Birth of Sir John Le Couteur.
1798. Birth of Harriet Janvrin, his wife.
      Battle of the Nile.
1799. His father's appointment as Inspector of Jersey Militia.
1800. Markets transferred from Royal Square to present site.
1805. *Battle of Trafalgar.*
1806. Foundation stone of Fort Regent laid.
1807. *Abolition of slave trade.*
1808. Sir John at Marlowe Military College.
1810. Commissioned as Ensign in 96th (Manchester) Regiment.
1811. Promoted Lieutenant in 104th Regiment (Munster Fusiliers). Sent to New Brunswick.
1812. *First steam vessel in the Clyde.*
1813. The winter march of the 104th.
      Westminster Bridge first lighted with gas.
1814. Present at Battle of Niagara and siege of Fort Erie.
      Peace declared with America.
1815. *Battle of Waterloo.*
1816. Appointed A.D.C. to his father in Curaçao.
1817. Returned to Jersey on leave. Became engaged. Returned to Canada.
1818. 104th Regiment disbanded. Placed on half-pay as Captain. Married Harriet Janvrin.
1819. Birth of his daughter Harriet.
      McAdam's road surfacing introduced in England.
1820. Birth of his son John (died 1821).
1821. Appointed A.D.C. to Sir Colin Halkett, with Militia rank of Lieutenant Colonel. Birth of daughter Mary. Acquisition by Britain of present Government House.
1823. Given command of the North-West Regiment of Militia.
1826. Elected Constable of St. Brelade. Opening of St. Aubin's Market. Birth of his son John Halkett Le Couteur.
1827. *Battle of Navarino.*
1828. Responsible for providing Jersey's first life-boat. Theatre Royal opened.
      Duke of Wellington Prime Minister.
1829. *Policemen introduced by Sir Robert Peel.*
1830. Re-elected Constable of St. Brelade.
      Revolution in France. Abdication of Charles X. Accession of Louis Philippe, the "Citizen King".
1831. *Accession of William IV.*
      Appointed A.D.C. to William IV (the first appointment of its kind).
1832. Cholera epidemic.
      Reform Bill. Others followed in 1867 and 1884.

1833.	*Act for Abolition of slavery in British Dominions.*
	Appointed Secretary of newly formed Royal Jersey Agricultural and Horticultural Society.
1835.	Elected Jurat (fiercely contested election).
1836.	Published book "On the varieties, properties and classification of wheat".
1837.	*Accession of Queen Victoria, on death of her uncle.*
	Confirmation of position as Q.A.D.C. Resigned position as Jurat.
1838.	Elected a Member of the (later Royal) Society of Arts.
1839.	*Penny post established in Britain.*
	Elected President of the R.J.A. & H.S. (also in 1847, 1853 and 1868).
1840.	*Marriage of Queen Victoria to Prince Consort.*
1842.	Marriage of daughter Mary to Rev. John Maunoir Sumner. Appointed Vicomte de Jersey. Exchanged from North-West to South-West Regiment of Militia.
1843.	Elected a Fellow of the Royal Society.
1846.	*Repeal of Corn Laws. Irish potato famine.*
	Royal Commissioners (Messrs. Ellis and Bros) in Jersey. Visit of Queen Victoria.
1847.	St. Catherine's Breakwater begun (completed 1852).
1848.	*Third French Revolution. Abdication of Louis Philippe. Republic declared under Napoleon III.*
8149.	Second cholera epidemic. Publication of Godfray's map.
1850.	Transferred to command of Town Regiment of Militia.
1851.	*Opening of the Great Exhibition.*
	Exhibited 104 varieties of wheat at the Great Exhibition.
1852.	*Louis Napoleon re-elected, and later became Emperor. Death of the Duke of Wellington.*
	Opening of Victoria College. Victor Hugo in Jersey (to 1855).
1853.	*The Crimean War (to 1855).*
	Appointed Adjutant General of Militia.
1855.	*Fall of Sebastopol.*
1857.	*The Indian Mutiny (to 1858). Relief of Lucknow.*
	Marriage of son, John Halkett Le Couteur, to Mai Low. Second visit of Queen.
1859.	*Italian war of liberation. Rise of Garibaldi.*
1860.	Royal Commissioners (Sir J. Awdry, R. Jebb and the Earl of Devon) in Jersey.
1861.	*Death of the Prince Consort.*
1863.	*Marriage of the Prince of Wales (Edward VII) to Princess Alexandra of Denmark.*
1865.	Death of his wife Harriet.
1866/7.	*The Fenian Conspiracy.*
1870.	Direct telegraphic communication with England. Opening of railway from St. Helier to St. Aubin.
1871.	*Franco-Prussian War. Surrender of Louis Napoleon.*
	Channel Islands Exhibition.
1872.	Published second edition of book on wheat. Knighthood.
1873.	Death of his son John Halkett. Opening of Jersey Eastern Railway.
1875.	Death of his daughter Mary Sumner.
	Death of Sir John Le Couteur.

A GUIDE TO THE SCOPE OF THE LE COUTEUR PAPERS

Sir John Dumaresq.

Militia Commissions, 1770, 1777.
Diaries and Accounts, 1786, 1788, 1797.
Statement of his inheritances, 1819.

General John Le Couteur.

Belle Vue Farm Diaries and Notebooks, 1803-1820 (intermittent).
Orders concerning the duties of Assistant Inspectors and Drill Sergeants, Royal Jersey
    Militia, 1807.
Letters to his son John, 1807-1813.
Form of Oath of Allegiance, Curaçao, 1810-1815.
Official Notebooks and Accounts, Jamaica, Curaçao and later, 1812-1817.
Account books, 1815-1816.
Will, 1821.

Mary, wife of General Le Couteur.

some 20 letters received from her aunt (probably Marthe Saumarez née Le Mesurier),
    1789-1795.
Narrative of travel on transfer with the General to Scotland, 1797.
Details of lessons given to her sons, John and Gordon, 1798.
Narrative of the stationing of Russian troops in Jersey, 1799.
Pencil drawing of a Jersey mill, 1802, and other sketches.
Water-colour panoramas of fortifications in St. Brelade's, St. Catherine's and Grouville
    Bays, Jersey, 1804.
Series of letters to her son John at school and college in England, 1808-1816.
Narrative of travel on transfer through Wales to Ireland, thence to Lisbon, and
    finally Jamaica and Curaçao, 1811.
Description of the Jamaica earthquake, 1812.
Sketch book, Jamaica and Curaçao, 1812-1816.
Journal, and sundry notes and observations, 1816-1839 (intermittent).
Letter to her future daughter-in-law, 1817.
Housekeeping ledger and diary, 1831-1844.
Sketch-book, Jersey and elsewhere, from 1839.

Colonel (later Sir John) Le Couteur.

Autobiographical Journal (Marlowe, Canada, West Indies and Jersey), 1796-1825.
Draft narrative of the Winter March of the 104th Regiment in Canada, 1813.
two retrospective water-colours of incidents in the Niagara campaign, 1813.
Army List, 1815, with his marginal notes on men he knew.
Diaries, 1815-1875 (with some gaps, notably 1831-1839).

15 Letter-books (containing drafts or copies of letters sent), 1817-1875, continued by his daughter to 1887. These books overlap in date, some being confined to a single subject, e.g. agriculture.

Story of the near-wreck of the "Young Phoenix", 1818.

Orderly Book, North-West Regiment, Royal Jersey Militia, 1826-1834.

Narrative of his attendance on King William IV as A.D.C., with a description of the Brighton Pavilion, 1830.

Census details, St. Brelade's Parish, 1831.

Memorandum of Jersey shipping plying to the British Plantations Fisheries, 1835.

Letters to Viscount Hardinge regarding care of cows, the Brunswick rifle and other subjects, 1850-1852.

some 50 letters from Colonel and Mrs. Le Couteur to their son J. H. Le Couteur, mostly to India, 1850-1858.

Letter to Evie Sumner describing the wreck of the "Express", 1859.

List of exhibits lent to the Jersey Masonic Museum, 1865.

Resignation as Adjutant General of Militia, and the thanks of the Lieutenant Governor, 1872.

Patent of Knighthood, 1873.

Will, 1873.

Partage of the Belle Vue inheritance, 1879.

Harriet Le Couteur, his wife.

Album of water-colours of fruit grown at Belle Vue, 1831 onwards.

Household accounts and records, 1847-1865.

John Halkett Le Couteur, his son.

copies of 15 Letters describing his voyage to India, and first impressions of life there, 1850.

95 Letters written while on active service in the Crimea, 1854-1856.

Will, 1857.

Harriet Le Couteur, his daughter.

Sketch book, 1836 onwards, containing original work and copies.

Diaries, 1851-1890, (with many gaps, notably 1861-1875).

Household accounts, records and menus, 1865-1876.

Will, 1889.

Copies of public documents preserved in the family, mainly by Colonel Le Couteur during his term of office as Vicomte.

many Extracts taken from public records in London relative to the history of Jersey, 1274-1771.

"Des Crimes". Extracts from criminal cases, appeals, sentences, and notes thereon, 1553-1801.

A document of 1542 regarding seeking sanctuary by means of a Perquage path.

Copies of Orders in Council concerning Jersey, 16th-18th centuries.

"Des Préjugés" (legal precedents). Extracts from 16th-19th century cases.

"Griefs de l'Isle de Jersey" by Moses Corbet: printed in London, 1770.

"A Statement of the mode of proceeding . . . . in the Royal Court of Jersey", by James Hemery and John Dumaresq: printed by the Jersey Press, 1789.

many Press cuttings about Jersey.

MS copy of Sir Frederick Thesiger's speech to the Privy Council about Jersey affairs, 1853.

Records of the Le Couteur and related families.

a large number of Deeds of sale, purchase, lease and inheritance of houses and land in Jersey, from 1611.

many deeds of Rente (Jersey mortgage), from 1620.

a bound volume of Extracts from Parish Registers concerning the Le Couteur family.

Partage of the Le Couteur property in St. John, 1685.

Partage of the Le Couteur property at Le Nord, St. John, 1720.

Ship's Log Book of a voyage in 1726 from England to Barbados, compiled by Jean Ballaine, with nautical and astronomical theorems and calculations. Re-used from 1730 by the Dumaresq family for accounts, and from 1737 for entries of births and deaths: and finally, from 1819-1862 by the Le Couteurs for garden notes and accounts at Le Bocage and Belle Vue.

Partage, Bertault family, 1731.

Assignment of Le Nord to Philippe Le Couteur, and Les Buttes to Jean Le Couteur, 1761.

Appariement, Fief du Roi, St. Brelade: Chef 17; 1775, 1786.

MS book of Poems by Jean Dumaresq, Bulkeley Bandinel and others, 1780-1808: also used for exercises in arithmetic, and finally as a commonplace book by Dumaresq's brother Philippe on board H.M.S. "Victory", 1809-1811, including specifications of the ship "Leda", launched in 1800; the state of the Swedish and Russian navies, 1810; many cooking recipes; and hints on how to make ginger beer, remove stains, make tooth-powder, make boots waterproof, cure headaches and rheumatism, and much other useful information.

Militia Commission, François Janvrin, 1812.

Will, Philippe Dumaresq, R.N., 1816.

Partage, estate of François Janvrin, 1838.

Genealogy, Le Mesurier family.

a number of Sketch-books by various members of the family, containing scenes in Jersey and abroad.

5 pencil and pastel Portraits of members of the family by T. Berteau, 1845-1848.

pencil Portraits of Halkett and Harriet Le Couteur, by Mrs. McNiven, c. 1850.

a large folder of prints, engravings, water-colours and other works of art collected by the family at intervals, chiefly on the continent, now dispersed.

CHAPTER ONE

INTRODUCING THE LE COUTEURS

TOUJOURS
PREST

This a tale of people who lived with gusto; who awoke with an appetite for each day's activity, and a flair for finding most of it interesting. Nurtured in religious beliefs as yet unchallenged, and trained in a code of conduct which knew nothing of permissiveness, they spent no time, as many are obliged to do today, in hesitation and controversy, but devoted all the hours at their disposal to the fascinating business of living life according to accepted standards. Like any other game, life to them would have made no sense without rules. If the hours in a day were fewer than they needed, they added to them by rising before dawn, or retiring in the small hours. Time was always set aside for private prayer: and at the end of a day they felt a duty to share its experiences with each other in letters, and with posterity in diaries. In the generous chronicles we here receive from them they speak to us in clear and confident tones, in the voices of Victorian days and those which preceded them. What they wrote is invigorating stuff to read. It has manifold variety and is of absorbing interest. In the pages of the great Le Couteur archive you may share with these competent people a way of life now largely obsolete, and converse with men and women whose names are part of English history. You are looking back on what in many ways was a golden age.

C

Who were these people? They were the Le Couteur family of Jersey. In the middle ages their name was spelt Le Cousteur, meaning the church sexton or factotum, the curé's right-hand man. One of his main functions was to calculate or cost the sums due from parishioners for tithes, baptisms, funerals, obits and the like, and it may be for this reason that he was known in this part of the world as the "cousteur", the man who told you how much it would cost. The title came to mean a lay reader, perhaps because the sexton, being literate, was among the few who could read.

Originating in Normandy like so many Jersey families, the Le Couteurs have been established in Jersey for centuries. In 1331 we hear of a Robert and a Jean Le Coustor in St. Brelade's Parish.[1] Sir John Le Couteur, the central figure of this book, traced his own ancestry back to Julian Le Couteur who married Catherine Querée in 1598, and Sir John once wrote to his son: "Mind you call your eldest son Julian, to begin another respectable run of 250 years". Julian was descended, it appears, from Thomas Le Couteur of St. John's Parish, born in 1460, and in that parish the family remained for six more generations, their home being Les Buttes, a house named after the archery butts which were situated, as always, near the parish church. Today Les Buttes has not the outward appearance of great antiquity, but contains many fragments of seventeenth-century carved stonework and a notable fireplace dated 1669. Sir John passed the old place in 1851 while on a Visite des Chemins (road inspection). "Rain came on and dispersed us", he wrote, and he took the opportunity to visit "old Betty Pinel (Aubert), my grandfather Le Couteur's old servant. She is past ninety, very active, turned me round to the light to look at me, and was delighted to see her master's grandson. I gave her a small piece of gold as a remembrancer. The old porch and steps to mount the chargers are still in existence at Les Buttes; the ancient keystone bears the date 1681". The dated stone may still be seen, built in on the north of the house. Les Buttes carried with it the feudal duty of "Sergenté du Fief de St. Jean La Hougue Boëte", or the office of sergeant to the seigneurial court of that fief.[2]

In 1793 Sir John's father, Jean Le Couteur, married Marie Dumaresq, having sold Les Buttes and bought from his father-in-law the property named Belle Vue, on the Fief du Roi in St. Brelade, thereby severing the connection of his branch with St. John's parish. The Dumaresqs were also of ancient island stock, having provided a Jurat of the Royal Court in 1292. Sir John's grandmother was daughter of Jean Le Mesurier, Governor of Alderney, and he had many relatives there and in Guernsey. His wife was Harriet Janvrin, of a Jersey family originally named Valpy-dit-Janvrin, shortened to Janvrin alone in 1826.

Belle Vue stands in a commanding position and its view over St. Aubin's town, harbour and bay fully justifies its name. Indeed, the prospect is breath-taking, and it is not surprising that Ouless chose it in 1847 for the "Royal Squadron at Anchor" in his album recording Queen Victoria's visit. There are relics here of the standard four-roomed house of the seventeenth century, two on the ground floor and two above, and these survive in the northern part of the present building. During the eighteenth century accommodation was doubled by adding rooms to the south, and a third storey. The stair from first to second floor, and on to the attic in modified form, displays an interesting style found in eighteenth-century houses in Jersey, with the baluster of the lower flight crossing the stringer of the upper in the form of an X, impressive and of great strength. The bedroom at the south-

1. Extente of 1331.
2. Registre Publique, 79. 155. 1793 Nov. 9.

The view which gave BELLE VUE its name.
(after P. J. Ouless and the Le Couteur sketch-books).

west is completely panelled in the early Georgian style which was so much admired in Jersey that it continued after it had become old-fashioned in England. Similar panelling in the library was recently found to be infested with death-watch beetle and has had to go. There are indications that the main front room, originally the drawing room, was also panelled. It is likely that these internal improvements were made in 1775 by Philip Le Vesconte, and at a cost of only 122 livres tournois, a modest one even by the standards of the time.

In 1816 Jean Le Couteur retired to Belle Vue, and added the kitchen wing. The elegant curved staircase from the ground floor may also have been erected by him. The alterations caused an upheaval in the household, and we can sympathise with his wife when she wrote to her son in Quebec: "We are plagued with workmen, and the work not going on so fast as we could wish; not so with the money .... your Father tired out of his life with building, and I teazed with house-keeping and want of convenience to give dinners . . . .". They entertained "General Skinner of the 16th foot[1] and his son .... we could not avoid giving them a leg of mutton, roasted on a string before the smoaky fire .... Then General Carey and his nephew, son of poor General Le Marchant[2], on a visit to Col. Touzel; and here again I was put to my wit's end to give them two dinners; after which I declared I would abandon the house if your Father invited anyone in before the kitchen was finished . . . ." The verandah, which has now been removed, may have dated from this period also. As the house had been a barracks for Russian troops stationed in Jersey from the autumn of 1799 to June 1800, and been let to tenants for some years, it doubtless needed renovation. But from 1816 to the present day there is no indication that any alterations took place at Belle

1. The Bedfordshire Regiment.
2. The General died on active service in 1812, when his son was but nine years old. The son was to become General Sir John Gaspard Le Marchant 1803-1874.

Vue, apart from routine repairs. Much of the garden design on which Sir John prided himself has necessarily vanished, but it is probable that many of the camellias which enrich the scene from Christmas to early summer are trees he planted himself. He made several additions to the estate, buying in 1827 (or possibly in 1832) Dell Farm, the small homestead immediately west of Le Bocage, from Jean Le Feuvre dit Filliastre, who reserved the right to take away two stone troughs, some stone paving, the contents of the woodshed, four plum and two cherry trees. In 1841 he bought from Jean Cutler, who lived opposite the Belle Vue entrance, the right of way to a spring on Cutler's cotil (hillside) and permission to draw water from it: and in 1836 Jean Allen sold him a small house opposite Dell Farm, which came to be called Allencot and appears from time to time in the diaries.

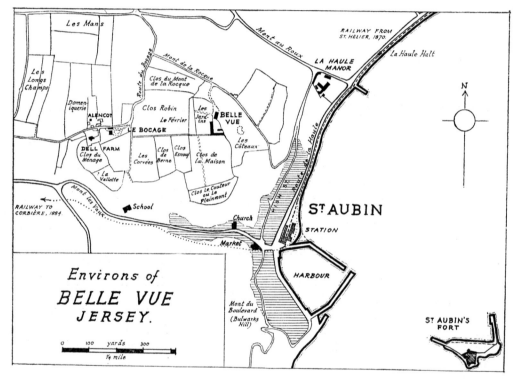

We do not know a great deal about Sir John's paternal grandparents. His grandfather was born in 1718, one of ten children of whom only two survived. He was Constable of St. John 1775-78, and apparently died away from home, for in 1822 Sir John went to the Père La Chaise cemetery in Paris to arrange for the placing of an epitaph on his grave. He chose a tombstone costing 410 francs, to be prepared by a mason named Bauche. He saw it later and wrote that it was "fort bien executé, et doit être expedié tout de suite". Of his wife we know nothing but her name, Marie Bertault, and that she was married in 1753. She may have been somewhat younger than her husband, who was 35 at the time. The artist Thomas Berteau, whom we shall meet presently, may have been a distant relative. She had two daughters who both died comparatively young, and unmarried. The only other child was Jean, who was to become a General, and father of Sir John.

1. BELLE VUE, St. Brelade, Jersey.

STAIRCASES
AT
BELLE VUE

2. The upper stair, c.1750.

3. The lower stair, c.1816.

4.   Sir JOHN DUMARESQ
(1749-1819)
Lieutenant Bailiff of Jersey.
(*painted by W. Hay*, 1869)

5. ST. AUBIN'S FORT
an example of Harriet Le Couteur's pencil work, c.1835-40.

Sir John's maternal grandmother Mary Le Mesurier, wife of Sir John Dumaresq, was the eldest of the seven children of Jean Le Mesurier, Governor of Alderney, and his wife Martha Dobree. She died in 1787 when her eldest child was only thirteen years of age. There are glimpses of her in her husband's diaries: thus, in 1786: "Bought a hat for Mrs. D. at Long's warehouse": and in February 1787 when she accompanied him to London: "Sailed from Jersey on board Capt. Wilkins the Liberty packet with Mrs. D. at eleven in the forenoon: wind S.W. gentle breeze". Six months later she died at the birth of her tenth child Louisa. We are told that she owned "a town house in St. Aubin's".

Sir John Dumaresq is amply documented[1], but here we shall deal only with the fresh material which the diaries provide about him, apart from mentioning that he served as Constable of St. Peter for 25 years and became Lieutenant-Bailiff in 1802, a period when non-resident Bailiffs threw the responsibilities of their post on the shoulders of a Lieutenant. He lived at St. Peter's House, "so called improperly", though we are not told what its name should be. His father had inherited it through the Robins, having in 1734 married Marie, daughter of Raulin Robin, whose family had lived in the parish since the middle of the fifteenth century. With the property went the fiefs of Orville, du Prieur de St. Pierre and Sauvalle, mainly in St. Peter's parish. The house was greatly altered and enlarged by Sir William Vernon, Bailiff, whose family acquired it in 1850, and little if anything of the Robin house has survived. But a vellum-bound book in these archives, later used for garden notes, has some family entries at the beginning, so torn and faded that they were far from easy to read. One of them says: "La néscence de mon fils Jean et de Ph. estai garite[2] dans un livre qui fut consumé dans l'embrasement de notre maison." (The birth of my sons Jean and Philippe were put for safety in a book which was destroyed in the burning of our house). No date is given, but the previous entry is 1746 and the succeeding one 1777. On the façade of St. Peter's House is a heraldic stone showing Dumaresq arms quartered with Payn, a combination not uncommon in Dumaresq heraldry, and the date 1754, which suggests that the house was rebuilt in that year, perhaps after a fire a year or two earlier. The Richmond map of 1795 shows a circular feature to the north-east of the house in a plot called Le Jardin du Hogard, which may indicate that the Dumaresqs or Robins were allowed a colombier (dovecot) in recognition of the small fiefs they held. The partage of Raulin Robin[3] in 1694 mentions: ". . . . maison, le colombier et un assez grand nombre de pièces de terre". The house was insured in 1792 in the City of London for £1600, which included £400 for furniture and £50 for printed books. In 1830 a General Orde enquired about renting it, and was told: ". . . . it is by a newly macadamised road through St. Peter's Valley, a beautiful drive of about four miles and a half from St. Helier and two from St. Aubin, where there is an English service every Sunday, either in the morning or afternoon. There is a French service in the parochial church every Sunday. The house is very spacious, having dining and drawing rooms about thirty by twenty feet, two smaller sitting rooms, a study, good cellars, very large kitchen, two sculleries, five pantries or offices, from ten to fourteen bedrooms, stable and coach house and large walled garden, and a smaller one containing about an acre, a green house, a good lawn and meadow of about two acres, sufficient to feed a couple of cows. The farmhouse which is close by and about twenty-six acres of land

1. Balleine, Biographical Dictionary of Jersey, p.240.
2. Meaning guarded: c.f. guerite, watch tower, look-out.
3. Bulletin of La Société Jersiaise, 1907, p.159.

are let to a respectable English farmer who has married an old servant of the family. He could supply a large family with potatoes, butter, cream, hay, in short the whole produce of the farm, without any trouble to the lodgers of the main house. I think it proper to be explicit, Sir, by saying that the house requires repairs, besides painting, which it could take two or three months time to do nicely, which I would undertake to do for a three year lease at ninety pounds a year". This correspondence was being conducted on behalf of Sir John Dumaresq's grandson George, then quite a young man.

Late in life, in 1870, Sir John Le Couteur revisited the place and wrote: ". . . . my grandfather's house, where my delightful early days were passed . . . . They admired the two fine rooms, in which I had seen three hundred guests. The India/China paper in the drawing room is still fresh and beautiful. The large garden is one of weeds, where hundreds of peaches and all European fruits used to flourish".

Sir John Dumaresq had been a scholar of Winchester College, and it was perhaps because of the fluency in English he had gained there that he was chosen no less than twenty-one times to make the journey to London to negotiate on the Island's behalf. Let us take one of these journeys to show what they involved. "1786. Jan. 12th. Sailed from Jersey on board the Guernsey packet Captain Mourant for England, wind SSW blowing fresh but clear weather. 13th: Made the Isle of Wight early in the morning and took the whole day to work up to Portsmouth against tide. Arrived there at $\frac{1}{2}$ past four p.m. Dined at the Coffee House with Mr. J. Dumaresq, Gros Puits, and about half past six set off in a postchaise alone for London. Wrote a line to Mrs. D. from Portsmouth. 14th: Arrived in town early". He then contacted his relatives the Le Mesuriers, who were influential in the City, and ". . . . was informed of what had been done respecting the Newfoundland trade, and was happy to find that my having been detained by the weather could not be prejudicial to the business". He then fixed up his lodgings, He kept accounts of travelling expenses, which follow a regular pattern, like this example from 1786:

By given the people of the boat going on board.	2. 6.
By ditto to a sailor carrying me on shore.	1. 0.
By given the sailor embarking a second time.	2. 6.
By ditto to the crew landing at Portsmouth.	5. 0.
By expenses of trunk and putting on shore.	5. 0.
By travelling charges from Portsmouth to town, by night.	£4. 19. 0.
By coach hire and porter to lodging.	3. 0.

Then, as now, travelling was a costly affair.

At this time his son John was at his old school, Winchester, as well as his nephew Bulkeley Bandinel[1], who was to become a well-known Librarian of the Bodleian in Oxford. For geographical reasons Winchester was the obvious choice for any Jerseyman with a promising son whom he wished to educate in England. Young John Dumaresq was a scholar of the College, but evidently failed to fulfil his early promise and was super-annuated in 1799. His father's visits, reflected in the diaries, will stir the feelings of parents today who for one reason or another can visit their sons but seldom at boarding-school, and the things Sir John Dumaresq did and recorded on these occasions have a timeless quality, as relevant to 1970 as to 1790. It goes without saying that after taking the boy out

---

1. Balleine, Biographical Dictionary of Jersey, p.23.

to supper he returned to College to search out old friends, all of whose names are to be found in College records: nor was he unmindful of those who had been kind to him in his own school days, such as Mrs. Williams at Sickhouse, to whom he gave 5s.; and Margaret the fruit-woman, to whom he gave 2s. 6d. Elsewhere in the accounts we find: "Six pairs of stockings for Jack, 13s. 6d.": and "Paid to Mr. Goddard being ye amount of Jack's bills and schooling at Winc. College, £40. 19. 4." His daughter Mary, and later her sisters Harriet and Marthe, were also at school in England, and he went down to take them out for treats as often as his duties permitted. Entries in his accounts show a fond parent always ready to indulge a large family. He paid for embroidery and painting materials, art and music lessons, clothes for the girls, toys to take home for the younger children, and things his friends in Jersey had asked him to buy on the mainland.

It is beyond the scope of this book to study the Dumaresq diaries in detail, but they merit attention as a mirror not only of Jersey affairs but of London life, conscientiously recorded by a relatively unknown official striving to conduct business, in the great metropolis, which was of great importance to him and his Island home. In off-duty hours he took full advantage of the cultural opportunities which these visits offered. In 1792 he went with "Mrs. Fiott, Bloomsbury St., Miss Le Geyt, the Misses Lee and Mr. Fiott to hear Mrs. Siddons act Ventura in the Tragedy of Coriolanus: also Mrs. Jordan as Nell in The Devil to Pay". On 15th April 1795 he took his son Philip to see Mrs. Jordan in The Country Girl and Alexander the Great at Drury Lane, having that same day seen ". . . . many curious animals, birds and beasts over Exeter Change, among them an elephant and an ostriche, and a very large black bird without wings and without tail or tong". On the previous Sunday he had "had the opportunity of seeing the Princess of Brunswick[1] on her arrival to St. James' Palace". In this year he created a mild sensation in Jersey by importing a post-chaise, the first vehicle of its kind to be seen in the Island. He had had it made by Messrs. Thomas and Meller, who charged him £75 for it, with three guineas extra for the lamps. There are many other points of interest in the diaries. In 1789 he experienced the frustration of trying to deliver, in face of endless delays, an address from the States on the "providential recovery" of George III. He took for granted, in a way which we never could, that a ship bound for Jersey might land him at any point on the coast. It is a different one on almost every homeward voyage: Grouville, Bonne Nuit, Grève de Lecq, St. Aubin, and even St. Helier.

To his political opponents Sir John Dumaresq was anathema, but by his family he was much loved. When writing to his grandson, the future Sir John Le Couteur, at Marlowe he used to place a half-sovereign beneath the seal. This was against the rules, and got Le Couteur into hot water. But there was true affection between them and when Le Couteur returned to Jersey in 1816 after long absence he wrote: "My dear grand father and Louisa embarked in the Scout for Southampton to remain a month in England for the recovery of his health . . . ." His health does seem to have improved, for in September of the following year Le Couteur wrote: ". . . . family dinner at Millbrook. My grandfather and I rode quietly together from St. Peter's and kept them waiting half an hour for us". The house at Millbrook was probably La Chaumière in the Rue de Haut, home of his uncle Thomas Dumaresq.

---

1. Future wife of George IV.

coming home up St Peter's Valley in the new Post-Chaise, 1795.

Sir John Dumaresq died on 20th March 1819, and Le Couteur wrote of him: ".... he was a man in whom were united the most endearing private qualities with the highest public virtues. His gentleness was only equalled by his probity, his truly Christian character by his solid talents. Brought up to the Bar of this Island he became its brightest ornament, he attained the highest dignities. Forty years devotedness to his country have at length worn out his own brilliant mind. He brought up eight children, the sons all brave, the daughters virtuous. The dear old gentleman after eleven hours sleep expired without a struggle or a groan, my aunt Betsy Pipon holding his right hand and I his left. Death never appeared lovely to me before". And again: ".... though at the heat of the party dissensions of the Charlots and Magots his great abilities were admitted on all sides, and his eloquence at the time said to be unrivalled. After many earnest and heated debates in the States he had the glory to carry the prospect for 'Trial by Jury'; which, however, was never confirmed, through the specious and mistaken representations of the opponents of this Palladium of British liberty; of whom it is said to have been basely reported to the then Government that Jersey would go over to France and to the Republican tendencies already incipient in that distracted country, if the measure were carried. Nevertheless to this hour it exists, a monument of his enlarged and just view of British law, and of unwearied labour. Advocate Dumaresq was sent as Deputy of the States to defend or to proclaim the rights and privileges of Jersey on one and twenty occasions. On one of these, after pleading before the Lord Chancellor, His Lordship observed,: 'Mr. Dumaresq, had you followed the English bar, you might have sat in my seat'".

Christmas always brought back memories of him to his family. Looking back in 1811, Sir John Le Couteur wrote: ".... that happy day of Xmas which for so many years had been my burthen of delight at my grandfather's most happy mansion at St. Peter's", and in Canada in 1813 he added: ".... he used to receive his children, his grandchildren, his nephews and nieces and more distant branches with the most joyous hospitality. As a college boy I used to look forward to that day for months with bright anticipation, to enjoy his dear bright countenance which ever received me with the most bland smiles. When I carry my recollections back to when we returned from Scotland, I was at that time six years old, when dear old Ma Suzon Colas[1], his housekeeper, my own mother's and my nurse, received me from the gig the day we arrived in Jersey, and clasping me in her arms at the entrance to the lawn: 'Man chier ptit, je te tiens oquorre un faie; tu ne me requitteras pont' (my dear little one, I hold you once again; you shall never leave me). I had been in the frozen north, but my little heart had not chilled to her warm embrace".

Sir John ends with a vivid description of his grandfather. "He was rather above five feet six inches high, of admirable form for any feat of activity or strength, his step light and airy with an inexpressible grace of manner. He used to whip me up on his shoulders and run or march about the lawn or room, to the tune of the British Grenadiers . . . ., which I verily believe did more to inspire me with the love of military than any one thing. Then his beautiful face was so sweet in expression, his features rather small but almost fault-less, a front of Jove, with rich hazel elongated eye and fringed with lashes under which, if roused, the fire would sparkle with immense power".

In his memory, which remained green to his family, a large and elaborate mural tablet was erected in the north-eastern portion of St. Peter's Church, surmounted by the Dumaresq arms. An inscription in French sets out his life's work and extols his virtues. Beside it are two smaller tablets to his sons John and Thomas. It is said that he is buried beside his wife. In 1839 his daughter Mary paid 9s. for "a new covering to my father's monument": and as late as 1869, fifty years after his death, we find his grandson Sir John Le Couteur saying: "Mr. Hay the portrait painter came to see me. I wish him to paint me a portrait of my grandfather": and a few days later: "Took Arthur Dumaresq to Mr. Hay the painter, who found him wonderfully like my grandfather, and his great-grandfather. He is to paint my grandfather from the miniature for me for twenty-five guineas". A little later: "Went to see my dear grandfather's portrait by Mr. Hay. It is very much like what I remember of him when I was a lad". The miniature cannot now be traced, but would have descended in the direct line, perhaps to the Arthur mentioned. It is tempting to think that it was the work of Jersey's famous miniaturist, Philippe Jean, a contemporary of Sir John Dumaresq. Mr. Hay executed many portraits of local persons, and several of his canvases hang in the Royal Court. In his portrait of Sir John Dumaresq he was handicapped by being unable to paint from life, which would explain why the face is so expressionless. Dumaresq is shown holding a volume entitled "Trial by Jury", and before him is a delicate silver filigree inkstand, which may be that inherited by his great granddaughter Miss E. de S. Dumaresq which bore the inscription: "A.D.1816. A Messire Jean Dumaresq, Chevalier, au moment ou il quittoit la charge de Lieutenant Bailli, les hommes de la loi de la Cour Royale de l'île de Jersey ont presenté cette pièce comme un faible tribut de leur respect et de leur reconnaissance".[2]

If so, whatever party politicians and political lampoonists may have said of him, this excellent man rested secure in the affection of his family and the respect of his colleagues. What man could wish for more?

---

1. Her tombstone is at the east entrance to St Peter's churchyard.
2. Bulletin of La Société Jersiaise, 1905, p.368.

CHAPTER TWO

MASSA FATHER

Sir John's father, General Le Couteur, first enters these papers when his future father-in-law, Sir John Dumaresq, was interceding on his behalf with the Governor of Jersey, General Conway, and others, and wrote: ". . . . the General told me he had recommended Captain Le Couteur to be appointed Major of the Brigade (of Militia) at Jersey . . . . Wrote an account of all this to Mary". Dumaresq did some shopping for the engaged couple, purchasing a tea urn, and perhaps some china, as he mentions "a case from Wedgewood for Le Couteur". He also bought them twelve yards of Kidderminster carpet for £2. 7s. and a hat for £1. 3s.

General Le Couteur's career was entirely military from the time of his first commission, in 1780, to the Sherwood Foresters, then stationed in the Island and destined to play a distinguished part in the Battle of Jersey in January 1781. He was on leave at the time, and as soon as he heard the alarm he rode to Grouville Barracks and marched, as a volunteer, to St. Helier. Many years later his son was in Bath, and wrote: "Frederick (Janvrin) took me to his club. I found my father's old friend Mr. Clephane there . . . . Two of his brothers were Generals . . . . His brother is the officer on Copley's painting of the Battle of Jersey, leading the 95th Grenadiers".

Immediately after this battle, General Le Couteur was sent to India, where he was captured and imprisoned by Tippoo Sahib. On reading a report of this episode his son wrote: ". . . . gives an account of the fall of Bednore, which the author says 'he has no access to the accounts of'. He never saw my father's book. Tippoo Sahib pretended that the officers had concealed treasure about their persons, for which he seized General Mathews and all the prisoners of war, and marched them off in irons to their various prisons, my poor father to Chitteldroog (3rd May 1783)". General Le Couteur's monument in St. Brelade's Church adds that he was kept "in chains 11 months, fed on rice and water. All his superior officers were poisoned, but the Lord preserved him". His son's note continues: "Tippoo then marched to the siege of Mangalore which Major Campbell, my father's friend and Captain, so nobly defended for nine months against Tippoo's whole force. He capitulated with all honors on the 30 Decr. 1783, but died of anxiety and fatigue at Tellicherry 23d March 1784. Col. Andrew Gordon the Lt. Govr. of Jersey afterwards was his second in command, the only one of my father's old comrades who knew and appreciated his value."

After the peace of 1784 he returned home, and published an account of the campaign in "Letters from India", referred to above as "my father's book". He then established "La Gazette de Jersey", in conjunction with Philippe Dumaresq, uncle of his future wife, the printing being done at this time at Belle Vue. He was also, in his son's words, "in charge of the secret service with the French Royalists with Georges, Pichegru and Laroche Jacquelin", from about 1793 to 1795. After his promotion to Captain, his regiment was disbanded and he devoted his energies and talents to local affairs, as Centenier of St. John and then as Jurat of the Royal Court[1]. It was in 1793 that he married, and on 21st October 1794 his son John was born in St. Helier. (He was baptized at home three days later and "presenté a l'église" the following June. His godparents were John Dumaresq, his grandfather, John Dumaresq, his uncle, and Harriet Dumaresq his aunt). Meanwhile his Militia duties were gradually absorbing more and more of his time, but in 1798 he was recalled to duty in Scotland. He said later to a friend: "You know I believe that I have always liked the Scotch, and my partiality for them augmented there greatly, in the company of the Governor Stuart, the present Lord Grey etc." The year before he had purchased a majority and lodged the necessary money for the purchase of a Lieutenant-Colonelcy but, as his wife wrote: ". . . . his Brevet rank of Lieutenant Colonel coming out in 1798, and having been disappointed of the purchase, he lost the amount paid, ... and was then ordered to join the 16th Regt.[2] as Major." He and his wife made the journey to Scotland with their only child, then aged two, and his nurse, "travelling post to Edinburgh in four days . . . . The Comte d'Artois, afterwards Charles Dix, was then occupying Holyrood House". They proceeded to their regimental station at Montrose, where they had introductions to the future Lord Panmure and others. "Whilst there we heard news of the escape of Sir Sidney Smith[3] from prison at Paris; he was an old friend." On transit to Aberdeen later on, she wrote: ". . . . arrived at Bervie at one o'clock and found neither beds nor accommodation . . . ., and no post horses . . . . We got two cart horses, which we got tackled with old ropes as no harness was to be had, and went on to Stonehaven in the midst of the worst weather I ever saw. Our driver was obliged to lead the horses part of the way over a shocking road and our tackling broke three times . . . . Whilst at Aberdeen . . . ., heard the news of Lord Nelson's victory[4]". The arduous journey continued, following in the wake of the regiment, with the observant Mrs. Le Couteur noticing everything she saw, and remarking: ". . . . almost all along this road quantities of peat are cut; on both sides of it we observed rotted roots and branches which we have always noticed among the peat. It is a proof that Scotland has not always been so bare of trees as it is at present . . . . As we got north we were surprised to find the language improved and that the people spoke better English than they do about Dundee". She visited an old woman of eighty living in a one-roomed hut without chimney or window, who remembered the battle of Culloden[5], and said; "A battle so terrible there never was; such numbers were killed and such numbers were hanged; even a year after the battle took place many were hanged who had taken part against the King". In March 1799 she wrote: "We heard this day of the death of Bonaparte[6]. My husband received a letter from General Andrew Gordon offering him the place of Inspector General of Militia of Jersey". Soon afterwards they set out on the long return journey, all of which is detailed in her journal. At the end she wrote: "It gave me a desire to visit other countries and a taste for travelling which I most likely shall never have it in my power to gratify. If it was of no further advantage to me, it at least helped to rub off some national prejudices which it is hardly possible to be exempt from when we never stir from the spot which gave us birth".

They arrived back in Jersey in July, after a rough passage on the Weymouth packet. Belle Vue was then a barracks, accommodating the Loyal Irish and Limerick Fencibles,

1. Jurat 1790-1795.   2. The Bedfordshire Regiment.   3. Sir Sidney Smith of the Siege of Acre 1798.
4. the Battle of the Nile, 1-2 August 1798.   5. 1746.   6. Clearly a mistake. Perhaps she meant 'defeat'?

and the Le Couteurs rented furnished lodgings from a Mr. Dolbel at 60 louis a year, and for a time he and his young wife lived in St. Helier, where his two sons were born. We do not know the address, but it may have been in King Street or Vine Street, for J. Dumaresq and B. Bandinel, his brother-in-law and cousin, whom we have already met as schoolboys, hint that it was in the shopping area. They do this in a book of poems, mostly addressed to an unidentified Betsey Dobree, who sounds a fascinating character. The poem is entitled "Verses addressed to Major Le Couteur on the delightful situation of his dwelling house at St. Helier", and reads:

"When from behind the slaughter'd ox is seen
and right in front a kennel dank and green,
when burning quick sands enter the back door
and sweep the passage to the street before;
twixt sundry dealers in fish, snuff and mugs,
and little Thoreau's mighty shop of drugs;
there, in a snug and most comodious house
an Eastern warrior and his youthful spouse
breathe the pure air: their darling infant tastes
the genial breezes wafted at both gates.
O Muse, if e're thy aid we might invoke
to sing the praise of filthyness and smoke;
if in poetic strains we e're did struggle
to paint the beauties of a standing puddle,
to tell delightful fancies of a pair
who smell Ambrosia through the foulest air,
'tis now . . . .   to be continued."

Sad to say, no continuation has been found. There were many Thoreaus living in the town at that period, but none was keeping a shop of drugs, mighty or otherwise.

Le Couteur's tenure of office as Inspector of Militia, for eleven years, was most successful and much commended by the Governor. His greatest innovation was the drill for boys, to accustom them to military discipline against the time when they could bear arms. He thrice received the thanks of the States for his work, "together with a piece of plate" on the third occasion, in 1811, It was a magnificent silver bowl, made by the celebrated English silversmith Paul Storr. Though designated as an heirloom by himself and his son, it passed out of the family and found its way to Canada, and in 1969 the States bought it back for the island of its origin for the sum of £2,100.

Soon after this he was posted to Ireland, on the staff at Armagh. His son John wrote: "I well remember the break up of the establishment in old Belle Vue, the sale of all the comfortable old furniture, the old horses on which I had learned to ride, farm stock and implements . . . . On the 23rd December (1811) we all embarked in the Government Scout, Captain Wooldridge, with a gun brig as a convoy, sent by the Admiral the Duke of Bouillon[1]. My father paid his respects to the Duke of York[2] to whom he owed his appointment but did not take me to the levée, fancying me, I suspect, to be too young looking for a Lieutenant." John had two months' leave, and set off from London for Dublin with his

---

1. Philippe d'Auvergne (1754-1816).   2. Frederick, second son of George III (1763-1827), Commander-in-Chief.

6. The Death of Major FRANCIS PEIRSON
6th January 1781
(*by J. S. Copley*)

7. SILVER TUREEN presented to Major General John Le Couteur in 1811.

8. THE ENTRANCE TO GOVERNMENT HOUSE, Curaçao.
(painted by Mary Le Couteur, 1815)

9. THE PRINS VAN ORANJE, (centre)
with other Dutch vessels, at Portsmouth, 1833.

The ship in which General Le Couteur returned from Curaçao in 1816.

(Aquatint, engraved by Robert Havell, after John Schetky, and published by L. A. Van Den Bergh)

parents on 2nd January 1812. They travelled through Wales, where "the roads were terrifying . . . ., and the country shockingly wild and barren . . . . The horses are very sure footed and the postillions excellent". Their first night in Dublin, as they sat down to dinner in the hotel, "a letter was received announcing to my husband that the Duke of York had changed his destination from Ireland to Jamaica". John's comment was: "a more troublesome and dangerous command, but of course of greater value. It made my heart sore to think of the climate . . . . However, my mother always concluded with: 'Whatever is, is right'". Her own journal remarked: "The necessity of making up my mind to go everywhere, if I wished to follow my husband, soon reconciled me to the idea . . . . of a West Indian climate . . . . Dublin is a fine town with a number of elegant buildings in it, but its filth is excessive . . . . The Irish gentlemen . . . . are not yet completely reconciled to the Union, and there still exists a party which entertains hopes of dissolving the tie". John was enjoying himself: "I nevertheless passed three happy weeks in Dublin . . . . The dinners of the Shaws and Needhams rivalled royalty. We met the great Plunkett, and choice company everywhere, the most lively and entertaining society I have ever met. Dr. Magee[1], the future Archbishop, was then in his zenith, polite, eloquent, handsome and a courtier of exquisite polish".

They proceeded to Cork where they had to spend three weeks, and it rained incessantly. "My husband went to Cove of Cork the day after our arrival to look out for the best accommodated West India man for Jamaica, and secured our passage for £150 to Montego Bay, three in the cabin and two servants". After a delay of eleven days they embarked on a ship named the Sarah and were on the point of sailing when "my husband received a letter from Lord Palmerston informing him that his destination was changed to Lisbon . . . . This threw me into the greatest consternation . . . ., but I determined at once to go also to Lisbon with my husband; if I became any encumberance to him in the way of his profession, to return to England . . . . The same morning our baggage was removed from the Sarah to a transport, and my boy was taken ill with the measles the following day . . . . We embarked on the 1st of March, the invalid, covered with measles, wrapped up in a blanket . . . . The accommodation was wretched, with only one berth. In this we placed my boy, and there was barely space for our own mattress on the floor. The cabin was occupied by four officers, passengers to Lisbon; in this my maid had to sleep, separated from the young men's berths by a mere flag . . . . The weather was so boisterous that I had to be lashed to an iron pillar in the cabin".

Mrs. Le Couteur told John more about it in a letter of 12th March 1812 from Lisbon: "We arrived here on the 10th after a very tolerable passage of ten days. The first four days the wind was not very favourable and the sea terribly rough . . . . Poor Gordon bore the passage uncommonly well. I was fearful it would be the death of him, but after his measles disappeared he recovered so fast that I believe a longer sea voyage would have done him much good . . . . The second night after we left the Cove of Cork we parted company with our convoy, and both fleets, which has proved a fortunate circumstance for us as they are not yet arrived. We had however a fine fright on the 7th. We were chased, as we thought by an enemy, and prepared all hands for action. Our ship had eight rusty guns, and 22 artillery soldiers (passengers) were armed with muskets, the Officers with pistols, your Father with his crooked sword, and we were kept a whole morning in suspence. As for Gordon and

---

1. There is some mistake here. William Connor Magee, the Archbishop, was not born until 1821.

myself, the station allotted us was among 42 artillery horses in the hold under water, which company we were determined to refuse until necessity obliged us. Gordon did not express the least symptom of fear, and it was but the day before he had got on his legs again. The supposed enemy was within hail of us before we discovered it to be English . . . .

"We are billetted in a large handsome house elegantly painted, fine sofas, chairs etc. We have ball room, dining and drawing rooms, dressing rooms, ante chambers; it has everything but comfort in it. I am starved with cold, and no possibility of making a fire for there is no fireplace in the house except a miserable one in the kitchen. We are surrounded by Venuses and Cupids painted on our ceiling, but certainly the houses of this country were not intended for flesh and blood to inhabit. We have scarcely anything to eat, and if we had plenty have hardly the means of cooking our victuals. Your Father is in a very unpleasant state of suspense, fearing his coming here is owing to a mistake of Lord Palmerston's. He has reported himself to Lord Wellington, but cannot get an answer before four days. If we have to go back to England to take another passage to Jamaica we shall be half ruined. Our cases of wine have been broken almost to pieces changing ships. The baggage has all suffered . . . . we were obliged to give £50 to the Captain of the West Indiaman we had taken our passage on board of.

"We dined the day before yesterday with the Commissary and Mrs. Pipon[1] who received us very kindly. The first persons we met on landing here were Charles Lemprière[2] of the 58th and G. Pipon[3] of the 26th. The first is as fat as a pig . . . . It is surprising to see the slovenly manner in which Officers dress here; your Father was quite shocked at their appearance; the officers with coloured waistcoats without belts or sashes and looking much more like militia than regulars. Your Father is the only General in Portugal with the new General's uniform; they had not yet seen the eguilette or the feathered hat".

After some frustrating weeks in Lisbon they re-embarked for the West Indies, and in a letter from Jamaica in January 1813 the General said: " I did not write to you on my arrival here as I waited to be settled, but before this took place, myself and my family were attacked with the delightful fevers of this country, which made a complete hospital of our house for about three months . . . . My servant has been so severely handled by sickness that to my great loss and disappointment I was obliged to send him home and the poor fellow has been taken in the Swallow packet . . . . It is reported that General Don is coming here in the room of General Morrison. I do not believe it and I do not think the country would agree with him. If it did, I should be delighted to see him here; he would make an excellent Governor . . . . This is a charming island notwithstanding its fevers, earthquakes and hurricanes. The mornings and evenings are heavenly, and when I am not obliged to go out in the heat of the day I never find it too warm, but everything is extremely dear. I live in a beautiful situation 1½ miles from Kingston, and although the house is hardly large enough for our family I pay £400 a year for it. I was extremely mortified . . . . ,to find when I arrived at Lisbon that Lord Palmerston's letter . . . . was a mistake, but you have heard perhaps how handsomely His Lordship behaved to me in paying all my expenses". In a letter to Sir Thomas Saumarez that retirement attracted him: "I shall be highly satisfied if they send me to Belle Vue as soon as they please, and I shall promise never to trouble

---

1. James Pipon of Noirmont (1770-1837) and his wife Elizabeth Hodges.
2 Charles son of Thomas Lemprière of Rozel: Northamptonshire Regiment.
3. George son of Thomas Pipon of La Moie: Cameronian Rifles.

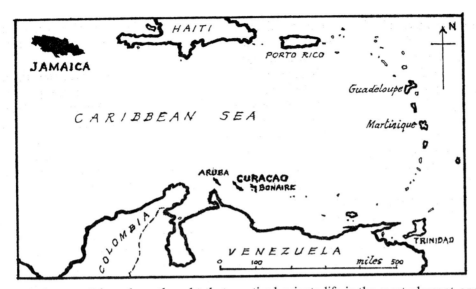

them again . . . . I have long thought that a retired private life is the most pleasant one".

Life in Jamaica was not without its stirring events. In a letter of November 1812 to her father Sir John Dumaresq, Mrs. Le Couteur said ". . . . I wrote to Louisa by the last and gave her an account of the hurricane we experienced on the 12 October . . . . I have now to describe to you the most terrifying earthquake felt in this island since the dreadful one of 1692 . . . . Last Wednesday sennight we had fixed upon to go and pay my first visit to Lady Caroline Morrison at Spanish Town, twelve miles from this place. My long illness and the bad weather in October had prevented my going before, and in order to perform our journey before the heat of the sun we got up very early. Gordon and I were just sat down by candlelight to take a cup of chocolate whilst the chaise was getting ready. Le Couteur was sitting on the opposite side of the room on a sopha, when all of a sudden an unaccountable noise and a shaking of the house took place. I at first thought Le Couteur moving on the sopha was the cause, and I called out 'What are you about?' A second shock more violent succeeded, when Le Couteur got up and said 'Lets go out'. To go to the servants' piazza, the door of which was the only one open, ... we had to pass through the dining room; and as I passed through the folding door which divides it from our drawing room, I saw the whole roof in agitation, a heavy mahogany sideboard was rocking from side to side; this was a third shock . . . . I cannot express my astonishment and thankfulness to find that we were all safe and the house standing . . . . During the second shock the house was twice raised up, and in the third and most violent shock it rocked like a ship at sea . . . Scarcely one house in Kingston has escaped injury and the church is obliged to have entire new gable ends . . . . Several Spaniards now here, who were at Caracas during the late dreadful earthquake, represent this as more severe, but account for the greater mischief done there by the houses being built on a sandy foundation and having very heavy roofs; here all the houses are covered with shingle . . . . The barracks at Up Park close to us which have been finished since our arrival, and which have cost Government £80,000, have suffered considerably. The 18th Regiment[1] (I suppose the Irish part of them) were pursuaded they had been

1. The Royal Irish.

taken up a high hill about five miles off and brought down again during the 30 seconds it continued, such were their sensations . . . . Some ladies of our acquaintance fell in fits, and many have not yet recovered from their fright . . . .

"The General and Lady Caroline see very little company. She is not liked here, though I see no reason for it. She hates Jamaica and makes no secret of it . . . . The people are so inhospitable . . . ., we have not yet dined at the house of a single inhabitant . . . . General Farley who commands the district is a stingy old bachelor; the largest table in his house will accommodate six persons only. I have called on him several times and done all I could to get a dinner out of him, but to no purpose; he has even asked Le Couteur without his Aide de Camp. He is for all that a very good man and goes to church every Sunday, but he is not much of a soldier . . . . No person here, I believe, thinks of anything else but of getting money and to return to Europe as fast as they can."

Then there was the row with General Morrison, who "altered the parade, but coming rather late, he was not expected, and the troops had begun their movements before his arrival; which so irritated him that he could not command his temper (at all times extremely irritable) and he addressed General Le Couteur, who had begun the parade in consequence of General Farley's desire, who was the senior on parade, in so uncivil and rough a manner as was the cause of coolness between them as long as General Morrison remained in the island. General Le Couteur could not help telling all the staff that since he had been in His Majesty's service he had never been spoken to in so ungracious a manner".

On Christmas Day 1812 they treated their servants "with roast beef and their favourite dish, salt pork, pudding, and as much bread and yams as they could eat, and as much punch as they could prudently drink . . . . They danced and played ball all the afternoon in the yard, and came in a body to thank me for their good fare and to wish long life to Massa and Missis".

We get a glimpse, in a letter which Gordon, then aged 13, wrote to his brother, of the General as a benign employer, and also as initiator of a simple form of malaria control. Writing of Up Park Camp, Gordon says: "When we came here first it was full of holes and the weeds were so high that you could not see any body. But since Papa has had command of the Brigade he has set the pioneers to work, and now it looks as well as a gentleman's park. Since he has done that the soldiers are much more healthy, and many less have died this year than before. Papa gets up every morning at day break, gives the pioneers a task. He shows them how to weed, and if they do all that he tells them, they get two holidays instead of one".

By September 1814 they had been transferred to Curaçao, the General being the last British Governor to serve there. An island with a troubled history, it had passed from hand to hand between the Spanish, French, Dutch and Portuguese, the British taking it from the French in 1800; but it remained a focus of attack and counter-attack until the British finally took possession of it in 1806. It had two small island dependencies, Aruba and Bon Air. According to General Le Couteur, the Governor's salary in 1764 had totalled £3333. 6s. 8d. sterling per annum.

After their arrival he wrote to Admiral Brown: "I return you mine and Mrs. Le Couteur's best thanks for the good ship which you had the kindness to give us, but particularly for putting us under the care of such an excellent man as Captain Milward. During the whole passage he has deprived himself of every comfort to render everything pleasant for

The Town of ARUBA, Aruba Island,
dependency of Curaçao.
from Mary Le Couteur's copy of a sketch.

us. He divided his cabin in half; one half he gave to us, and the other he gave to Mrs. Clark; as to himself, he slept over a gun, not half as well off, I think, as his men . . . . I could not have believed that things could have been carried on on board ship in the quiet manner observed on board the Herald. You never heard a word louder than another. Not once did I hear 'Damn your eyes'."

Had he remained there longer he would doubtless have introduced reforms. In another letter, in which he was interceding for a Jerseyman named Vibert who had been captured with his ship, the Rover, he wrote: "You can have no idea of the distressed state of this Island. You know it is mostly supplied with poor men from the Spanish Main, and as the privateers of both parties take everything they find at sea, nothing can venture to quit the coast; in consequence of which this island . . . . is on the point of starvation". He thought the Governor's powers "too much for one man . . . . I have the power to forgive all crimes. One of my predecessors forgave a murderer . . . . If the island remained in our possession and I stayed here, I would certainly apply for a judge". The scarcity of corn, the cause of

the General and party at a picnic

adaptation of Mary Le Couteur's sketch: 'View of the sea from my sitting room, Government Pen, Curaçoa, 1814:'
left: wine cellar, with A.D.C.'s room above. centre: jetty of coralline blocks, and (apparently) the General fishing: between him and us, 'Turtle Crawl'. extreme right: bathing house. see also inset.

D

18

starvation, was due to "the high fees on all small vessels of 15 tons and under that come into this port. As part of these fees were mine, I thought I could fairly use my supreme authority, and I abolished them for six months". But his humane efforts were not entirely successful: "I have done all I could to relieve the poor people, but I am afraid I shall not succeed as well as I at first expected. I have courted all countries to bring provisions, even Petain, who has applied for permission to trade with this colony. For the last act Lord Bathurst[1] will, I am afraid, be angry with me, but it is the only chance I have of saving the lives of thousands".

Like every conscientious colonial administrator, the General toured his parish though he does not say so. We only know it from the lively sketch-book of Mary, his wife, who was always at his side as he travelled, extracting enjoyment from each new scene, proud of a distinguished husband many years her senior, and fond of him to a point which permitted caricature. Her pen had already shown him, with his crooked sword, defying the King's

FORT GEORGE, CURAÇAO, 1815.
after a sketch by Mary Le Couteur.

enemies at sea, and fidgetting on a sofa to a degree resembling an earthquake. In the sketch-book her brush gives us the only surviving portraits of her red-coated veteran, usually from behind, fishing on the pier at Government Pen[2] in Curaçao, or at a picnic beneath a sapodilla or naseberry (she spells it nasburry) tree. Together they inspected Fort George (later Fort William), and Fort Caraccas, and made excursions to the estates of the settlers, whose names have a ring of the Netherlands: Duyckink, Gaatman, Scotburgh (of Santa Martha), and Jutting (of Santa Barbara).

---

1. Lord Bathurst, third Earl, (1762-1834), Secretary of State for War and Colonies.
2. A West Indian word for a small country house, often in the mountains. While in Jamaica the Le Couteurs lived at "Hind's Pen".

General Le Couteur
and party crossing the Santa Barbara Lagoon
to Fort Caraccas, Curaçao, December, 1814.
from a sketch by Mary Le Couteur.

While the General racked his brains to avert famine, Mary worried over their delicate son Gordon, and interested herself in the life of the islanders. Finding them unaware of Christian matrimony, she rejoiced at persuading many of them to be married in the church. Her elder son John was now at a loose end, his regiment, the 104th, having been disbanded after the Canadian war, and the General made strenuous efforts to secure him as his A.D.C., and in the end succeeded. But in fact he was not there more than a few weeks. His bill for provisions on the voyage amounted to about 80 dollars, and included mattress, blankets, pillows, sheets, 1½ dozen port wine, two dozen English porter, a gallon of brandy, a pound of Souchong tea, chocolate, loaf sugar, cheese, biscuits, ham, pepper, mustard, 1½ dozen fowls, butter and (wisely) 50 limes and (surprisingly) 200 pots of oysters. He had a happy trip of a fortnight, seeing flying fish and experiencing a "white squall". When they arrived he enquired for his parents, and the native pilot, on being asked if the American sloop would be allowed to enter the harbour, replied: "Oh, yes, Massa Sir, you be de best passport". He was soon at Government House, where "my dearest mother did not know my person, but hearing my voice flew to embrace me, looking young and really blooming with colour; my dear father looking strong and active but pale".

Britain was about to hand over the colony to the Dutch, and Admiral Kikkert, who was to replace General Le Couteur, had already arrived; "a rough, pompous old sailor, very kind to us, with every seeming disposition . . . . of taking full and despotic power over his new Government. He meant, he said, to relax no fees, fines or privileges . . . .; I afterwards heard that he had kept his word . . . . My father, Gordon and I generally rode out at four o'clock in the morning 8 or 10 miles. I had a nice pacer who took me along in his namby pamby pace, two legs on a side together in a most agreeable way . . . . Colonel Captain Lewe van Edouard, the commander of the Princes van Orange, a stately Dutch eighty-gun ship to mount 104 guns, gave General Le Couteur, Admiral Kikkert and all the authorities a superb state dinner on board of the liner. It was a superb turn out and very well done. The health of the respective sovereigns, and many more, warmed the hearts of the Orange Bovens as well as the John Bulls". There followed a succession of dinners, balls and return dinners, culminating in a farewell dinner given by the General: "a very gay affair it was. The Dutch beauties are plump, not too rosy, but frank and pleasant . . . . Never in my life did I see so many ugly baggages in the shape of women". The final handing over took place on Monday 4th March 1816. "The General proceeded in state to Fort Amsterdam passed in front of the Dutch and English troops, from whom he received salutes, proceeded to the Council Chamber to deliver the Proclamation by which the Island is restored to the Netherlands. By this, the gentlemen in British office and pay, up to this day, with all the inhabitants, were absolved from their oath of allegiance[1] to His Britannic Majesty. As soon as the Proclamation had been read the General, the absolved Governor, and the Admiral, the new Governor, appeared together on the balcony. Royal salutes were fired from all the forts, the British Union was lowered and the Dutch tricolour waved aloft in its place. The flank companies of the 7th West India Regiment formed a street from the Fort to the point of embarkation, and saluted as my father left his easy command, the band playing the National Anthem. We all went through the official ceremony of embarking, and then landed to dine with Mr. and Mrs. Scates. The Prins van Orange saluted with yards manned and colours flying in compliment.

"I shall never forget the impression I received in witnessing the hearty feelings of real love and attachment which the poor blacks especially evinced on the departure of my father and mother. All classes testified to their affection, many shed tears, which my mother said appeared to be genuine. To see and hear the poor negro race implore blessings on the head of their poor Massa Father in the presence of their new Dutch Governor, a man of their own country as it were, while the ex-Governor was a Briton, was a testimonial never to be forgotten". Already, 150 years ago, the British had learned to hand over a colony with dignity. The farewell address which the General received on leaving testifies to his "mild administration, ... paternal solicitude for our welfare, which prompted you to take such immediate and effectual measures as happily to avert from us the dreadful visitation of famine with which we were nearly threatened . . . . You have incessantly watched over and promoted the best interests of the colony . . . ., displaying a frank and kindly demeanour . . . . we express our fervent wishes for the continued health of yourself and amiable family . . . ."

One of the effective measures he introduced was the establishment of a police force. He insisted that the men should be under thirty years of age and of irreproachable character, and thirty-one recruits were attested, some white, some mulatto, some negro. They were given uniform, and paid well. "The system worked admirably. The policemen were scarcely required to be on duty by day, the people being of orderly and temperate habits. Their duty was so active and regular at night that security to property became assured . . . . The extraordinary diminution of offences of magnitude afforded unbounded satisfaction to the public, and satisfied the Governor as to the propriety of his police system . . . ." This experiment was duly reported to Earl Bathurst, then Colonial Secretary. Not long afterwards, in 1829, Mr. Peel, Secretary for the Home Department, who had known Le Couteur in Dublin, established the force known as "Peel's Police". Like the Curaçao Police, they used the term "Superintendent", and there were other points of similarity. It is not unlikely that Peel's system was based on Le Couteur's.

On 5th March 1816 the Le Couteur family left Curaçao. Before sailing they were showered with gifts by the Dutch administrators and the people of the island, including sheep, coconuts, limes and sapodilla fruit, milk and eggs. Mary Le Couteur was touched, she said, by the number of poor people who redoubled their affectionate attentions after her husband was no longer their Governor. Finally "at nine o'clock the pilot came on board and we left the beautiful harbour of St. Ann, the Prins van Orange like a magnificent castle sweeping alongside the houses of the town of Amsterdam. Many persons had been apprehensive of so large a vesssl getting safe out of the harbour, but we passed along the

---

1. There exists in these archives a large sheet of parchment headed with the oath of allegiance to King George III, followed by about 50 signatures (or marks in case of illiteracy), with dates from 1810 to 1815.

reefs in capital style at the rate of six knots . . . . The Captain's cabin was divided into two parts, one of which we occupied as a sitting room. The fore cabin, in which is the quarter gallery, was my son's sleeping room, with a small room where the General's cot is slung . . . . We dined in the Captain's room on an excellent dinner, which I did not expect to partake of, having suffered from seasickness in the morning. All the other ladies and Gordon were ill". After a severe storm, while going at the rate of 14 knots, San Domingo was sighted, and the next day Cape Tiburon, by when the storm had abated and they were almost becalmed. On the 10th March they sighted Jamaica and landed there, being entertained by many friends, including General Fuller who had recently married. "We were all delighted with Mrs. Fuller, a most interesting young Frenchwoman, without any of the levity attributed to that nation". She was twenty years of age, and the third wife of General Fuller, who was a grandfather. In the course of various expeditions they met a Jamaican aged 140, who "perfectly remembered the famous earthquake which destroyed Port Royal in 1693". A few days later they re-embarked on the Prins van Orange. A detailed account of the voyage follows, including a storm which carried away their main top-gallant sail. One day, near Inagua, "we were within three miles of the beach, but not being able to beat round the extreme point, attempted to tack, which the vessel could not effect, and had to wear, but so near to a ridge of breakers close inshore that we feared to shipwreck. An ominous sight was before us, the hull of a large vessel high and dry on the shore. I placed money in my pockets", Mrs. Le Couteur continued, "and filled our greatcoats with biscuits in case of accident".

The voyage lasted from 6th March to 11th May, and as it neared its end there was further excitement. John wrote: "May day. I was getting up to dress . . . ., and looking out of my stern gallery window . . . . I saw land about five miles off, and to my astonishment thought I recognised Torteval Church in Guernsey . . . . I flew to my father's cabin and told him, and he called it nonsense". But the General soon saw that it was so, and told the Captain the ship was in great danger being so close to land, emphasising the point by shouting "Donder und Blixam". By the time John got on deck the land had disappeared, for a thick fog had descended. Before long they were hailed by a fishing boat, which warned them that they were in great peril with so large a ship. That afternoon they arrived in England, "the blessed land of freedom . . . . Our noble ship gave and received a salute on anchoring at Spithead, when we soon after parted with our worthy host, afterwards Admiral van Leue, killed at the siege of Antwerp".[1]   The discipline on board had been rigid to the point of severity. "A midshipman, for having disobeyed some order, was chained to a gun and, though a tall clever youth of 17, would have been severely flogged but for the intercession of my mother, through my brother, with whom he was on friendly terms". Of the Prins van Orange, John said: "(she) was one of Bonaparte's Antwerp-built ships, and still had the "N" on all the stern PLATE glass windows. She was an admirable sailor, outstripping everything we came near". Curaçao was the General's last command, and after it he thankfully retired to Jersey, re-establishing himself at Belle Vue. Many of his letters during his absence had been pre-occupied with efforts to save money while in Curaçao, to ensure a fair income for his retirement.

His character is not easy to assess. Letters to his son are of a very stern though affectionate nature, admonishing him to uphold all the virtues, and offering sound advice on justice

1. In 1832.

and mercy in military matters. His official correspondence from the West Indies is somewhat querulous, and coloured by the necessity to solicit favours in order to gain promotion
or transfer: and in the background was the uncertainty of mails during war time, and the
long delay before a reply could be received from Europe. As a precaution he often sent
duplicates of important letters by different ships. He was much concerned with the matter
of pay and allowances, knowing that Heaven, and the War Office, would only help those
who helped themselves. While in Curaçao he avoided lavish hospitality, unlike his successor,
mainly for reasons of economy. When official entertainment was unavoidable, it could
run into a lot of money. Notes at the end of one of the books tell us: "Ball and supper
given by Gen. Le Couteur, King's birthday, June 1815, upward of 100 people who sat
down to supper; costing 324 (pieces of eight)".: and: "Expense of dinner given by Gen.
Le Couteur on Prince Regent's birthday, 12th Aug., to the Council, Commander, Field
Officers and Captains of the staff, 26 in number: 110 pieces of eight".

The General did not resume any civic functions in Jersey, being content to live quietly
in the enjoyment of his home, his farm and garden after a lifetime of strenuous service.
His son did not write a great deal about him. One gets the impression that he held him in
great respect, even awe, but perhaps with not as deep an affection as the grandfather had
commanded. 'Twas ever thus.

Both son and father missed Waterloo, on the 18th June 1815. But Sir John Le Couteur's
sketches of Hougoumont and La Haye Sainte, which he visited many years later, are
among the most interesting items in the archives.

CHAPTER THREE

A GENERAL'S WIFE AND WIDOW

Enough has already been said of Mrs. Le Couteur to gauge that she was a woman of courage, a devoted mother, intelligent and keenly observant, compassionate, religious and witty. Her son remembered her as "bright, pretty and lively, accomplished in drawing, music and literature".

She was the eldest child in a family of eight, and was only thirteen when her mother died in childbirth in 1787, being thus obliged to take the place of a mother while herself still a child. Her old London schoolmistress thought that her "steadiness of temper would go a great way towards the family's future welfare". Her aunt Martha de Sausmarez (née Le Mesurier) wrote her an unbelievably long letter of advice and admonition, full of religious precept and moral uplift. In her view women friends, after marriage, are a serious menace and should be eschewed. On the subject of "matrimony with all its horrors" she says she had married for love, as had the youthful Mary's parents. She and other members of the family appeared to approve of the girl's wish to marry Captain Le Couteur, while deploring his lack of fortune and the fact that he had no house; an unfair comment, as he only relinquished ownership of Les Buttes in order to buy Belle Vue.

Mary was but nineteen when she fell in love with this warrior, fourteen years older than herself. Returning from stirring adventures in India, and a cruel imprisonment which she believed had permanently affected his health, he seemed a glamorous figure to the young girl. Regarding the length of engagement, her aunt wrote: "If Papa thinks as I do, he will shorten the term of your probation and not suffer you to stop until a house shall be built; which, considering the known activity of your countrymen, is a work of some difficulty and great time. In the meanwhile, my dear girl, I admire the way in which you prepare yourself to be all obedience, and resolve as a prelude 'never to contradict your husband'."

The wedding took place in 1793 in St. Peter's House, the home of Mary's father, the ceremony being conducted by the Rector of the bridegroom's parish, St. John, and Mary became a soldier's wife. The vagaries and adventures of following the drum at that period have been hinted at in the last chapter. By the time her husband was posted to Scotland, Mary had a son, the future Sir John Le Couteur, and while there she set herself to improve her painting, taking lessons from "Wilson, the best landscape painter of the day, to great profit". This was not the famous Richard Wilson, who died in 1782, but one of two other Wilsons in Edinburgh at the time: either John (Jock) (1774-1855), or Andrew (1788-1848), who studied under Nasmyth and was called "The Scottish Claude". Her own natural ability, and this tuition, made her a competent artist, as her West Indian sketch-book, already mentioned, shows. She did other capable drawings, of which her pale wash sketch of "a mill[1] in St. Peter's Valley, 1802" is a good example.

---

1. It could be Tesson, or Le Moulin de Tostain.

24

Fort Henry and Barracks, Grouville Church and Mill, and Prince's Tower, 1804.
from a panorama by Mary Le Couteur.

As time went on she undertook the task of giving lessons to her two sons, John and Gordon, and when John entered the military college at Marlowe she used to write him long letters, full of human interest. The sojourn of Russian troops[1] in Jersey was an exciting time for her, and her account of the wonderful balls and dinners she attended is full of gaiety. Her husband made allusion to her fondness for dancing in a letter of 1809 when he said: "Your cousins at the Bulwarks give a Grand Fête on Thursday. They have invited 150 persons, and your mother means to kick a great stunt there, after she has put poor Gordon and me to bed". Whilst always writing affectionately to John, she does not shrink from reprimand: "I fear that you have got some bad advisers . . . . What can have occasioned the alteration in your opinion of your Captain ? . . . . There are those who are devilish good-natured fellows over a bottle of wine, or at a card table, but will never become a Duke of Marlborough or a Mr. Pitt . . . . I entreat you earnestly to study the control of your temper whilst you are

MONT ORGUEIL CASTLE in about 1800, before the erection of Gorey Pier, and the removal of Martello Tower No.6.
from an unfinished sketch by Mary Le Couteur.

1. Bulletins of La Societe Jersiaise 1914, p.416 and 1968, p.327.

young . . . . You are too fretful and easily offended". Nor do faults in literary composition escape her: "A great deal of the elegance of writing consists not only in the choice of expression, but in the use of those words only which are necessary".

We have already recorded her flash of indignation in 1816 when she was expected to play hostess at Belle Vue before the workmen had finished the alterations. She felt strongly about this, and went on to relate that she now had "a decent cook, a decent Jersey girl, instead of that fat animal you left here. The kitchen range was put up last week and made use of last Sunday. The cistern is not finished; no water; the pump has got dry". Then, moving on to other matters, but still smouldering a little: "You will see by the papers the death of the Prince of Bouillon; the poor man, it is supposed he could not survive the loss of his titles and supposed riches. Two days illness have rid him of the cares and disappointments of life, the greatest part of which has been spent in the enjoyment of (imaginary) wealth and honours, now declared to be the property of another. If he has been happy in the pursuit, he is not to be pitied. He leaves few people to regret him. His two natural daughters are both well married, the youngest to Captain Aplin, only two days before they heard of his death".

From 1816, when they came home from Curaçao, until the General's death in 1835, he and Mary lived contentedly at Belle Vue, its tranquility broken only when the General was seriously ill in England in 1831. The news of this illness caused much dismay at home, and Sir John decided to go over to England to help his mother, taking with him the faithful Ann Luce. This exemplary woman had come to the family from her home in St. Mary's in 1819 as a nurse to the children, when only a young girl herself, and remained at Belle Vue for the whole of her working life, retiring to live her last few years in the little cottage Allencot. There were tearful scenes in the Belle Vue nursery when it was known that not only was poor grandpapa ill, but that father had to go to England with Ann to nurse him. Through his sobs, the small boy said: "Oh yes, she must go". One little girl abandoned herself to prolonged crying: but Mary, who was only nine years old, rebuked her for this: "Look at me: though I feel as much as you do, I only cry in secret, but though Papa cries, I do not, and try to cheer him up". In time of grief, most Victorians, by our standards, were extroverts.

John Le Couteur thought his journey to England very fast. Passengers were allowed to board the night before, and were asleep at sailing time. "The packet started . . . ., but I was so tired that I did not hear her . . . . We got to Guernsey at a quarter past 6". They left at 7 and "thanks be to Almighty God for permitting man to invent steam, we arrived after a beautiful passage and landed at Weymouth at half past 6 . . . . I found two horrifying letters from my mother. I called for a postchaise, ran for my luggage, which the Customs House Officer examined instantly as he sympathised with me, having lost his own father the week before. I left Weymouth at 7 and got to Dorchester in 40 minutes". A breathless journey followed, bringing the anxious son to Farrington[1] in the middle of the night, where he found his father a little better. "He was lying on two beds laid on the floor . . . . His spirit had not forsaken him a whit, for he told Ann that 'he did not look much like a lover now'." For three weeks his health fluctuated, and during this time he was subjected to treatment which today would seem vicious, his condition evidently being one of acute lobar pneumonia. In those days the only known treatment for a man as ill as he was a

---

1. Probably Farrington Gurney, south-west of Bath.

succession of violent purges and emetics, combined with the scantiest possible diet, and it is a miracle that his heart survived the ordeal. Every, but every, detail of his symptoms is recorded. But he pulled through, and by the end of July was strong enough to undertake the journey home. A carriage was hired at 25s. per week. Then, "all preparations being duly completed, ... we carried my father down . . . . and placed him in the carriage, where he laid himself down very comfortably". They travelled fifteen miles to Ansford[1], but "the rain had soaked the top of the carriage so thoroughly the evening I came from Bath that yesterday's hot sun suddenly dried the leather, and the top opened of itself, nor could I close it again; which made me fear my father might take cold, and wish all landaus at the moon. I got the Hostler to wet the leather thoroughly, then saturate it with oil which stretched it properly and made it close well; but to secure it from opening I got two leather straps . . . ., which effectually secured it".

The journey continued, the poor old General standing up to it very well, and one day "my father talked of going off after dinner for Weymouth. He almost wished to eat a third slice of dry toast with his tea". A few hours later he was not so well, his pulse slow and irregular, and "I immediately suspected the toast dry had caused an indigestion". Castor oil was at once administered, a doctor was called in, and prescribed only castor oil, a little broth and sherry in water. On the 4th August, a month after his son had crossed over to see him, the General entered the last lap of his journey to Weymouth. Arrived there he was placed "in a comfortable reclining bed . . . ., carried to the wharf, and placed in a boat very comfortably . . . . We had some difficulty in getting him from the boat to the steamer, the new one, the Flameur . . . . Though it was a rough night he was not sea sick for the first time in his life. We started at 9, and got to Jersey at half past 10, and landed my dear father near the tower[2], where the carriage was in waiting for him".

The General had another four years to live, which he passed peacefully, surrounded by his family. Mary Le Couteur's diary and account books show that he ailed and weakened gradually, but with no serious illness until March 1835, when he was again subjected to constant purges, alternating with solid foods "which disagreed". On the 23rd March Mary wrote: "John arrived at 11 o'clock by the packet, just in time to receive his dear parent's blessing, who gently breathed his last about 12 o'clock, with very little struggle, although he told me but two hours before: "I fear it will be very severe with me. All the family were present at his death. Praised be God for this infinite mercy, to have brought him to this good old age". He was 75. Four days later he was buried at St. Brelade's.

There is a list of "Cloathes of my dear departed husband, given in his name by his desire to William McDermott". There were gifts of money to the house servants; £15 to Ann Luce, a considerable sum at that time, with lesser sums to Nancy and Rachel Le Cras and Mary Cox. Two visits from the Doctor cost 10s. A sum of £57. 18. 11. was paid to Godfrey Helleur & Co. for the funeral, and for a suit of clothes for Mathew the coachman, Peter Nolais the gardener, Stansberry the ploughman and labourer; George Mitchell, John's servant; and altering his master's best suit for William McDermott. Then £22. 13. 11. for "Ramie Le Brocq for dress for self, Harriet, Mary and Sophy; and for Ann Luce, Mary Cox (the cook), Nancy Le Cras, and Thérèse (the new maid): a further £1. 10s. to Miss de Boursier for making three bonnets for Ann, Nancy and the cook: £2. 2. 8. to Adams

---

1 Near Castle Cary.
2. Presumably St. Aubin's fort.

for engraving the brass plate on the coffin: £1. 9. 6 to Mrs. Marett for "my crape bonnet, frill and cap": and £3. 18s. to John Leigh for coffin attendance.

Like her husband, Mary Le Couteur was deeply religious, and this strain of piety runs right through the family, being intensified when the Sumner marriage united them with that episcopal family in England. As time went on, religion became the main pre-occupation of Mary's widowhood. She greatly valued contacts with the famous Elizabeth Fry, who visited Jersey with her husband and children in connection with her Quaker work. The Fry family often dined at Belle Vue, and they went on drives and picnics together. On the first occasion, in 1833, Mary wrote: "We had the high privilege of giving a dinner to the celebrated Elizabeth Fry with her husband Mr. Joseph Fry, two daughters and young son". In 1835, with a friend named Miss Irvine, Mrs. Fry stayed at Belle Vue, and in the morning "I breakfasted in bed . . . ., dear Mrs. Fry came into my sitting room to read in the Bible to us all, and to make a beautiful prayer . . . . fervent and sincere . . . ., invoking the blessing of God upon this family".

The work of the British and Foreign Bible Society took up much of Mary's attention in latter years. Soon after her husband's retirement she had undertaken parish work and, "with the Clergyman of the parish, instituted a Sunday school and later an Infant School. At that period few children in the parish could read or speak in the English language. Her first teaching led . . . . in half a century to have the whole body of parishioners, old and young, talking both French and English familiarly". In 1818 she founded an auxiliary Society, and the record reads: "At a meeting of ladies held at Mr. Le Sueur's Hotel in St. Helier, on Friday the 13th November 1818, a society was established under the name of The Jersey Female Auxiliary Bible Society. President, Mrs. Le Couteur: Vice Presidents, Mrs. La Cloche, Mrs. Nicolle, Mrs. Pipon (Bulwark): Treasurer, Mrs. Gordon: Bible Secretary, Mrs. Perrot: Minute Secretary, Mrs. James Le Couteur: Cash Secretary, Mrs. (Captain) Pipon, R.N.: with a committee of twenty-three ladies, then present".

In 1836 she visited France on Bible Society affairs, and wrote: "On the 5th of May, the day after our Bible Society meeting, I left Jersey, a solitary widow, with my new maid Ann Batty and embarked on board the Ariadne steamer for Granville. The concourse assembled on both piers to see the Ariadne going to France, and the Lady de Sausmarez to Southampton, gave to Jersey the appearance of a very considerable commercial country. The pier was crowded with vessels . . . . The fine pier of Granville exhibited a large assemblage of rabble, but did not give the same idea of commerce as that of St. Helier". At the hotel, "Who should I see but Sir Thomas Le Breton; we shook hands. He looked fallen. I felt an emotion I cannot describe . . . . At Caen the dinner was very good but the room and the stairs were filthy". At Evreux she attended the cathedral service, which was most impressive, but "I suppose there were ten women to one man". In all it took her four days to get to Paris, where she joined her daughter-in-law and three grand-daughters, the elder girls being at school. Contemplating the memorials to Napoleon she remarked: "He was invincible as long as he felt invincible. Arrived at his meridian sun he committed one fault, and that sun set, never to rise again". While in Paris she had trouble with her teeth and "went to the dentist . . . . and had my upper mâchoire measured for a couple of biting instruments which I am to try on next Thursday". She saw M. de Pressom on Bible Society affairs, and tried on all occasions to persuade people to read the Bible for themselves, and particularly to their children. On 16th May she witnessed an eclipse of the sun, which covered nine-twelfths of the sun's disc "and attracted an immense concourse of people in the Tuileries Gardens". She took her grand-children to see Les Précieuses Ridicules at Le Théâtre Français, and "as good luck would have it, the pieces had been called by the Queen. We were agreeably surprised to see Her Majesty[1] with some of the Princesses and a young Prince in their box. No more notice was taken of her entrance than if she had been a private person. She looked old and careworn, has very gray hair and dresses very plainly. The actors and actresses were tolerable, but being the best in Paris, I should deem them mediocre". She was given two tickets to see the Chambre des Députés: "It is a beautiful amphitheatre . . . . newly fitted up since the last revolution . . . . The Budget was the subject of debate and I heard a very interesting discussion on prison discipline." As regards her grandchildren's drawing lessons she wrote: "The drawing master was there, spoiling their taste, in my opinion. I was very glad to find Harriet inclined to dismiss him. He is quite incompetent to teach, a mere dauber. The fine arts are certainly not just now in fashion in Paris. The sciences, where cultivated, stand on higher ground. The succession of revolutions which have agitated France during the last forty years have not been favourable to elegance and refinement".

Mr. Billing, the agent for the Protestant Bible Society, called to see her. "He gave me most interesting information concerning the progress attending the distribution of the Scriptures, and its influence on society in general. This has been the work of the Protestants, and of OUR society". On the subject of the distribution of literature, she said: "Thus you observe the Catholics are getting acquainted with the Scriptures and, if they do not become Protestants, it will make them Christians". She believed fervently in the work of her Society: "When Bible Societies shall have spread the Holy Scripture to the utmost of their power, they will have fulfilled the task which they had engaged to perform; but we would affectionately entreat everyone to lay the scriptures to heart, and to cherish them as the crucible through which all human opinions and motives of action are to be sifted". Again: "In January 1834 I read in the newspaper that the Government of France had ordered that every child in the National schools of France shall be supplied with the New Testament. Who would have supposed twenty years ago that France would be foremost in Europe to supply her national schools with the Gospel?" She was President of the Jersey branch for twenty years, during which time they distributed 6501 Bibles, and sent £4376 to the parent society in London.

Mary Le Couteur's accounts, carefully kept with every detail mentioned, show that she paid a substantial part of the Belle Vue expenses after her son and his family moved there from Le Bocage in 1830. It seems to have been a happy arrangement and when, years later, her son was discussing with friends the problem of a mother-in-law living with her children, he said: "My mother lived with us as a visitor and never interfered in anything". As with any fond parent, her accounts are full of presents and treats for the grandchildren and other young relatives. She certainly paid her way, at the following rate:

"I give John and Harriet towards housekeeping	£200
I pay William's wages	32
Coachman's	20
my maid who is also housemaid for half the house	9
wines, deducting £20 from what we drank formerly	40

1. Queen Amélie, consort of Louis Philippe.

I pay besides for my coals, candles, soap, starch, coffee and sugar, washer and ironing woman's wages, half stabling in town. I also pay for half the rates on this property". Another entry reads: "Given to my children since their parent's death in 1835, to December 1843, £3223. 18. 9".

In health she was a comparatively strong woman. She was seriously ill with fever in the West Indies, but almost everyone was. She suffered a great deal from gout, which had already attacked her in 1826, when she was but forty-two. In later years the gout, with rheumatism and cramp, gave her considerable suffering. While nursing her husband in England, she wrote: "I was very poorly, but not being dangerously ill my state of health was unnoticed. Severe rheumatic pains in my back, loin and belly continued upon me for some months". A variety of doctors prescribed a series of remedies: showers, different diets, "blue pills" and colchicum. But she continued to suffer keenly, particularly at night, when cramp was sometimes so acute that she had to ring for her maid to assist her. Towards the end, her ailments naturally occupied her thoughts more and more, and the entries in the diary become very sad.

Mary inherited from her father the little fief of Orville. This was situated partly in St. John, and called des Mouriers, from early holders of that name, with a small enclave in St. Peter only half a carucate in size. Her son inherited it from her, and it reappears in 1873, when he wrote: "The Bailiff, Lieut. Bailiff Bisson, Jurat Le Montais with Mr. Solicitor Giffard came to pass a contract between the Rev. Mr. Le Hardy, Rector of St. Peter's, and churchwardens Malzard and . . . . ,[1] me, as Seigneur du fief d'Orville et du Prieur, to surrender my seigneurial right to a playground adjoining the school in case of mortmain. Gave them cake and wine". Not long before her death she also inherited the house Elysée, up Mont au Prêtre. It no longer exists, but the name is preserved in the Elysée Estate which has been built on the site. It came to her from Frederick, son of her brother Captain Philip Dumaresq, R.N. Frederick died in 1845 without issue and his other relatives claimed his inherited property. But he had acquired, not inherited, Elysée and was able to leave it to his aunt. Poor Mary did not live long to enjoy this bequest, but her son was much concerned with its upkeep and tenants for the rest of his life.

On the 4th April 1845 Mary died. Her devoted son said: "My dear and venerable mother departed this life . . . . with scarcely a struggle. It was a happy relief from great and distressing restlessness". A few days later he planted a cedar of Lebanon, willow, yew and hydrangea over the graves of Gordon and his parents, and a hydrangea over Sophy's. "The sepulture is divided into three, the edges being of box, my parents next the wall on which is engraved Le Couteur of Belle Vue; Sophy's at the other extremity; the large middle space is free for succeeding generations. The vault which contains Sophy can hold us all, if it pleases Divine Providence to grant us fulness of days. Sowed grass seed all round the other graves which we had disturbed. Three heads and many bones had been disinterred by old Clarke the gravedigger, which I had placed as deep as convenient. Clarke is like Hamlet's gravedigger, a moralist, has similar notions of fitness and sentiment. He asked me whether there was any objection on my part to have my father's coffin in view. 'Certainly do not uncover it', I answered, 'but as it is sound, by all means see the side of it and place my dear mother's coffin close beside it; I wish them to lay side by side'. 'Which will be very pretty, Sir', said the gravedigger, and he meant it in its most refined sense. The graves

---

1. Illegible.

are seven feet deep and need not be disturbed for a hundred years. Mark this, ye who succeed me!"

By Mary's direction all her clothes were given to her maid, Maria Warden, and it may be of interest to read what they were: "2 bonnets, 2 cloaks, 4 shawls, 2 merino dresses, 1 silk and one poplin, 2 aprons, 3 night caps, 5 bedgowns, 4 shifts, 6 pockets, 14 neck handkerchiefs, 12 pocket handkerchiefs, and two silk do., 3 pairs of drawers, 4 flannel waistcoats, 1 dressing gown, collars, cap and bodice, stays, 13 pair of stockings, 9 pair cloth or merino half boots, 2 pair white satin shoes, 3 pair slippers, 2 pair overall boots, a fur cap, 2 pair clogs, 1 merino petticoat, and six pounds."

Of her appearance when young, we are told she was pretty, rosy, gay and lively. There is a portrait of her in old age, though it was painted five years after her death, her son having "settled with Mr. Fisher the artist that he is to paint a portrait of my late mother and one of my wife, in the style and size of Lady Reynett's, for thirty guineas". There is a distinct likeness between these two portraits, which is not surprising as the daughter-in-law was also a niece. Mary's portrait shows her seated at a window of an upstairs room at Belle Vue, a bible on her knee in recognition of her work for the Bible Society, and behind her the view of the bay which they all loved. She looks a little sad, but serene and contented. Let us bid adieu to this excellent woman with a quotation from 1830: "Dr. Valpy[1] came to dinner. He was looking remarkably well, in very good spirits, seemed very glad to see us, and kissed Harriet. He proposed my mother's health, and said he considered her to be one of the cleverest, most conscientious and powerfully minded women he knew; indeed he knew none who surpassed her".

The younger son Gordon[2], named after his godfather General Andrew Gordon, then Lieutenant Governor, was delicate all his life and died at the age of 16. The first positive evidence of him, when he was but six years old, is in a postscript to a letter to his elder brother: "I wish much to see you, my dear John. I hope you are well. I long for next summer, that you may come. I love you dearly. Gordon Thos. Le Couteur". Then: "Gordon is to have a birthday party next week. He was told that if he knew his multiplication tables he could treat all his friends on his birthday. He knows it perfectly, so we are to have a great feast: Fred de Veulle, Millais, Butler and God knows who are to be of the party . . . . He has a fine kite which he says will fly higher than the town hill". By the name Millais is the note "the Royal Academy artist". A little later Mary wrote to John: "A watch and a gun are promised for Xmas, and Gordon is determined you shall have what you are entitled to, and will not let us rest until the gun and the watch are forthcoming. He gains strength fast, but the abscess still runs a good deal".

The period in Curaçao must have been the happiest in his short life. It may be that the hot climate was of advantage to him. His mother gave him lessons, and he went riding with his father, and on expeditions to collect sea shells. He wrote a most competent description of the island to his elder brother, which enabled the latter to recognise the island when approaching it for the first time, when the captain of the ship thought otherwise. From time to time a small painstaking copper-plate script makes a welcome appearance in the almost illegible scrawl of the General's manuscript books, and one guesses that on these occasions Gordon was acting as his father's secretary. Of his appearance, his brother

1. Dr. Richard Valpy (1754-1836), Headmaster of Reading Grammar School.
2. He was born in St. Helier in 1801.

found in him a likeness to a statue of Paris, and wrote that one lady has said to another that "he was the most beautiful creature she had ever seen. No wonder, when he was so like Paris. He had the most magnificent azure eyes I have ever seen, with a noble brow and long eyelashes to a longer eye. Chiselled features . . . . His mind was as bright as his countenance". There are no portraits of him, but if you look carefully in the Curaçao sketch-book you may discern the figure of a child in a picnic party, in a boat on a lagoon, and exploring a fort: too small for recognition, but enough to show what he looked like to his mother. The General once wrote: "I have the pleasure to inform you that Gordon's disorder entirely left him about two months ago and he is now, thank God, as well as we could wish, except his shape, which is shocking and can never be recovered". This is perhaps explained by the following: "Thrown from a restive horse when riding before a groom who had taken him up in kindness, when a beautiful robust boy of six years of age, he fell upon his back; which caused a disease of the spine, cared for by Sir Astley Cooper[1] and other eminent men; but which finally, through a gentle, studious, loving life, with the fondest of mothers, led to the disease which she so greatly but religiously mourned". It was almost certainly some form of tuberculosis.

Soon after the General's return to Jersey, in 1817, he wrote to a friend: "We have another son who has been long in a bad state of health, but he recovered in the West Indies and is now, thank God, much better". Only a month later he had to write: "I have the melancholy task of acquainting you of the death of our dear little Gordon". The elder brother John, whom he had idolised, was much shocked at the news and wrote: "Went to the de Lisles. Found there from my dear mother's letter . . . . of the loss of my poor little brother. It came very hard upon me as I was totally unprepared for it. Mama's excellent letter discovered her great resignation to the will of Providence". His mother's account of his death shall not be laid open in print. Owing to his illness he had been her constant companion, entirely dependent upon her, and she utterly devoted to him. One day he had told her that he did not expect to live long, and she answered; "As long as it shall please God". "Oh yes", he replied: "I know that, my Mummy".

---

1. Sir Astley Paston Cooper F.R.S. (1768-1841). Celebrated Surgeon who operated on George IV.

CHAPTER FOUR

B. 100

Having arrived at an assessment of Sir John Le Couteur's background through his "aieuls", we now return to him personally as the principal actor in this drama of eventful lives.

From the several portraits and photographs of him at various ages we see that he had the wide forehead and determined chin of a strong intellectual character. The picture in militia uniform shows clear, penetrating, light blue eyes. He mentions this characteristic in describing his own brother, and his great-granddaughter, Miss Ethel Utterton, has them to this day. Before her forthright, honest yet witty gaze I had the feeling I was looking into his eyes. Several clues show that he was short in stature but of upright military bearing. The sterner features of the young A.D.C. in all the pride of his new uniform have softened and rounded by the time of the portraits by Stonehouse and Berteau, and bear greater resemblance to the early picture of the young cadet. There is no doubt about the authenticity of any of these portraits, for the evidence in the diaries is conclusive.

Even at this early stage an appraisal of his character can be made, as it altered little through his long life, except for the natural modifications of age. He was of the utmost honesty of mind and conduct, incapable of a mean act, and with it went strength of purpose, integrity, loyalty and conscientiousness. These deeply rooted characteristics were fostered by religion and strengthened by the background of a happy childhood, and a belief in goodness for its own sake. He was convinced that in order to fulfil his purpose on earth, each man should do his best for the benefit of his fellow men. Family devotion was a strong element in his life. There was a keen sense of humour, which in his boyhood bubbled forth in mischievous frolics and quick back-answers. Generous in praise of goodness, he had no mercy on behaviour which fell short of his standards, and comments on some of his contemporaries in Jersey are strong, almost vicious. He was not averse to telling a doubtful story, provided it was witty. Of his faults, and one would not wish him to have been without any, it cannot be denied that he was overconfident, well aware of his own abilities and success, and perhaps too ready to remind the reader of them. His weakness for signing KADC or QADC after his name on each and every occasion might be taken for conceit, but stems, one feels, from a true pride, in the best sense of the word, in having been chosen for that distinction. According to his mother, he was inclined to laziness as a lad and, like many parents, she bemoans the fact that he does not write home often enough. But it is hard to comprehend a charge of laziness, as his whole life leaves one exhausted at its speed and intensity. She also accuses him of being hot-tempered. This also may have sprung from her own almost impossibly high standards. On the other hand we shall see that he could be very irritable with his wife and elder daughter on occasion, though the younger daughter never receives a word of censure.

The first episode we have of his childhood, which occurred when he was two, is a hilarious one: "I was first breeched by being laid out "al fresco on a piece of cloth, while my

10. MARY LE COUTEUR (née Dumaresq)
(1774-1845)
(*painted by Fisher*, 1850).

11.   THE FORTIFICATIONS OF ST. BRELADE'S BAY, Jersey, c.1800.
(*a water-colour by Mary Le Couteur*)

mother was at St. Helier's and I at St. Peter's, when three merry young aunts cut out my first dress on my shape. It was so tight that my mother hardly knew her walking sausage". Allowing for the rose-coloured spectacles which doting mothers constantly wear, one must admit that he was a highly intelligent child, showing an early ability in mathematics. His mother wrote: "Jack read English tolerably at four years. He began to write a letter legibly at five, but about this time he had sore eyes which prevented him reading and writing for near six months, which put him very back. He began arithmetic at six, but it was discontinued for near two months whilst I was in childbed of Gordon . . . . He knew his multiplication table perfectly before he was seven, and before he was eight he began the rule of three[1]. I began him in grammar at seven, without book, by making him understand the nature of the different parts of speech; and before he was eight he made very few mistakes in telling the part of speech of any word. He began to read Euclid at seven . . . ., also French and Geography . . . .; finished the fifth book of Euclid in 1804, for which his father gave him a silver spoon with his name on it . . . . In 1802 he began vulgar fractions with his father, and could by then translate French into English or English into French pretty correctly. He began algebra with his father as soon as he was eleven years old. He had then gone over the whole arithmetic, and could extract the cube root . . . . I then sent for Dalby's mathematics book, taught at Marlowe, and he began geometry. In August 1805, before he was eleven years old, he began to learn German with Mr. Kerpedron, a French emigrant who came to him twice a week . . . .; the Abbé Cabri came three times a week to teach him the upper branches of . . . . mathematics. He attended Boy's drill under his father, the Inspector of Militia". Of these drills he himself wrote: "I had striven to gain a prize, though only twelve years old, when at drill with the boys at St. Helier. De Quetteville and Phil de Carteret were my rivals: de Quetteville, being a stronger boy, tired us out on the day of trial and got the prize. We commanded squads, nevertheless, as officers". At school the following year he heard of the militia prize-giving from his father: "We had the last delivery of prizes for the year a few weeks ago, Sir G. Doyle[2], and Generals Don and Leighton, and a great number of officers and ladies both from the Island and Guernsey were present . . . . Your friend Le Sueur, who is not much taller than you, drew the admiration of everybody, but particularly of the ladies: he had the fourth spoon".

In 1807 he was sent to a preparatory school for Marlowe, the college for training "Gentleman Cadets". The active life of Marlowe was short, from 1801-1812 only, its place being taken by Sandhurst, founded by Major General Gaspard Le Marchant[3], a Guernseyman. The master of the preparatory school was Mr. Sproston, Rector of High Wycombe, "a worthy sincere man with whom I was very happy. The French master thought me his best scholar, thanks to the Abbé Bourge in Jersey. On the French master quitting our school, Mr. Sproston made me act as French master, which I did for some months". He was rather too young to take the Marlowe entrance examination, but General Le Marchant, the Governor, recognised him and asked: "'Are you come up for examination?' 'No, Sir, I am not of age for it yet'. 'Do you think you could pass?' 'Yes, Sir'. 'Will you try?' 'Certainly, Sir'. Up I went to old Black Swat (Professor Dalby)", the story continues, "and got through my arithmetic". After the examination, Le Marchant said: "Write to

1. A method of finding the fourth number in a proportion sum, when the first three are given.
2. Lieutenant-Governor of Guernsey. 3. (1766-1812). Governor of the Royal Military College, 1801-1810.

E

your Father and Mother that although you cannot be admitted yet, you have earned your admission. I give you joy".

In February 1808 he went on to Marlowe, where he was allocated the number B.100. "This was considered the crack company of the Royal Military College . . . . My weekly allowance was a shilling . . . . The drilling which I had undergone in Jersey told wonderfully . . . . Drilling was under the clear comprehension that when the Sergeant says: 'As you were', I means: 'As you was' . . . . At this period the cadets had to clean their own shoes, gaiters, coats, buttons, belts, plates, arms and accoutrements. We had heel ball, pipe clay, plate powder, buff sticks, brushes, all to buy". Promotion to Corporal and then Under Officer followed swiftly. "I then had three stripes on my arm, and a sword instead of a bayonet; we did not draw our swords, but carried our arms at the advance like Sergeants".

These young lads had plenty of fun. "The hospital, when it could be reached by a sham, offered an agreeable break in the dry and laborious course of study. Many and clever were the dodges devised to deceive our Scotch Esculapius, a dry but kind old gallypot[1]. . . . . a knocking of elbows against walls, washing the eyes with a solution of goulard[2] to redden them, gargling with vinegar to furr the tongue, rubbing chalk powder on the cheeks to give a pallid hue . . . . In the hospital, low diet was indeed close upon starvation, just weak tea and gruel. Full diet was plentiful . . . .

"B.64 was an ingenious deviser, a youth of fertile invention and ready resources. We were a demure half dozen on the starving diet, plenty of money in the room but no servant was to be bribed: all thought to be too ill to be indulged with meats or confections, even by the gentle-hearted maids, when they were visible, and theirs were angel visits. So, two sick and four shammers, hungry as wolves in a Siberian winter. B.100 had a smooth face, something like a girl's and the sauciness was tempered by the danger . . . . He was deputed to the maids' room while they were sipping their tea. He borrowed a bonnet, gown and shawl. These were speedily put on, and the bonnet, gown and shawl walked to the front door, which was readily opened by the Janitor. Off ran the maid cadet to the pastry-cook, a trusty and tried friend. The astonished and alarmstruck piewoman was unwilling to supply the hospitallers". But at last Le Couteur persuaded her, and "tongues, sausages, shrub rolls[3] and confections were deposited in a basket, and off went the little maid cadet, while the well-placed sentinels watched her advance. Janitor was called from the door by one, for a case of fainting and dread alarm, while another opened the door, while the little cadet maid skipped upstairs, deposited the supplies under a bed", and returned the disguise to the maids' room. "Then, when all were sound in the arms of Morpheus, came the repast".

There was a sequel to this affair. "We felt bound in gratitude to give a boating party to the pastrycook's daughter and one or two of her fair friends, with a picnic up the river . . . . Our boat was taken some distance to a place of concealment . . . . Off we pulled up stream, so fast as to distance any Sergeant-Major on the banks . . . . The gay painted barge flew through the silver stream. At the end of a seven mile stretch, 'Row easy in bow': out with the landing board, hand out the ladies, get out the baskets. No sooner said than done, when just beyond us from a sort of shrubbery emerged a fair damsel with a beau: 'Oh, what a pretty boat, do let us go and see it'. Murder and confusion, Jeannette Butler, the Colonel's daughter, and an opposition picnic'. 'Jump in, girls, with the baskets. She won't

---

1. For gallipot, a small glazed medicine-bottle.　　2. A lead lotion.
3. Shrub was a delicious cordial made of fruit juice and rum, but I do not know what a shrub roll was.

know us, and if she does she won't peach[1], provided the Colonel does not see us'. Jeannette twigged[2] us, but did not peach, we fancied . . . . We enjoyed our picnic lower down, but within a mile of Marlowe were two Sergeants, one on each side of the river. 'Look down, lads, and pull your best'. We quite distanced and fagged out the runners, got to a safe landing, left the boat in charge of the ladies and ran for our lives. Got to the pastrycook's in safety, on uniforms, and in College in time".

Marlow Bridge

Intermittent but bitter war was waged between the cadets and the Thames bargees, the battle-ground often being one of the bridges, from which cadets used to throw missiles to bring the enemy to the boil. Marlowe was then "a sort of port for barges", and strong forces of bargemen could be mustered. "Sometimes the bargemen would land, assemble and thrash the first cadet they could lay hands on". One day they were out in force and would not let a cadet cross Marlowe Bridge, but a cadet "who had the form of Mercury, with a giant's strength and pluck for any row, was named the General. A hundred and fifty volunteers were soon armed, some with cudgels, others with pockets full of stones. These slingers and throwers were the light troops and advance guard. As they came to the bridge end, they were to extend to each side and commence rapid and independent fire on the enemy who, having been reconnoitred, were found to be in force, three or four deep, armed with oars, boathooks and bludgeons, holding the pass in quiet and stern defiance. The forlorn hope were the strong, big boys, the reserve . . . . On taking up the points of attack, which the bargees looked upon with the calm determination which the Duke did at Waterloo[3], the word was waited for. Once given, a shower of missiles nearly blinded the enemy, who were quite unprepared for such a cannonade. An indication of retreat led to the charge, when bludgeons, oars, boathooks and stones came into active and serious play. One cadet, a Lord, was in the hands of two bargemen, who were in the act of giving His Lordship a pitch into the river. But the sword of Achilles was flashing to the rescue, and two strokes right and left over the body of the cadet sent a broken jaw and broken head to the ground . . . The bridge was cleared in ten minutes of all but the wounded. The officers and sergeants soon appeared, and all were confined to College for the day".

1. Inform on us.   2. Recognised.
3. This shows that the narrative was written retrospectively. The story also reveals that these adolescent pranks were conducted as tactical exercises, and that participants had a grounding in classical mythology.

One day this boisterous cadet, B.100, became a genuine inmate of the hospital with an attack of pleurisy. By chance, another patient in the same ward was George FitzClarence, eldest son of William IV and Mrs. Jordan[1], afterwards Earl of Munster, and they became great friends. "I was weakly dozing one morning, when suddenly a fair being, with a sweet, compassionate and beaming countenance, beautifully dressed, with a voice like a seraph, sat by me and gently took my hand . . . . 'My dear young friend, how are you? You are George's friend, and I am his mother; therefore you are my friend. How do you feel today? You have been very poorly, but the danger is over. My George is still dangerously ill, and I have come to nurse him myself'." She asked him, as soon as he was well enough, to move to another room so that she might stay with her sick son. Not long after, and partly as a result of this encounter, B.100 was asked to assist in taking care of Henry, the next eldest son of the Duke of Clarence, a boy who had been removed from the Navy because he was unmanageable. The Duke wished him "to be under the care of a steady cadet" at Marlowe, and B.100 was selected to solve this royal problem. He was greatly perturbed at such a responsibility and asked for time to consult his parents. His mother advised acceptance, which he gave, on condition that the boy should sleep in the room which, as Responsible Under Officer, he occupied alone. "The afternoon of his arrival I showed him his bed, explained to him that I had required him to be placed in my room because, if he had gone among the cadets in the larger room, he must have been fag to someone, bullied, misled and played tricks with; and, if he had borne this impatiently, beaten and misused. Alone with me he would merely have to take care of his own kit, and fetch water in the morning for himself and me. I would show him how to clean his clothes, shoes, arms and accoutrements, after which he must learn to do it for himself . . . . I would never punish him without warning, and if I moved my hand to my face in speaking to the Company, (it meant) he was unsteady. After that he would be punished as any other cadet. 'Where is your kit?'

"The boy burst into a flood of tears. 'I have nothing. They destroyed all my things, cut up my bedding, cut me down, beat me, made me drink. I have been cruelly used on board of His Majesty's ship, and never got a good word from anyone. I was never so kindly spoken to in my life before' . . . . The youth was, for his station, shamefully destitute of comforts, owing to the ill usage on board ship. He was untidy and rough looking, from the Middys having resolved to take all the polish out of him".

B.100 and this disorientated boy became great friends, and Henry was soon one of the smartest cadets in the College. "Some months later the Duke of Clarence, with his lovely daughter (afterwards Lady De Lisle) came to the College to see his son. The Duke said: 'Le Couteur, what have you done with my son?' I coloured and felt droll, looked at the sweet and beaming eyes of Miss FitzClarence: all must be right from that beautiful smile. I bowed. 'What have you done, I say, to my son? He was reported to me as being too unsteady for the Navy, quite intractable, discontented, slovenly: and here I see a fine smart lad, contented and bearing an excellent character. How you have effected this transformation I know not, but this I will assure you, that at any time, or under any circumstances that may happen, if ever I can be of service to you, you need only remind me of this circumstance to insure it'." At that time the Duke had little expectation that he would become King.

---

1. There were five sons and five daughters. The sons were, George (1794-1842) (Earl of Munster), Henry (1795-1817), Frederick (1799-1854), Adolphus (1802-1856), Augustus (1805-1854). The Miss FitzClarence mentioned was Sophia, who married Lord de Lisle and Dudley.

In 1810 came the climax of examination for commissions. "I was given the third case of trigonometry, with the attendant problems and theorems. The room was full of magnates and ladies, some fair beating bosoms, anxious for brothers or friends . . . . While, rod in hand and bold in voice, (I was saying) 'the angle RSF is equal to . . . .', B.86 whispered in my ear: 'Johnny, look at that lovely girl eyeing you: wouldn't you like to kiss her?' This to me, in the midst of an examination. I gave a kickback and felt that I had lost my place, hesitated, and thought my commission in jeopardy. Sir Howard Douglas[1], the accomplished, the learned, the kind Sir Howard, had overheard the mischief and saw my distress, and whispered: 'Very well, the angle RSF is equal to the angle FGP', ... and so I was able to go on".

He passed, gained his commission, and was posted as Ensign to the 96th Regiment, the Manchesters, who by a twist of chance were then stationed in Jersey. At the end of the academic year he found himself in his home Island in the Light Infantry Company under Colonel Lee. "They were all Welshmen, as active as goats, very smart nice fellows, but quarrelsome". In 1810 "I mounted perhaps the first guard at Fort Regent, for on that day Sir George Don, the Commander in Chief, then General Don, came to visit the still unfinished works. After presenting arms and turning in my guard, he asked what sort of a guard room I had. 'Indeed, Sir, a very uncomfortable one, for if your Excellency were to alight, I could not offer you a seat'." General Don perhaps the most popular Governor Jersey ever had, asked to be shown the situation, There was only a stretcher and a table in the guard room. He said: "Well, that is scanty indeed, regular campaigning accommodation. Now, write out an order for anything you like, and I will sign it". So the young officer asked for a table, six chairs, a bedstead, one cupboard and a wash-stand. "Is that too much, Sir?". "What did I say?" "Very true, Your Excellency, but I did not wish to be unreasonable. A fender and fireirons and a few utensils". The General signed the order, and it "made our guard room very snug".

A race occurred at this time, which must have been the greatest fun for all concerned. "One evening at our rollicking mess they got up a race, the Light Company officers against the Regiment: a sweepstake: the distance, from the sands below the Blue Barracks where the 96th was quartered, to St. Aubins: up the slip: through the street: down by La Haulle, and back". Earnest training took place for about a month, and then "the eventful day arrived. We were all clothed in flannels, mine trimmed with green. My Marlowe training led them to back me freely. Off we started, I in no hurry at the steady slow trot was soon left behind, but by the time I had held the same pace to St. Aubins, there were only O'Halloran, Calomb and Rickards in company, and I took the lead up the hill at a running pace. Well do I remember the cheers and waving of handkerchiefs from the thronged windows, for half St. Heliers was out to witness the great foot race . . . . Capt., now Sir George Arthur, rode by and urged me not to hurry . . . . Off again over the sands . . . . I lengthened my pace in the last mile and quickened it in the last hundred yards, distancing all but the Welsh Corporal in the Light Company, who could have run past me like a greyhound; but the honour of the company was his also, and he only cheered his sub. He and I ran five miles two furlongs and a half, measured, in thirty-one minutes and a half, and I won the sweepstakes. The moment I got to the winning post, to my utter astonishment I found

---

1. Sir Howard Douglas (1776-1861), General and military writer.

myself whipped off my legs and muffled up in blankets as if I had been a baby in arms. Four of the light bobs ran up the sand hills with me amidst the cheers of the company, who relieved the bearers by turns, till I got to the barrack room where I was unceremoniously stripped naked, popped into a warm bed; then the Doctor stood by, saw me rubbed down by a detachment, who were laughing, full of joy and triumph at the victory". After a drink of negus[1] he fell asleep. His mother, on this occasion rather a spoil-sport, made him promise never again to run for money, and said she had been very worried at the thought of boys running against grown men; though he assured her that he and Carey Le Marchant had done an even more arduous run at Marlowe in half an hour.

In November 1811 he was promoted Lieutenant in the 104th, the Munster Fusiliers, and "regretted parting with my 96th friends but was delighted at the idea of going abroad". His father was at this point ordered to Ireland and applied for his son to accompany him as A.D.C., which was refused as the son had not then done two years of regimental duty. But he spent his leave in Ireland with his parents, as mentioned above. In February 1812 there were "rumours of a war between Great Britain and the United States . . . . I received orders to rejoin my regiment in New Brunswick". He proceeded to the depot at Newport, Isle of Wight, and "joined the mess of the depot, which was made up of officers from a variety of corps, some of the worst looking scamps I had ever seen wearing the King's uniform. In those days of raging wars, all sorts of men obtained commissions, some without education, some without means, some without either . . . . It was a society so vulgar, so drunken, so vicious and so disorderly that on meeting one absolutely dreaded who to sit by or who to converse with".

Whilst there he was ordered to sit on a court martial. "At this period of our military era corporal punishments were ferocious . . . . from three hundred to a thousand lashes might be awarded, and I have known the latter figure to be sentenced. The prisoner was on trial for being drunk while waiting for guard . . . ., but he proved in mitigation that he had not had due warning because it was not his turn for duty . . . . I considered he had justified his plea. On being asked my opinion first, as junior member, I stated my opinion, why I only found him guilty of simple drunkenness and awarded him the least punishment of those bloodthirsty days, one hundred lashes". The next two members of the court agreed with this, but the two senior members thought the case was quite made out against the man and awarded three hundred lashes. The majority having recommended the lesser punishment, the case was forwarded to General Taylor, who was highly dissatisfied and ordered a retrial, at which Le Couteur, when again asked for his opinion first, replied that his father, a General, had taken great pains to teach him how to judge a court martial and, "if there were any mitigating circumstances, to lean to the side of mercy and to judge according to my conscience". The lesser sentence was again passed by majority vote, and Taylor was displeased, issuing "a severe censure on three members of a court martial for an ill-judged sentence; which the whole garrison thought very ill-timed and uncalled for, and I was complimented by many old officers".

"The General thought to punish me after a fashion of his own by sending me, then a youth of 17 only, to take charge of a detachment of wounded soldiers, two hundred Peninsula heroes, who were on board of a transport then lying at Spithead, on passage

---

1. Hot sweetened wine and water.

to Deal to the military hospital. I found the Harford, Capt. Landels, a fine ship of 600 tons, among the fleet. What a glorious fleet it was, some forty or fifty line of battle ships and a bevy of frigates and sloops of war, beside 300 sail . . . .; never did I behold such a sight. My uncle Philip Dumaresq was then captain of Lord Nelson's famous ship the Victory. She was at anchor, with the flag of Sir James Saumarez flying, as commanding the Baltic fleet.

"I found . . . . Dr. Bradley in charge of the wounded invalids, a well educated and amiable companion; we became real friends. As soon as I got on board I mustered my detachment. Never was such a disorderly set of veterans, old and young, all wounded. I was resolved to treat them with great indulgence . . . . Some squads . . . . had no non-commissioned officer whatever. The senior sergeant . . . . of the Fusiliers . . . . I made acting Sergeant Major. Some had no legs, and others no arms. I went below to visit the sick, when the heat and stench were so great, from a number of women and children being among the men, that it was quite unbearable . . . . When the dinner hour arrived the grog was served, as to the seamen. The consequence was that, some of the men having sold their grog to others and to the women, many got very drunk by the evening parade or roll call and were insolent in the last degree. The Doctor wrote to me officially to say that the grog issued at that strength would endanger the health of the men, many of whom should have none what-ever . . . . So the following day I ordered water to be mixed with the grog, explaining to the men that it was the Doctor's desire. There was a regular mutiny. They threatened to pitch me overboard, a brat of a boy who had never seen a shot fired, to ill-use veterans in that way. One of them tripped up my one-legged sergeant, on which I knocked the fellow down and called on the Captain and his crew to assist in quelling the mutiny. Many flung away their weak grog". This was not the end of his trials. When all was quiet after the dis-turbance he went ashore to get provisions for the ship and, on returning with them to the hard, was told by the watermen that the ship had sailed. Fearing a court martial and loss of commission, he ran back to find his Uncle Philip, whom by good fortune he met coming down to the hard. His advice was: "You must go by mail to Deal, get on board your ship the instant she arrives, and land your men. No one will report you, as you are commanding officer; even so you would not be to blame, as you were without provisions". Le Couteur had another stroke of luck. A ship in the convoy arrived, was hailed, and asked to assist Captain Dumaresq's nephew, who had come ashore for provisions. "His ship is under your convoy but has got under weigh, and he may miss her in a shore boat. I shall thank you to give him a cast on board when you near her". During dinner on board the convoy ship the story of the mutiny was told, and the captain said: "If that should happen again, hoist a yellow burgee[1] at the peak and I will send a boat crew for the offender".

Then came the day of reckoning. "The next day, when the grog was to be mixed, a most riotous scene occurred. I drew my sword and declared I would cut down the rascal who again knocked the sergeant over. I instantly hoisted my signal for aid. The boat with a crew manned and armed came off, and I had the two most violent offenders siezed . . . . I promised to send off any women who misbehaved, and this brought them to some order. In about two hours our delinquent returned, as tame as a lamb". This man, who had been

---

1. A small swallow-tailed pennant.

beaten, was paraded before the whole company, and "I declared if they disobeyed me I would carry out the articles of war with full vigour. There was no more trouble".

A few days later there was a fierce gale. "I was sound asleep in my berth . . . ., when all at once I heard an immense crash, and perceived a great beam poking through the stern windows, tearing and breaking all it met with in a violent jar which shook the ship to her keel. I flew on deck, where I saw we were driving on and riding down a sloop of war. We had carried away her sprit sail yard, knocked some of her guns over, stove in her bow, and the Jacks were striving to shove us off and swearing at us manfully. We soon got clear of her with little damage to ourselves . . . . The hurricane continued all that day . . . ., but next morning the pilot boats, splendid little boats, came about in a heavy sea, offering to land for a guinea a head . . . . The weather was too boisterous all that day to land my invalids but, the next days being calm, they were all landed safely; legs without arms agreed to carry arms without legs".

He spent about two months at Deal with the 104th, and in May 1812 received embarkation orders, "with directions to provide our passage as we might". This turned out to be a most unpleasant voyage, very crowded, and with extremely dirty weather at the start. In those days passengers on long journeys like this took their own provisions, including live poultry, which on this occasion was put in charge of a farm-bred man. But he failed to keep the poor birds in good condition. A better place having been found for them, the poultryman was told: "Old fellow, you are no farmer. You are starving and killing all our poultry with your West Country kindness". "Well, why don't you try your hand at it, Johnny, and see what your Jersey farming will do?" "Done. Jersey for ever against the world!" It was apparently a successful take-over, for at the end of the voyage all birds not killed for the pot were well and healthy.

This trans-Atlantic trip took from 18th May to 21st June 1812. On arrival at Halifax "I found my old friend and countryman George Lemprière, the Second Lieutenant on board the flag ship Africa . . . . He was most kind and took me to parties . . . . Sir Thomas Saumarez applied for me to become his A.D.C., but the fated regimental duty still stood in my way . . . . On the 26th I was dining in the gun room of the Africa with Lemprière when it was announced that the Belvidera coming in had made her private signal. A moment later an officer hurried down . . . ., 'She has no boats, no anchor and shot holes through her sails'. Up flew all, and she soon came alongside, when indeed we saw signs of battle. She has been chased by Commodore Rogers in the President, and by an American squadron . . . . She cut away everything weighty, fired her starn chasers and got off."

Next day, war with America was declared, the sad, futile, unwanted campaign of 1812-1814. The 104th were immediately sent under convoy to St. Johns, Bay of Fundy. A small engagement took place, and an American captain was taken prisoner, who said he had known friends not half so kind as his enemies. This was the youthful Sir John Le Couteur's first taste of war. "Now I had seen the reality, a brave handful under a dear friend, seeking the bubble in the cannon's mouth[1]. I had seen wounds and death in real war". On arrival at St. Johns in the new uniform of that day they were "looked upon as dandies of the first water and finest fashion. The old uniform had been a long coatee with cocked hats , . . .; knee breeches with black gaiters, with some fifty little round buttons up

---

. "The bubble reputation, even in . .". Shakespeare, As you like it, II.vii.139.

their sides; a sword belt, gorget and sash. The light companies wore jackets and wings, with a cap like a sugar loaf, the peak square and turned up, a bugle in front, with long cords with tassels of gold or silver and a green plume. The new uniform was a perfect contrast. A cap like a straight quart mug only the side (size) of the noddle it was meant to fit, a sort of screen risen above the front half of it, a rich large gilt cap plate, a small feather and very rich cords and tassels of gold, intended to secure the cap from being lost while skirmishing; a short jacket with small pockets . . . ., while loosish grey overalls, with six buttons in two figures like a brace, ornamented the front over pockets in pretence . . . . A vile dress it was for service . . . . The neat hessian boot and tight pantaloons, the most dressy of all uniforms, was the evening or full dress".

In such splendid apparel the young officers enjoyed strolling around the town and attracting female admiration. "We saw two very pretty women laughing very heartily at our droll caps and clipped tails. 'I won't be laughed at in that style', I exclaimed to my companion. 'I'll kiss my hand to that sweet one'. No sooner said than done". But there was a sequel to this gesture. After delivering his letters of introduction at Government House, he was summoned there by General Smyth and received "politely, but with much stately dignity", and told that he had been entrusted to the care of Mrs. Smyth, who desired to see him. Ushered in with great pomp, he tried to remember all he had been taught about bowing correctly to a grand lady, but to no avail, for "I felt rooted to the ground . . . . I felt my face redder than my new coatee. My sin was before me, for I had kissed my hand to the Governor's own wife. . . . . I felt like a chien fouetté". They had recognised each other. The girl who had laughed at him in the street was none other than the Governor's wife, far younger than her husband, and of surpassing beauty. The situation was saved by the appearance of her daughter, who was fascinated by the uniform, and made friends with the young man who wore it; so much so that when the child was at loggerheads with her governess, she ran a full mile to find her friend in his barracks, and insisted that he should give her a lesson in drawing in colours before she would go home. "I was on thorns for fear some of my playful brother officers should have caught me at my task". But there were no intruders, the lesson was given and the little girl returned to her mother.

He described St. John's as a large town with some good houses, but poor barracks. Major Drummond was in command, "a splendid looking man, kind hearted and noble". The cold was intense. On one occasion a sentry was found insensate on duty, it was assumed he was drunk and he was severely punished. Long afterwards Sir John asked himself if this unfortunate soldier was not in fact benumbed by the bitter temperature, and marvels that this explanation had not occurred to any experienced officer or doctor at the time. The regiment was not long at St. Johns, leaving for Fredericton by way of the St. Johns River, "the most beautiful I ever saw". As they moved up it the country became more and more fertile, and on landing on an island they found quantities of wild strawberries and raspberries. Arrived in Fredericton, there was much jollity and entertaining. Although it was war time, with drills, guards and pickets at night, and duty was pretty hard, they had at this stage none of the horrors of war. Nevertheless in his three months at Fredericton he attended thirty-five dinners or balls. When orders came for them to march to Canada, they were sorry to leave "our noble barracks, for though they were wooden I have never seen any so good; were as warm and comfortable as possible, close to the river, with a fine parade ground, good stables; messing was very cheap, as from 1st to 30th September my account shows £3. 11s.".

The famous march of the 104th to Canada started on 16th February 1813, Colonel Halkett leading with the Grenadier Company, and one Company following each succeeding day, the Light Company (Captain Shore's) being the last to leave, on the 21st. About 550 men took part in the march. Sir John was in the Light Company, and naturally related their experiences only, but with minor variations these were probably shared by their comrades. He wrote as though he kept a diary of the march. If so, it is lost. We have, however, the draft of a narrative he wrote in 1831 for a New York magazine named Albion,[1] and W. Austin Squires says[2] that most of the detailed accounts of the march are based on Le Couteur's story. The narrative is quoted extensively in the next chapter[3], and is firsthand evidence of a remarkable achievement. "Our Regiment", wrote Sir John, "was the first British Corps that ever performed such a march during the height of a northern winter, a great part of it on snow shoes".

---

1. Reprinted in the Canadian Defence Quarterly, 1930, Vol.VII, pp.490-500.
2. In his "The 104th Regiment of Foot".
3. Any material differences between the draft narrative in these archives, and the Albion version reprinted in the Canadian Defence Quarterly, are shown in footnotes, with the letters CDQ where the latter is quoted.

CHAPTER FIVE

THE MARCH OF THE 104th

When war broke out with the United States in June 1812, Sir John's narrative explains, the British Commander-in-Chief in Canada, Sir George Prevost[1], found himself with only 3000 regular troops to defend 1100 miles of frontier from Quebec to Michilimackinack; a frontier assailable at many points, particularly along the River St. Lawrence from Cornwall to Kingston, and from Fort George to Fort Erie in the Niagara area. For a time the firm measures of the gallant General Brock[2], a Guernseyman, assisted by a formidable force of Indians whose confidence he had won, saved the Upper Province from enemy invasion. But in October 1812 he was killed at Queenston. Owing to the Peninsular War, England was unlikely to spare any re-inforcements, and Sir George took the risk of weakening his force in New Brunswick, which was less vulnerable than Upper Canada, by bringing the 104th Regiment westwards. Winter descended, but no matter. A winter march must be performed; and Major-General Smyth, commanding in New Brunswick, put the men through intensive training on snow-shoes without disclosing the reason. They guessed, of course, that something was afoot, and on the 5th February 1813 a garrison order announced the intended march. The Regiment greeted it with enthusiasm "as an effort yet unknown in British warfare and therefore well worthy of British soldiers to accomplish".

The 104th were admirably suited to the assignment, having been raised chiefly in New Brunswick "from the descendants of the veterans who had served in the former war, ..." There were a number of Canadians also. In fact most of the men were indigenous to the country, inured to cold and hardship, marksmen, fine axemen "able to build a log hut with an axe alone; good boatmen . . . ., many of them as expert as Indians in a canoe, and as alert as hunters on snow shoes". Morale was high, "as there is a characteristic cheerfulness in the Canadian soldier, inherited from his French ancestry, which being both lively and good tempered, tended much towards lightening the labours of a heavy march . . . . and kept . . . . in good humour the more dogged and varied characters of the English, Irish and Scotch which completed the Regiment".

They were equipped with snow-shoes[3], moccasins and toboggans. The snow-shoe was designed to "support the weight of a man on the light and frail surface of his own height of snow, so as to enable him to walk with ease and comfort over it, and where without such assistance he would infallibly perish". It was made "somewhat like a racket. The frames of my own were just three feet in length by fifteen inches in width, of hickory, which is tougher and more elastic than ash, with two cross bars to connect and render them firm. The network to support the foot is of dressed cariboo deer or buffalo hide, strongly inter-laced and drawn very tight. That which is perfectly dressed never slackens by moisture but continues quite elastic, which is of great importance. For if the net of the shoe becomes slackened . . . ., the fatigue of the wearer is greatly encreased from the want of elasticity . . . . At nine inches from the front of it is an aperture behind the cross bar with a leather strap

---

1. Sir George Prevost (1767-1816), British General.　　2. Sir Isaac Brock (1769-1812), British Major General.
3. Most of the next four paragraphs do not appear in the CDQ.

over it to secure the toes from slipping, to allow the toes to play in, and the foot is firmly secured to this spot by a long bandage of list or cloth, crossed over the toes and behind the foot, round the heel, that it may not slip. The shoes weigh one pound and a half each when dry; they were full half a pound heavier when wet, and cost 16 shillings the pair".

The moccasin or slipper worn with the snow-shoe "should fit comfortably over three or even four pair of woollen socks, to keep the feet both warm and soft". It was disagreeable to prepare, but if badly made "it wets through directly in wet snow, which in a long and cold winter's march is absolute misery . . . . It should be made of moose deer or ox hide, well tanned, then soaked in strong brine for 24 hours, in order to soften the leather and keep it moist: when drained and half dry, steeped in train oil for several days until completely saturated, and afterwards gradually dried at a distance from the fire. Thus prepared they will last a great while without being penetrated by snow or water. Even shooting shoes or boots prepared in this way are softer and more useful to sportsmen than all the anti-attrition compositions I have ever tried". The moccasins issued to the men were quite unsuitable, "being contract articles, of hide that had never been properly dressed. Moreover, few of the Officers or men then knew how to prepare them . . . . The Officers prepared flannels for clothing themselves from head to foot, besides fur caps, mits and collars", the men receiving these also.

"The tobogin or Indian sledge . . . . is made of a hiccory or ash plank scarcely a quarter of an inch thick, about six feet in length and a foot in breadth, so as to fit the track of a snow shoe. The head of the tobogin is turned up, in order to throw off the snow, like the fingers of a hand half shut. Attached to it on each side are two light sticks secured by thongs which form the side of the vehicle, which, when it is packed, prevent anything from falling off it. We added a pole to it behind in order to assist the man who dragged it in front, by another pushing it on, or keeping it back when going down a hill. Each tobogin was supplied with a large tarpaulin, cut so as to pack in the most snug manner, the men's knapsacks being laid on the bottom of the tobogin and the arms stowed on the sides. The provisions were packed on separate tobogins, the daily allowance . . . . being one large biscuit and $\frac{3}{4}$ lb. of pork to each man. The allowance was thus shortened to lighten the draught, as the men had to drag seventeen days' provisions besides the articles already enumerated, and

thirty rounds of ball cartridge per man. A man can drag this carriage with a hundredweight on it easier than he can carry his knapsack".

In addition to practice marches on snow-shoes, the Light Company was "drilled to draw a three-pounder on a kind of sledge . . . . , but the light bobs abominated being 'made dray-horses of', as they called it", and the gun-dray experiment was a failure, the gun sinking into the snow,

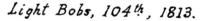

Light Bobs, 104ᵗʰ, 1813.

and its attendants after it. Tuition was also given in getting out of deep snow, unrehearsed, by the excellent General Smyth. At drill one day, anxious to correct some movement, he tripped over his snow-shoes and disappeared under four feeet of snow which instantly covered him, leaving only an "indenture" to show where he lay. Eager rescuers hurried to the spot, the vanished commander was located and everybody burst out laughing, the General joining in. Refusing help, he declared he "would then shew us the proper mode of getting out of deep snow: which he performed, having been in the country before with the Duke of Kent[1], very neatly". He untied one of his snow-shoes, placed it firmly on the snow, laid his elbow on it and levered his body up, knelt on the shoe and refastened it, and so regained the surface. That year the winter was exceptionally severe, more snow having fallen than during the past nine years, and on the 5th February the thermometer had sunk to 17° below zero.

On the 16th all was in readiness, and Colonel Halkett led the exodus of the 104th from the friendly and hospitable community of Fredericton, "where a British uniform, worn with credit and conduct, was a sure passport without a further introduction"; and five days later the last Company moved out. "I shall never forget", wrote Sir John, "the morning parade of that Sunday, ... it was impossible not to feel . . . . low spirited as our bugles struck up: 'The girls we leave behind us'; most of our gallant fellows being . . . . destined never to revisit their sisters or sweethearts. The Company presented a most unmilitary appearance, as it marched without arms or knapsacks in Indian file, divided into squads, so many to each tobogin, the rear of it being nearly half a mile from the front". They were off.

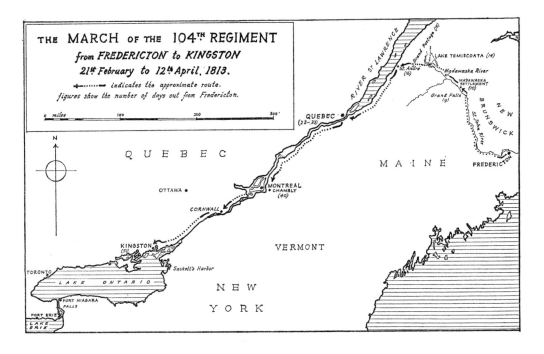

---

1. Third son of George III.

The Light Company's first seven days' marches, 21st to 27th of February, were through inhabited country: "we found them comparatively easy, though sometimes the snow might be 8 inches or a foot in depth, from the circumstance of the foundation of it being a beaten road; and at the close of each day's march, houses and barns to lodge the men in". On the 26th they were overtaken by the sleigh of a man named Wilsea[1], who had travelled in the winter of 1789 on snow-shoes with Lord Edward Fitzgerald[2] from Fredericton to Quebec. Wilsea said that Lord Edward had supported the acerbities of the journey with the greatest cheerfulness and fortitude[3], and remembered him as "a most amiable young man".

It had been understood that Indians would be sent on ahead to build wigwams every 15 miles for the men, but the Light Company saw no trace of them, and on the 29th February[4] they "hutted" for the first time after a tiring day's march during which snow had fallen incessantly, and so heavily that they often lost the narrow track of the snow-shoe, and fell into deep snow. One man falling like this kept all those behind him at a halt "until he had scrabbled[5] out from his cold bath", which might take ten minutes. This was such a strain on the men behind that it was decided to march on in future and "leave the straggler to regain his place when he could", which was so exhausting that everybody took care not to fall if they could help it. A straggler trying to catch up would have to march some distance in deep snow, lifting his snow-shoes up to fifteen inches at each step, an exertion which produced in those unaccustomed to it "an excruciating pain in the tendon Achilles, which the Canadians call 'le mal de racquette'." In order to distribute fatigue evenly, each officer and man took his turn at "breaking the road", by marching as leader for fifteen minutes and then stepping one pace aside and letting the whole company pass him. Each succeeding pair of snow-shoes improved the track, and when all the marchers had passed it was so firm and hard that the original leader could walk without his snow-shoes, and the toboggans could come on easily. "We generally marched close along the edge of the river, marching on it whenever no rapids intervened . . . ., and always constructed our huts on the windward side of it in the woods, in order to gain a little shelter".

"Hutting" was a gruelling business. "The men's hands were frequently so cold that they could scarcely work; however, as they were divided into squads, the best axemen immediately set to felling young pine trees to form rafters . . . .; these being trimmed of all their lateral branches were cut to about 15ft in height. Others felled hard wood and cut it into logs for burning. Others trimmed branches of pine for thatching the hut. While these were at work, some were clearing away places for the areas of the huts, which was done by taking off our snow-shoes and using them as shovels to throw back the snow, till we got to the soil destined for the floor, four or five feet deep. The snow that was thrown back formed a high wall round it, which served to shelter us somewhat from the chilly wind. Within this area the trimmed branches were placed in a conical . . . . form, and tied at the top, and were then covered with pine boughs thickly laid over each; the points of the branches being downwards, made it an excellent thatch quite impervious to the snow, with the exception of a hole at the top which was left for a chimney. A blazing fire was then lit in the centre of the hut, and all around it we strewed a thick layer of small pine branches,

---

1. CDQ. 'Wilson'.   2. Lord Edward Fitzgerald (1763-1798), Irish politician. Served in New Brunswick.
3. CDQ. 'aptitude'.
4. He must mean 28th. 1813 was not a leap year.   5. CDQ. 'scrambled'.

which formed a delicious and fragrant bed. Here were no feather bed soldiers. The next precaution was to close the only other aperture in the hut, which was intended for a door-way, made just large enough for a man to creep through[1], and a blanket, which everyone in turn grumbled to give up, served as an inner door to shut out the cold if possible. But I may well say if possible, as those who have not experienced it cannot figure to themselves the extreme frigidity of a temperature varying from 18°-27° below zero, that is from 50°-59° below freezing. While our feet were burning, which was sometimes literally the case whilst asleep, our heads were in a freezing temperature, as water immediately froze if placed near the inner circumference of the hut. It generally happened that we were as completely enveloped in smoke as an Esquimaux family, but like them we found it much more agreeable than having no smoke at all, as it warmed the hut. Moreover, I imagine that sleep without fire in such cold would have proved the sleep of death". In a later paragraph Sir John advises that for future marches of this kind, troops should do practice marches daily for a month before the event, in snow shoes, learning how to tie them on and wear them with comfort, how to dress their moccasins, and how to pack and drag toboggans. Indians should be sent a day's march ahead to prepare huts, cut wood and boil water in readiness for the arrival of the troops, who should be given warm tea, or broth made from portable soup, instead of "the bit of pork that was allowed to the 104th Regiment".

The story continues: "On the first of March we reached the Grand falls of the River St. John, 150 miles from Fredericton, where there was a small English settlement. We could not judge of its state of forwardness, everything being covered with a mantle of snow, but the inhabitants appeared to be happy and contented. They said they went down to Frederic-ton once or twice in a year to sell or barter their furs for what commodities they required, and added that their wants were few and simple". After dinner the officers went to view the falls, which in summer were 84 ft high and 900 ft wide, but at that season much reduced by freezing. Rising spray, as it froze, had formed a fantastic arch, supported by the glassy buttresses of the frozen banks. The surrounding trees were fringed with frost, and when the sun shone, prismatic colours played on the ice. It was a lifeless, soundless scene, except for the river rushing through "its restricted and fringed bed of ice into the gulph beneath . . ."

Grand Falls was the last military post in New Brunswick, and Sir John considered it a key point of defence, close to the American border and on a level 200 mile road on the St. John and Madawaska Rivers and Temisquata Lake. This road was the only winter mail route to Canada, and a strategic line for movement of troops, who would otherwise have to battle through forest. He also thought that "we should gain a little more extent to our boundary, in a line from the South Bay on the Grand Lake to Quebec, a little within that followed by Lord Edward Fitzgerald; land in itself unimportant to the Americans but of consequence to us, as it would prevent the likelihood of their hereafter wishing to gain the western bank of the St. John's River for a boundary, which would be fatal to our communication with Canada.

"The weather was so cold that several of us got frost bitten whilst marching this day (1st March), and one person, an inhabitant of the vicinity of the Falls, was frozen to death.

"On Wednesday the 2nd March we arrived at Laronciers[2], the head of the Madawaska Settlement. Here I began to find French language of the greatest service to me, as I did

---

1. CDQ. 'through edgewise'.   2. CDQ. 'Larouciers'.

through all Lower Canada. The worthy curé, Monsieur Rabbi, was delighted to meet a British officer who could converse with him freely, and . . . . not only invited me to take my billet at his house but also insisted that one of my brother subs should accompany me, where he treated us with the greatest hospitality. This insulated settlement is entirely separated from the busy world; a few hundred French Canadians are here settled in peaceful retirement". The pastor assured Sir John that crimes were quite unknown. "He was their confessor, their advisor and their Judge, and if a difference ever did exist amongst them it was speedily referred to him, and his decision was final. Their habits and manners were simple and kind, altogether French; like the Ant in Lafontaine's Fable, they told me they grew enough in summer to supply their wants for the winter, which they passed in mirth and friendly intercourse. From the worthy curé's description, and the lively and contented air of the people, I would take this to be the only Arcadia now existing in the world. I am not aware that these good people considered us as great intruders, but they certainly did not give us much time to corrupt them, as they mounted the whole of us, officers and men, in sleighs and drove us through their settlement, 21 miles in a day; which by the way was a great treat, and the men vowed it was by far the pleasantest day's *march* that we had had.

"On the 4th of March the cold was gradually increasing, and an incessant snow storm filling up the track rapidly made the dragging of the tobogins exceedingly laborious, especially as we occasionally had to quit the Madawaska River owing to rapids in it which had not frozen, and the thickness of the brushwood and forest along this edge. When we got to the end of our day's march the cold was so intense that the men could scarcely use their fingers to hew down firewood or to build huts, and it was dark before we could commence cooking, if sticking a pit [1] of salt pork on the end of a twig and holding it to the fire could be so termed by Monsr. Ude[2] or Mrs. Glass[3]".

The morning of the 5th of March was even colder, with the thermometer at 27° below zero, and "a gale, a North Wester, in our teeth which scarcely left power to breathe; indeed the intensity of the cold was indescribable. The Captain of the company anticipated the effects of it and went on with an officer and a few men to arrange the huts and to prepare fires for our reception. At about midday, on turning a corner or angle along the river, I was surprised to find that the head of the company had stopped, which caused the centre and the rear to halt as they came up. Knowing the dangerous consequences that might ensue from a prolonged halt in such excessive cold, I hastened in the deep snow to the head of the company, and going along I observed that almost every man was already more or less frost bitten, and was occupied in rubbing his cheeks or nose or both with snow. In my progress I also was caught by the nose, and when I turned the corner in the river I really thought I should not have been able to proceed; the cold wind appeared to penetrate through my body in defiance of flannels or furs. I however urged the men on, as soon as we had taken time to lay one poor fellow, whose whole body was frost bitten, on a tobogin and covered him with blankets. By changing the lead every four or five minutes we at length got to the huts, having about ninety men out of 105 more or less frost bitten on that occasion . . . . At the huts we found that the company which should have been a day's

1. For bit, unless pit is a local abbreviation for pitance, which originally meant a small daily ration issued in a monastery.
2. A famous chef at Crockford's, and the Reform Club, who served dinner for 2000 on the day of Queen Victoria's coronation.
3. Mrs Hannah Glasse, author of "The Art of Cookery", 1747.

12.   JOHN LE COUTEUR
(1794-1875)
Lieutenant in the 104th Regiment, 1811, aged 17.

13.   The gold watch given him by his mother.

14. A WOUNDED HORSEMAN, possibly Lieutenant Gladwyn, 19th Light Dragoons.

(an unsigned water-colour)

(see page 58)

march ahead of us were still hutted. They had attempted to cross the Temisquata Lake in the morning, but the cold wind blowing over it was so exquisitely keen that after marching a mile the Captain [1] of it faced about and returned to the huts. It was impossible to get warm that night. One officer literally scorched his moccasins on his feet in his sleep by being over anxious to keep them warm.

"The next morning (6th March), the wind having abated, both companies crossed the lake. The marching this day was very different from anything that we had yet experienced in our journeys; the sun, having begun to have some power on the snow, had thawed the surface of it, which froze again in the night and formed a surface of thin ice sufficiently strong to bear a light person; but a heavy man would frequently break through and sink into the substratum of snow till he was arrested by the firm ice on the lake. This was very troublesome and laborious work, but those who chose to keep their snow shoes on avoided it and marched at a great pace over the ice . . . . It may not be amiss to observe that some persons have a great objection to wearing snow shoes, as they suffer from 'mal de racquette' in a greater or less degree, while to others snow shoes are quite a relief. It was an 18 mile march, and we were delighted to get to a habitation on the edge of the portage . . . . We had to leave poor Rogers who was so severely frost bitten . . . ., in charge of a Corporal, with the woodsman at the portage, who promised to recover him speedily by means of simples and herbs, though his life appeared in danger. He was quite a hideous spectacle, altogether one ulcerated mass, as if scalded all over from boiling water. However he rejoined us in Kingston in six weeks, perfectly recovered.

"The next day's march (7th March) was through a mountainous country which is called the 'grand portage'. Some parts of the pine forest through which we passed had been burned for clearing and presented a curious picture. The black tall grim pine trees, rearing their scathed heads to the sky, seemed like the ghosts or rather skeletons of the noble forms they once possessed, and contrasted strangely with the virgin snow on which they appeared to stand. It was altogether a most dreary and laborious day's march, as the snow drift in some places was ten or twelve feet deep, and the constant ascent and descent made it excessively fatigueing for the tobogin men. The descent of the hills was even more dangerous than the ascent, for if a tobogin once got a fair start in the track there was no stopping it, and man and all went down hill to the foot of the hill [2] with amazing velocity. In this way there were several upsets, to the great amusement of all who escaped an accident. However it delayed the rear of the company so much that the head of it had finished its marching by ten or eleven o'clock in the morning, whereas the rear guard only arrived at half past five". After a frugal meal of biscuit and pork, the story continues, they turned in as usual round the fire but their sleep was disturbed by a novel accident. The high wind had dried the top of the pine thatch and it caught fire. ". . . . On waking from a sound slumber I found myself in a blaze, a complete auto-da-fé, for there was no appearance of a doorway or outlet, so instant was the blaze. However—a yell of despair from the giant form of an officer of the Regiment, who dashed into the hut through the flames exclaiming: 'Holy J . . . s, my money box!', which he snatched up with the fondness of a father saving his only child from the flames—enabled me to dash out after him, dragging my all with me, a change of suit, in a historical fit of laughter at the strange lamentation of our brother officer. We were some little

---

1. Captain Armstrong. 2. CDQ. 'like a car down a "montagne russe"?

F

time occupied in snowballing the fire to extinguish the flames, for fear the men's huts should have also caught fire, but it was a most ludicrous sight as we were floundering in the deep snow up to our middles, or shoulders, not having time to put on our snow shoes. Several of the men and officers got frost bitten in this adventure".

Next morning, 8th March, they started hopefully on what they believed was their last day in uninhabited country. They had been a fortnight in the wilds with only the snow, sky and "the interminable silent forest to look upon, and the possibility of being frozen to death, which sometimes crossed our minds . . . ." It was therefore with delight that they saw a horse-drawn sleigh coming to meet them. In it was "a worthy gentleman of the commisariat, Mr. Anderson . . . ., who had been sent from Quebec to receive us". He brought not only Government rations and rum, but fowls, veal, ham, and other provisions. They then had "the best meal we all vowed we had ever tasted, and gratitude proclaimed our worthy friend ever after a standing toast amongst us. After our repast we moved on to a village in the parish of St. Andrews, from whence we saw spread before us the magnificent St. Lawrence, 18 miles wide". Here they obtained comfortable billets, "regularly washed and dressed for the first time in 17 days", had a well cooked dinner and good beds.

"Our march from hence", he goes on, "to Quebec was along a good beaten snow road, and marches of 18 or 20 miles mere exercise for us, so that our last seven days passed away merrily under the cheering smiles of the worthy Canadians, who welcomed us as a non-descript race that had never been seen in those quiet parts before, being the first Regiment that had ever been there; and our merry bugles were quite a novel treat to the Canadian lasses. The country along the river up to Quebec was cleared in a belt ranging from half a mile to three miles in depth. We passed through several villages almost entirely built of wood, with neat looking churches roofed externally with zinc, so that when the sun shines on them they present a brilliant and elegant appearance. On the 25th[1], our twenty-fourth day's march, we entered Quebec, greeted by an immense concourse of people, who appeared to consider us quite the Lions of the Army after our unexampled march. The Quebec paper called us, in the words of the poet, fine young fellows, fit 'to pluck bright honor from the pale faced moon[2]".

They spent the next ten days in Quebec. Then, "on inspecting our six companies, 550 rank and file, Sir G. Prevost paid us the highest compliments, and to show us that he really thought us in good wind and order, he ordered the Grenadiers and Light Company to march on the 25th for Chambly, 200 miles". This they duly did, but it seems that their reputation for fitness had preceded them, for as they approached Montreal "Colonel Drummond sent me on to General De Rottenburgh to report our speedy arrival; when, on my honestly avowing we were in excellent wind, the General said: 'Then he should send us on two hundred miles further to Kingston'. When I reported the circumstance to Colonel Drummond, who was marching at the head of the companies, one of them exclaim-ed: 'It's no wonder. They think we are like the children of Israel. We must march forty years before we halt'". Another view was that, as it was the 1st of April, the General was merely making April fools of them, "but the second of April undeceived us. We were then off for Kingston".

---

1. He means the 15th (of March, 1813).   2. Shakespeare, Henry iv, Part i, 1.3.201.

Sir John does not describe the march from Quebec to Kingston, which many other regiments had performed, though none, he remarks, in so short a time. But conditions were, he says, severe. The sun by now had the strength to thaw the small streams, some of which they had to ford to their waists. The water was intolerably cold, causing a shock to pores open from perspiration which was trying even to the strongest constitution.

Then came the finale. "On the 12th of April we were marching up a gentle ascent, and just as the head files were rising it there was a general exclamation of: 'The sea, the sea[1]; the ships, the ships'. The whole of us spontaneously broke and ran to see this novel and interesting sight. Some of us had been marching between 800 and a thousand miles in six weeks, with only ten days halt, during which time we had never lost sight of a forest. When suddenly there lay before our astonished and delighted view the town of Kingston, the magnificent lake Ontario and, what was far more surprising still, a squadron of ships of war frozen on its bosom. It was a striking and indescribable sensation, as none of we Europeans appeared to have reflected on the circumstance of being sure to find a fleet of men of war on a fresh water lake. After having feasted our eyes for a while, the companies resumed their wonted order; and after having washed the mud off our legs in a rivulet, that we might appear very clean in getting under the scrutiny of the fair sex, we made our triumphant entry into Kingston to our merry bugles".

Then comes a warning against liquor. "The comparative repose which . . . . followed our long march, together with good feeding, occasioned disorders amongst the men; and although we had not lost a single man during the march, many were ill, and a few died from the effects of it. But it was observed that these were all the hardest drinkers. Indeed there is no doubt whatever that dram drinking is highly injurious in a very cold country, as the heat that is momentarily conveyed to the body is followed by a reaction which the cold turns quickly into a numbness, and retarded circulation".

This remarkable narrative ends on a justifiable note of pride in the 104th Regiment. "Brother soldiers will pardon the Esprit de Corps which leads me to say that during this long march, under considerable privation and hardships, not one single robbery was committed by the men; nor was there a single report made against them by the inhabitants to the Commanding Officer".

At Kingston the troops were given poor accommodation, the town being over-full, and Sir John could find none until an elderly lady, Mrs. Robison, took pity on him and his companion and offered them lodging. This was the beginning of a deep friendship with the Robison family. Later he became godfather to a grandchild of his hostess, called Mary at his request after his own mother, and the association between the Le Couteurs and Robisons extended through the generations.

Both sides were now working strenuously to gain naval superiority on the lake. "It was a war of carpenters", as Sir John puts it, the shipyards launching vessels as fast as they could build them. On 25th April 1813 Captain Grey the British D.Q.M.G., "a half-horse, half-alligator sort of soldier-sailor, launched a small frigate, the Sir George Prevost of 24 guns. She went off prettily, but the cradle broke . . . ., and there she stuck: It was a serious check . . . ." Another handicap was ice. On 10th April 1814, ". . . . on jumping out of my bed, a singular sight presented itself . . . ., the Sidney was floating out of the harbour in a

---

1. Whether he knew it or not, Sir John was quoting Xenophon.

large cake of ice, with all the bushes and trees, also a part of the road which led to her. She was helpless: while the Beresford was sailing after her to her assistance". The sketch of H.M.S. Regent illustrates Sir John's description of her launching on 14th April 1814:

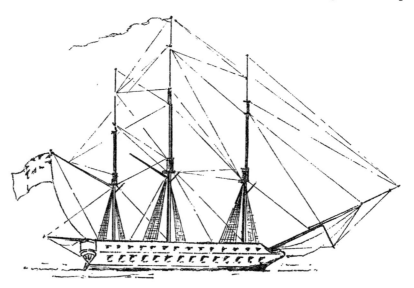

H.M. Frigate REGENT, (6o guns).
launched on Lake Ontario, U.C. 14. April 1814.
(after a sketch by Lieut. J. Le Couteur, 104th. Regt.)

"she followed the Princess Charlotte, as a lover to guard his Belle, ... plunging into the calm water; then rode in triumph, a real Lord of the Lake". On 26th December that year the "Psyche, a fine 38 gun frigate", was launched. A week or two later an exhausted man was seen struggling through the ice in a canoe and was brought to shore. He turned out to be Sir James Yeo's coxswain who had been captured, kept on short commons in a block-house in Sackett's Harbour and offered every inducement to desert. But "the noble fellow was a true Jack Tar", tore sheets into strips, escaped from his prison to the lake shore, found a broken canoe and propelled it or pushed it on the ice all the way round from Sackett's Harbour. Sir John had dined some time before with Yeo and other senior naval officers and remarked: "How frank and pleasant these marine big wigs are on shore, and what awful tyrants some of them are on board ship. I have seen a Captain of a man of War fling a round shot . . . . at his men's legs to make them trot round the windlass faster. Flinging his speaking trumpet at them was a joke. Yet this tyrant could be most winning in the society of strangers on shore".

Late in April 1813 the Journal tells us: "Very disastrous news received from York, the capital of Upper Canada, which was assaulted and taken by the Americans, and that our army was in full retreat. Our Grenadiers were marched off to its support under the command of Major Drummond, though the place could ill afford to spare men as it was expected to be menaced, the enemy being anxious to destroy the ships of war that we are building here". On May 5th: "The remnant of the King's Regiment marched in from their defeat at York; their splendid Grenadier company, which left this last month, 112 rank and file, returned here 25 in number". In preparation for an expected attack, Sir John had to take out a detachment and prepare a defence, and gave an interesting description of felling trees. "The mode was to commence with what the axemen called a key tree, a monarch of the wood. Two men opposite each other, sometimes four, cut an enormous wedge as smoothly as if done with a plane, from the two sides of the tree, in the direction it was meant to fall; one great cut, the outer, being about six inches below the other, the inner cut, thus. The tree was then left, and the two next to it were cut partly through; then the three next, then four, five, six, to a hundred, in one lengthened wedge to any desired extent. Then the forest was ready for the fall, and grand was the fall thereof. All the party

'.. and grand was the fall thereof.'
Lt. J. Le Couteur. 9. May 1813.

went back to the key tree, the four axemen gave a few finishing rapid strokes with their ponderous axes; down went the monarch, sweeping the two next; and so on through the forest with the rushing sound of the fall of many waters; a forest Niagara".

In about June 1813 Sir John was apparently seconded as Adjutant to the 2nd Battalion Militia Light Infantry, and when this battalion was disbanded in the following November, he stayed on as Adjutant to Colonel De Haren, who commanded bodies of light infantry on the Niagara frontier until the end of the war. He tells us that he took part in one siege (Fort Erie), three general engagements (probably Sackett's Harbour, the battle of Niagara and Cross Roads), and thirty-three skirmishes. Details are given in 100 pages of a calf-bound volume measuring 10 by 16 inches, entitled "My Journal", and their contents would fill a book on their own. Here we can do no more than take a glance at some of them. There were three incidents which lingered especially in his memory, a brush with an Indian sheep-stealer, night fishing with Indians, and the occasion when his own picket fired on him, and he painted retrospective water-colours of these.

Of the Battle of Niagara on 25th July 1814 the Journal records, inter alia: "Colonel Drummond rode up . . . . 'My lads, will you charge the Americans?' He put the question instead of giving the order . . . . About midnight the whole of the American army had retired . . . . there was a rumour that General Brown was coming to renew his attack on our small but victorious army . . . . Col. Drummond made us draw all the dead horses into a line on the crest of our position, and if attacked to kneel behind them as a breastwork. I was on duty that night. What a dismal night. There were 300 dead on the Niagara side of the hillock and about a hundred of ours, beside several hundred wounded. The miserable badly wounded were groaning and imploring us for water, the Indians prowling about them and scalping and plundering. Close by me lay a fine young man, the son of an American General, Hull. He was mortally wounded. I gave him some brandy and water, and wished him to give me his watch etc . . . . to send to his family . . . . Our men's heads and those of the Americans were within a few yards of each other . . . ., so close had been the deadly strife".

There is a copy of a letter he wrote, in camp before Fort Erie on 6th September 1814 to his mother: "General Brown and his army retired to Fort Erie, and on the 2d (August) we followed them up, and took up a position about a mile from the Fort . . . ., opposite Black Rock, a small village of the enemy's, where at that time they had a great number of tents pitched. Before daylight on the 3rd the General sent our division . . . . on an expedition to the other side . . . . to bring off the tents from Black Rock and destroy the village and a battery . . . . We accordingly crossed in batteaux, but unfortunately landed below a very deep creek which was not fordable, and a bridge over it had been destroyed by the enemy, and was defended by 250 British deserters (riflemen) who, posted behind a heavy breastwork, ... killed and wounded 25 men and compelled us to return . . . . On the 5th we . . . . commenced a 4 Gun battery within 1100 yards of the Fort, which was compleated on the 10th . . . . the fire of the Fort . . . . was silenced by us on the 14th and the General then determined upon storming it. It was necessary to gain possession of Snake Hill, which commands the Fort, at a distance of 800 yards . . . . Fifteen hundred men were to attempt Snake Hill: and the 41st, 103rd and us were the storming party for the Fort, supported by the Royals. On the 15th (August), about two in the morning, the Snake Hill party commenced, and about 3 we advanced under a heavy fire of grape and musquetry". The Journal describes Fort Erie as "an ugly customer for fifteen hundred men to attack.

Six thousand, it was said, placed behind breastworks and ramparts, with a blockhouse and guns bristling in every direction. The fort was of irregular form, with demi-bastions that flanked the ditches. The faces were of earth, but the embrasures seemed to me to be of masonry". The party "got to the ditch, jumped in, reared the scaling ladders . . . . I jumped with our company into the ditch. It was slow work to get up the ladders, of which there were not one quarter enough. There were palisades too to be cut away . . . . I was in the act of jumping into the place when I saw it full of combatants. Our men had carried the fort, all but the blockhouse", which the letter calls two stone houses, loopholed for musquetry, and these were manned by a party of deserters who had climbed to the upper storey, cut loopholes in the floor, and were firing at all who entered, and on the intruders in the Fort as well, shouting: "Come on, you rascals; we're British deserters and Irish rebels". Drawing in turn from the letter and the Journal, we continue the narrative thus: "I was just on the scaling ladder when the rascals exploded a mine . . . . I only remember seeing a black volume rise from the earth, and I lost my senses. After I recovered them I was lying in the ditch . . . ., where I had been thrown by a tremendous explosion . . . ., which cleared the Fort of 300 men in an instant. The platform had been blown over and a great beam had jammed me to the earth . . . . What a horrid sight presented itself; some 300 men lay roasted, mangled, burned, wounded, black, hideous to view. On getting upon my legs I trod on poor Lt. Hazen's[1] broken leg, which made me shudder to my marrow . . . . The explosion had caused a cessation of hostilities on both sides for a few minutes . . . . We did all we could to rally the men, but the enemy sent a body of men and a field piece to enfilade the ditch and it was no longer possible to remain in it. I then told Shore if we did not wish to be taken prisoners, we had better run for it and take our chance of being shot. We were the last officers that left it. Some staid and did not venture crossing the plain. Thank God, we both escaped unhurt, though the enemy kept up a roar of grape, canister and musquetry as we recrossed that vile plain. I lost Shore in the wood, and for two hours thought he had been taken . . . . Our gallant and good Colonel Drummond was killed . . . . We marched from Kingston 8 officers and 120 men, and we had remaining 4 officers and 27. The remainder were killed and wounded in the skirmishes which we had constantly in the wood. The Snake Hill division were ordered to take out their flints, à la Whitelocke, and were also repulsed. We lost 14 officers killed and many more wounded, and over 1000 killed and wounded, on that most melancholy day . . . . We have since erected two batteries within 600 yards of the Fort, and our Picquets are intrenched at the edge of the wood; our army very strong, and in high spirits". The journal brings the dreadful total to 1003 "killed, wounded, missing, burned or prisoners: Lt. Cols., 2: Majors, 1: Captains, 10: Subalterns, 21: Staff, 2: Sergeants 64: Privates, 903: or one strong regiment put out of the way".

Sir John was absurdly young, celebrating his nineteenth birthday at Kingston in October 1813, and in spite of the hardships of the campaign enjoyed robust health, suffering only from boils and attacks of dysentery. He seems to have been universally popular in military circles, and with many families in Fredericton, Kingston and elsewhere; amongst them the Coffins, of whom he wrote that General Coffin was a fine old veteran, and his daughter Sophy "a splendid girl. She and her father were crossing the lake one morning when a great bear attacked them, and would have swamped the boat, if Sophy had not

---

1. George Hazen

stood by the General with discretion and courage; for while the General was battering Bruin with the butt end of an oar, Sophy pushed the point of the boat-hook in his eye, which made Bruin scratch it and retreat". His youthful high spirits sometimes made him rather a handful to his superiors. In January 1814, for instance, "Shore rowed me for being a little late for parade . . . .". He had been running to keep himself warm, when he perceived "a fair lady", wife of a Captain of the 100th Regiment, with a umbrella, "feeling for a point where to cross . . . . a shallow stream . . . . she cast an imploring look at me". She was "a very nice armful", but not having been introduced to her he "could scarcely offer to take her up in an embrace and carry her over . . . . , still less as they land you at low water in Jersey, on my back . . . . I placed my nice clean boot . . . . into the middle of the running water: 'Now, Madam, if you will favor me with your hand, and place your pretty foot upon my instep, you may skip over dry shod'. Over she flew. 'How very gallant, I declare. To whom am I indebted for this happy expedient?' 'Lieutenant Le Couteur of the 104th. Beg your pardon, but I am late for Parade'. Off I flew". While on secondment in August that year he was busy constructing a battery before Fort Erie, but his superior officer, on inspecting it, "got into a violent passion and wanted me to take it down again, which I declared I would certainly not do . . . . we had such high words that I said I would no longer serve under his orders: and the next day I rejoined the Company". Soon after that, on reserve night picquet, he, Brown and Basden told stories in turn, "which made us, men and all, laugh so loud that the Fort fired at us, and the Field Officer of the night came up and gave us a precious wigging". There was much badinage among the younger officers, and from having lost his scabbard, and been obliged to carry a naked sword for a month, "the wags had called me 'Bloody-minded Johnny'." Accustomed at that time to the admiration of most of the damsels he met, he had a setback one evening which was probably very good for him. He was rebuffed on the ball-room floor. He had booked a dance with one of three sisters, all dressed alike, and on advancing to the wrong one with: "May I have the grati-fication of placing you in the dance?", was greeted with: "'Sir!', with an eye of fire and a haughty toss of a nez retroussé: 'I never forget. I am not your partner'".

As a soldier, he was conscientious and enterprising. When manning a breastwork before Fort Erie, and hearing "the well-known sharp ring of the American rifle", he ordered his men to place their caps on the breastwork, away from themselves: "the riflemen knocked the men's caps over nicely, which greatly inspirited my men", and the sortie was driven back with heavy loss. When lost in a forest he learned that the moss grows thickest on the north side of the trees, and a general direction could be maintained, provided there was visibility. But at night, or in fog "it is all chance; you may wander for days and nights". It was not, however, an inspiring first campaign for a zealous subaltern. Many of the combatants had little heart in it, regarding it as a civil war between compatriots, and desertions were frequent, in both directions. Nor was there complete confidence between officers and men, as was shown in the order sometimes given to remove flints from the muskets, presumably to prevent reckless firing, or to ensure the use of the bayonet. When such an order was discussed in the attack on Snake Hill Sir John said "Such a proceeding must ensure defeat. If troops could not be trusted with their flints, they had better leave their arms behind them. I would answer for our men. If ordered not to load, not a man would think of it". Nevertheless the Snake Hill party went into action without flints, "a scandalous want of confidence in the brave men . . . . The Americans, finding only cheers to oppose them .... shot the unarmed men .... like so many sheep". In one skirmish, when a British force of 700 were ordered to retire, the Americans, numbering 1800, "came out of the woods; officers and men; did not fire, and I verily believe cheered us while admiring the beautiful military movement we were executing in slow time". It was, in fact, what was known in 1939 as a "phoney war", and many of the participants, Sir John included, tired of it. Writing from Montreal to his mother on 19th July 1815, he said: "I am heartily tired of a Subaltern's life. To compleat my disagreables, just now, on my arrival here, I found every article of linnen and cloathing wet: my poor drawing box ruined: the colours well mixed: my dressing case in pieces: my books and papers spoiled: and my desk full of water". The fault lay with the "blockhead of an officer" who came down the St. Lawrence rapids with fifteen batteaux of heavy luggage and only one guide.

Some memorable characters appear in the pages of the Journal. There is Lieutenant Jobling, overheated at a Government House Ball at Fredericton, who decided to cool off by skating back to barracks on the frozen river, and set off at top speed, only to plunge into a fissure in the ice, and find himself below the ice on the further side of the crack. Pausing an instant to feel which way the current ran, he struck out against it, his head rubbing the under surface of the ice, and was soon out in the open water, and skating on again to barracks where a hot brandy and water set him to rights. Later on Jobling, by then a Captain, is called "as bold a fire-eating Northumbrian as any man in this army". Then there is Captain Shore's servant Nickerson, a Highlander, who kept on standing up when under fire at the battle of Niagara. "Nic, lie down". He was soon up again. "Don't you hear? The shot all around you. Lie down!" Again he was up. "What's the use of my speaking to you? .... This is no place to be finding fault with a good soldier". "Wall, Sir, do ye no see Colonel Drummond sitting on that grit horse, up there among the balls, and sall I be laying down, sneaking whan he's exposed?" Then there was Lemery, "a true recruiting Sergeant, a handsome, gay, chattering humbug". And the ferocious Pearson, with a heart of gold, who was "in a moody humour" when one of his Militiamen applied for leave, and replied: "'Go to Hell'. The man quietly said: 'Has Your Honor any orders for the devil?' Pearson looked at him. Smiled. 'What leave do you want?' 'Six days!' He doubled his leave, and gave him a pound to take him home". The Marquis of Tweeddale was a man after their own heart: being "wonderfully vigilant; he sits up with us and watches by the hour. A fine gentleman and soldier". Moorsom, D.A.A.G., killed early in the battle of Niagara, was greatly missed, and on 27th July 1814 "we buried our excellent friend Moorsom at Queenston this day, by the side of the gallant General Brock".

He pays tribute to the bravery of the Indians as allies but deplores their cruelty, especially to prisoners. A young American prisoner was being held by a Mohawk Chief, who had lost his only son in battle, "to be immolated when they got him into the back woods", and the lad begged the British to ransom him. But "no sum would tempt" the Chief. Eventually he was persuaded to adopt the American, who was divested of his clothing and dressed as an Indian. No attempt was made to rescue him, which would have alienated the tribe, and he was advised not to try to escape until he had been with them for a year or two. An interesting description is given of night fishing with Indians at McPherson's Bay. A torch consisting of pitch pine in an iron basket was fixed in the bows of the canoe, there was a noiseless paddler in the stern and a man with a long fish-spear in the bows. "Presently off went the spear with the speed of an arrow ....., up came a fine large pickerel; a yard in length; then a salmon; he reversed his spear and the helmsman released the fish, and off again over the clear transparent water". The Indians had their own codes of honour, and many lives may have been spared on this account. For example: "Lieutenant Gladwin of the 19th Light Dragoons came galloping along the road from a clearing, evidently badly wounded. He pulled up, on coming to me, and dropped into my arms. He had ridden among the American Indians, mistaking them for ours, shook hands with them and 'Sago Nitchee'd' them all round. They were greatly admiring his fine person and splendid uniform, when five or six riflemen rushed from the wood and shouted 'Seize him, stop him'. Gladwin saw his error, turned round and galloped off with his two orderly dragoons. The magnanimous Indians, having shaken hands with him, did not fire a shot at him or his men, but discharged their volley above them. The riflemen however fired well; one hit Gladwin in the thighs and the others hit his corporal". This incident may be the subject of a water-colour in the Belle Vue collection, reproduced here.

By the 24th September 1814 he was at Queenston, and here his chronicle of martial events is relieved by a homely episode. Whilst sleeping in an empty attic he heard a faint cry, oft repeated, and was sure it came from a dying baby, but a search revealed that it was a tabby kitten, starving to the point of death. St.Germain, his French Canadian servant, recommended putting it out of its misery: "Il faut la jeter par la fenêtre"; to which Sir John replies: "Nous l'avons sauvée, il faut la secourir". Thus reprieved, the kitten became devoted to him, even following him on parade, and when this happened the Light Bobs used to chant: "See Le Couteur and his cat coming on parade". Eventually he got her a home, hundreds of miles away, with the doctor's wife at Fredericton, who for long after used to send him news of Queenie, her health and progeny.

On 18-19th October he took part with a force under the command of the Marquis of Tweeddale, in the successful engagement at Cook's Mills. After this the 104th were in no major actions, but the war was not over, there were sundry alarms and skirmishes, intense cold, and much distress from dysentery. But at last, on 24th February 1815, the diary announces: "Heard the American official news of peace!", and next day: "Several American officers came over from Sackett's Harbour with the news. We received them very well, gave them a dinner and made our Band play Yankee Doodle on drinking the President's health, which gave them great pleasure . . . . Col. Moodie came to my quarters and asked me in what time I could start express for Montreal with the despatches and news of Peace. 'In five minutes', I said. 'Good. Well, Johnny, you shall have a quarter of an hour . . . .'". He used it to finish a long letter to his mother with: "I saw the first shot holes in the sails and hull of the Belvidera Frigate when she came to Halifax . . . ., and I witnessed the second engagement between our sloop of war's boat and the Rover of Salem . . . ., and now I am the bearer of the blessed news of Peace at the close of a hot and unnatural war between kindred people. Thank God". Steps were taken to get him to his destination as fast as possible: "the sleigh soon came to the door and I, well enveloped in furs, started at speed. I had no great difficulty to obtain conveyances by day, but after midnight it was 'une autre affaire'". At one point he drove up to a prosperous Dutch farm and aroused the farmer, who appeared at the window with: "Vat's all dat? Vat de teufel maks you mak dat noise?" "I want horses . . . . I am travelling with Government despatches express". "I got no horsen. Vat de teufel you come freiten de hause vor? I got no horsen". But on hearing that the stranger was a messenger of peace, "Vat you say, vat you say, Peace . . . . Oh, I zall zee my two boys dat are in de Mileetia . . . . horsen, yees, you zall have de best horsen; myzell I will droive you . . . ." The whole family was now aroused, and he was given food, drink, horses, blessings and a fur-lined sleigh which carried him 16 miles in an hour and twenty minutes. It took him 43 hours to get to Montreal and lay the news before General de Rottenburgh, only to find he had heard it the night before!

Sir John now decided "to quit a country of which I had seen all I desired, but I would go through the States, to see the domestic habits of the people to whom we had been opposed . . . . They had turned out very good soldiers. Their officers were gallant and enter-prising and, although our Engineers said they do not understand fortification, they had shewn that the rules of common sense guided them. They would have a fine army ten years hence . . . ." He applied for a little leave, which he spent enjoyably in Montreal, falling in love more than once, and attending a grand ball and masquerade given by the Marquis of Tweeddale to 700 persons. He and a French-speaking friend went as "a respectable young Jean Baptiste farmer and his wife". During his stay a Montreal lady offered him her daugh-ter's hand, "but I said I had nothing beyond a guinea a week and my Sub's pay, which was quite out of marrying conditions". Speaking French so easily, he passed in Montreal as "un de la vieille France".

He was messing with the 8th (King's) Regiment as an honorary member. The hero of that corps was Major Billy Robinson, "an Irish Falstaff" whose wit had restored the men's spirits in the camp at the Black Swamp, and had divine service read to them one day in the forest, "in God's own temple for a church. The Brigade was formed in a close column at ordered arms . . . . it was the most solemn (service) I had ever heard".

Soon afterwards he was ordered to return to the Regiment at Kingston, and was sad to find that he had to discharge his old servant Mills for misconduct during his absence. In his place he took on St. Germain, and fifty years later Sir John is corresponding with St. Germain, sending him money, and arranging for his pension to be increased by threepence a day. In July 1815 the Regiment received orders to move to Quebec and Sir John, rather to his disgust, was required to act as Quarter Master on the move, being in charge of all "the women, children, sick, sorry or lazy, besides all the heavy luggage . . . . Never was I so pestered: 'Mr. Le Couteur', the officers' wives imploring, some commanding: 'see to my luggage: do place us an awning to the batteaux . . . . see to the baby'". In spite of this they had a delightful trip down river, with fine scenery. There was some panic among the females when the boats negotiated the Long Saut and La Chine Rapids, a region "celebrated in Tom Moore's pretty song 'Row, Brothers, row'," but Sir John managed to calm them and they made Montreal in safety. He thought the approach to that city very lovely, and parted from his "fair friends, the ladies and women and chicks of the Regiment" with a sigh of relief. The only mishap during the journey was when the baggage got soaked and all his possessions damaged, including a bible his mother had given him[1]. He was disgusted with the dirty barracks allotted to them, and the absence of cooking stoves to prepare meals for the main body of the Regiment, expected at any moment from a long and arduous march. Finding the delivery of stoves enmeshed in red tape, he resourcefully collected some of his men with barrows and helped himself to what he needed, in spite of the protests of the

1. It found its way latterly to Ireland, and was bought by La Société Jersiaise in 1968. In 1857 he had it rebound by Eyre and Spottiswoode for £2.

Barrack Master General. He was threatened with court-martial for this irregular act, but argued his way out of the difficulty. In July he was in command of a recruiting party.

In December he was appointed A.D.C. to his father, General Le Couteur, Governor of Curaçao and its dependencies, Aruba and Bon Air, and proceeded to his new post.

United States Mail, 1816.

The first part of the journey was 588 miles by American mail coach, the stages being Quebec to Three Rivers, 85 miles: Montreal, 99: Burlington, 89: Albany, 150: New York, 165. He reached New York, "this beautiful city", on 5th January 1816, and noted that Broadway was "so spacious, so long and so many fine houses in it". At an inn there he found he was expected to share a bed in a dormitory, and refused, saying that Britishers were "partikler on that pint", to which the landlord replied: "I guess if you don't chuse to take half a bed with someone, you'll jist sleep in a cheer". He was surprised "in this new country to observe schools at almost every two miles distance, which accounts for their being so intelligent a people". He was taken to parties at the Watts, Gracie and Ogden homes, which were "superbly furnished, damasks, India papers and furniture, much plate glass which has a noble and dressy look at night when brilliantly lit and filled with well-dressed women: the style an attempt at French, but a gauche imitation of it. The girls were not well got up". He made the acquaintance of the great Dutch merchant Mr. John B. Graves, who had sent him letters from his parents at Curaçao during the war, and supplied his needs for his voyage there; "a man of grave, gentle, most kind habits", who at once introduced him to Mrs. Graves, "dear Mrs. Graves, what a nice specimen of the ancient Dutch gentlewoman she was, dressed all neatly and starchy, like one of Rembrandt's ladies". She sent for her daughters to introduce them, "nice, rosy, merry girls; very soon at home with them all. A ten days' daily acquaintance made me fancy one of them . . . . Ten months instead of ten days might have given me a Dutch wife".

On 18th January 1816 he left on board a sloop, with a cargo of flour, to join his parents at Curaçao, and his stay there has already been described. On the 6th of March he and they left Curaçao. Sir John was not at home long, but the time was spent to advantage. "In the short six weeks I was allowed to continue on leave, I engaged my cousin Harriet Janvrin, then only eighteen, to become my wife, whenever I became a Captain. This affair came off at a Pic Nic at Rozel Manor, in the arbour half way down in the wood. Thus it is that youths and maidens at the inexperienced age of 22 and 18 risk their earthly fate. To my consternation, I was ordered to rejoin my regiment at Quebec owing, I afterwards learned, to a fresh rumour of war with America". Elsewhere he mentions driving Harriet and Louisa to the picnic, and how beautiful the view was, "but my attention was too much engrossed by a declaration which, with the blessing of God, may one day be my lasting happiness". He refers to Harriet as a fine, lively girl. Her father, Francis Janvrin, gave a "splendid ball to the whole Island. My old belle, Ann Marett, is still the Belle in my opinion. The ladies, near seventy in number, were well dressed and very gay and the party went off admirably. Harriet did her honours so as to give satisfaction to all, and very much like a lady. The Island is certainly the most beautiful spot I have yet seen, and is much improved as to town and roads since I left it". The midsummer day fête in St. John's parish used to be an occasion of great jollification, and in June 1816 he says of it: "La St. Jean. Drove out with my uncle and Harriet to St. John's, where we had a view of the fair sex of this island in their gayest mood. The country girls are certainly handsome and blessed with sparkling eyes".

In August 1816, after driving with Frank Janvrin in his spree gig with grey thorobred to Richmond to see little Loulou Janvrin at school, he embarked on the Sterling clipper for Quebec, paying £35 for the passage, everything but wine and bedding included. Among his fellow passengers were two ships' carpenters turned missionary, ". . . . not such as would by their appearance convert savages. They will have some difficulty with the Mohawks . . . . Our cards they called the books of Satan, our lively songs, obscene". They proved dreary companions on the voyage. On 26th September 1816 the Sterling ran into a severe storm off the banks of Newfoundland: ". . . . every sail was . . . . in ribands . . . ., the strips of canvas being flicked like a cartman's whip in a quarrel with his team; the sound was like a rapid volley of musketry . . . . the sea broke over us every time it struck the ship. I never witnessed anything so awful . . . . I got a severe fall and soaking in going to assist at the pump". By October, "All our spirituous liquors out, and our good spirits with them . . . our coffee being all used, the steward burnt pearl barley, which answered very well . . . ." After being on short commons for a fortnight they reached Quebec on 20th October, the voyage having taken just on two months.

After a stay in Quebec, revisiting old friends and receiving much hospitality, he and his Colonel, Moodie, went up to Montreal by steam boat, "my first voyage by steam". Arrived there, he saw more old friends, including fellow-islanders Harry Le Mesurier and George Pipon . . . . "The society of Montreal is excellent, the style of parties sumptuous. At all dinners you are given claret and champagne . . . . in short, the style of £4000 to £5000 a year in England . . . . my friend David Ogden, ... a lawyer, makes about £2000 a year and lives accordingly".

In February 1817 "Captain Holland called at my lodgings and offered to sell his company to me for fifteen hundred pounds, to which I instantly acceeded . . . ." In May, "The Regiment having received notice from England that it was to be disbanded, I obtained leave to proceed to England via New York, and was allowed my passage money". At New York he called on the Graves; on hearing he was in the house Mrs. Graves ran down stairs and "absolutely embraced me, as if I had been her own son. She told me much about Curaçao. The poor people sadly lamented the loss of my father's Government, and the gentle English rule. They would readily surrender themselves back to England". On 23rd June, "Landed once more in dear old England and found myself a Captain. Adieu to all other professions". This resolve, however, he was unable to keep, as his parents "distinctly stated they wished me never to leave them again". It is hard to understand why the General, a soldier to the core, should have taken this standpoint with the son who had only just purchased a captaincy, nor why the son acceeded so readily to his wishes. But it is clear that by this decision the Army lost a promising officer.

CHAPTER SIX

THE CIRCLE

The letter which Mary Le Couteur wrote to her future daughter-in-law, Harriet Janvrin, in 1817 would not be well received by a bride of 1970, but nevertheless it contains much sound common sense, and is not so formidable as that which Mary had herself received in similar circumstances from her aunt a quarter of a century earlier. What Mary said was: "I will not, my dear girl, wish you joy on becoming a wife, so very uncertain is it . . . . I am however certain . . . . that it is not likely you could be better suited than with a man bred up in the same community with yourself, with similar habits, way of living, equality of fortune and . . . . early imbibed sentiments of piety and good morals . . . . It was the fervent wish of your poor mother[1] that you and John should one day make a match . . . Mutual love is the first step towards (happiness), without which it cannot take root; but it is not all . . . . You doubtless think it easier to please a husband than to please a father. A short time will undeceive you in this respect . . . . The age of tyranny over our sex is nearly at an end, ... but there still exists a stumbling block against which reason will never be fully able to prevail, that is the love of power . . . . Very few men will ever allow that a wife can have reason on her side; it is all one whether she be wise or foolish; if she thinks not as he does, she must be wrong . . . . Our lives are much more sedentary than those of men, and therefore we have much more time for reflexion and thought . . . . You must make yourself acquainted with the exact state of your income, and with that which you can and ought to afford yourselves . . . . I cannot command your love, but I hope to acquire it. Come here when you like, be open with me, and you may do with me what you please".

As soon as Sir John arrived back from Canada the wedding was announced, but Harriet adopted an unexpected course. "My sweet Harriet was on a visit to her aunt Patty Pipon at Falmouth from September 1817 to January 1818, where she had gone to be away from the gaiety of Jersey and my importunity, my mother and Mrs. Touzel having given her great credit for this step". In January he went over to fetch her, and on the 25th they embarked in the Young Phoenix, a Jersey-built ship, full-rigged, three masted, carvel-built, with square stern, a billet head and of 183 tons burthen. Some details have survived about her, and those interested in ships of the past may welcome a short digression to include them. She was 86 feet in length and 22 in breadth, and was first registered in 1803, being owned throughout her working life by the firm of Philip and Francis Janvrin. She was granted a charter to act as a privateer. In 1812 she was altered and re-registered. In August 1818 she sailed from Gaspé, bound for the Mediterranean, and was never heard of again, being reported as missing in September 1819.

With Sir John and Harriet on the voyage was her father Francis Janvrin, part owner of the ship. Captain Asplet was the master. They started with a fresh north-west breeze which took them fast out to sea, but the weather deteriorated and the sails were taut.

---

1. Harriet Janvrin, née Dumaresq, Mary's sister.

"Captain", asked the landsman, "do you mean to carry on thus all night, with the sky overclouding and the wind increasing?": to which Asplet replied he was proud of the speed his ship was making, and they would soon be at Gorey. "True", said the landsman, "but she is rather going under it than over it; for I have crossed the Atlantic five times, and never yet saw a three masted vessel straining along with her gunwale under water". The Captain was contemptuous of this warning, but the landsman insisted that it would be wise to "take in your royals and make under a reef. You will lose some of your sticks yet tonight". The Captain went below and Sir John conversed with the Mate, who said that Asplet never would take in a reef, and had had the Young Phoenix on her beam ends once, in the Mediterranean; and added "though she is a good sea ship she is very crank[1]". The Mate then took precautionary measures on his own initiative, for which the Captain took him severely to task later. In the morning, still uneasy, Sir John was on the look-out and was the first to see rocks, shouting "Breakers ahead". Nobody seemed to know what rocks they were, but thought the Minquiers the most likely. The fog was thick, but for one instant it lifted, showing that the ship was behind Icho Tower, "over the whole bed to St. Clement's rocks". Philip Janvrin, who was on the sands in his gig, "drove violently to the pier to get boats ready to save our lives, for he thought it impossible that the vessel should be saved. Such was the danger, the foolhardiness and imprudence of the Captain. The next trip was his last; the noble little ship, crew nor Captain have ever been heard of since".

On 23rd March 1818 Sir John and his "dearest Ha", as he always called her, were married by the Rev. Mr. Bertram[2] at St. Brelade's Church. It appears that only his mother and her father were present, though one does not know the reason why. They chose as their wedding day the anniversary of the General's release from prison by Hyder Aly, only they made a mistake of one day, the General being too kind to undeceive them. The following day they left for Granville. When they arrived there, "the Douaniers were on the point of handling my young wife, when my military rage exploded and she was handed over to the celebrated Marguerite, the examining matron, whose potent influence was accessible under silver control. I was astounded at the filth and discomfort at the leading pothouse, miscalled a hotel. The bed was so small that it could only be intended for a just newly married pair". They proceeded through the countryside by coach at leisurely pace. At Caen they ran into a bunch of young Jerseymen studying at the University or Lycée. It was the 1st April, and one of them refused the invitation to dinner, fearing they were making a "poisson d'Avril" of him, but he was persuaded, and the party consisted of Tom Pipon, John de Veulle, Touzel and Aubin, Hammond being ill[3]. They went shopping and he bought Harriet some lace. After a gay and happy time in Paris they returned home, and the diary of a near neighbour and friend, Philippe Marett of La Haule mentions "my cousin Harriet Janvrin" and "John Le Couteur, which charming couple, after having travelled together through part of France for the space of two months, was now returned to enjoy domestic and conjugal happiness at home. Visits were received at Belle Vue and Belmont[4]".

---

1. Weak, shaky.   2. Rector 1788-1818.
3. Pipon was probably of La Hague: de Veulle, later Sir John (1799-1848), became Bailiff: Touzel, probably Percival, son of Col. Touzel. Aubin, perhaps Clement Aubin, who was having treatment for deafness: Hammond, John Hammond (1801-1880), became Bailiff.
4. Later Government House.

The first thing they did after their return was to demolish the old farm barracks at Belle Vue which had formerly been occupied by the Russians, and then let, and Dart the builder "contracted to build a new cottage for us at 3s. 3d. the perch for stone masonry and 2s. 6d. for 9 in. brickwork . . . . The house ran up quickly", and was called Le Bocage. There was already an older house on the site, with a front door lintel inscribed HLR ELB 1751, for Helier Le Rossignol and Elizabeth Le Bas, who had been married a few years before that date. The old house has other interesting features. On the first floor the eastern room has one attractive small window, a fireplace with plain unchamfered corbels and a depressed arch lintel in brick, probably replacing one of wood. On the ground floor is a better fireplace with chamfered uprights and stops. The north wall, which abuts on the road, appears earlier than 1751. There are several blocked windows and doors, and a curve in the masonry suggests that once there was a tourelle staircase. The ground floor rooms are cobbled, literally, with perfectly matched sea pebbles, the only example recorded in the Island.

Sir John, however, required something more up to date for his bride, and started building immediately in front of the old house, choosing the "cottage orné" style which was very popular in England at the time. The finished result was very like Houghton Lodge[1] in Hampshire, built in 1801. Apart from the fact that the original thatched roof has been replaced by slate, Le Bocage has changed but little and is a charming example of the period. In 1832, when still thatched, it was insured for £500. The illustration shows a wedding which took place there during the tenancy of William Baker. Le Bocage took a year or more to build. Messrs. Booley of Exeter were consulted about a stove, and the cost of a cast-iron verandah, which is still there in perfect condition.

In April 1819 their first child was born, Harriet, always called Tit, perhaps her own childish effort to say "chick". They were at this time living with their parents at Belle Vue, though clearly starting a garden at Le Bocage, for the first peas of the season were picked there the day that "Little Chick and Mama went out for the first time". A new well was needed, and "Mr. Clement Ingouville, the spring finder", came and divined the water, and a well was sunk 24ft. deep where he recommended, midway between the two houses. Gardening continued, and the next year Sir John recorded the planting of "one *dahlia purpurea*, a Mexican plant with tuberous perennial roots, to be propagated by seed and by offsets from the roots. Believed to be the first dahlia brought to Jersey". The dahlia was first introduced to Europe from Mexico in 1789, and from then on attempts were made to grow it in England, Lady Holland sending seed home from Madrid in 1804, and other stock coming from France in about 1815. Bulbs were planted in the Le Bocage garden from Hamburg, from Mr. Poingdestre at Grainville and from many other friends. Always on the look out for rare plants he recorded in 1826 seeing a loquat in the greenhouse at Noirmont, and that it had a sweet malic flavour. He planted a kernel of it at Belle Vue.

Poor Harriet suffered from a serious stammer, and before they were married Mrs. Le Couteur remarked to her son that it would not do for Harriet to be a chatterbox. Sir John never mentioned this impediment and had evidently not minded it. But in 1825 he wrote: "Having heard that Mr. Broster made perfect cures of stammering, my father wished Harriet to place herself under his care. So he gave her a hundred pounds towards the attempt,

---

1. Christopher Hussey's "Late Georgian Architecture", p.21.

15. LE BOCAGE, ST. BRELADE, Jersey,
built by John Le Couteur in 1818.
(*photograph taken in 1872 at the wedding of a relative of the tenant at that time, Mr Baker.*)

16. HARRIET LE COUTEUR (née Janvrin)
(1798-1865)
wife of Sir John Le Couteur
(*portrait by Fisher*, 1850)

17. Mourning Brooch of pearl and onyx, in memory of
SOPHY LE COUTEUR (1832-1844)

SALE OF PROPERTY,
At Gaspé.

On THE 1st JANUARY, 1842,

WILL BE EXPOSED FOR SALE, IN THE ISLAND OF JERSEY,

IN ONE LOT, THAT

LUCRATIVE ESTABLISHMENT IN THE DISTRICT OF GASPÉ,

LOWER CANADA,

The Property of FRED.ᴷ JANVRIN, Esq,

COMPRISING

1st.--His principal Establishment, situate at Grand Grève, in Gaspé Bay, four miles from Gaspé Point, including a large DWELLING HOUSE, with suitable FISH STORES to contain about 7000 qtls Fish, Shop, Stages, Cook Rooms, Forge, &c., &c., the whole measuring about 19 chains front by 46 chains long, bounded on the West by Gaspé Bay, and on the East by the River St. Lawrence.

2d.--His Property at the Basin of Gaspé, about 15 miles distant from Grand Grève, including a WHARF with sufficient depth of water alongside to admit two Ships of 300 tons, each loading at the same time, with several SALT and FISH STORES, the latter sufficiently spacious to contain 10,000 qtls. Fish. This point of Land is situated on a space of 1 acre, 2 roods, and 22 perches of ground.

3rd.--Malbay, another Establishment, situated to the Southward of Grand Grève, distant 20 miles, with a DWELLING HOUSE, Stages, and Fish Stores, to contain about 1,000 qtls. Fish, where 10 Fishing Barges are kept. This Fishing place measures 162 feet front by 470 feet deep.

4th.--Cape Roziers, another Fishing Establishment, situated in the River St. Lawrence, distant about 2 miles by land from Grand Grève, where 8 Fishing Barges are kept, with DWELLING HOUSE, spacious FISH STORES, &c. The lot measuring about 100 feet front by 180 feet in depth.

5th.--Also a beautiful new Establishment, at Griffin's Cove, a well settled spot and sheltered, distant 6 miles from Cape Roziers, with a new Stage thirty-four feet by sixty-four. Also, a new FISH STORE to contain 1000 qtls. Fish, a SALT STORE, Flakes, Cook Rooms, for 10 Barges and Shoresmen. Also, a DWELLING HOUSE,--the whole completed in 1840. Besides Inventory of Goods remaining at the close of the year's navigation at the above Establishments, with Debts, &c.

For Particulars and Plans, apply to the Proprietor, in Jersey.

JERSEY, 20th APRIL, 1841.

18. Sale Poster of Property of FREDERICK JANVRIN at Gaspé, 1841

(*see page* 72)

19.   probably
SOPHIA DUMARESQ
(née Lovelace)
(1786-1885)
widow of Thomas Dumaresq of Millbrook.
'Dear old Aunt Sophia'

20.   probably
ROBERT PIPON, R.N.
(1815-1872)
Midshipman, H.M.S. Belvidera.
(*see page* 73)

which induced us to start for Edinburgh where he practises". In these archives there is an engraving of John Broster, F.A.S., saying that he cures impediments of the speech, and that the engraving had been made at the request and expense of his patients. The cure seems well-nigh miraculous, and can only be explained as some sort of mesmerism. It took just one hour. Harriet was first asked to sign an undertaking that she would not reveal what had occurred, would never attempt to tell anyone or to cure anyone. Always a devoted mother, she refused to sign, saying it was inhuman to expect her to promise not to cure her children. By this time she had two little girls, but there is no evidence that either of them suffered from stammering. After a while Dr. Broster agreed to waive this proviso, and she signed. An hour later her anxious husband returned to fetch her and was told that she was cured. He was amazed, as she conversed, and even read Milton to him, without hesitation. They were both deeply grateful to God, and to Mr. Broster, for this miracle. The cure seems to have been permanent.

They had reached Edinburgh by an unusual route. Leaving Jersey in the Ariadne, they spent a few days in London, and then secured berths in the "James Watt, a fine Leith steamer, for which paid nine guineas board included". They left Blackwall on 10th August, by the 12th were off Dunbar and arrived in Edinburgh that evening.

They had not been married many years when they decided that their French was not fluent enough and a trip to Paris must be made, and they set off, accompanied by Harriet's sister Louisa, the two little girls and two nurses. Sir John attended a course of lectures at Le Collège de France, took lessons in the violon-cello, went sightseeing everywhere and met the Egyptologist Bonzoni. He found him very entertaining, "and would have been more so had not a vile discussion, about dates before the Christian era, stinted the information he would have treated us to. Savants are really asses when they lose facts for speculation". They often went to the theatre, and saw the great Talma[1] playing Auguste in Le Mercure Galant; and Voltaire's Tancrède, "très mal joué, excepté le role de Tancrède par Vigier". After a stay of three months they returned to Jersey, having worked extremely hard at French, art and music lessons. There were also trips to London, on one of which they bought a phaeton, ordering it "to be painted drab in colour and to be sent off tomorrow fortnight". A little later, back at home: "Drove to Vinchelez in our new phaeton. It runs very light and was much admired by Carteret[2] and Tom Pipon at La Hague".

In 1826 Harriet was expecting another baby. One can guess with what anxiety it was awaited, for she had had a daughter, Harriet, in 1819, and a son, John, in 1820, who died the next year, and whose existence is only known from the parish register, the diaries for those two years having disappeared. In 1822 she had had another daughter, Mary. It was the day after Sir John's own thirty-second birthday, and they had all had a gay family dinner at Belle Vue, when "my dear Harriet called me up at half past one and I sent off for Dr. Struvé at 2, who arrived about 4; and at 5.15 she was in smart labour pains, and in about ten minutes was well delivered of a smart boy. Went to Chapel to offer my thanks to the giver of all good, and to pray Him to grant wisdom to my boy; to make him a just and pious Christian. Went off for Government House to request Sir Colin to stand as his godfather; met him on the way, when he kindly consented and said he wished Halkett to

1. François Joseph Talma (1763-1826), French tragic actor.
2. Probably Colonel John Daniel de Carteret of Vinchelez de Bas.

*a phaeton
c.1830.*

be placed after John. Had him baptised by Mr. de Joux. Dined with my father-in-law, who was highly delighted with his grandson".

Sir John was at this time A.D.C. to the Lieutenant-Governor, Sir Colin Halkett, a Waterloo hero[1]. Only a few months previously Lady Halkett had given birth to a son[2]. "I went up to wish him joy of it, and found she was still in great danger at 12, but all right in the evening". Sir Colin and Lady Halkett had a large family, including a daughter they named Jersey, and they remained firm friends with Sir John always. Only once did he criticise his chief, after a long discussion with him about "those persons who have no horses being obliged to furnish them (for the militia). Astonished and shocked to hear the b . . . . attribute motives of disloyalty to those who decline on the pleas of ill health or want of means". This was but a passing comment, and for the rest he thought the world of Sir Colin. In 1849 he visited them at Chelsea Hospital, of which Sir Colin had been made Governor, and reflected how fitting a position this was for "my old chief, who had bled so often for his country and had led some of its best soldiers to their most glorious efforts, at the head of its hardy veterans . . . . Lady H. took me through the wards and seems to take a real interest . . . . Their own house is everything an old Governor could wish, with fine rooms . . . . all furnished by themselves at considerable cost . . . . She recapitulated with

1. Sir Colin Halkett, (1774-1856), served in the Peninsula and at Waterloo.
2. Frederick John Colin, born June 10th 1826.

inimitable grace their history in India, and her dislike of the coarse habits of the ladies there, a vulgarity which her dear genteel little society at Jersey never dreamt of". The Halketts seem to have left India under some disfavour[1], after which they went to Italy, which they had enjoyed.

On 3rd July 1832 Harriet had her last child, a girl, Sophy. Her mother-in-law wrote: "At half past six o'clock Dr. Struvé was sent for to attend Harriet, who was brought to bed of a fine girl a quarter of an hour before the doctor came": and later on, to a cousin George Dumaresq, then in Rio de Janeiro, he said: "Harriet is very well. She has presented me with a lovely little Sophia, who has not had a day ailing in three months from her birth, and if she goes on improving as she has begun . . . . (she) will be a Vénus de Caesarée". Everyone seems to have loved this child, who was in Paris with her mother when she was only four years old. Her grandmother was there also, and wrote: "Took her to the Palais Royal and as far as the Passage Panorama beyond the Bourse to get her a bonnet. She passed all the bonbon and toy shops without the least desire to get anything from either. I never witnessed such philosophy and forbearance in so young a child . . . . She at length stopped at a toy shop to look at some hoops . . . . I bought her one, which satisfied all her desires . . . . After enjoying her hoop for a while in the Tuileries Gardens I took her to dine with me at a restaurant . . . . She was quite satisfied with a mutton chop and a charlotte de pommes . . . . The little dear often kissed me during the day . . . . So pleasing to Grand-mammas!" But in 1844 her father had to record: "Took my sweet child Sophy home from school for the last time. She seemingly only ailed from a slight bilious attack, but there was an uneasy look about her which alarmed me, so that I consulted Dr. Low who was passing the gates of Belle Vue. He thought nothing of it and sent her some pills". The next day she was "quite poorly . . . . She said 'Come closer' several times, but did not smile when I kissed her". During the night she was "stricken with a convulsion", from which she never recovered. In a letter to a doctor friend, Frederick Roberts of the 59th Regiment[2], he said that a post mortem examination had revealed water on the posterior part of the brain. It was almost certainly meningo-encephalitis. He decided to erect a memorial, and when in London consulted William Rogers, Illuminator to the Architectural College, "the Grinling Gibbons of our day", who designed a lily. Rogers' drawing is pasted into a bible belonging to the family, but the flower carved on her memorial tablet in St. Brelade's Church is smaller and less elaborate. A mourning brooch made in her memory was given to her friend and contemporary Julia Marett of La Haule, the future Lady Marett. It is in onyx, with pearls, and is inscribed with her initials and dates. Such brooches and rings are a fashion of the past, and would be thought very curious now.

Sophy's lily.
1844.

Once she had overcome her stammering, Harriet seems to have been a strong and healthy woman. In 1830 she had a dramatic accident. Sir John was on his way back from England, having a merry party on board with friends. Captain White "had kindly offered to land me in his boat at St. Aubin, but which I of course declined as being too troublesome. I heard from Bouton of dear Ha having had

1. Perhaps due to their disapproval of coarse habits.   2. The East Lancashires.

an upset, though she was not much hurt, so I hastened home and found her with black eyes and her arm in a sling . . . . Last Monday . . . . Robert was driving her to town, and going down Mont de la Rocque the braking gave way. Off started the mare at a gallop, and in trying to check her the reins broke, which caused them both to be violently thrown forward over the mare's back . . . . It seems after the accident that Robert scampered off after the mare and phaeton as soon as he had picked himself up. Harriet did the same when she recovered her senses, and was met at La Haule by Mr. John Fox, bleeding and breathless, running after the fugitives, not a bit frightened or concerned . . . . The mare and phaeton were stopped past the third Tower[1] by Mr. Guille, not a bit injured . . . . When Johnnie saw his Mama come home wounded and bound up, he cried and said: 'What will Papa say?'"

There have been several outbreaks of cholera in Jersey, always worse in the town, as would be expected, and one of the diaries remarks that the principal cause of cholera in George Street "had been owing to the bad water, into which some of the privies drained. It was poison the people had been drinking". It is possible that Harriet herself had a mild attack during the epidemic of 1849, with other members of the household, for Sir John recorded: "Poorly all the week. So was my wife, old Ann and Susan, George the coachman and William. Symptoms of cholera". For the week after that the diary is mute, and a month later in a letter he wrote: "Harriet has been with myself on a tour through the lakes for a change of air, having suffered much while the cholera prevailed in Jersey". There are hints that in middle age she may have become delicate from some unknown cause, as she seldom accompanied Sir John when he went away, and he often attended some function with his daughter instead of his wife. On the other hand the daughter, writing in 1850 to her brother in India, described a New Year's Eve dance at the Assembly Ball Room in these words: "Lord Limerick and Mamma led the way. She was by far the lightest dancer in the room and entered into the fun of it with all the spirit imaginable".

Of Harriet's appearance we know only what is shown in one portrait, painted by Fisher at the same time as that of her aunt-mother-in-law. There is a strong likeness between the two women, the common element being the Dumaresq ancestry they shared. Harriet sits at an upstairs window at Belle Vue, painting, and before her is one of those pears which she so exquisitely portrayed in her album of fruit. This album was started while she was still living at Le Bocage and continues through the Belle Vue days. It shows great talent, and presents a large number of specimens of fruit, pears predominating a little over apples. Each is labelled with its name, and sometimes with a historic footnote such as: "sent some of these to King William". It is a sparkling record of fruit which could be, and was, grown in one garden in Jersey at that time, and the fidelity with which each specimen is portrayed, blemishes and all, makes many of the paintings veritable "trompes l'oeil". Other sketches she did show her to have had as great facility with pencil as with brush. She was an efficient housekeeper, keeping meticulous accounts, and keeping her husband's books for him also. Her complete devotion as mother and grandmother is testified by her memorial in St. Brelade's Church, but even more so by entries in the diaries.

As was then customary, her daughters received their education at home. In 1826 a Miss Wilton was engaged as governess, mainly for Harriet, who was then seven years old, and she has a claim to immortality from a new adjective which Sir John coined for her. He

---

1. At Beaumont.

said: "Drove Miss Wilton home. She is a clever girl, independent of her great acquirements, which she quite avoids making a display of. It is rare that a girl of seventeen should be musical, dansical, a Latin, Greek, Hebrew and French scholar, and withal very lively, a pretty poetess, with modesty and unassuming manners". He felt they were very fortunate to have her as a governess. One would like to hear more of the dansical Miss Wilton, but the diaries are dumb. Later on the girls shared lessons with the daughters of Noirmont Manor, and Harriet's "New Zealand Tale", written at the age of twelve, speaks as well for her mentors as herself. The handwriting and spelling are perfect.

Complete as was the devotion between Sir John and Harriet, and of this there is no shadow of doubt, he did get irritated with her sometimes, in circumstances which show that she richly deserved it. She could be unpunctual, and he found her life too tightly bound to social engagements and shopping. On occasion she could be downright selfish, taking out the carriage for a drive, staying in town on a whim to lunch with friends and forgetting that neither coachman nor horse had anything to eat. Or taking the carriage without telling him when he needed the horse for mowing hay, which would make any farmer lose his temper. He was once laid up for several weeks and things went badly wrong: "Interference will never cease in this house. I order the gardener to go and fetch me a box in which to send apples to a friend. Harriet flies from the room, in which she is reading over a letter of advice to Johnny, does two things at a time, and goes to send a box which will not suit, though I have begged, entreated, ordered and quarrelled about never being interfered with when I give orders to my men servants. The maids, I dare not, in her presence". Next day a penitent Harriet said: "I will go because I see I fret you", but he continued to grumble that she so often interfered.

His daughter Harriet could be equally irritating, and he sometimes found her vague and unable to concentrate. When he sent her to his study to fetch books and she returned with the wrong ones, he confided to his diary: "It is quite surprising to see how little her mind reasons or acts upon one thing at a time; a fatal habit. She would have left the three volumes in my room before she went to search again . . . ., till I called her back to replace the books. Then she went and found the book which I wanted". One does not know with which of them to sympathise more, the tetchy patient or the girl who dithered because he barked at her. Probably the latter, because he was so tough. "I shall read a few of these wants of fixity of purpose to her, as I note them, with a hope of cure, as she is earnest in trying to do right, but a regular wool-gatherer". Was she wondering, poor soul, when a beau would come and rescue her from this demanding household. When, her duties done, she sat at the piano to sing "Ah, vous dirai je, Maman?", he could only say that though this was the most beautiful of all French ballads, she was "quite losing sight of its meaning". The gulf between crabbed age and youth has always been a wide one. As he grew older, he came to depend more and more on her, especially after her mother's death, and was acutely aware of his debt of gratitude to her. Bred in an exemplary household, she was perhaps over serious all her life, but there had been golden days when she was young, knew everyone in the Island, and met the officers of the regiments stationed in it. But somehow she never made a match, and when she was only thirty her younger sister called her "the old lady".

Of the younger daughter, Mary there is never a word of criticism. The first mention of her was when she had colic, as an infant, on a journey to France. At the age of nine, she was already showing a strong character, and more self control than her elder sister, as has

Lively with children, a great walker.'

been shown, when her grandfather was so ill. On one of her father's visits to London, he made a note: "Buy a muslin gown for Mary, with a very small neat sprig worked in blue." In 1842, at the age of twenty, she was ill and her parents took her to England to see two doctors, Mr. M. Tupper and Mr. Lawrence, both of whose names appear later on her father's nomination as a Fellow of the Royal Society. In explaining the case to them, Sir John described Mary as mild, placid, studious, yet very lively, even boisterous with children, a great walker, but suffering from severe headaches and complaining of double vision. The specialists declared that "the disease was caused by the general want of regularity in her system", and set about regulating it with doses of mercury and chalk. The double vision may have been caused by cerebral pressure, or perhaps she simply needed spectacles. The information is insufficient for diagnosis, and in any case she apparently recovered.

Thirteen years earlier, in 1829, Charles Richard Sumner[1], Bishop of Winchester, the first holder of the see to visit the Channel Islands, came to Jersey. His wife was Jennie Fanny Maunoir, daughter of a Genevan minister, and his son, the Rev. John Maunoir Sumner, was in attendance on his father during this first visit, which was one of several; and during them a deep friendship sprang up between the Bishop and Sir John, who were of the same age, and it lasted for the rest of their lives. The Bishop's daughter Louisana also came in 1829, and kept a diary, in which she wrote: "There was no good service of steamers to the Islands in those days, and Government put a steamer at my father's disposal, the Lightning . . . . My chief friend was the daughter of the Bailli of the Island, a Miss Touzel, who took me to see all the interesting spots . . . . She was 15 or 16, and we took long walks, taking our lunch with us". Louisana was not entirely accurate, as Miss Touzel was not the daughter of the Bailiff, but of General Touzel of d'Hautrée.

In due course John Sumner met Mary Le Couteur, and by 1843 her grandmother was writing: "Mr. Sumner, the Bishop of Winchester's eldest son, arrived with consent of parties to court my granddaughter Mary and to ask her in marriage. He came, he saw, he conquered. Everything being settled, and no love lost[2] on either side, he returned home on Friday to prepare the parsonage, and the Bishop's family, to receive his pretty little wife. He takes Johnny with him to keep up his spirits till Wednesday, when he purposes to return on the wings of love". A week later Grandmamma wrote: "Love making all the week". In after years Mary's father said that she proved to be a perfect parson's wife. At first they lived at North Waltham, where Sir John visited them and attended service in "John's cold church", but soon afterwards were transferred to Buriton in Hampshire, where they spent almost all their lives, administering the combined parish of Buriton and Petersfield.

Sir John and Harriet's son John was known as Johnnie until his marriage, when he became Halkett, or Hal. There are details of his progress during childhood: at five weeks, we are told, he "knows his nurse when washed in cold water of a morning": at eleven weeks he knew his father and no longer minded being washed in cold water: at ten months he could walk alone, and on his first birthday "Mr. Johnny trots along famously for a one year old". When he was three his father bought him a desk in England for £1. 16s. In 1839,

---

1. At one time Librarian and Chaplain to George III.   2. A phrase which later changed its meaning.

then aged thirteen, he was taken to London to school. He and his father embarked on the Atalanta, Captain Babot, and had a rough crossing, the boy being very sick. Arrived in London, they found that the Queen was at that moment proroguing Parliament, so they went straight to the Palace. "Johnny was greatly delighted with the bands of the Blues and Guards, and we were close to the Palace in front of the crowd when 'Bang' went the cannons to announce that H.M. had left . . . . The procession soon arrived, first the Guards . . . ., then Her Majesty in the state coach, drawn by eight cream coloured horses. When Johnny saw the Queen, with her coronet of diamonds, bow . . . ., he said he was all of a tremble and called her a 'dear little Queen' for bowing to him. The Master of the Horse, Lord Albemarle, was the only person in the state coach with her. Johnny thought the Palace perfection, but very large for a young lady to live in". The Queen was then unmarried.

The next few days were taken up with sight-seeing. They went to a comedy at the Haymarket, the Horse Guards stables, the Zoological gardens and then to the Gallery of science, where "Johnny and I went down in the diving bell . . . . It affected our ears and created an uneasy sensation of pressure". They got a shock from an electric eel, marvelled at a microscope and saw "the electrical experiment to exhibit Mr. Marks' system of light-ning conductors, carried through a ship's bottom . . . ., (which) appeared conclusive". The boy was then taken to the school he was to attend, kept by Dr. and Mrs. Major in Bloomsbury Square. At parting his father said: "He is a little fellow to be thrown on his own resources among big boys, but so was I at his age". In 1842 at the age of sixteen he was with a Mr. Barry at Woolwich, who advised Sir John to send him to the Rev. Mr. Groze to work up his algebra for the army examination, a service for which he apparently charged no less than 40 guineas. In May 1844 he was commissioned into the 87th, the Royal Irish Fusiliers, was an Ensign for two years and became full Lieutenant in 1846, serving in Scot-land, and then at Newport in Wales. His military career at home, in India and the Crimea is dealt with in Chapters 13 and 14. There is a masterly portrait of him by Berteau holding the Regimental Colour of the 87th, on which some of the battle honours of this famous regiment can be discerned. The particular stand of colours he is holding was laid up in 1860, and its successor in 1938.

This may be a convenient place for a brief review of the Le Couteur relations whose names appear in the archives. They are many in number, owing to the large families which were normal at the time, and more closely integrated than is usual today, when ease of travel makes for dispersal. With so many relatives living so close together, there was inevitably a large family circle who knew each other well and spent much time together. This was especially true of Jersey, with its strict geographical limits. Until Victorian times many Jerseymen and most Jerseywomen never left their native island; and although many of the menfolk served in the Army or Navy, or plied the Atlantic in the cod fishing fleets, the majority married local girls and returned home to retire. Within the island itself there were even smaller microcosms, and one of these was the little port and village of St. Aubin's, five miles west of St. Helier, which was dominated by the families of Pipon, Marett, Janvrin and Le Couteur, with the Dumaresqs in the neighbouring parish of St. Peter. There was a great degree of inter-marriage between them, making their genealogies rather confusing. Sir John actually had no near Le Couteur relatives. His only brother died in childhood, and his father was an only son with two sisters who died unmarried. Being a first cousin of his wife's, they were equally connected with the numerous Dumaresq family. It would be wearisome to the reader to follow all the intricacies of relationship, or to introduce to him all the members of what they themselves called "The Circle" but some of those most closely connected and mentioned most often may deserve attention.

Harriet had a brother and sister only. The brother Frederick lived most of his life at Bath, and was intimately connected with the Janvrin family business at Gaspé. The sale poster of 1841, shown here, advertises his property as a "lucrative establishment". In 1816 somebody described him as an "engaging boy". He had small-pox in 1845, a diary entry saying: "Saw poor Frederick. Dreadfully marked". He also married his first cousin Jane Janvrin, daughter of Daniel, and they had three children, Adolphus, Emily and Francis William. Whenever members of the family went to England they stayed with Frederick and Jane at Bath, and it was in their house that Johnnie met his future wife, Mai Low. Frederick and Sir John became widowed at about the same time, and were of some comfort to one another. Jane seems to have had the feeling that Sir John disapproved of her, and he confessed that "when you were younger I thought that your wit and spirits sometimes led you into danger, and that you had a cold heart . . . . When your excellent husband had been so ill in London of the small pox, and I witnessed the desperate alarm in which you were . . . ., a veil was suddenly rent from my eyes . . . ., and I have ever since loved and honoured you". Indeed he felt that it was the news of the death of Jane which precipitated his own wife's seizure and death, so attached had they all become.

Harriet's sister Louisa was younger than herself, and always very close to her. She went to school at Petersham in 1816. Ten years later, "Loulou told me with a downcast look she was engaged to Dan, and asked me if I was pleased at it; to which I said I really was, as I had ever considered him a very amiable man". This occasion was on meeting "my father-in-law, Louisa and Dan land from the steam boat: found them on the beach, all sick and well". Daniel Janvrin was a cousin, a generation older than Louisa, and widower of Anne Marett of La Haule. In 1830 Louisa had a son, Charles, who died young, and then two more children, Louisa who married George Charleton, and Daniel. This Daniel was never well, always too fat for his age, and developed gout when quite young. In 1862 he married Harriet Nicolle, who had "a beautiful voice but no fortune. But she looked very pretty in white muslin, and sang and played sweetly . . . . What a sacrifice that sweet young girl is making, marrying an heir to gout . . . . She has been admirably educated by a judicious mother. So much may be hoped for my idle and good natured nephew". They lived at Belmont, Mont au Prêtre. But by 1867 he was an invalid, and an entry said: "Went to see Dan who is wretchedly ill from gout; a miserable object, smoking in bed". Three weeks later he died: "a happy relief from much misery to himself and his sweet wife". Two years later she married a Captain Ewart.

The Dumaresq family were far more numerous. It will be recalled that Sir John Dumaresq had a family of nine, three surviving sons and six daughters. The eldest son was John who, like his father, was educated at Winchester College, and became Attorney General, but died at the age of forty-three. There is a memorial to him in St. Peter's Church. He married Mary Janvrin and they had eleven children, six of whom left no descendants. The eldest to survive was George, who in 1842 married Rachel Le Geyt and lived at Font Hill, Beaumont. After having a stroke he lived on for many years, devotedly nursed by his wife. The next son of Sir John Dumaresq was Henry, who became an Admiral. He married Anne Janvrin and they left three children, the only male descendant of this large family being their son Arthur. On 17th May 1850 the ship Cuckoo was wrecked at the entrance to St. Helier's harbour, while engaged in ferrying men of the 26th Regiment[1] from H.M.S. Birkenhead and embarking the 54th.[2] She struck the Oyster Rock and "by using every possible effect of steam she reached the head of the pier, so as to save all the lives on board. Boats immediately surrounded her and in five minutes . . . . she sank, leaving only the tips of her masts above water". Henry was in command of the Cuckoo, and it was said that it was due to his coolness in this emergency that there was no loss of life. H.M.S. Cuckoo was repaired, and in commission again the following year. Henry's promotion to Admiral in 1875 was very gratifying to his godfather, Sir John Le Couteur who, though old and blind, drove out to congratulate him.

Sir John Dumaresq's next son, Philip, we have already met as Captain of the famous ship Victory. Her keel had been laid down in 1759 and she was launched in 1765, remaining technically on active service until 1922. This Philip died in 1819, and the partage of his effects show him to have had a considerable library and a certain amount of silver. The sale of his property, conducted by Philip Le Gallais, produced the substantial sum of £1178 for his widow. He had three children: Philip, who was killed on board H.M.S. Asia at Navarino in 1827: Frederick, who married Marguerite Le Geyt, and owned, perhaps built, the house Elysée, which he bequeathed to his aunt in 1845: and Amelia.

The third son of Sir John Dumaresq, Thomas, known in the family as Thomas of Millbrook, may have lived at La Chaumière, Rue de Haut. His memorial at St. Peter's says "He served in Egypt, the Mediterranean and the Peninsula, and had charge of the army of occupation in Paris in 1815". He was also Deputy Assistant Commissary General. Like his brothers he died comparatively young, in 1825, leaving a widow, Sophia Lovelace, and three sons, Charles, Albert and William. Aunt Sophia died at the age of 99, outliving her nephew Sir John, of whom she was very fond. At every Christmas party there is mention of her name, how wonderful she was for her age and how, when an octogenarian, she "ran for her parasol".

A few words about Sir John Dumaresq's daughters will complete the review of this large family circle. The eldest was Mary, mother of Sir John: the second, Harriet, wife of Francis Janvrin and mother of Harriet: Martha, known as Aunt Patty, who married Charles Pipon: Elizabeth (Aunt Betsy) who married his brother Philip Pipon. Philip and Betsy had a son Robert, who entered the Navy, and is probably the young officer in the striking engraving in this book. Sir John was fond of this young cousin and took a great interest in his education and career, this attachment continuing to Robert's son, his godson, of whom he noted in 1860: "I had a long and very nice letter from Beaumont Pipon who is acting as mate on board the London screw liner . . . . He is in charge of the Captain's barge, 18 oars; writes with ease, a fine bold hand; good style for a lad of fifteen; no mistakes in spelling, which the Etonians are famed for". The youngest daughter, Louisa, married Philip Bouton, and had two sons, Philip and Charles.

If the reader feels bemused he will see from the genealogies at the end of the book: that the relatives mentioned are only a proportion of an even larger band, who constantly stayed at or had lavish meals within the hospitable walls of Belle Vue, and therefore qualify for membership of "The Circle".

---

1. The Cameronians.   2. The Dorsetshires.

CHAPTER SEVEN

THE YOUNG CONSTABLE

The terms Constable and Jurat need some explanation to anyone who is not a Channel Islander. They are both of great dignity, and carried with them a seat in the States (the Legislative Assembly), while Jurats also sat on the bench in the Royal Court (the Judicial Assembly). Both posts are entirely unpaid. In simple terms the Constable was the father of his parish. He had wide powers for settling disputes, maintaining law and order, care of the sick, needy and orphans. He also had multifarious duties including holding of parish assemblies, collection of rates and taxes, maintenance of roads, and many other functions, which are reflected in this chapter.

Early in 1826 Sir John had thoughts of standing as Constable for his parish of St. Brelade. "Captain Duval called to say that the general wish of the parish was to set me up as Constable, as Mr. Orange would resign in June. Agreed to accept, provided it did not cause a division in the parish". A few days later: "T.L.B.[1] hinted to me it would not be quite dignified in a Colonel being a Constable . . . . I told him I was not ashamed to occupy any post my grandfather had filled". In fact both his grandfathers had been Constables, Jean Le Couteur for St. John and Sir John Dumaresq for St. Peter. He called on the retiring Constable, Jean Orange of Franc Fief, who assured him that it was "son voeu et celui de toute la campagne que je le remplace". Nevertheless a Mr. Remon decided to contest the election, though Sir John was assured by his friends that "the country interest is mine". He was perturbed at the suggestion of bribery for votes and declared "there will certainly be none ʋn my part", but he was reminded that he could not be answerable for all his friends.

The next three months were overshadowed with anxiety about the outcome of the election, and occupied with canvassing for votes, his friends and relatives touring the parish to secure promises of support at the election. But there were snakes in the grass. "As I find John Pipon is doing everything he can against me, and I am told it is by threats and promises, I commence from today making and securing my own votes". By and by "Colonel Pipon came up to me and said he heard that 'I was making use of his name'. I told him I was; in this manner, that if he made votes against me by threats or promises I would report it to the General in order that it might be brought before the Court. We had high words, but I ended by repeating the same thing, from the Market Place to the Hospital,[2] where I told him I would not interfere with his men as he was going to drill". The forecasts were good, but only two days before the election there was still some doubt: "Herault and I went to try and recover Jean Cadoret. Great fun with him about his jackass." Electioneering continued up to the last moment: "A party of staunch supporters at Bocage in the evening. Duval, Herault and others went round by La Moie, I with Marett and others

---

1. Thomas Le Breton.   2. Half a mile or more.

round St. Aubins and Noirmont. Talked Ph. Le Ray's wife into preventing her husband voting against me".

In those days elections took place on Sundays, at the parish church, a practice soon to be discontinued. The detailed account we have of it is therefore worthy of preservation. "Sunday July 9th. The day of trial arrived. Prayed the Great Disposer of all events to grant me moderation if successful and fortitude if defeated. My father came by Bocage and made Capt. Le Feuvre vote en passant. My friends mustered in great force near the church and went in, after the bell had rung, peacably and quietly. Mr Filleul[1] preached an excellent sermon on brotherly love from the 133rd Psalm: 'Voici, O, que c'est une chose agréable que les frères s'entretiennent, qu'ils s'entretiennent, dis-je, ensemble'. It was full of feeling and point and he concluded by imploring the Divine assistance for the person on whom the choice might fall, for the establishment of God's word and the due administration of the laws. The table, a small round one, was placed in the corner of the vestibule. R[2] attempted to secure it for himself. Mr. O[3], however showed him out pretty unceremoniously, got and kept possession of it. I motioned and requested R. to come and stand by me. That would have been too friendly by half, so he declined. Colonel John P. stood at the foot of the stairs, trying to hold up a threatening look to the voters who should dare to vote for me. It would not do. His eye withered and his head sunk as my father came to give me his vote. He dared not meet his patron veteran's eye, nor could his friend. They were equally beholden to my father. My honest friends came up and cheerfully gave their votes. Some looked their Colonel eye to eye, with the expression 'We are free men': others, more nervous, passed on. When Ph. Ami came, his vote was questioned by the Judge (Benest) as being a poor man: he ought not to have been rated. I observed that although it was possible he ought not to have been rated, since his name was on the book, his poverty ought not to deprive him of his right, his privilege of voting as a Jerseyman and freeman.

"The whole went off perfectly quietly with a result of 79 votes for me and 37 for Mr. Remon . . . . My electors waited outside the door to hear me as I came out, but I slunk out by the back door as the triumph was sufficient. We all met at Mr. Benest's, where they all sat down with me to a cheerful dinner". In the evening there was a family celebration, with champagne insisted on by Harriet, to drink the health of Monsieur Le Connétable. A few days later he was sworn in, and attended and voted at his first session of the States, remarking that "The States are held in the Court House upstairs"; a reminder that at that date the States assembly still had no room of their own.

Sir John was rightly anxious for the abolition of Sunday elections. In 1830, having been re-elected Constable at the expiry of his first three year term of office, he wrote to Sir Robert Peel: "The transferring of an election from the Lord's day to a week day is of itself an act so proper and natural to any Christian mind, that one is at a loss to discover why it should be opposed. But it is so . . . . Strong and influential parties are hostile to the change . . . . . Our laws respecting elections and the rights of electors are quite undefined: indeed unfortunately so are most of our laws". After consulting the Bishop of Winchester and Lord Beresford[4] on this problem, he remarked to Sir Colin Halkett: "The latter appears

---

1. Rev Philippe Filleul. Rector 1818-1829.
2. Remon, the opposing candidate. 3. Orange, the retiring Constable, in office 1820-1826.
4. William Carr, Lord Beresford (1768-1854), Peninsula hero. Governor of Jersey 1821-1854.

to know more about the matter than the former . . . . His Lordship assured me that Lord Bathurst was in full possession of the case, but that under the present circumstances that is to say the King's illness, no cabinet council could be held". This measure was at first defeated, but later carried by 28 votes to 2, and the first week-day election in Jersey took place on 22nd March 1831.

Soon after taking office he was advised by Sir Thomas Le Breton, the Bailiff, "that as Constable I need not interfere in any private grievances. Public wrongs were all that a Constable had to notice. So that although a person has an undoubted right to a thing, a litigious neighbour may deprive him of that right if he has no means to carry on a lawsuit against him. Oh, fie!" At this period it appears that the post of Constable had fallen in public esteem, for he wrote: "the Constables, a class of men perfectly respectable as to character, but frequently not possessing weight or education enough to prevent their being led. The leading gentry of the Island will not act as Constables, unfortunately, considering the situation beneath them, though it is one of the highest importance, and very superior to persons holding that office in England". Some years later he was explaining the position to the Lieutenant Governor, General Reynett, in these terms: "The Constable in Jersey is not what a constable is in England. He is the representative or M.P. of his parish. He reports to the Court, whereas his Centeniers, who are police officers, report to him; a marked distinction noticed by Le Geyt, the law historian".[1]

Macadam's road surfaces appeared in Jersey at a surprisingly early date. In the year 1824 Sir John recorded: "Appointed to the Committee of roads, and introduced Macadam's system in the western parishes". At that time it was still a very new idea in England. As soon as he became Constable he set about getting island roads macadamised ("macadamisé" in the parish records). The first road surfaced in this way was near Le Pont Duval in St. Brelade's, and he noted: "the contrebanques near the Pont Duval to be built. The hillock in the road between Mr. Edward and Mr. Francis Marett's fields to be levelled . . . . The road leading to the church to be broken up and macadamised . . . . To look over McAdam's principles for hills". In 1830 the main street in St. Aubins' was macadamised, and at about this time, in a letter describing Jersey to Colonel Heriot, whom he called a (fellow) country- man, he remarked: "As every true Jerseyman has the true amor patriae at heart, you will be glad to learn that all our narrow lanes have made way for macadamised roads". The St. Peter's Valley road is said to have been so treated at this time. In a letter discussing corvée (compulsory road work) with Colonel Guille, his brother A.D.C. in Guernsey, he wrote: "I told my parishioners that if they would allow me to macadamise their small roads, in the course of six years . . . . there would not be occasion to call them out three days for repairs of roads, instead of the six days they were then subject to. The result is, as I antici- pated, there is scarcely occupation for two days of cartage, and as most of the parishes have adopted the system we are on the eve of modifying the law, in order to admit of commutations of money, in lieu of personal service and cartage, as efficient work is never obtained by such means". Soon after the introduction of the system, the cost of macadami- sation was said to be 12s. a perch on roads of 8 foot width.

As member of the States Sir John was chosen to serve on the Comité des Chaussées (Roads Committee), and in 1826 he "ordered a breakwater or quay to be built, 120ft. long

---

1. Philippe Le Geyt (1635-1716) wrote the "Constitution, Lois et Usages de l'Ile de Jersey", published 1847.

and 46ft. high, to cost £2500, to secure the fishing boats at Bouley Bay. There will be from 8 to 10ft. water at the pierhead in low spring tides, and 26ft. in the entrance. Rode on at 11 to Rozel, where another quay was proposed, 200ft. long and 26ft. above the rocks: to excavate all the inner space as a harbour, estimated between £2000 and £3000. Went on to La Rocque, where we ordered, or rather confirmed a previous act of the Committee to expend £500 in building a breakwater to secure the fishing boats". A little later he said: "Incessant rain, so went by water to a Comité des Chaussées at Bouley Bay .... The Committee adhered to their old (plan) of having a breakwater between La Gouttière and the land rocks .... Allowed me to have drains cut in the new quay, not to exceed £16". A further meeting there considered tenders, three firms competing. One competitor remarked that it would be patriotic to use only Jersey

BOULEY BAY PIER

stone, but Sir John knew that another intended to use Ecréhous stone and ruled out this stipulation. "The plan had been altered to one which I suggested ...., to join the breakwater to the bank and make a quay of it; because the sea would have acted like a sluice inside the breakwater and have literally washed out a vessel from it. After holding a levée of gentlemen, contractors, farmers, sailors and pilots for two hours, the accuracy of the plan was doubted; so I went home with Le Gros and the surveyor and measured it afresh, which satisfied all parties". The contract was awarded to the lowest bidder, Mr. Abraham de la Mare, who next year had brought the works "to a five feet level. The old man is very active and good tempered. He allows no one to be idle a moment. He has 42 men at work. His foreman, Josué Coutanche of my regiment, has four pounds ten sols (livres tournois) a day. The whole of the rock ought to be made into a pier to make it complete". The Bouley Bay pier is still there, a fine example of local masonry. On one corner beside a flight of steps the following letters are incised in a block of granite: "A.P.F.DLM: E.D.E.T. 1828". One wonders what the inscription can mean. The first line must refer to the builders. In 1803 a François and Abraham de la Mare contracted for work on St. Helier's harbour, and there is record of a Philip, born 1823[1], son of François (1794-1865), son of Abraham (born 1766). The "old man" is presumably Abraham, and the A may stand for him. If so the P between him and F (for François) is a puzzle. It could represent a Philip, brother of François, not otherwise known, or stand for "père", in which case A.P.F.DLM would mean "Abraham father of François de la Mare". A speculative suggestion is that the inscription was composed by a Latin scholar and stands for: "Artifices pontis, familia De La Mare: eximia diligentia, exiguum tempus" (the builders of the jetty were the De La Mare

1. He emigrated to America in 1852, and his descendants are still there.

family, with exemplary diligence and in record time). This would accord with the picture we have of Father Abraham as a man who could get the best out of his gangs, and deliver the goods on schedule.

Banon is a word deeply embedded in Jersey tradition, and means the right to turn animals loose to graze land from which the harvest has been taken, between September and March. Sir John was determined to see this right maintained in his parish, and on one occasion "went to La Moie early to settle a dispute about the banon which is not yet proclaimed". Apparently the sheep of Mrs. Seale and Mrs. Bisson had invaded Mrs. Gruchy's corn, "which ought to have been got in, so they say, a fortnight before. However they admitted the corn to have been eaten and trodden down, and I recommended them to pay 20 sols for each sheep to settle the matter, which they agreed to do". He considered banon to be "of very ancient date and therefore should be respected. It would be a serious grievance to the poor to (stop) it suddenly, though no doubt it is a source of litigation as it now exists".

As Constable he had a good deal to do with vraic or varech (seaweed) which has been used in the Island from time immemorial as a fertiliser. His opinion of its value is given in his book on wheat, to be discussed later on. "It attracts", he said, "moisture from the atmosphere; it materially increases the volume of grain and fineness of the sample; it does not add to the weight of the straw, though rendering it whiter and more nourishing to cattle. It causes the wheat to assume a rich healthy appearance and is an excellent application after a crop of potatoes or parsnips, both of which require land to be richly dressed with stable or other strong manures, and has not the effect of decomposing them as lime has. It is also destructive to insects and their eggs, which lie in the soil or turf. It forces the earth worms and wire worms from their lurking places to come to the surface and die, particularly when laid on in a larger quantity than I have named; some farmers being in the habit of putting on double or even treble the quantity . . . . Vraic thrown up by the tide may be collected and spread on the fields, but the best quality is that weed which is cut live from the rocks at low tide".

The dates when vraic might be collected were strictly controlled by the Constable, and he had often to give a ruling as to who was entitled to collect it. On 21st March 1826 he recorded: "Vraicing commenced today"; and a few days later: "went to see the vraicers at St. Ouen's Bay . . . . (They) think the law of 1771, which allotted vraic in proportion to property, was better than the present one; and that those persons who have purchased estate with the anticipation of so many shares, are thereby cheated; moreover that the poor were not anxious that the division by lots should take place. . . . . Spoke to Amice Cadoret, a poor man, who told me that he and all those who were poor like himself thought that the 'vraic venu' was the gift of providence, and that he and all the poor were equally entitled to it with the rich . . . . Cadoret told me there would be plenty of time in a tide for a poor man to save his lot. I fear otherwise". In the following January he described a division of vraic. "Went to La Pulente to see the partage of vraic. There is a large stone in a small pool which has been known from time immemorial. When the tide has ebbed sufficiently to show the summit of it, the Officier des Vraics called those persons together to claim shares. They then divide themselves into two companies of nearly equal landed property. The vraic which has been left by the tide in a curved line on the shore is then marked by a line into two lots. Then the two companies of sharers toss up for the north or south share. Each company then subdivides again, and so on, until each man has his own lot, which he then carts away. It was my duty to see this performed once and to learn if there were any complaints, but my duty proved an amusement. I considered about a slip leading from the bay, which would be highly advantageous to the vraickers, but how to get the means just now, except by the sale of vraic?"

When the vraicing season came, even militia drills were curtailed, so important was it recognised to be. The scenes on the beach must have been most impressive. "I reckoned upwards of 250 carts and 17 boats. Averaging each four loads, would make about eleven hundred loads cut and brought up, besides what was sold as vraic venu. Some of the single horse carts had cut six loads; . . . . averaging the loads at 5s. each there will have been £275 worth of vraic brought in today". A few days later: "At vraic. Sold the vraic venu or écapillon by lots to the amount of a hundred livres". In 1829 he proposed a new vraicing law and wrote to Sir Robert Peel urging that the new law, drafted by himself and passed by the States, should be placed before His Majesty in Council before the coming vraicing season, "in order to put an end to the spoliation and violence which takes place every day"; and he assessed that the vraic of St. Ouen's Bay alone could be assessed at £5000 annually. His law was passed, and entitled every parishioner to have his share of vraic according to his property.

At his first parish meeting as Constable, when he "assured his parishioners that the new Constable will not remember who voted against Col. Le Couteur in the election", the question of a market for St. Aubin's was posed. The existing building had proved too small for modern requirements and a new one was erected from the proceeds of lotteries. Several people applied for stalls at once. Sir John supervised this market carefully, examining produce, and weights and measures, and confiscating bad meat when he found it.

The administration of the little port of St. Aubin came under his care as well. In 1830 the Harbour Master complained that masters of vessels were refusing to pay the pilotage dues, on the grounds that pilots were often not available when required. He wrote: "As this complaint, if correctly grounded, may be highly prejudicial to the mercantile interests of the island, I beg leave to recommend that the subject may be immediately laid before the Committee of Harbours; in order to . . . . enforce the regular and certain attendance of the pilots; as well as to establish some fixed point where Captains may send to the pilots on duty, in order to ensure their sailing when it suits them. I have to add that the pilotage revenue has lost a certain sum by this non-attendance of pilots". There was also the case of the recalcitrant Remon, his opponent in the election for Constable, who "refused to haul his vessel from the quay in order to allow a large brig of Perrée's, the Doris, to come into the shoalest[1] part to have a false keel put on". The dispute was patched up, after some hard words on all sides.

During his term of office dozens of other cases of every description came up before him for decision. He tempered justice with mercy, and some examples of his clemency and common sense may be interesting. One day he was called on board the Calliope to punish a sailor who had stolen apples, and had offered to give himself up, but "as the honest Jack seemed to consider it all as a frolic and was penitent, I let him off with a lecture". Then a man named George Taylor had insulted his master, and already been in gaol for two days, and as he also showed remorse "I interceded for him, so he was released". Then "Mr. Le

1. Shallowest.

Cras came to tell me our neighbour Mrs. Arthur declared he had bewitched her; so I went to see her, and found the poor woman out of her mind". Speaking in the States about hospital affairs, he "proposed that the dens in which the unfortunate maniacs are confined should be warmed . . . ., which was carried". When suddenly called to avert a murder, he arrived at the place and "had a curious scene with a drunken sailor, who did not care a damn for all the constables in the world. Jack swore he'd 'take another opportunity to mend my jacket for me'. At length, finding he bore a good character when sober, sent him back to his ship rather than to jail". He constantly settled small disputes by advice, or by small fines, giving the proceeds to the poor box, and took practical action where it was needed, resolving family squabbles with sensible compromise, securing work for orphans or pensions for widows and performing acts of humanity to alleviate distress. "Sent a hearty meal to the Baudains family", he once wrote.

Much of his time was devoted to road work, which involved riding out to visit road gangs at Pont Duval, La Pulente, Pont Marquet and Mont ès Croix, and recording minutiae of the work: and time could be wasted by visits from incompetent officials, for example: "a Vue de Vicomte at the entrance to St. Brelade's Bay to see if the communes of La Moie and Noirmont join together. Blockheads. They are miles apart, and besides there was a flaw in the act of the Court, for the question was about campagnes, not communes".

In April 1828 the building of Jersey's first lifeboat comes to our notice. In a letter to the Admiralty Sir John wrote: "In consequence of the lamentable shipwreck of the cutter Fanny in January last, by which Lord Harley and a number of other passengers met with an untimely end . . . . within a few hundred yards of St. Helier's harbour, I . . . . moved in the States that two or more lifeboats should forthwith be purchased". Plans went forward and Captain (later Admiral) White, R.N. was consulted, "being the person who knows more than any other the coast and tides of the Island". Soon afterwards he wrote to Captain Symonds, R.N.[1], at Trinity Manor, asking to meet him and discuss details, as "you had kindly consented to give us the use of your valuable talents to superintend its construction . . . . I shall also have much to say to you about its crew, station, regulations, and objections which have already been stated as to its efficiency". Regulations were drawn up but only partly adopted by the States. By May 1830 the boat was all but ready, though Captain Symonds was suffering from the effects of a fall, and on 17th May the launching took place. "Went off to Trinity to see the lifeboat launched at Rozel, and others were there. She is a noble boat, and four and twenty of us on her side could not bring her gunwale under water. Symonds had taken out the plugs, when she was about 25 minutes in filling, but did not sink, even with us all in her beyond her air pipes. After we were all out, she emptied herself out to her flooring in about an hour, by her specific gravity being so much lighter than water. I hope she may soon save one life, when she will even then have repaid her expense". Her actual builder was a Mr. Lillington of Weymouth. A second boat was proposed to be stationed at Havre des Pas, and the officer commanding the Royal Engineers was asked if the Board of Ordnance would cede a small piece of land bordering the sea, only 40 by 20ft., for the purpose of building a boathouse.

The theatre was always a keen interest to Sir John and his family, and whenever they visited England or the continent they went to as many theatres and concerts as they could. In 1826 he wrote: "Early to town to make arrangements for the first oratorio ever given in

1. Sir William Symonds C.B. R.N. married Elizabeth de Carteret, heiress of Trinity.

21. The DE LA MARE STONE
on Bouley Bay Pier,
1828.

22. ST. AUBIN'S MARKET in 1959. Built in 1826.

23. ST. PETER'S PARISH CANNON, JERSEY
cast by John Owen, 1551

The inscription on it reads:

"IHON OWYN MADE THYS PESE ANNO DNI 1551
FOR THE PARYSHE OF SAYNT PETER IN IERSSE."

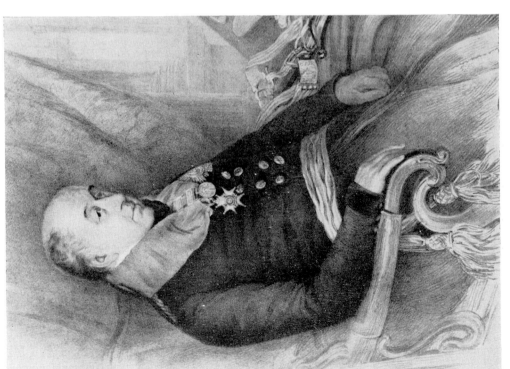

TWO OF JERSEY'S LIEUTENANT GOVERNORS

(See Chapter 10)

24.   Sir EDWARD GIBBS, K.C.B. (1838-1847)

25.   Major General Sir FREDERICK LOVE, C.B.
(1852-1857)

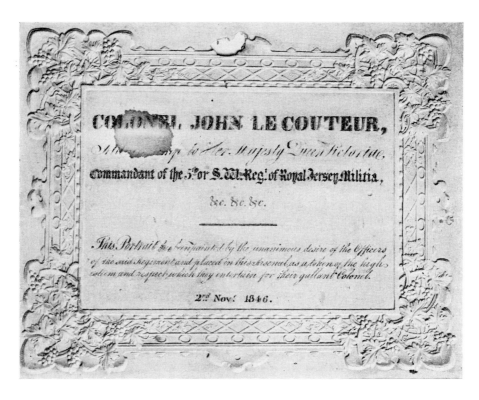

COLONEL JOHN LE COUTEUR,

Commandant of the 5.th or S.W. Reg.t of Royal Jersey Militia,

&c. &c. &c.

2.nd Nov.r 1846.

26. Embossed card presented with the STONEHOUSE Portrait, 1846
(see page 126)

27. ST. MARY'S ARSENAL, Built c.1830
(see page 131)

I   Lieutenant JOHN HALKETT LE COUTEUR
with the Colour of the 87th Regiment (Royal Irish Fusiliers)
(*from a pastel by Thomas Berteau,* 1846)

II   ROYAL CRESCENT and THEATRE ROYAL, JERSEY, built 1827-28
(from a water-colour by George Sidney Shepherd, 1833)

the church. It went off extremely well, being very well attended and carried on with much decorum. £35. 9s. 6d. were received at the doors. The Dean returned us many thanks for our exertions". That year it was decided to build a theatre in a commanding position in the splendid sweep of the Royal Crescent. There were constant meetings of the Theatre Committee, who were acting for a group of subscribers, and signed the contract and building plan with a Mr. Way. But its meetings were not always harmonious, Sir John complained of jealousies and intrigues, adding "my countrymen are unfit for committees where their interests are concerned". One meeting, however, was highly satisfactory, being attended only by Benest, Simonet and himself: there was a quick dispatch of business, "a plain proof that committees should only consist of three members". While in Paris he went to see Ciceri, a scenic painter who had decorated all the royal theatres there, with a view to employing him, but found his prices higher than the Jersey theatre could afford. He was asked by Hocquard the surveyor to examine "the linen roof", whatever that was, and neither of them thought it would answer. By September 1827 bookings were being received, and "Mlle. Léon of the Odeon, now Madame Balbyno Cortes, 61 St. James' Street, Piccadilly offered to take our theatre. Two sky lights ordered". In 1858 the subscribers were trying to sell the theatre, which had not been a financial success, and it was finally burnt down in 1863, being replaced by a large Methodist chapel.

In 1832, at the end of his second term of office as Constable, Sir John gave up the post, and wrote to a relative that he had done so "in good time to escape from a stormy sea of politics which now disgraces us; and am now turned farmer, which I am very fond of and gives me plenty to do. I find it much more agreeable to deal in corn, potatoes and turnips than laws, politics and police". Indeed the next ten years were the most productive in his life, including as they did his agricultural experiments, and it is most unfortunate that we have no diaries for them. He did not, however, remain out of public life as long as he had intended, for in 1835 he was persuaded to stand as a Jurat of the Royal Court. In this capacity he wrote many pages on legal and constitutional problems, but this interesting material cannot be treated in depth in such a brief survey, for Sir John was nothing if not thorough when he put pen to paper. He held this, the post of highest dignity in the eyes of Jerseymen, for only three years, resigning from ill health, and in 1837 wrote about it to Mrs. Elizabeth Fry: "I avoided society much when you were last in Jersey, which was a very different practice with me when you last visited us. The fact was that I had such frequent headaches from attending the, to me, anxious and laborious duties in court, that I avoided society as it fatigued and distressed me to exert myself. Still I thought that temperate habits and diet would get the better of them. About four months back they became constant, and after consulting Sir B. Brodie, Dr. Tupper and my own physician here Dr. Hooper, finding from their treatments that no other remedy was left but to give up my duties at court, I have forwarded my resignation as a Jurat to H.M. in Council".

A problem which had come to the fore during his term of office was the quorum necessary to permit a meeting of the States or the Court. In those days of horse transport and no telephones, it was difficult for a country member to report that he was unable to attend. But his absence might mean there was not a quorum, in which case others who had come to town from equally distant parts would have wasted their time. Sir John pointed this out in 1839 to the Home Office: "very frequent delay has taken place in public business here from the . . . . constantly recurring absence of members of the States . . . ., which had

H

indeed so much obstructed it as to call forth the animadversion of Lord John Russell. It requires 21 out of 36 members to form a quorum, seven from each body, which is the chief cause of the mischief. Some now propose to make the quorum 24 of any members who may be present . . . ., which would not strike at the root of the evil . . . . It is now suggested . . . . that there should be thirteen new 'members of parliament', two for the town parish and one for each country parish, selected from persons of independent fortune, to act merely as legislators without having any other duty to perform . . . . This would form a sort of preparation for the office of the Jurat, and men selected from these would be infinitely better qualified to hold that responsible office than those taken from among gentlemen who are quite unacquainted with legislation". Sir John was in fact recommending the creation of the office of Deputy, but it was not for another eighteen years that this forward-looking suggestion bore fruit.

At about this time he found and recognised, at the Ordnance Department the cannon which now stands at the foot of Beaumont Hill, and was instrumental in bringing it back to the Island. It bears the date 1551 and the name John Owen, who made it for the Parish of St. Peter. It is thought that Owen worked for Hugget, who had a furnace near Mayfield, and that he is the John mentioned in the old couplet:

"Master Hugget and his man John
    they did cast the first cannon".[1]

Who were the Bailiffs who guided the Island's affairs during Sir John's lifetime, what were his relations with them and his opinion of them? Henry Frederick, Lord Carteret, was the last of the de Carteret line to hold the post of Bailiff, which had become in effect, though not legally, hereditary in that family. For the whole of the eighteenth and the early part of the nineteenth centuries the Bailiffs had been non-resident, some never coming to the Island at all; with the result that Lieutenant-Bailiffs, such as Sir John Dumaresq, had done the work without enjoying the title. At Lord Carteret's death his Lieutenant-Bailiff, Sir Thomas Le Breton, was chosen to follow him, an unexpected and not entirely popular choice; and when a dinner was being arranged to mark his appointment, Sir John wrote: "At a committee for Sir Thomas Le Breton's dinner. Stuff and nonsense". The dinner was, however, a splendid affair and on the Tuesday (7th September 1826) the stewards were "busy decorating Deal's saloon for the grand entertainment". On the Wednesday, "went in early through heavy rain to a Committee of stewards: found everything going on well but no venison come, in consequence of the gale". On Thursday, "Sir Thomas Le Breton was sworn in as Bailiff. Messrs. de St. Ouen, de Ste Croix, d'Auvergne, commonly called the radical judges, did not chuse to attend, tho all the others did. Sir Thomas was a good deal moved in delivering his speech, expressive of his good intentions. We all went to take wine with him at The British Hotel, and at length came the dinner, which was laid for 227 persons. There were a few over the number. The dinner and wines were good, the company cheerful but not over select. I took occasion to observe, on rising to propose a toast, that I thought the toast I was about to propose would be drunk with satisfaction, for it was generally admitted that it was well to have a friend in the Government; and the Right Honourable gentleman whose health I was about to propose had given us a pretty substantial proof of it, by recommending the appointment of Bailiff to be conferred on the learned and talented gentleman we had the honour to entertain this day. I hailed it as an auspicious

1. "Decorative Cast Iron Work in Great Britain", by G. Raymond Lister.

day, for it held out the first civil dignity the Crown could bestow to the young men now at the bar, and those who might succeed them . . . . so I proposed the health of that minister most directly concerned in the business of the Island, the Right Honourable Robert Peel . . . . My father's health was drunk with acclamation as the friend of his country. We broke up in good humour at 12 after lots of speeches and songs . . . . Slept in town. Put Fred to bed". The sole entry for the morrow is :"Poorly".

Sir Thomas' tenure of office was neither long nor illustrious and he resigned in 1831. His successor, John de Veulle, was a young man in his thirties, who had been an Advocate and Jurat, but was very delicate. There was anxiety about him in 1847, when we read: "Sir Thomas told me he knew that de Veulle had had a fit; if so he certainly could not continue Bailiff". In fact, the poor man died the next year. Years later Sir John referred to a son of his, next to whom he sat at a St. Peter's farmers' club dinner, as "the youth whose arm I persuaded him to have set when broken . . . . He was five months in the Crimea". In 1851 Lady de Veulle, who was a neice of Lord Justice Tindall, died, and Sir John attended the funeral, of which he said: "Advocate Godfray, who abused poor Sir John beyond all endurance, and got him into a lawsuit which cost him seven thousand pounds, was one of the pallbearers! That was carrying forgiveness a long way beyond the grave. Who could have invited him? . . . . the young men scarcely shed a tear. Mr. Tindal her brother seemed rather affected."

The next Bailiff was another Sir Thomas Le Breton, son of the previous Sir Thomas. We learn that he kept a good table, and Sir John records of one of his dinners: "Met Mons. de Salvandy[1] and his son Paul at Sir T. Le Breton this day: a very handsome dinner provided by, or dressed by a late cook of the Duke of Wellington. Sir T. has adopted the French mode, which Sir James has done, of handing the wine round all dinner time, a great piece of economy". In July 1849 Sir Thomas was given a dinner by the Jurats, the Crown officers being invited as well as the Bailiff's brother Frank, who was a close friend of Sir John's. Jurat Nicolle offered to provide "all the wine but the hock and the champaign, which I said was very handsome and liberal on his part. Harriet helped Bisson and I to order the dinner from Mrs. de Rue, while the soup we ordered from Clarke". A dozen each of champagne and hock were ordered from Hemerys, and on the day: "Bisson and Nicolle thought H should have been asked rather than S and G: Le G was a crafty person, The dinner went off very well. Sir T on coming in shook hands with no one but Bisson and me, bowed grandly to all, in very good spirits . . . . We had an excellent dinner, a regular Pontac supply. There were 11 Jurats, three Crown officers and two dénonciateurs, 18 in all. Sir T said that he felt too much gratified to be able to utter all he thought. It was a mark of confidence he little anticipated . . . . Union was strength: with their support he would maintain (our institutions) to his utmost . . . . Judge E. Nicolle said that the B's impartiality had been his admiration". But Sir Thomas' popularity seems to have waned rather swiftly, mainly through his weakness. Some entries in the diaries show this. In 1851: "It is rumoured that Sir Thomas Le Breton is about to resign, and that Frank Godfray has gone back to England to endeavour to succeed to the Bailiwick". Later: "Judge de Quetteville tells me Sir Thomas Le Breton takes few or no notes. The Jurats would be guided by him if he expounded the law to them. He has never read much, and was ever very indolent. Dupré is the finest man in Jersey". Again: "Captain Taylor came to see me. He opposed the painting of Sir Thomas

1. *See* Chapter 10.

Le Breton's portrait at the meeting of the club last Saturday on the ground that there was no quorum . . . . The matter was dropped for the moment by his firmness". Then: "Three Orders in Council arrived three weeks since, for a Police Superintendent and men on the London plan, a sitting Magistrate for the recovery of small debts, and a Court of Requests. Sir Thomas is gone with his secretary, sans lequel il ne peut agir, to try to get the stringency of some of the provisions slackened. As the Police is to be paid by means of a house tax, there will be a rare uproar when it is known. Sir James[1] showed me a draft of an Order in Council to abolish the Royal Court and to name three Judges, which he opposed, or the recommendations of the Royal Commissioners would have been enforced . . . . He deserves more thanks from the Bailli and Jurats than he will receive. I told him that with an able, energetic Chief Magistrate our Court could act perfectly well. He observed: 'I do not think that Sir TLB is quite what you describe. I find him changed from what he was, but I found him an able man formerly; he has changed much of late'".

In 1852 the diary said: "The Orders in Council for a Police Court for the recovery of small debts, and other reforms, have created a mighty stir. The Bailli has gone to London to endeavour to suspend them, because he will lose £300 a year by them". Then: "Dupré told me . . . . that the Court under Sir Thomas . . . . was far worse and less business done than under Sir John de Veulle. The lawyers abused . . . . each other while Sir Thomas seemed to enjoy the fun. He never interfered with them; all he did was to escape from business . . . . The court was an amusement for loungers but was a disgrace to the bar". Then: "Sir Thomas Le Breton saw Sir William Joliffe, the Secretary of State, in London . . . . (who told him) a considerable body of the people (wished for) reform". His comment was: "Men of straw merely, Sir", but when confronted with the names of signatories to the petition he was nonplussed and had to admit that one of them was the Seigneur of Rozel, another James Robin, "a respectable, large merchant". Joliffe then asked if he knew a certain Thomas Le Breton, to which he replied that he was a paperhanger. "Oh, I see it is William, not Thomas Le Breton", said Joliffe, and Sir Thomas had to admit this was his uncle. "Well, Sir Thomas, these are not men of straw", said Joliffe.

One day the diary complained: "Sir Thomas sat in Court, but soon after got up and gave the Lieutenant Bailiff charge, and went off for a promenade with his two nephews . . . . He might as well not have appeared . . . . Godfray the Advocate dictates to the Bailiff, who seems quite afraid of him. He says: 'Vous ne comprenez pas le billet', and talks to him sitting". In 1855 Sir Thomas was said to be "trying to resign in favour of Hemery Le Breton". He was certainly losing grip, and in 1857 he had an attack of paralysis, became very ill and was unable to attend a meeting to raise funds for sufferers in India. A few months later he was lingering and said to be dying.

On his death in 1857 the able, brilliant Dupré was surprisingly passed over and John Hammond was appointed, being sworn in on 27th February 1858. "An immense crowd, and many ladies in Court. I conducted Mr. Hammond from his room into Court, where his patent was presented . . . . Dupré was a little choky at starting, but read the lengthy document, which closed his own preferment for ever, very well . . . . The Bailiff . . . . made a short and very appropriate speech, making no professions but relying on the Jurats for support . . . . He invited us all to Le Veslet's according to an ancient and appropriate custom, to drink his health . . . . I believe that his appointment is well received generally throughout

1. The Lieutenant-Governor, Major General Sir James Reynett.

the Island. The Godfrays and their Court party are vastly annoyed". Unfortunately "that ruffian Godfray" managed to intimidate this Bailiff also, and "'Oh, Oh', is all he ever says to him". The indignation of the Lieutenant Governor, General Douglas, was stated to be "unqualified at the supineness of the Bailiff and Attorney General in the . . . . case".

Bailiff Hammond was a kind-hearted man: "The Bailiff called. He had had his leg tied up after an operation when he was 19, ... and so could sympathise with me". He lived at La Fantaisie, where one day his wife showed Sir John "the improvements in the out-houses and kitchens", and then the Bailiff came "and showed me the finest crop of chaumontels I ever saw on standards". He outlived Sir John by several years. In later life they became firm friends, and used to enjoy going over each other's gardens and remarking on the fruit which grew in them. He was the most congenial of the Bailiffs under whom Sir John served, and was one of the most kindly, just and honourable of men.

In reading Sir John's assessment of his contemporaries, it may be as well to bear in mind General Dwight Eisenhower's warning. He disapproved of diaries, reasoning that diarists record day-to-day annoyances which assume false importance under the hand of a biographer. So it may have been with some of our Bailiffs. Requiescant in pace.

CHAPTER EIGHT

A.D.C. TO THE KING

Those who fear that Friday the thirteenth is an unlucky day may be reassured by the following entry in the Le Couteur diaries: "1830, Friday, August 13th. This morning to my great surprise and joy I received the kindest note in the world from my old friend Colonel FitzClarence, congratulating me on my appointment as Militia A.D.C. to the King for Jersey[1]. I called dear Ha, and my sweet little girls to express to them how great an honour had been conferred on their Papa by his gracious Sovereign, for services rendered to his son when I was but a few years older than my Harriet; services which, however trifling, were then performed with faithfulness and integrity; which nevertheless won the affection of my charge, Henry FitzClarence. Ran to my father and mother, who shed tears of delight". Thus was the news received of the first appointment of its kind in Jersey.

The next day Sir John left for England, his wife observing that it was the first time she had ever seen him quit the Island with satisfaction. He was not sped, however, returning home for another night as the gale was so strong that the passengers refused to sail. Next day he was off. On the way up to London from Southampton his coach pulled up to examine a steam-coach, "which had stopped for a supply of water. It was on three wheels, the driver sitting in front on a coach box, directing it by a curved bar in a similar way to a garden chair. The water is below the body of the carriage, and the fire and copper behind. The fire is fanned by a revolving fanwheel. The weight is too much on the fan wheel, so that the conductor cannot turn rapidly, if at all, on a soft road. The Engineer . . . . said he ascended hills at the rate of 16 miles per hour. He could go down hill as slow as he pleased . . . . . I shall be curious to know the result of this first experiment. It will be very difficult for it to turn in and out of Winchester, which is shamefully narrow". Arrived at the Horse Guards next day he was received by Colonel FitzClarence, who was delighted to see an old friend. Sir John had in fact applied for the appointment, through Sir Colin Halkett the Lieutenant Governor, and he asked FitzClarence if his application had been in order, and was reassured. "My good fellow", his friend replied, "the King was quite happy about it . . . . He was very glad you had applied". Upon enquiry about the appropriate uniform, he was told: "Exactly like the King's, only in silver, as His Majesty has made a very proper distinction between the Line and the Militia, as the former are to have gold lace, and all the Militias, Yeomanry and Volunteers, silver lace".

This lace on uniform was quite a controversial matter. "Holbeck, Fox and Webb went to Windsor with a petition from the lacemen . . . ., and were received by Sir H. Taylor . . . . They complained that if the whole lace of the army was uniform, gold for the Line and silver for the Militia, all the lace would be made in Paris, (where) labour is four times

---

1. The Jersey A.D.Cs to the Sovereign have been: Col. John Le Couteur (1830): Col. Clement Hemery of Plaisance (1873): Sir James Godfray of Grainville (1880): Col. C. P. Le Cornu of La Hague (1898): Brigadier General James Godfray (1911): Col. Voisin (1921): followed by Col. Albert Le Gallais of La Moie, and Col. Henry Vatcher.

Steam Coach near Winchester, 16. August. 1830.

cheaper, and owing to the genial climate silver thread can be spun one-fifteenth longer and finer than in England, where it snaps from the coldness if drawn out too fine . . . . In short, the London trade would be utterly ruined . . . . The King sent off an express in consequence to the Horse Guards to suspend all further alterations in the dress for the army". Nearly thirty years later the right to wear gold lace was still a live issue, and the Under Secretary of State was told that "the Royal Militia Artillery of Jersey is a very ancient corps, always composed of the best yeomanry in the Island. So far back as 1560 the gunners were sufficiently considered as to be sworn in as such . . . . That force has ever worn gold lace. The officers at their own charge. without pay or horse allowance, supply their horses and wear gold embroidered uniforms . . . . These were confirmed by his late Majesty William IV". A final letter, to Colonel Hemery of the Artillery, confirmed that "the Artillery will continue to wear gold lace", with a white piping instead of red, to distinguish them from the Royal Artillery.

At first Sir John was to have been named A.D.C. for the Channel Islands, but Guernsey's Lieutenant Governor, General Ross, applied for Colonel Guille, "a very nice fellow", to represent that Island, which our Jerseyman thought preferable, "to prevent jealousy on the part of the Guernsey people".

On Sir John's first night in London there were illuminations for the King's birthday, which were "very gay, but the most brilliant by far were those of gas, which is as splendid as a diamond . . . . There were hundreds of thousands of people on foot, in carriages, on horse back, pouring along the streets in streams". In France the July revolution had just taken place, Charles X and the Duc d'Angoulême were in retreat in England, and the latter is recorded as saying: "Le peuple Français l'avait fait sans reflexion, mais ce n'était fini pour lui et sons fils": on which Sir John commented: "Poor King, he is not yet arrived at the hope deferred which makes the heart sick[1]".

After a deal of red tape in Whitehall, about exactly when and by whom he was gazetted as A.D.C., he proceeded to Brighton at the suggestion of FitzClarence, got there on 11th September 1830, and "lounged about the town, admiring the new squares, Bedford and Brunswick". When he returned to his hotel he found a summons to dine with the King that evening. "At a quarter before seven I went to the Pavilion by the north entrance gate

1. Proverbs, 13.12.

and was shown in . . . . Found Colonel FitzClarence . . . ., I asked him what forms were to be gone through and he said: 'You will have to kiss hands'. 'And what ceremonial is to be observed towards the Queen?' 'I believe a couple of bows will do' ''. The distinguished party began to assemble, and after some court officials had arrived, "the Princess Elizabeth of Hesse Homburg, and the Princess Augusta[1] came in. They are both very stout, but with most amiable countenances, and the Princess of Hesse must have been very pretty. They were dressed in black satin with caps on their heads. All the ladies are still in black. Soon after the King came in and asked Col. FitzClarence for me, who said: 'Here is Col. Le Couteur, Sir'. I bowed and stepped forward to His Majesty, who graciously extended his hand . . . ., which I knelt and kissed". Sir John then expressed gratitude for the honour conferred upon him, saying it was an honour not only for him but for the Island, and "another link in the chain of affection which the inhabitants of Jersey have entertained for Your Majesty's family for centuries past". The King then said, "in a firm and dignified tone of voice which the whole Court, which was as still as death, listened to: 'Colonel Le Couteur, you have been recommended to me in the strongest manner through the Governor of Jersey, and by my Secretary of State for the home department, Sir Robert Peel, as an active, intelligent and deserving officer, and I could not refuse such a recommendation. I did not know you from the Man in the Moon when you were recommended to me, but I hear you are a *very good officer* (with peculiar emphasis) and I am exceedingly happy at having an occasion of thus publickly expressing it. I am very happy to have you about my person. I have received a communication from a certain quarter, but I never listen to such communications. Your recommendation came through the regular official channels, and that was quite sufficient for me. I am very happy to see you. I congratulate you' . . . . The King then made me step forward two or three steps and presented me to the Queen: 'My aide-de-Camp for Jersey, Your Majesty'. I bowed very low and withdrew. The King then turned round to a gentleman I was sure I had seen somewhere but could not recollect. 'How d'ye do, Captain. But I must knight you, I believe. Lygon, give me your sword. Don't be afraid, Captain Erskine. I am not going to chop off your head'. His Majesty then gently laid the sword on each of Captain Erskine's shoulders, who was on one knee. 'Rise, Sir David Erskine', who kissed hands and bowed.

"The King then made his bow to all the company and came back to me:
'Colonel Le Couteur, when did you arrive?'
   'Last night, please Your Majesty'.
'What brought you to England? Have you been here long?'
   'I came over, Sir, a month ago, Sir, on hearing of my appointment, in order to offer my dutiful and grateful acknowledgements to Your Majesty, at the very first occasion that might suit Your Majesty'.
'Did you come on purpose?'
   'Yes, Sir, for no other purpose'. I think the King appeared pleased at it.
'What is the strength of your Militia force?'
   'The aggregate strength is about 5000 men, but it being peace time there are many non-effectives'.
'What regular troops have you there now?'

---

1. Daughters of George III.

'Only the depots of two regiments, Sir; a company of Artillery who look after the fortifications, batteries and guns; and a few engineers'.

'What force would you consider sufficient to defend the Island?'

'Ten thousand men at the least, Sir, and if Your Majesty will permit me I will say why an increase of force would be necessary. During the last war, Sir, our rocks and tides were our greatest security, as no fleet could be assembled upon any given point without giving us timely notice. Indeed it was next to impossible to rendez-vous a squadron in Jersey unless everything, wind and weather, favoured it. But now, Sir, all those natural advantages have been rendered unavailable by the invention of steam vessels. A fleet could be collected on any given point in three, four or five hours. Thus a much larger force would be required in the event of another war for the defence of the Island than was necessary last war'.

'Your observations are very just. Have you Martello towers in the bays?'

'Yes, Sir; four, three, two and one in the accessible bays in proportion to their extent'.

"Dinner was then announced. The King bowed graciously and left me, to hand in the Princesses, one under each arm, but waited until the Earl of Errol , who handed the Queen in, had passed . . . . Seeing Miss FitzClarence had no beau, I offered her my arm, which she accepted. I found myself seated between Miss FitzClarence . . . . and Miss Wilson the Queen's bedchamber woman. As soon as the soup was over, the King said, to my great surprise: 'Colonel Le Couteur, will you take a glass of wine with me?' " He then collected around him all men present who had been at Marlowe. "When dinner was over, the King said: 'I must give a toast. The land we live in. Colonel Le Couteur, tell our friends in Jersey that we do not forget them, but include them in this toast. I drink to the health of our friends in Jersey' ". The A.D.C. then asked the Chief A.D.C., Sir Herbert Taylor, what his duties were, and was told that there were none unless the King should visit Jersey; but that he might attend Court from time to time if he wished. He said he would do so once a year.

Later in the evening the King resumed his questionnaire and "asked me seventy-three questions, which I have already written down, besides many others that I shall be able to recollect as I write my answers opposite to the queries . . . . I must either have been a walking army list or a travelling map to answer them:

'Come here, Le Couteur. Sit down by me. I want to have some conversation with you about Jersey . . . . How many regiments have you?'

'Six of infantry and one of artillery, Sir'.

'How strong are they?'

'The Town Regiment about 700 men. The others from 350 to 200 men according to the population of their districts, Sir. The Artillery is a very fine corps, Sir, with twenty-four guns, formed into car brigades which manoeuvre at a gallop as the Line Artillery do, Sir. Their practice also is admirable. They were formed by Sir Colin Halkett, Sir'.

'How often is the militia called out?'

'In consequence of the system of boys' drill . . . . , it is not necessary to call them out more than ten or twelve times a year. Before that system of drill they were called out twenty or thirty times in a year, and were not half so efficient'.

'What are you paid when out?'

'Nothing, Sir'.

'What, not at all paid?'

'Not a farthing, please Your Majesty', and I smiled with triumph.

'But are not the officers paid?'

'Never, Sir'.

'Nor the Non-commissioned officers?'

'Not one of them, Sir. The Adjutants and drill sergeants are the only persons paid, which is for drilling the boys . . . ., and they are only paid 3s. 6d. a day'.

'But you are in war time?'

'Never, Sir'.

'What, and do the men mount guards, then?'

'Yes, Sir, all round the Island in their respective districts'.

'Well, that is surprising. And how many nights abed do you think they had?'

'I cannot precisely . . . . answer that question, Your Majesty . . . ., but I . . . . have heard that the men were on guard every week'.

'Now, in St. Helier's Bay, how far do you think the sentries might have been apart?'

'Why, Sir, the accessible extent of the bay I take to be about three miles. There may have been fifteen sentries round the bay within watch call of each other'.

'How many accessible bays have you?'

'Five, Sir. But St. Ouen's bay, though the largest to the westward, is so open to the Atlantic ocean, its first shelter being North America, that there is almost a constant surf there . . . . St. Helier's is the finest landing place of all'.

'What other defences are there in that bay besides Elizabeth Castle?'

'Fort Regent crosses its fire with Elizabeth Castle over St. Helier's harbour, Sir; and St. Aubin's tower also crosses fire with Elizabeth Castle over the Anchorage. There are also four Martello towers and batteries which, being very near the level of the sea, would almost act as water batteries'.

'Very true indeed. A very just observation'.

'Another bay, Sir, though small and not very accessible, is of very high importance, and I have the authority of Sir James Saumarez, Sir Philip Carteret, Captain Symonds and some of my own relations, captains in the navy, for stating it to be so. It is called Bouley Bay, and lies directly opposite to Cherbourg. We have commenced a pier in it, Sir, at the head of which there is always nine feet of water in low spring tides; but if a breakwater were carried out in a south-east direction, from the head of the pier about a hundred yards out, it would, so Sir James Saumarez says, shelter half Your Majesty's fleet of line of battle ships to watch Cherbourg. It would be the best port in the channel.' "

The conversation continued with questions about distances from Jersey to various ports, and the defensive work then being carried on at Cherbourg, which was said to have been "much strengthened and improved since the war". The King then asked where Rullecourt had landed, and was told about the Battle of Jersey, and that the next year, 1831, would be its fiftieth anniversary. The King resumed his enquiries about the militia:

" 'By whom are they clothed, and how are they dressed? In scarlet?'

'Yes, Sir. By Your Majesty, like the Line, except that we have old clothing' ".

The A.D.C. urged that all facings should be uniform, not different for each regiment, which caused much alteration of jackets when men moved from one regiment to another for any reason.

" 'That is your opinion?'

'Yes, Sir, and that of some other militia officers'.

'Then go to Sir Robert Peel and state it to him as the result of your own observation. Mind you do so before you leave town' ".

The conversation then turned to the outgoing Lieutenant Governor of Jersey, Sir Colin Halkett:

" '. . . . He was one of Your Majesty's Generals, and was wounded at Waterloo'.

'I know it. I know it' . . . . 'You had Andrew Gordon there, I recollect . . . . Who since?'

'General Don, Sir H. Turner and Hugh Mackay Gordon'.

'Ah, it is a Lieutenant General's command in war time?'

'Yes, Sir, with two Major Generals under him' ".

There were searching questions about the laws and government of Jersey, in comparison with those of Guernsey, at the end of which the King was assured that the States were:

" '. . . . a most loyal body, entirely and devotedly attached to Your Majesty's dynasty'.

'I know it. I believe it. Have you many emigrants in Jersey?'

'Not many, I believe, Sir . . . . But I saw that poor Prince Polignac[1] had almost effected his escape to us'.

'Ah, poor Prince Polignac. I wish to God he had. It would have been well for him . . . .'

'You said you had many fishermen in your regiment that went to Newfoundland . . . ., and is your trade general, all over the world?'

'No, Sir, it lies chiefly to Newfoundland, the South American states, Spain and the Baltic. It has wonderfully increased of late years. Thirty years ago we had not 8000 tons of shipping. Now we have 20,000 tons; and in 1828 . . . . 138,000 tons cleared in and out. We rank the fifth port in Your Majesty's dominions'..

'You have very fine harbours, have you not?'

'Yes, Sir, we shall soon have five completed, but St. Heliers is the finest little dry harbour in the channel and there are never less than fifty ships in it'.

'What is your revenue?'

'About £13,000 a year, Sir . . . .'

'I hear it is a very pretty Island'.

'Yes, Sir . . . . Nature has been very bountiful to it . . . . I should like to see Your Majesty there . . . . The Kings of England have not often rejoiced us by their presence'.

'So should I like to go there. I should like to see it very much. Is French yet generally spoken?'

'Only among the elderly people, Sir. The younger persons and children all speak English as well as French. Besides, Sir, there are English schools in every parish, which it is become the fashion to send the children to . . . . The mischief is that

---

1. Prince Jules de Polignac (1780-1847). On the Revolution of July 1830 he fled to Normandy, being finally arrested at Granville.

our States and Courts of law speak in French, but I think in another half century it will be discontinued altogether; though it is not of essential consequence, as we have a true hereditary Norman dislike to everything French'.

'I know it' ".

The A.D.C. mentioned to the King how his father and grandfather had told him that there had been a ministerial proposal to hand over the Channel Islands to France "for some important consideration", but that George III had been quite indignant at the proposal and said he would never consent to give up "the last remaining portion of his hereditary Norman possessions . . . . Besides, it would be forming a nest of Privateers against his merchant vessels.

'I never heard that. No, no. It couldn't be'.

'Oh, indeed, Sir, I fear it was true . . . .' "

Near the close of this long colloquy[1], which appeared deeply to interest (him), His Majesty appeared fatigued at length and, leaning his head on his hand, dropped asleep, while I sat watching my Sovereign . . . . However, as Miss FitzClarence was playing some very pretty airs, I beat time to them, when Colonel Frederick FitzClarence stepped up to me on tip toe: 'The Queen sends you this paper to amuse yourself with while the King sleeps. Sit quite still and be silent'. I looked back on Her Majesty, caught her eyes and laughing bowed very low. She and all her coterie were laughing and giggling at my droll dilemma, and Her Majesty nodded graciously to me. The King every now and then roused himself and plied me with new questions. He appears to have the faculty of being able to reflect and question tho' asleep. A man must look sharp who is near him".

The splendours of the Royal Pavilion were described in great detail by Sir John in a letter he wrote to his wife and children, in a way which would have delighted the hearts of small girls, with every room described for them to the last particular. As this remarkable building is so well known, it will suffice to take one extract from all he wrote. It is about the banqueting hall: "It rises forty feet to the dome, which is 30 feet in diameter and 85 in height, so that Bocage put upon wheels could drive into this dining room quite comfortably. The paper, or rather the silk hangings, are of a large magnificent pattern, white, in superbly rich gilt panels, and in each panel is a beautiful picture of Chinese figures as large as life, representing the customs and manners of the Chinese. A celebrated artist was two whole years in painting them. You may imagine it must have been difficult to make the silk fit the roof, but it is so well adapted that it glitters like rich silver. The top of the whole is like an immense cocoanut tree, whose magnificent leaves droop over the whole roof, so finely painted that they are quite deceptive. From the centre an immense gilt Chinese dragon holds in his talons a superb lustre which hangs down about thirty feet. There are I think four other magnificent lustres in the corners of the room, held in the claws of flying peacocks as large as life. Each of them have beautiful glass shades to hold the lights in this form, supported by dragons heads gilt. The curtains of the superb windows are of rich crimson damask. The sideboards glittered with gold plate. The carpet is of a rich, large, light pattern . . . . The table was laid I believe for thirty-two on Saturday".

Sir John had promised the King a return of the Jersey militia, but found to his dismay that he had left it in London, so he hastened there to get it. On returning to Brighton,

---

1. This and subsequent paragraphs are drawn partly from the diary of 11th to 15th September 1830, and partly from letters written at the same time.

FitzClarence told him the King had sent him an invitation to dine the night before, and when he failed to appear, the truth was out. "I exclaimed: 'I hope the King was not displeased with me'. 'Just the contrary. He said you were a smart, zealous fellow . . . . and had done just what was proper' . . . . The King presently caught my eye and I bowed. His Majesty said: 'That is for me, I suppose'. 'Yes, Sir'. I stepped forward and bowing presented the return to the King, who said: 'I thank you', and placed it in his pocket, nodding graciously . . . . I withdrew at once, for the Prussian Minister, Count Bulow and the Hanoverian Minister, Count Munster and their wives and daughters came in. It was a state dinner given to the Austrian Ambassador, who returns to the Emperor today, so that I was in great luck to be present. When all the company had arrived the Queen came in attended by her maids of Honor. She was neatly and elegantly attired in black satin, which set off her figure to advantage. She had on a handsome set of pearly ornaments and a very becoming Spanish hat or tocque of black satin and feathers . . . .

"I made myself acquainted with Sir Augustus D'Este, the Duke of Sussex's son, who *might* have been King of Hanover:

'I believe you have been in Jersey, Sir Augustus?'

'Oh, yes, indeed I have. I remember Jersey with feelings of great delight'.

'You may then recollect Sir J. Dumaresq. He was my grandfather'.

'Indeed, a charming old gentleman. He was very kind to me. Dear me, how is Miss D? Your name is Dumaresq, then, I presume?'

'No, Sir'.

'Pray, how is my first love Miss Marett at the large house near St. Aubin's?'

'What, rivals on first acquaintance. She was *my first love* too, just when she came from school'.

'Excellent (he burst out into a loud laugh). What has become of the charming creature? She would have graced a Court'.

"When dinner was announced . . . ., I handed out Miss FitzClarence and found myself seated between the two handsomest ladies at Court. I turned to the lady on my left and said: 'I believe I have the honor to address Miss D'Este[1]. I have just made the agreeable acquaintance of your brother'; after which we all three were very friendly and sociable. Miss D'Este is a most beautiful girl, perfectly elegant in her style, dress, manner and conversation. She dances like a fairy, and is the woman of the best fashion I have ever seen. Miss FitzClarence is sweetly pretty, a very neat figure, dressed quite plainly, very unaffected and cheerful, as great a laugher as you, but perfectly well bred, and industrious withal. For after dinner I found her at a work table embroidering, with a great bunch of thread-papers, like Grandmama's. I observed: 'Well, I did not expect to see a homely article of this kind in a palace'. 'Don't you think it does just as well as a gayer one?' 'Certainly I do. I much admire the unsophisticated taste that uses it'.

"The Princess Augusta was very condescending to me, and said to me: 'How do you do, Colonel Le Couteur. So you are back from Town?' 'Yes, your Royal Highness. I thank you for your obliging notice of me. That was a sad scrape I got into. I went to repair it as fast as I could'. 'You were quite right. It was just what you should have done. It was thought so (nodding towards the King)'. The King honored me by asking me *three* times to take wine with him, which I attributed to the goodness of his heart, in order to dispel

1. Daughter of the Duke of Sussex.

any idea in my mind that I had incurred his displeasure at having left my return in London".

After dinner he asked FitzClarence: " 'Now tell me candidly, how did I come off in my ordeal on Saturday?' He hugged me and laughed: 'With éclat, Sir, so all at Court say. Few so well, none ever better. The King said to me, but don't let it make you vain, 'that Le Couteur is a nice, shrewd, clever fellow. I like him'. You are in luck, Le Couteur. Stick to the King. He likes you'. 'My dear FitzC, how much indebted I am to you'. 'Stay, not a bit. Now it is all yourself. Look sharp'; and away he went". Then there was dancing, but the new A.D.C. did not venture to waltz with Miss D'Este, fearing he should not perform well enough, and she took the floor with the Duke of Clarence. "None of them waltzes as well as Sir Colin", he wrote, and went on: "Her Majesty is by far the most graceful and elegant dancer in the court. She appears to great advantage then, and has a very good foot and ankle which, as our poor Uncle Pipon used to say, she handles beautifully". The Duke of Clarence, the eldest of the King's large family of sons, was in high spirits and "ran among them, shouting and laughing, and tickling the young ladies; just as our kind Uncle Pipon used to play with his nieces . . . . The Duke is just such another charming gay person. No wonder they idolise him in Hanover".

For a third evening in succession he was summoned to dine with the royal family, and arrived in gloves, but was told that it was not etiquette to wear them before Their Majesties unless one were going to dance: "so I put my hands behind me and slipped them into my pocket". This was a grand state dinner, with toasts to the Emperor of Russia through his Ambassador, Prince Troubetskoi, next to whom Sir John sat at dinner, and the King of Prussia, followed by a fulsome toast to the Empress of Russia. These were proposed by the King in French, faultless it appears, unless Sir John edited the words as he wrote them in his diary. "A little while after", he tells us, "I said to the Prince (Troubetskoi) who was whispering to me: 'Monseigneur, ne croyez-vous que notre Roi est très affable?' 'Ah, quelle bonté, quelle grandeur de voir un Roi entouré d'un peuple riche, fier, poli et instruit, dont il jouit des affections sincères—quel sublime spectacle! C'est singulier, mais tous les jours je crois que c'est le Dimanche; le peuple est si bien mis, les voitures si propres, tout parait si elegant. Chez nous et dans le continent ce n'est que le Dimanche qu'on se met ainsi' ". The Prince was delighted with Sir John's French speech and said he could not believe he was an Englishman. After dinner there was a ball, with waltzes, quadrilles and galoppades. He danced with Miss FitzClarence but considered Miss D'Este the belle of the ball, and when an unwanted beau approached to claim a dance with her, she whispered to Sir John: "Chat to me as fast as you can, and he will be afraid to ask me". The band was the Prague minstrels, six musicians and three singers.

Next morning the King granted his Jersey A.D.C. a brief audience, in which he asked him: " 'Pray, now: and when were your Militia organised?':

> 'The origin of the Militia law, Sire, is very ancient . . . ., but the present system of organisation was introduced by Colonel Le Couteur in 1798. A little time previous to that period, Government named an officer of the line to organise the Militia, who could scarcely speak French. The consequence was that, being unacquainted with the language or customs of the people, and accustomed to military discipline, he was too rigid, he became unpopular and was nearly ston'd to death. The project then failed'.

'Ah! Just like the Government, naming entirely inefficient and incompetent persons for peculiar and important stations, which require a knowledge of local usages and customs . . . . How often were the drills?'

'Weekly, Sir, in their respective districts, except in harvest time, or at particular periods which might give offence'.

'Very right. Much better to consult occasional convenience' . . . ."

The A.D.C. then mentioned the anonymous letter opposing his appointment, and said: " '. . . . I hope that Your Majesty will be pleased to believe that I never gave occasion for such a letter'. The King appeared kindly moved, and said: 'Never mind it, never mind it, Le Couteur . . . . As to that letter, it is not of the slightest consequence. You must not mind it. You know that there are mischievous persons who always like to be fishing in troubled waters . . . . I never listen to such communications. Your recommendation came through the regular official channels, which was sufficient'. 'I am deeply grateful to Your Majesty . . . . I will take my leave, Sir, if you please'. 'When do you go?' 'Tomorrow morning, Sir'. 'Then you had better dine here today, and I shall see you again' ' ". The diary concludes this episode with: "May God bless and preserve the King with a peaceful and long life, such as he bestowed on the righteous Kings of Israel, is the fervent prayer of his attached and devoted servant, J. Le Couteur, his A.D.C. Wed. 15th September 1830, at Brighton". He was overwhelmed by the condescension shown him, and in some ways this was the most exhilarating moment of his whole career.

The following October he was again in London to attend a levée, and when the Lord in Waiting, to whom a card had been handed, stumbled in pronouncing the unfamiliar name, the King looked up and said: "Oh, this is Le Couteur". It was entertaining to watch the varying reactions of those who came up to be presented. Some seemed to panic, others almost to eat the King's hand, others to back away from it, causing the young Princes of Cumberland and Cambridge to "laugh out, rudely enough". Next day there was a review of the 2nd Battalion of the Coldstreams, with the King in Field Marshal's uniform. He was loudly cheered, and the same evening he and the Queen were cheered when they attended Drury Lane Theatre.

In February 1831 the new A.D.C. went over to attend a Queen's Drawing Room. "The waiting room was thronged with superbly dressed nobility . . . . The throne room presented a magnificent scene . . . . The maids of honour were drawn up on the left of the throne. Miss D'Este, the belle among them all, was most becomingly dressed in white blonde oversatin, with an elegant head dress of diamonds and plumes . . . . The Queen's dress . . . . was of Honiton lace over a white satin dress. A beautiful train of rose coloured velvet was supported by a page. A magnificent tiara of diamonds, from which rose a superb plume of feathers, and a magnificent stomacher of diamonds, and shoulder ornaments of brilliants . . . . The Duchess of Kent and the Princess Victoria, a nice plump little girl, with a good tempered cherub face, simply dressed except that they had spoiled her hair by dressing it womanly". The next day he had an interview with the King, and presented a report on the Island defences, illustrated with a sketch of St. Aubins Bay, "made to correspond with Capt. White's chart, three times enlarged"; all of which the King said was "beautifully done". In a lengthy conversation the year before, about the Militia, Sir John had asked if the prefix Royal might be added, to which the King had replied: "Royal? Oh, certainly". He now enquired if the people were pleased with the new title, which had been granted in time to be announced on 6th January 1831, the jubilee of the Battle of Jersey.

The Coronation of King William took place on 8th September 1831. From early morning Sir John, from his rooms on Regent Street, heard carriages rumbling past, and saw gaily dressed peeresses in them. A few days before he had seen Lord Frederick Fitz-Clarence, who told him he was to ride in the procession, and promised him trappings and bridle. He saw the royal horses, and declared them "magnificent, with three distinct breeds, being white, cream and black Hanoverian breeds. One of the cream coloured horses is $17\frac{1}{2}$ hands high and was bred at Hampton Court, but they cannot find a match for him, and he is a vicious devil moreover. . . . I found a nice looking little mare at Maynards in Prince's Street, which will suit me very well if she stands fire . . . . Went to the King's mews to enquire after my housings . . . . I am to chuse which I like from among several superb sets which are to be lent to those A.D.C.'s who have none". On Coronation morning at 8 o'clock "my servant brought down my horse, which attracted a crowd as the mare, being black and showy, looked remarkably well in her superb trappings, which were: a very rich shell bridle[1], silver bridoon[2], shell surcingle[3], martingale[4] and crupper[5], covered with a superb shabrach[6], very long, with a broad rim of silver lace, and the Prince of Wales' arms richly embroidered in the corners . . . . Our A.D.Cs' rendez-vous was the Royal Mews, where the sight was gay enough . . . . ten royal carriages with six showy horses to each, covered with glittering harnesses . . . . The state coach if divested of its gilding would be as ugly a vehicle as can well be imagined . . . . The King's six led horses in superb trappings also had a magnificent appearance. One of them, a cream, has a mane a yard and a half in length. They were led by two grooms by a long red silk halter . . . which gave the horses plenty of room to play and throw up their heads and appear very fine, which the noble creatures seemed to think themselves". We have a detailed description of how the procession wound its way to the Abbey, where the A.D.Cs' servants had miraculously arrived in time to take their masters' horses. Having dismounted they were ushered to the "places allotted to the King's household".

The King had rightly felt that some economies should be made in the costly ceremony, and it is generally believed to have been a drab one, but after reading Sir John's description one is inclined to think otherwise. There was, however, a moment of anxiety, and some very disorderly scenes. Immediately after the crowning, when coming up the steps, "the King appeared a little faint and almost tottered under the weight of all his insignia. Then came a regular scene of riot, for medals were thrown about by the treasurer of the Household's officers, which set all decorum at defiance. The very judges opposite to us, to the discomposure of their rams' wigs, shoved and jostled each other to get a largesse, which set the House of Commons in a roar, clapping. They threw some amongst us, which equally discomposed us, but by stooping while a Lifeguardsman took a ride on my shoulders, I obtained three, one for each of the children . . . . One of the purse bearers was regularly rifled, being thrown down, his sword was broken, his purse bag taken from, him and all his medals snatched, and all this close behind the King's chair . . . . The homage of the

---

1. Enamel or lacquer ornamentation.   2. Snaffle bit of the double bridle, or possibly referring to both snaffle and curb.   3. Girth.   4. A strap from girth to noseband.   5. Strap along back and under tail, to secure saddle.   6. Cavalry saddlecloth. A Q.A.D.C's saddlecloth is on view in the Castle Cornet Museum in Guernsey, presumably similar to the one mentioned here.

III   Colonel JOHN LE COUTEUR, K.A.D.C
in the uniform of A.D.C. to King William IV for the Royal Jersey Militia.
(*from the portrait by John Boaden*, 1831)

Two pages from Harriet Le Couteur's album of apples and pears grown at Le Bocage and Belle Vue, 1831-62

IVa   Apples: Reinette de Hollande: Madame Le Brun: Seedling Pearmain from the Valley.
Pears: Rivilète?: Brown Beurré.

IVb   Apples: Royal Codlin: Derbyshire: Petit Jean
Pear: Louisebonne of Jersey (delicious).

peers took a great length of time as they all kissed the King's left cheek, except the Bishop of Exeter who preferred the right one, which created a great laugh". Many of the peers were loudly cheered as they did homage, most of all Lord Brougham[1]. As soon as the cortège came out of the Abbey it began to rain, but the crowds and the police were cheerful and mutually cooperative. "Never was the utility of the new police more conspicuous".

Next day there was a Coronation Service in St. Paul's, at which the Bishop of London preached, "but it was not oratory", being more of a political discourse, to which Talleyrand, "who was sitting very near . . . ., lent a very attentive ear". Talleyrand, Prince, prelate and diplomat, was then French Ambassador in London and a world famed figure. Sir John had already seen him at a levée, "seated at the head of the room, the most remarkable person there beyond a doubt. The hero of thirteen revolutions, he is bowed down with years and cares; was originally about 5 foot 8: had a mild, pale, placid countenance, wrinkled but not so much so as his years might command; a profusion of silver locks give an air of dignity and veneration to his appearance, which his talents alone would not command. He was paid universal attention and conversed much with Baron Bulow and Count Munster". At a later levée he saw him again: "When the Duke of Wellington came in, Talleyrand got up and hobbled up to the centre of the room to shake hands with him. Everybody made a large circle round the lions, and it was really curious and interesting thus to see the two most remarkable men of the age, surrounded by peers, generals and sages, all intent upon them". To return to St. Paul's: "Nothing could be more ludicrous than the appearance of two of the judges, peers, with their coronets over their caxons[2] . . . . It was funnier still when Lord Lyndhurst's[3] tumbled off, but he has been a good cricketer in his day, for he caught it cleverly and stuck it on his wig, not his head, again".

In a conversation with the Garter King of Arms, Sir George Naylor, Sir John remarked that he was surprised to find that the arms of Jersey were not registered. Sir George was amazed, and asked how he knew this. "Because the King wanted to see the arms last year, and I went to your college, where they were not to be found". Sir George said this must be put right at once, and added: "Jersey and Guernsey should have claimed a place at the Coronation, as remainder of the Duchy of Normandy".

A few days later there was a Coronation Drawing Room . . . ., "perhaps the most splendid ever seen". The Queen wore gold tissue with a mantle and train of purple velvet . . . . and a radiant crown of diamonds . . . . The Marchioness of Londonderry was a jewel set in diamonds . . . . Old Lady Talbot . . . . had been created Baroness in her own right at 93 years of age, and came all the way from Dublin for the Coronation". There was an embarrassing moment at the entrance of the one of peeresses, who "walked in on her privilege, curtsied to the King who looked away, faced him and curtsied again, who again looked away and reddened. She then quickly and firmly and impudently told the Lord in Waiting, who had thrown her card in the basket, to return it to her; walked stately, looking rather pale but not alarmed, up to the Queen, who also cut her, curtsied and walked on. It was a scene. I stared and looked down. The Duke of Devonshire planted his gold stick and looked up. Lord Hill looked down. The King looked annoyed, as well he might".

---

1. Baron Brougham and Vaux (1778-1868), Statesman.   2. Wigs.
3. John Singleton Copley, son of the artist of the same name who painted the Battle of Jersey. An eminent jurist, who became Lord Chancellor, (1772-1863).

I

CHAPTER NINE

LIONS OF THE CENTURY

In the last chapter we found Sir John watching an encounter between the lions of the court, Wellington and Talleyrand. But there are many other famous names which sparkle like stars in the pages of his diaries. A recital of them all would read like a page from Debrett or Whitaker, and we shall choose some of the brightest in the firmament, and read what our Jersey diarist had to say about them.

He first saw the Duke of Wellington at an opening of Parliament, carrying the Sword of State before the King, but "he had been so much hooted and hissed that he returned with Prince Esterhazy (the Austrian Ambassador); but was soon discovered in the carriage and groaned at more than ever. Why, I cannot guess, unless it was owing to the new Police system, which is very annoying to thieves and pickpockets and strumpets". Some years later, in 1845, when again in London, "I met the great Duke, getting out of his own phaeton without assistance. I should have liked to have done the civil, but knowing his independence I avoided intrusion. He looked remarkably well and smart". After an interview with him then, he noted: "The Duke is feeble; his voice still loud and distinct in conversation, rather otherwise when he reads. Bought the daguerrotype likeness of him, just himself as he spoke and looked at me". At the opening of the Crystal Palace he was "admirably received" by the crowd. Soon afterwards, on 17th September 1852, news was received in Jersey of his death. At the opening of Victoria College a few days later, Sir John, on his way there, "drove into town by 8 o'clock, got a crape scarf added to my mourning, according to the Queen's general order"; and his daughter Harriet's diary remarks; "Papa in full fig and deep mourning, according to the Queen's regulations in respect of the memory of the dear old Duke".

For the state funeral windows were let out at high prices, one bay window costing a hundred guineas, and an ordinary one in the Strand three guineas. Seats in the Abbey for the service were jealously contested, and "the Dean and Chapter had monopolised an immense number . . . . If the daughters of the eldest sons of peers claimed theirs, and the Baronets' wives, there was no pleasing all". The Duke's body lay in state at Chelsea Hospital. "It was a grand and imposing sight, and far more gorgeous than the catafalque which covered the remains of William IV at Windsor".

On the day of the funeral, with Colonel Priaulx, the A.D.C. for Guernsey, and a friend Colonel Wymer, he set out for St. Paul's by carriage, but "got into a regular fix on turning into Waterloo Place. Five rows of carriages crossed our path, and no one would let us in, and there we remained for an hour". Then a policeman came to their rescue and they proceeded. "It was wonderful to see the myriads of heads in every street, opening, churchyard, window, gallery or roof from where the procession might be seen. Policemen at every yard's distance kept all in order. The people were behaving marvellously well, with the greatest order and almost silence . . . . The Temple Bar was gaudily and citically (sic) decorated for the occasion, but without taste or solemn grandeur . . . . We got in and found our places among the Order of the Bath, next to . . . . the Peers. I had the good luck to find myself seated by . . . . Sir Charles Trevelyan[1]. His brother-in-law, Macaulay, suggested to Dr. Milman the beautiful dirge 'A Prince has fallen in Israel' . . . . The Ambassadors' Gallery was being marshalled by Sir Edward Cust, who looked as grand and stately as anyone. The Marshals of Russia, Spain, Portugal, Prussia etc., seven of them, took their seats at the head of the bier . . . ., in the centre under the dome. Though there was a flood of light and heat round the frieze and the upper circle of the dome, gas gems burning brightly, yet they were so elevated that though there was a fine sombre light they sent down no heat, and it was excessively cold to one's head. Many of us put our white handkerchiefs on our bald heads. The Commons came in, about 600 strong . . . ., and dropped into their seats like a well drilled corps. The Lords came in like a rabble and looked very undignified". They were followed by the universally popular Princess Mary, mother of the late Queen Mary, and then the Chelsea pensioners, many of whom must have served under the Duke. "It was a stirring and awestriking sight to perceive seventeen thousand heads stretched out, silent and observant . . . . As the procession entered the nave the grand organ played, and 230 canons and choristers struck up 'I am the resurrection . . . .' The banners and heraldic emblazonments, the Guidon, and Marshals and Royalty all preceding the coffin of the great deceased. When the coffin, which was of lead covered with rich crimson velvet and gold handles, had to be slid from the carriage bier to the sinking bier over the grave, there was a hitch for two or three minutes that caused a sensation of apprehension . . . ., but at length it slid gently to its place". As it did so, the organ played the Dead March. "It was most impressive and affecting. The faces of the heroic generals who were the pall bearers became visible, and their handkerchiefs and sobs witnessed their love for their great commander. The young Duke quite gave way. After the Grace, Garter King of Arms, Sir George Young declared in a loud but nervous tone the titles and honours of the late Duke, and the Chamberlain broke his white wand of office, dropping the pieces into the grave beneath". Yet, as Sir John recorded elsewhere, the Iron Duke, the personification of Britain, the demi-god, was a modest man withal. When asked whom he considered the greatest General of the age, he instantly replied: "In this age, in past ages, in *any* age, Napoleon".

There are references to Gladstone's policies in these papers, but apparently Sir John never met him. Of D'Israeli, as he spells the name, he wrote: "the most able writer, but always with a political design, to raise the Jews into the first people in the world; and in favour of agricultural protection, and the liberty of the subject". When in 1852 the Whig Parliament fell and Lord Derby took over, the comment was: "he has named the clever Jew as his leader in the Commons. He is equal to the task and will rebuild the Temple of Solomon and make us all good Jews". The Globe newspaper was much dissatisfied with what is called the "Blockhead ministry of second-rates, the dull tools of Derby and Dizzy"; and the Daily News called it "the Derby-Disraeli Ministry". By 1855 he was writing: "If he was not the leader and tool of a party, his home truths would be telling". Two years later, when Disraeli was in opposition, Sir John wrote, in reference to Lord Panmure's economies: "The Government sank every expense to get rid of the 9d. income tax. D'Israeli would have turned them out otherwise". At the end of a rather wearisome Queen's Ball

---

1. Sir Charles Edward Trevelyan (1807-1886).

which went on until 3 a.m., he found himself standing beside Palmerston and Disraeli as they all waited for their carriages. The two great men were chatting ."Oh, you don't like commissions?" asked Disraeli. "No", replied the other, whereat "Dizzy gave a satirical smile, which I reflected by a laugh. He observed it, saw he was noticed, and walked off".

Of Lord Palmerston, Sir John wrote: "He is the most truly English gentleman that can be met with, very popular with the Whigs, much the contrary otherwise. All the foreign courts hate him". Others also had cause to dislike this rebellious spirit. The 1851 diary referring to recent events in France, relates: "Lord Palmerston wrote to the President approving of the coup d'état. The same afternoon (the President) received a letter from Lord John Russell in the name of the Cabinet, regretting the very wholesale and unconstitutional measures which had been resorted to, so entirely at variance with preconceived notions of liberty. Yet the Government was quite prepared to acknowledge any form of government which the French people should accept. Louis Napoleon was in a towering rage at this discrepancy, and wrote to the Queen to know which of her Ministers he was to credit. The Queen sent for Lord John, desired him to express her highest displeasure to Lord Palmerston at the unauthorised step which he had taken, and ordered him to return to her the seals of the Foreign Office on the morrow. But the Tragedy was to end in Comedy. Palmerston was warned to attend the Privy Council at 12. Her Majesty and Russell were punctual. No Palmerston. No seals . . . . 1 o'clock . . . . two o'clock . . . . 3 o'clock . . . . He had sent the seals to Lord John Russell, and cut the Queen and all his old colleagues. He thought to make Majesty without its externals a reality. A good republican temper his Lordship has".

In 1853 Sir John saw Lord Palmerston at his residence in Carlton Gardens, about his position as Vicomte in Jersey, and recorded: "He has grown old since he was in Jersey in 1846. He recollected me and shook hands . . . . He listened with all attention, and then asked my opinion as to the state of affairs in Jersey; which I told him unreservedly because I thought it to be my duty to do so". Later that year news of his resignation reached Jersey. It "took us by surprise, and deep regret, independently of his relations with us as Home Secretary. His removal from office at the moment when his services to the country . . . . on an impending war[1], is highly to be regretted. Surely he is not playing a game to become Prime Minister?" In 1856 this ebullient man was seen again by the diarist at a Queen's levée: "Lord Palmerston and the group of Ministers seemed as happy as if they had just taken office. Their victory on the 'Kars' debate has set them up for a twelvemonth". Kars, in Transcaucasia, had just been taken by the Russians from the Turks.

Sir Robert Peel is often mentioned. Sir John was present in the House of Commons in 1830 when Sir Robert Peel resigned, and "this announcement was received in the most respectful manner by the whole house, not a cheer, not a murmur". Sir Robert's sister, Mrs. Dawson, told Sir John that her brother found working with the Queen a pleasure, "as she was so very attentive to business. Even in the middle of dinner she would rise to answer any communication of consequence". In 1845 the diary says: "Many Conservatives support Sir Robert Peel, for fear of getting a worse government, but the least split between Sir Robert and the Duke would break it up. They know of no one to succeed him just now, no one with fixed principles. They consider Sir Robert to be constantly duping them". At a meeting of the Royal Society, Mr. Jonathan Peel was blackballed from entry, although

---

1. The Crimea.

his relative Sir Robert was one of his sponsors. It was said he had done nothing for science and only desired to enter from motives of curiosity. In December of that year there was talk of Sir Robert resigning, but ten days later his ministry was in again, and the diary remarked: "I said in London to Mr. de Lisle and others that I thought Sir Robert Peel would take the repeal of the corn laws in hand, mount on the top of the wave which Lord John Russell's letter to his constituents in London had created, and safely steer the vessel through the dangers, with Lord John and his party as a portion of his crew. Was I right or not?" In the opinion of Sir James Reynett, Lieutenant Governor of Jersey, Peel was a republican at heart and no friend to monarchy. In 1850 Lady Peel, who had recently been widowed, came to Jersey with her daughter and two sons. It was said that "Sir Robert has left her the house in Whitehall with plate and furniture, with a jointure of £3000 a year and £3000 in cash. He has left £75,000 to each of his children . . . . It is not enough for her to keep up that house in Whitehall, with the expensive habits of her children". Sir John assisted her to find accommodation in the Island, and went to call on her at Pontac, as did the Bishop of Winchester.

Lord Panmure, previously Ramsey Fox Maule, Secretary for War, was a wealthy man. He had said he was "tired of office and sacrificing his fortune, but would not desert the Queen, or throw up his commission while the country was at war. His new house in Scotland was to cost him £110,000 . . . . His fortune was £42,000 a year". Sir John went on: "When he was here as a sub, he looked as heavy a youth as could be. So he did in Canada, until he broke out into all sorts of dissipation, when he found his tongue. He has a powerful memory, and invincible courage and perseverance". As Secretary for War he took some interest in Sir John's work on the Enfield rifle, of which more presently.

Another eminent Victorian who flits across these pages is Lord John Russell, appearing first as Chairman of a meeting of the Royal Humane Society in 1843. In 1845 "we received the astounding news that Ministers had resigned, and that the Queen had charged Lord John Russell to form a ministry". In 1847 he was said to be "ill and weak". Some years later: "he finds himself at the last hampered by his relatives, and nepotism". The tale was told that "the Reform Bill, which he made such a fuss about giving up, was none of his own, but a concoction of Lady John's and Elliott's; that he did not care a straw about it, but had to father it; and the tender scene in the House was all fudge and crocodile tears. He got a good rating from Lady J. for his tergiversation".

Sir John became very friendly with the fifth Earl Spencer through agricultural channels, the latter being Chairman of the English Agricultural Society in 1839, and he was invited to stay at Althorp in Northamptonshire. This famous house was in origin a Tudor mansion built in 1580, altered in 1665 and again in 1790 by Holland, and its many chimneys pierce the skyline like a forest. The library is still famous, and Sir John recorded that it contained 50,000 volumes, one rare book alone being worth £25,000. A Boccaccio for which the Duke of Marlborough paid £2600 had been bought by Lord Spencer's father for £760. One printed page was dated 1423 (sic). There were paintings by Raphael, Correggio, Titian, Teniers and Gainsborough, and Lord Spencer remembered sitting to Gainsborough when he was five years old. They went all over the farm lands, which the visitor found extremely interesting.

Lord Spencer gave Sir John his impressions of contemporary statesmen, and these were carefully recorded in the diary. He himself, he said, was very nervous when speaking in the House. Lord Plunkett, he considered "the closest reasoner he had ever heard"; and Sir Robert Peel "a very good and useful debater . . . . difficult to reply to . . . . never commits himself"; and again, "very cautious, distant, not a single personal friend, a cool ready debater". Spencer said he disliked speaking in the Lords because, having been leader of the House of Commons, so much was expected of him; and "there are no cheers to spur one on there; it is a dead awful silence, and no one knows whether he is making an impression or not. . . . No one peer will be turned by your speech, as all their minds are made up previously". Stanley he found "very violent, but honest and sincere". Melbourne "very literary, of silent habits, seldom speaking in the Privy Council, very energetic when roused to action . . . . very private". When Spencer's father was about to die, and his son to inherit the title which would exclude him from the Commons, he wrote to warn Melbourne of this, in order that another Chancellor of the Exchecquer might be found. Melbourne replied: "You need not be uneasy about a successor. We are all out. The King has dismissed us". "The fault was", Spencer explained, "the King had great confidence in Grey and the Duke, but in no one else; and when he found I quitted the Commons he thought the Duke would be able to form a Government, but he could not". He went on to comment on political life; "It is most harrassing to be obliged to receive all deputations, and to have no time for preparation for debates . . . . I never laid my head down at night without wishing it might be my last". Returning to individuals: "King William was most straight forward and confiding on business: George IV the worst that ever reigned . . . . Peel certainly never would be considered a great man by after ages; he was too cautious, and an ungenerous enemy. The Duke, on the contrary, was a noble antagonist, a much greater man . . . . Lord John a very superior man, very good tempered, patient, with excellent judgement and great skill, and now a capital man of business. Quite a mistake to remove him from the Home Department to the Colonies". In 1845 Lord Spencer died. Lord Beresford said of him: "He was indeed an honest statesman, and no man of any party ever questioned his integrity". A fund was established in his memory "to relieve the widows of decayed farmers".

Viscount Beresford, a Peninsula veteran, was Governor of Jersey from 1821-1854, the last to hold that office. Sir John went to see him in London in 1830 to discuss Jersey affairs, and wrote: "It is impossible to have a worse notion (with some degree of truth tho) than His Lordship entertains respecting our Court . . . . It is unfortunate that he thinks this, as his opinion, delivered with great warmth, must influence the Council more or less". Beresford had visited Jersey in 1821, but apparently not after that, though retaining a close interest in Island affairs, and Sir John always called on him when he was in England. In 1840 he was invited down to Bedgebury in Kent to see Beresford's farm, but had to defer the visit until two years later. There he joined a most distinguished house-party, shot, saw the school endowed by Lady Beresford, went to church and inspected the farm lands. Mrs. Dawson, Peel's sister, was there: "noted as an historical and most agreeable person . . . ., she led the conversation with considerable brilliance and perfect ease". Each evening they played something called "Earth". The return journey was by carriage to Tonbridge, and thence by coach to London in $5\frac{1}{2}$ hours. Beresford must have had a splendid household staff, for he recalled that when he entertained the Duchess of Gloucester there were a hundred people in the house for five days, consuming 2000lbs of meat. He complained that he was constantly robbed by his farm stewards, having to buy 19 tons of hay a year, in addition to what he grew, for 32 head of cattle. In 1845 there was another visit to Bedgebury: "dear Lord Beresford looking wonderfully well . . . . Lady B. welcomed me . . . . she looked very well and handsome". In Kildown Church Sir John noticed a window to St. Alban and wrote: "He should be in one of our windows", meaning in St. Aubin's Church in Jersey. He made the acquaintance of the Vicar of Goudhurst Church, Mr. Dupré, a relative of the Solicitor General of Jersey who, Sir John told him, was "a person of the highest power of mind". One day the house-party visited Battle Abbey and the diary remarks: "I, a Norman, of ancient Norman descent, saw it with reverence". They had enormous meals. The menu one night was fried sole, haunch of mutton, pheasant, fillet of beef, partridges, calf's head, mutton cutlets, a charlotte, an apple omelette and cauliflower au gratin. Sir John stayed up one night talking to the old Marquis about Military matters, and asked whether Marlborough's army was in as high a state of discipline as the modern army. "Probably it was", replied Beresford; "there are no positive means of knowing it, but it is likely . . . . Marlborough was a great man, a very great man . . . ., of immense resources all drawn from his own store".

In 1849 Sir John paid them another visit, and took the opportunity of seeking Beresford's support in the claims of a relative, James Janvrin, to the Deanery of Jersey, but Beresford replied that Lord John Russell had deprived him of the right to name the Dean. By 1850 the old Marquis was in failing health, and died in 1854. Sir John's letter to his widow shows that there was real friendship between the two men, and that the three knew each other so well that a touch of spice was permitted in their correspondence. For in sending her pears from his own garden and apologising that they were not so good as he could have wished, he said: "but the climate is an inexorable mistress; like some wives, sometimes too hot and sometimes too cold".

Among the eminent military men he met were the Napiers, a family which produced so many famous generals that one is not always sure which one is meant. In 1846 General Napier[1] was Governor of Guernsey, and Sir John met him in company with the Royal Commissioners to discuss the defences of Alderney. "The General talked to me of the defences, of the affairs of war, of all things he touches en main de maître. What a pity that such a man should not pull well with the authorities here. He did me the honour to confide his confidential report on the defences to me, with leave to take notes, an invaluable privilege to a man who desires to save Jersey, aye and the Channel Islands, from the grasp of France". When in London in 1852 for the Duke of Wellington's funeral he met Sir William Napier[2], brother of the above, and they discussed military matters; and two days later he rode out to Sir William's home, Sinde House at Clapham Park, and "found the old hero and historian in his dressing gown, not quite so well as on Thursday". In a conversation about defence, Sir William spoke highly of Jersey's Governor, General Love, and said: " 'There should be a rallying point for the troops to concentrate on to defend Fort Regent . . . .' I said that I thought that with scarping the northern coast, and making heavy breastworks all round the bays by a levy en masse, they ought not to be allowed to land; especially if we had two men of war, steamers, in each bay, and a scout steamer of the swiftest build to convey alarms to us. 'Yes, get that, and you may be safe. But where will you get it? Our people won't believe that there is danger. They laughed at the Duke for saying so' ". Sir William recalled being told by a pilot at Grève de Lecq

1. Sir Charles James Napier (1782-1853).   2. Sir William Napier (1785-1860).

that there were one or two inlets there into which a steamer might creep; to which Sir John replied that it was just those places he wished to see "scarped perpendicularly and rendered inaccessible".

In 1853 Sir John visited Sir John Byng, who had become Lord Strafford, "an elegant old gentlemanly soldier", who assured him that any officer recommended by Lord Raglan would be well received by him. This referred to Sir John's efforts to gain a transfer from the Royal Irish Fusiliers to the Coldstreams for his son, soon to leave for the Crimea. A year later he and his son were dining with Lord Strafford, who was almost blind, and discussed getting a stock of cattle for his son Mr. Byng. "His memory", wrote Sir John, "is surprisingly good; and he spoke on home and foreign affairs, and remembered Guernsey well". On another occasion, "He told me that he remembered Guernsey as a most delightful quarter. The breakfasts were the best he knew, and the butter and cream so good. The old captains of invalids then lived on their pay like kings. I assured him that the living was as good as ever, but the cheapness had disappeared".

In 1827, when dining with the Lieutenant Governor of Jersey, Sir John met the Marquess of Douro[1] and Sir John Burgoyne[2], noting: "The Marquis appears to be a perfect gentleman without any silly airs about him". In 1846 he was discussing with Burgoyne, then Lieutenant General of the Ordnance, the problem of defence; "He looked at the map of Jersey, and I showed him why Noirmont peninsula should be defended". Further interviews occurred with him concerning arsenals, and in 1852 Burgoyne came to Jersey with Lord Hardinge, not apparently a harmonious pair, for one diary remarks: "difference of opinion between them at New Orleans, not yet forgotten". In the following year Burgoyne was in Jersey again, inspecting the building of St. Catherine's breakwater; and Sir John met him yet again, and discussed Jersey affairs, at the Queen's presentation of Crimea medals.

Whenever he went to London, Sir John called on Lord Fitzroy Somerset, later Lord Raglan, who always received him most kindly, whether in his office or at official levées. On these occasions he met many old acquaintances, some of whom had become distinguished men, such as Sir James Denniss under whom he had served so many years ago in Canada. Denniss remembered visiting Jersey a long time before, and meeting "a fine handsome young fellow, Brigade Major there". This was General Le Couteur, Sir John's father.

Admiral Lord Saumarez, or de Saumarez was a distant relative of Sir John's through the Le Mesuriers, and whenever the packet stopped at Guernsey when Sir John was on the way to England, he paid a quick visit to the de Saumarez home, now called Saumarez Park or to the family's town house. The Admiral had some fine naval pictures, including a pair connected with two different Captains Saumarez who had sailed round the world with Lord Anson. When the Admiral, then Sir James Saumarez, was first presented at court "by old Sir Hyde Parker, (the King) said: 'Saumarey, Saumarey? Is that a relation of my father's two captains who went round the world with Anson[3]?'; and Sir Hyde said: 'Yes, Your Majesty, and as good an officer as his uncles'. Sir James was writing to Admiral Codrington[4] on the 20th October (1827), at the very moment the battle of

1. Son of the Duke of Wellington.   2. Sir John Fox Burgoyne (1782-1871), son of General John Burgoyne.
3. George Anson (Lord) (1697-1762), Admiral.
4. Admiral Sir Edward Codrington (1770-1851).

Navarino was being fought, that he hoped 'he would be an instrument under divine providence of chastising the Turks, and relieving the Greeks from their state of slavery'. I have seen Sir Edward's answer, in which he says how highly he values Sir Jame's opinion . . . . Sir James told me his object in the Baltic was to sever the Russians from Bonaparte; and when the Swedes wished to have Bernadotte[1] as their Crown Prince, there were three parties soliciting his support. First, the King and Swedes for Bernadotte, because they said he was sincere in his opinion of Boney, from his quarrel with him at Versailles and his jealousy of him: secondly, the Duke of Augustenburg: and thirdly the King of Denmark: all pressing their solicitations on him. Sir James told them all he would represent their views . . . . When England gave in, in Bernadotte's favour, the Swedes wrote him that he had been their arbiter and saviour, and the first instrument of Banaparte's downfall, and voted him a sword worth three thousand guineas . . . . (It) has a hilt of brilliants. He calls it a sword of peace. I also saw the letter which accompanied it, which was very flattering".

Sir James was most anxious for a peerage, and we are told that he "shewed me the Duke of Wellington's letters to him, so that I cannot imagine that they can refuse to give him one". But some sharp correspondence passed between Saumarez and the Duke on the subject, which was "perfectly bearish and betrayed jealousy". But in 1831 the peerage was announced, and Saumarez was presented as a Baron at the Coronation Drawing Room, where "he appeared greatly delighted and in capital spirits". A tale is told about the granting of this peerage: "When Earl Grey made his batch of peers, the name of Sir James Saumarez appeared on the list . . . . The King said: 'What has he done?' 'He drowned a lot of men in the Baltic'. Captain Seymour, then Master of the Robes, was told this . . . . 'That is not correct, Lord Grey. Sir James had nothing to do with the loss of the line of battle ships. Grenville wrote the order for them to remain until December'. 'Then tell that to the King. You are a sailor; he will believe you . . . .' When the King told him Lord Grey wished to make Saumarez a peer, 'Why not, Your Majesty? He has seen more shots fired than any man in the navy, and has commanded and won a victory'. 'But he lost those men in the Baltic'. Seymour denied it . . . . They had a three hours discussion, when Seymour said: 'It will be a great honour to the Channel Islands. They will like it'. 'Ah, aye, and do you think the navy will like it?' 'On my honour they will' ''. Thus was the peerage won.

Sir John's friendship with the Bishop of Winchester has already been mentioned, and frequent were his visits to Farnham Castle and to Winchester House in London. The Bishop's eldest son, it will be remembered, married Mary Le Couteur; and a younger son married Mary Heywood, revered as the founder of the Mothers' Union. The Bishop's elder brother was Archbishop of Canterbury, and a deep devotion existed between the eminent brothers. We meet the Archbishop at a Sumner family party in 1857, looking remarkably well . . . .: "His spirits are most cheerful and his conversation most attractive and smooth, at times quite playful. Benevolence is his true characteristic . . . . He enquired . . . . in the most feeling manner after the health of the Bishop of Exeter, who used him despitefully last year . . . . It is a remarkable sight to see these two . . . . in so remarkable positions . . . . so brotherly and affectionate".

1. Jean Bernadotte (1764-1844), King of Sweden and Norway.

So many more famous names pass across these pages that one cannot discuss them all: Statesmen, Generals, Admirals, Peers of the Realm, Members of Parliament, Prelates, Doctors: all the élite of those days; and Sir John found it exhilarating to meet and converse with them. But in many ways the most stimulating event in his varied career was his election as a Fellow of the Royal Society, the chief of all learned societies in the land, fellowship of which is coveted by all who have made contributions to scientific knowledge. How did this come about? Let us see what clues the diaries give, and then trace the contacts with a few of the most famous Fellows with whom Sir John became friendly. On 25th January 1843 he was taken to the Society's rooms by Sir Marc Isambard Brunel (1769-1849) to hear a lecture on "polarisation of light and prismatic colours: too deep for me, and long enough to give a nap to several of the members. At this meeting Captain Belcher, R.N., a Surveyor, was declared not elected, "not a very pleasing prospect for myself, whom Sir Isambard, Mr. Tupper and other friends wish to become an F.R.S. Sir Isambard said: 'Bah, bah, that is nothing. You will be elected' . . . . The conversatzione is very amusing and intellectual . . . . Sir Isambard in leaving said: 'It is a singular fact that when I came from America in 1799, a poor unknown foreigner, I drove to this place, Somerset House, not in a cab (there were none in those days) but in a hackney coach, to find the brother of my future wife, who was an Under Secretary in the Admiralty Office . . . . I little thought then that I should have the honour of sitting in the chair of Newton, and being the first foreigner who was elected President of the Royal Academy[1]". He went on to describe how his wife, known as La belle Anglaise, had gone to France to learn French at the age of 16, was imprisoned by Robespierre and remained there for a year. Her family disliked the idea of her marrying a Frenchman, and he fled to America and worked there for six years, and returned to claim the hand of his first love, married her, and 'all has gone on well since' ".

Turning to the subject of a Thames tunnel, this remarkable man said: "It is more difficult to construct a tunnel under the Thames than a bridge over it . . . . I will tell you what first gave me the idea of the shield, without which the attempt to sink a tunnel would have been hopeless. I was in the dockyard at Portsmouth, about my block machinery, when I accidentally saw a piece of oak, black and decomposed. It was full of perforations, the work of the *Teredo navalis* (ship-worm). I thought it was strange how this little creature should proceed and not be drowned, when I perceived that its instinct led it to form a shield to work, as it were, in compartments, to enable it to exclude the water. It instantly occurred to me that with such a provision a tunnel under a river could be constructed".

Sir John continued: "He kindly urged me to banish any fears about being elected a member of the Royal Society. I assured him that I considered it to be a singular honour that so great a philosopher should condescend to second me; and that I would procure all the little essays I had written and submit them to him". In spite of this diary entry, Brunel's signature is not amongst those on Sir John's nomination paper, the list being headed by the Duke of Richmond[2] and Mr. Pusey[3]. The diary goes on: "It may do honour to Jersey, if not to the individual. Allons. Nous verrons, en tremblant". On 15th February 1843: "Received as F.R.S. at 8 p.m. Marquis of Northampton in the chair". Later in the

---

1. This may refer to the French Académie des Sciences to which Newton was elected in 1699.
2. The fifth Duke (1791-1860), President of the Royal Agricultural Society in succession to Lord Spencer.
3. Philip Pusey (1799-1855), eminent agriculturist.

year he attended a meeting under the same chairman, seeing there "the Bishop of Norwich, Colonel Sabine[1] and the room full of savants, some of whom distressed me by chatting while Professor Faraday's[2] report on the analysis of a ray of light was being read. It was too elaborate for common minds". In 1862 he was able to vote by post for the President, officers and council, Major General Edward Sabine, R.A., D.C.L., L.L.D'., being elected President. In 1870 he attended the closing meeting of the season: "My dear friend the President, Sir Edward Sabine, recognised me so warmly at the doorway . . . ., and introduced me to Admiral Ommaney[3], by whom I sat in the front row. The President took the chair . . . ., and the newly elected fellows were severally brought up by their godfather and congratulated . . . . Lord Rosse[4], a fine tall, aristocratic young man, about 28, explained his own papers on the heat of the moon and sun very neatly, and was much applauded . . . . Admiral O. whispered to me that the Doctors were getting in numbers into the R.S., and they found it gave them weight".

The next year he attended again: "I made a point to be punctual in my attendance on my early friend and chief Sir Edward Sabine who had a learned staff of constellations in a semi circle behind him. He shook my hand kindly and said: 'It is a long while since we first met. I am intensely happy to see you here': and made way for the three or four hundred savants who were streaming in to be presented. Four other rooms were open to us, to view new experimental machines, telegraphs, spectrums, photographs etc. The House of Commons could not show forth the same amount of learning and talent". The subscription during those years was £4 annually, high indeed, allowing for the value of money at that time. Sir John had first met and admired Sabine in the Canadian war in 1813, the diaries recording: "Dispatched under Captain Sabine's orders to assist him in setting up telegraphs from the islands to Kingston and Point Frederic. A most delightful, amiable companion". A little later, after a skirmish: "We found our excellent friend Captain Sabine. He gave us a hearty welcome, a capital dinner and a bottle of port, a luxury we had not enjoyed for a length of time".

The diaries never tell us in so many words on what grounds Sir John obtained his Fellowship of the Royal Society, but as early as 1835 he had written to the President of the Board of Agriculture: "I am preparing a short minute or essay on my mode of obtaining pure crops of wheat, for the Royal Society": and in a later chapter it will become apparent that he was accorded this honour for his pioneering work in agriculture. The exhibition of his wheat specimens at the Crystal Palace later on was a logical outcome of his researches.

A fellow, and President of the Society whom he knew well was the eminent surgeon Sir Benjamin Collin Brodie (1783-1862), to whom he had come also as a patient in 1830: "Called on Mr. Brodie, a mild, gentlemanly little man, and explained to him the nature of my headaches . . . . He asked me to be cupped, and to lose 10 ounces of blood . . . ., and to drink no wine at all". A few days later, there being no improvement, "he told me I must have a blister on . . . ., and to go on with the mercurial pills". Later still, he was told to go into the country in order to wash his head, "but not to take a shower bath, and 'Mind your diet' ". Brodie was in attendance on King George IV at this time, and

1. Sir Edward Sabine (1788-1883), astronomer and physicist.   2. Michael Faraday (1791-1867), physicist.
3. Admiral Sir John Ackworth Ommaney (1773-1858), whose daughter Anne married Thomas Pipon of La Moie.
4.   ? William Parson, third Earl of Rosse (1800-1867), astronomer: the suggested age does not agree with this identification.

said that for many days beforehand the doctors had known he would not last much longer. Sir John did not always agree with his friend's pronouncements: "Sir B. Brodie told a party of gentlemen where Mr. McN. was dining that there was more gluten in the bran than in the meal of wheat, and that therefore bread made of bran and all was the most nutritious. Was he dreaming?" Or was Sir John, on this occasion, quite wrong?

Before his election to the Royal Society, Sir John had become, in 1838, a Fellow of the Society of Arts, later the Royal Society of Arts, "for the encouragement", he wrote, "of the Arts, manufacture and commerce, which has already given such an impulse to the various branches of industry": and he assured them of his support for their admirable objectives. They seem to have become muddled about his name, and in 1856 he wrote to say that while he did not really mind being addressed as William Martin Le Couteur on paper wrappers, he would like his name correctly given in the list of members. In 1862 he proposed as Fellow Edward Mourant of Samarès Manor, who was duly elected. Notices announcing meetings tended to reach Jersey only on the previous day, which he thought "a case of double mortification, because it precludes the possibility of my personal attendance, or of my availing myself of the privilege to admit a friend to the evening lectures". He offered to propose a resolution for arranging this in the interests of members living far afield. One day he attended a lecture "on the new screen breakwater, very ingenious but not practical". His book on wheat, he noted, was to be "taken into consideration by the Society of Arts".

Brunel once took him to a meeting of the Humane Society, with Lord John Russell in the chair. For some reason undivulged, host and guest diverted themselves by weighing each other, and the verdict on Brunel was: "He weighed 166 lbs without his hat, and noted it in his pocket book. Weighed and not found wanting by me!"

A rewarding contact he made in these palmy days was with Mr. Whitbread, "son of the great brewer, a friend of Charles J. Fox, who is on a visit to Mr. King. A very pleasant superior man, ten years in Parliament himself, and his son there now". This meeting was in Jersey. A few days later "Mr. Whitbread and Mr. King came to breakfast here, walked round the grounds; took them round the prison, with which he was much pleased . . . . Mr. Whitbread a good astronomer". He renewed the acquaintance later that year, 1854, in London: "I dined with Mr. and Mrs. Whitbread, 22 Eaton Street. I was punctual, which they ascribed to military habits. Mr. W. told me who were the party to be: the Duchess of Inverness, ex Lady Buggin or the Duke of Sussex' Widow, Lord and Lady Dacre, Sir Hamilton and Lady Seymour, the ex-Ambassador to Russia[1], and Miss S., a love. I was to hand out Lady S., sister to Mrs. Whitbread, who he said was a very agreeable person. Mr. F. C. Russell, M.P., a pleasant man: Lord Thynne, a man in mustachios, his two sons, and a daughter on a fine scale. They kindly named them, that I might know the party. I took down Lady S., a very delightful person. She was all in all at one time with the Emperor of Russia. He was most kind and attentive to her. The habits, manners and living, even the language, was mostly French. The Emperor had, however, urged the cultivation of the Russian language, and founded a fine college for young ladies and governesses. The duplicity and disregard to truth was amazing . . . . The Duchess of Inverness is very lively, enjoys life thoroughly. The 21st Lord Dacre is not the most talkative peer in the realm. Mr. Russell, M.P., an old Foot Guardsman, a very nice person. Mr.

1. Sir Hamilton Seymour (1797-1880); appointed Ambassador at St. Petersburg, 1851.

Whitbread's table is quite 'comme il faut'. Lady Dacre had to walk home. She would not be set down by anyone".

A little later he was invited to dine with Mr. Whitbread at the London Tavern in Bishopsgate Street at 6.15, and to ask for the Brewers' Room. He arrived "at the hour, and found Mr. Whitbread and Sir Hamilton Seymour there . . . . We were 27. About 7 dinner was announced. The room is a beautiful one, and was resplendent with light and a table covered with gold plate. Four angles of the room were ornamented with gold shields and plateaux, of regal splendour. The dinner: thick and thin turtle soup, various sorts of fish, Gloster salmon, Thames trout, whitebait plain and devilled, venison, turtle pastry: in short every delicious French and English (dish). East India madeira, Queen Adelaide's sherry, Louis Philippe's champagne, hock, burgundy etc. "One cannot resist the feeling that they overdid it. "I replied to the toast of the army and navy, assuring them as an old soldier who had seen service in America that our army never was in a more efficient state than now: that competent judges declared the navy to be equally so: that with two such services, and the martial spirit of Britons, they might rely on them to maintain their ancient fame.

"Sir Hamilton Seymour gave us a very full and frank account of his mission in Russia, and heartily abused the Emperor, whose bad faith he fully exposed. We came home together. I told him the country gave him great credit for the discretion and firmness he had shown".

The following day "Mr. Whitbread took me to call on the Speaker, Mr. J. Le Fèvre[1]. He has two houses in one. His reception room is beautiful and spacious. He is a very fine man, very courteous and fine looking, six foot two at least. Told us he was glad the Government were beat last night, on the schools and colleges question, as he was a Wykehamist and wishes the schools and colleges to be continued".

Next year "I called at Mr. Whitbread's brewery in Chiswick St., Finsbury Sq. . . . ., he took me to the Apothecaries Hall to see Mr. Warington's vivarium. He is the Director there, a very nice person. He has had his fish and actinae in their glass cases these last six years, since 1849, without shifting the water; merely create the sea water, adding a little distilled or rain water to replace the evaporation. He covers the ponds, which are about a foot to two feet deep, with green coloured glass in order to keep them cool, and to give the water the quiet colour of the sea . . . . The sea snails and shells, such as we have in Jersey, are good scavengers: so are the molluscs which are found among oysters in deep water".

As he wandered around London sightseeing in 1855, he said: "I was strolling in the morning round Smithfield market, when I came upon the Old Jerusalem Coffee House or tavern, which is the scene of Garrick's first essay or play as an actor in London. The hall of the tavern is over the archway of St. John's Gate, Clerkenwell, a square room rudely ornamented with armour, and bearings of a club calling itself the Knights of St. John. I got a couple of nice mutton chops and some excellent ale in the hall, and was shown the room in the tavern in which Dr. Johnson, and all the great wits of that day, used to keep the table in a roar".

There is one celebrity of the Victorian age, known to Sir John, who was actually of Jersey origin, but achieved a fame which ran far beyond the Island's shores. She was the

---

1. Probably C. S. Le Fèvre, admitted to Winchester College 1806, Speaker 1839, 1841, 1847

famous beauty, Lillie Langtry, daughter of Dean Le Breton. We meet her first when she was only ten, in a diary mention of "Mrs. Dean Le Breton and her pretty little girl". By 1866 she was showing a touch of wildness, which led to a riding accident, and the diary remarks: "Called to hear how the Dean's daughter was. Imprudent to allow a girl of 13 to ride a racer with a snaffle". Next year her exceptional looks again secure her the complimentary adjective: "To call the Dean this morning at 11, to proceed to examine the lads at the Industrial School in St. Martins for my annual prize. Mrs. Le Breton and Lilly, their pretty girl of 13 or 14, came with the Dean": and later on: "Took Mrs. Dean and pretty Lilly to their dresssmaker", and finally, in 1874: "paid an engagement visit to Miss Le Breton, the Dean, Mrs. Le Breton and Mr. Langtree". Sir John was unorthodox in his spelling of Lillie and Langtry, but followed the rest of mankind in sincerely admiring her beauty.

You may draw from this recital an impression of a popular man who was always away in England, enjoying the city lights and the luxury of house-parties in the country. Sir John, in fact, went to the mainland for one of three reasons: to attend functions as Royal A.D.C.: to further Jersey interests in matters concerning the Militia, agriculture or the work of the Vicomte's office: and, an item he always squeezed in if he could, to visit his daughter and her children in Hampshire, where he was always welcome, and always happy. But I have wished, as I have followed his pen over the endless pages, that Harriet had sometimes been there to share the thrills and excitement of it all. Perhaps she preferred to remain at Belle Vue. This is a private matter and none of our business. There are hints that he, too, wished she would accompany him oftener.

CHAPTER TEN

SOJOURNERS IN THE ISLAND

It is time now to return to Jersey and take a look at its successive Governors, and other people of importance who came here during the period covered by these archives; and the impression they made on a man who was working with or under them. But let us first examine the arena in which they gave their performances, the small Island of Jersey, and the conditions then obtaining in it.

In 1847, at the request of Captain Martin White, R.N., Sir John wrote an account of the Island, in which he said: ". . . . The arable land is excellent and of great depth . . . . Some portions of the uplands have the appearance of moors, being composed of black soil. One district to the westwards is a range of sandhills, of considerable elevation, over St. Ouen's Bay, now being reclaimed and successfully brought into cultivation of lucerne . . . .

"Some learned persons have insisted that they discern two races to this day, the black eyed, dark haired and bright eyed brunette look of the Norman; from the grey or blue eyed, light haired fair complexioned maid of the Celtic or Saxon (race) . . . . By the census taken in 1831 the population was 36,582 souls, being an increase of nearly 8000 in the preceding ten years, the increase having been steady and progressive since the use of steam power[1]. In 1841 the census taken was 47,556. Of these 33,784 are indigenous, with 11,000 being natives of Great Britain and Ireland. The number of inhabited houses was 4090. The most surprising increase has taken place, however, in the capital of St. Helier . . . .

"The average crop of wheat is about thirty bushels to the acre, of very fine and pure sorts . . . . Apples are in great cultivation for cider, and the average produce may be twenty hogsheads per acre . . . . Potatoes are a great staple produce of Jersey, the crops which were raised previous to the potato disease having reached thirty tons to the acre . . . .[2]"

"In 1824 weekly intercourse by steam was established between the mother country and the Channel Islands. From this period a rapid increase in population, wealth and trade is perceivable. In 1830 there were 200 vessels belonging to Jersey . . . . In 1843 the general commerce had more than doubled. Several fine vessels are on the stocks and a steady augmentation is anticipated. Piers at St. Helier, St. Aubin, Gorey, Rozel and Bouley Bay, all of them, however, dry at low water spring tide, have been constructed, suitable to the wants of the smaller trade but unfit . . . . for large ships . . . . It is to be hoped that the noble harbour of refuge at St. Catherine's Bay, which is now in progress and has already reached the base of La Pierre Mouillée (where there is a perfect shelter from every wind but the south-east, and twenty feet of water in the lowest spring tides), may speedily afford protection to a large class of merchantmen that should not take the ground. Here indeed may be a magnificent port of entrepôt, where deeply laden vessels may lie in safety with a constant fair wind to run, south-westerly winds prevailing in Jersey nine months

---

1. Sic.   2. See Chapter 16.

out of the twelve, according to the statement of Captain Martin White, the Surveyor of the Channel . . . .

"The Protestant faith is universal among the inhabitants, not a single Roman Catholic family being of Jersey origin. The people of Jersey, taken as a whole, are highly religious, fully observant of the sabbath and of the decencies of religion, industrious and moral".

In 1838 he had written to General Sir W. Thornton, a previous Lieutenant Governor: ". . . . Jersey is pretty much in the state you left it, never quiet, always an intestine war, the parties cordially detesting each other as much as ever. Sir John de Veulle has made peace with the Godfrays and D'Avranches, who is Lieutenant Bailli, which in some measure must make his situation pleasanter. But Le Breton and the Bailli are still as distant as ever.

"Your offspring the Agricultural Society, of which I am the President this year, still flourishes, increasing daily in utility and support. It always thinks of you with regard and respect. The cattle are wonderfully improved in form and beauty, and of course in price. The farms also mend in cleanliness and appearance, and the vegetable market is now superb".

Some years later he wrote to an old friend, Major General Arthur, Governor of Upper Canada: ". . . . trade, that disturber of the tranquil retirement of man, with its giant infant steam, has converted the rural and pastoral simplicity of Jersey. All this has vanished before the formal but useful rules of McAdam, our vallies being cut up into wide roads carrying constant traffic on them. The old families are dwindling away owing to the law of gavelkind, and new ones occupy their houses. Our Jersey fortunes, which were ample for our own wants while the intercourse with England was occasional, are insufficient for the same style of living when ten thousand gentry visit us in the summer, and half as many make this an occasional residence to nurse their fortunes in. Keep therefore in your recollection its early unadorned beauties".

In fact, in the middle of the 19th century, Jersey was a land where every prospect pleased, and only man's enmities were vile. As he wrote to Jeune, when congratulating him on elevation to the bishopric of Peterborough: "Little Jersey, with all its political agitations, is looking very pretty. Would that the feelings of all were in harmony with the beauties of this lovely and beloved Island".

Let us now make the acquaintance of the Lieutenant Governors whom Sir John knew. In 1825 he became A.D.C. to Sir Colin Halkett[1]. At that time the present Government House, Belmont was a new acquisition, Mathieu Amiraux having exchanged it with government for the previous Government House, situated where Woolworth's store now is in King Street. Amiraux had bought it a few years previously from Sir John's father-in-law Francis Janvrin, which explains the following entry: "Called on the General. He showed me into the small boudoir upstairs where they had been obliged to take down the chimney piece, as the smoke had nearly dried all the woodwork to a cinder. The masonry behind it was shamefully done, although my father-in-law had spent so many thousands upon the house". The Lieutenant Governor was not provided with furniture and had to supply his own, at a cost in those days of about £2000. Soon after this "Lady Halkett told us in confidence that Sir Colin was to be removed, and General Thornton to have Jersey. She bears it very well indeed. The folks here will soon repent of losing so kind a

---

1. Sir Colin Halkett (1774-1856). Served in the Peninsula and at Waterloo.

Belmont. (Government House, Jersey).

governor as he has proved". Sir Colin was well thought of in high circles. The papers quote Lord Hopetoun as saying to Lord Hill that "Sir Colin deserved anything the Government could give him. He had seen many men in service . . . ., but never one who could lead a troop on as Halkett did". When Sir Colin appealed for help to Lord Fitzroy Somerset, saying "I am a poor man with a large family, and look up to you to befriend me", Lord Fitzroy replied: "Pooh, nonsense, man. Don't look up to me; look to your services; they will get you anything". Halkett and his wife were gay and convivial spirits, and good dancers, and in an interview with the King, Sir John described him as "rather an expensive man; and I know he thought it to be his duty to keep up a certain appearance and see a good deal of company, which there is in Jersey from the influx of strangers". Though very friendly with Sir John, Halkett never allowed his children to visit Belle Vue, which hurt the Le Couteurs deeply. The diary makes this final mention of the Halketts on the eve of their departure: "Lady Halkett appeared low. He is in very good spirits, and is in treaty for a house at Southampton for £2400, which they are to furnish from Government House. They think General Thornton very shabby at not taking their furniture in the drawing room, which is quite new. But he writes to them he means to hire furniture, a cheap plan with a vengeance".

Major General Thornton arrived in 1830. Sir John, who had discussed local affairs with him previously in London, wrote: "We shall find him a clever, intelligent person, I suspect, besides being a thorough man of business". On arrival, "The General was received by Touzel, Tom Le Breton and the flank company of the Town Regiment, all in state, to contrast their neglect of the worthy Sir Colin. The General landed in full uniform and looked well". He left again in 1835, and there is little about him in the papers, except a hint that his term of office was marred by political controversy. This comes in a letter Sir John wrote him in 1836, in which he said he felt that Thornton was far happier away from the petty party strife, "the absolute curse of this Island", and added: "You are too honest in your purposes for most men". The only other crumb of information about him is that he got his swords from Messrs. Tathams near the Horse Guards, and used Russini's

J

tooth powder; for both items appear in a list of shopping Sir John did in London for friends in Jersey.

We are deprived of his impressions of the next Lieutenant Governor, General Campbell, by the absence of diaries for the period, but in a letter he said: "General Campbell has steered clear till now and is well with us all, but his day of trial is not distant, and I dare say the impartial straight forward course he will take will be the signal for a declaration of war from some". The diary of Mrs. Le Couteur, senior, for 10th May 1838, says: "General Campbell died of dropsy". It is generally thought that his death was hastened by a cold caught during the revolt of the oyster fishermen at Gorey.

Then came Sir Edward Gibbs, sworn in in 1838, whose term of office was overshadowed by illness. In 1843 Sir John wrote: "Called on Sir Edward. He leaves on Monday for six weeks or two months. Will he ever return?" He did, and seemed very well, and soon afterwards was "in trouble for a coachman, his young fellow being on passage to Buffalo as a settler amongst the Yankees". Then his servant Tellis was assaulted by one Le Breton, and his eye much injured, though it transpired that Tellis had spent the evening in "a pot house in the Trooper's Yard (near Queen Street), where he ought not to have been ".Gibbs gave a dinner party for the Bishop and Mrs. Sumner and various military officers, "a capital party, with a gentlemanly regard for the clergy present". When Queen Victoria came in 1846 poor Sir Edward was too ill to receive her, and Sir John explained that he was "a fine old officer who has been severely wounded on many occasions. He was wounded at the storming of Badajos, and is in high favour with the Duke of Wellington". In 1847 he had a sale of cattle which "went off well", and the diary records that he was "determined to go nowhere but to Poingdestres", the owners of Grainville Manor, to whom he was related. The owner at that time was named after him, Edward Gibbs Poingdestre. A little time later he "had another attack of apoplexy . . . ., and is in a dying condition so Dr. Dickson told me". Two days later he died just after the arrival of his successor. Sir John attended his funeral: "There were 27 carriages . . . . I commanded the battalion of flankers . . . ., Colonel Dixon, I and James Hammond on the left; Sir John de Veulle and James Robin (on the right). There was a great concourse to see the fine old soldier committed to the vault of the Poingdestres".

Sir James Reynett became Lieutenant Governor in 1847. "I called on him and found him to be an old acquaintance . . . . He is a very courteous nice person . . . . He seems to be a young man for so high a place of trust". He announced that he did not intend to be present at States sessions usually, though there might be occasions when he should do so. There was a question of raising a storey on Government House, but he decided to "play it safe". In contrast with some other Governors he was "a quiet tempered man". The Reynetts often went to Belle Vue. One day when he called at Government House, Sir John was told that Admiral Sir Charles Ogle and party were on their way to his house; whereupon the practical host drove to town and "got chickens, chops and fruit; drove off home; prepared lunch; when the fine old warrior soon came, with Mrs. Ogle, his daughter and son-in-law, Lieutenant Cochrane, Flags, and Captain Dumaresq. Had a very long conference on the defences . . . . Louis Philippe told him that it was a horrible crime in two great nations like England and France to engage in war. He had personally, by his own influence, prevented a war and while he lived none should ever take place between them. The feeling in France, however, was that as soon as he died a casus belli would be sought and a blow struck at England". Reynett made improvements in Government House gardens, but did not "intend to remain here after his five years". He seems to have been averse to early rising, and an unpunctual man, for at a militia review he "was to have been on the ground by 3, and the men stood broiling in the sun till 4, and I made sure he would not come". But come he did, attended by his staff, and was delighted with the review. During this period the Port Admiral, Sir Bladen Capel, with his Lady, visited the Island and went out to Belle Vue where they were shown over the gardens and admired the cows. Next day there was a dinner for them at Government House. Reynett was executor to the Duke of Cambridge's [1] will, and was much distressed at being unable to arrive in time for the Duke's funeral in 1850. He soon gave up this function, as Prince George of Cambridge was of age and no longer needed executors to assist him. He was given a snuff-box used by the deceased and appointed Deputy Ranger of Richmond Park by the new Duke. His time in Jersey was drawing to a close and he appeared "to be sorry to give up his government". The diary comments: "Whatever relaxation he may have shown in the militia, he wishes well to Jersey, and I am sure will live in the grateful recollection of the people of this Island hereafter, by having founded the College". The diary also compares him, to his advantage, with his successor: "Wonderful contrasts between them. One never speaks of his acts: and the other tells them all". Lady Reynett was evidently a woman of sense and talent. She and her two daughters all drew and painted well. The family remained in Jersey for some time after retirement, moving on to Brighton and finally London. Sir John always kept up with them and visited them when he went to England.

General Love, gazetted as the next Lieutenant Governor in 1852, entered office with a setback, "the loss of the vessel which he had freighted at Carmarthen with his luggage and furniture. He bore it admirably. So did Mrs. Love. They showed me the insurance for £1000 which only half covers them". He was said to be "as minute in his inspection as General Thornton was". Sir John was much in contact with him over militia affairs. "On Gallows Hill with General Love. The highest ground should be occupied by a low fort with sunken ditches, so as to be tenable against an escalade. Approves of the site for the (Town) Arsenal and drill ground up to Blandy's road". When reporting to him about militia defaulters, Sir John said the problem would never be solved until there was a new militia law, to which Love replied that the worse it got, the sooner should we obtain the new law. He showed Sir John correspondence he had received, and his reply, "which was quite to the point, though a little rambling for want of stops [2]". He seems to have had a weekly levée for men, but often failed to attend it or give notice of his intention to be absent. Nor was he the soul of discretion: "At the General's levée I told him how completely Lord Aberdeen had cleared Prince Albert . . . ., as the Duke of Wellington had proposed to him to succeed himself as Commander in Chief, which the Prince gave him good and cogent reasons for declining. The General, before Fraser and Gardner, said it was a libel on the Duke; that Lord Aberdeen and Lord J. Russell were l(iars) and not to be believed; the P(rince) has grasped at everything and interfered everywhere . . . . He was very indiscreet to say all that before two other persons, and much more that I could not commit to paper". At the outbreak of the Crimean War in 1854 he expected to be recalled for active service, but Sir John calculated his age as 65, "too old to have hard work of that sort". In London,

1. Tenth child of George III.
2. The typist here remarks: "A failing not unknown in the writings of Sir John himself, and of his son".

Sir John was asked by General Yorke "how old Love was getting on, and if he could ride yet", to which he replied that Love disliked being thought old, and rode everywhere; and Yorke retorted: "Wants a strong horse. Would like to have had a division in Turkey, not a brigade". In 1856 Love received the Order of the Bath and became Sir Frederick Love. He took an interest in farming, and went to Belle Vue to see the cows and Sir John's farming enterprises. Shortly before giving up his command he was distressed by a libel, which he showed to Sir John, saying: "This has been shoved under the doors of houses in St. Helier". It was "an unsigned paper, printed here no doubt . . . . a dialogue between the Emperor Napoleon III and General Love, in which the Emperor is made to thank him for banishing the French refugees from Jersey by an arbitrary act of power". It went on to suggest that Love was prepared to hand Jersey over to France for a million pounds. The Attorney General had advised him to prosecute the Editor of the paper concerned. Sir John, on the contrary, strongly advised him to ignore the whole affair, which he agreed to do. In 1856 Love heard that he had been made Colonel of the 56th[1], and on New Year's Day 1857 he held his last Jersey levée, "numerously attended . . . ., his appointment to the camp at Shorncliffe being certain". The Colonels of Militia presented him with an address, written by Sir John, and on hearing that he was doing this, Love "desired me to write the rough draft of a reply. As I had written the address, I could best do it". One of the Colonels refused to sign the address, at which Love "was in high dudgeon".

When the next Lieutenant Governor, Major General Mundy, arrived the "packet was decorated with flags". But his reign was a sad one, clouded by illness and closed by death. On first meeting "I was much pleased by several remarks of our future Governor. He is a very travelled man, who had roughed it in Australia . . . . His wife is a botanist". At the quayside he "dispensed with the band, guard of honour and mob, and did not land until they had retired". He said he was leaving all the management of house and garden to his wife, and wished she would take on the horses too, which Sir John remarked was the first time he had ever heard of a soldier giving up his horses to anyone. He was obviously tired out. He complained that nobody had told him he had a pew in St. Helier's Church, when in fact he had "a very nice one, a seat of State, just opposite to the pulpit". Mrs. Mundy sounds a lively creature, enthusiastic in her garden and, in 1858, "in great glee at having got eleven prizes" in a show. She showed Sir John "an ugly cow which Le Bas had sent her for £15. She had a hideous claw, was cat-hammed, with a head like a fiddle . . . . I said she was unfit for Government House grounds, so she sent her back and ordered a pretty cow". In the fullness of time the pretty cow calved a bull calf, which Mrs. Mundy presented to Sir John, and he named it "Governor". It was "of a brown red colour, with a white star on his forehead, and prettily spotted". In 1860 poor Mundy became ill, and after a trip to consult London doctors Mrs. Mundy "imparted in confidence that she thought the General would never return here. The doctor said the climate of Jersey did not suit his constitution, and he must have an entire change of air". A week later he was dead. The diary's epitaph reads: "a kind amiable fine-toned mind he possessed; over-anxious to discharge his duties, and long since feeling unequal to the task he felt he ought to do. A friend to Jersey, lost among the selfish, unpatriotic, worthless men he often had to deal with. He is a real loss to Jersey, and in him I am sure we have lost a true friend".

His widow stayed on in Government House for a while after the arrival of her husband's

1. The Essex Regiment.

successor, General Douglas, in accordance with a decision that she should not be pressed to leave. The Douglases arrived on 18th September 1860 after a boisterous passage, both looking rather ill, and were met with a salute from Elizabeth Castle and a guard of honour. "He was pleased with the appointment, liked Government House, though the stables were bad and not well drained . . . . would buy furniture from Mrs. Mundy and bring over some of his own". He decided to rent a house for a while, and Sir John, being charged to find one for him, "went to see Blythe's house in St. Saviour's Crescent. It is badly furnished and too small for the Douglas family". After seeing others which would not do, he chose "Theshie's Belgrave House[1]. It is very well furnished, and a thoroughly good house . . . . He asks £35 for the three months, including stable and coach house". On being sworn in General Douglas read his declaration in French, with a remarkably pure accent. On the death of his father, Sir Howard Douglas, in 1862, he inherited a baronetcy, and the next year, after a very short tenure of office in Jersey, he was appointed Governor of the Cape of Good Hope. The diary notes regretfully, "He is popular with the English and lower classes of Jersey; not so with the States and Militia officers . . . . I could not prevail on them to give him a dinner . . . . Personally I regret his departure. An honest, straight forward, earnest man".

It sounds as though, a century ago, it was difficult to be both an efficient and popular Lieutenant Governor of Jersey.

General Burke Cuppage, with wife and two daughters, arrived to take up his post on 22nd October 1863. A contemporary of Sir John's, they had been at Marlowe together in 1812. There was the usual wrangle about the value of the outgoing Governor's furniture, and Cuppage said "his means were not large, but he wished to see the Jersey gentry, those he was come to govern. He could not visit the great body of English gentry". In due course he complained that his salary was inadequate, that he had been promised £1500 a year, but the War Office had withdrawn £200 allowances, thus "cutting into his private fortune". One gets the impression that Cuppage was usually annoyed about something, and failed to establish a modus vivendi with the local hierarchy. But he had a genuine grievance about his A.D.C., Captain Lerrier Godfray, who was seeing more of his daughter Jane than Victorian propriety could tolerate. In 1866 Cuppage told Sir John "he was very sore about the anonymous abuse he was getting about Jane and Godfray . . . . People will talk. It will raise scandal when a handsome married man leaves his wife day after day to ride about with a girl". The tolerant Cuppage said: "Godfray lets her know when he has an arrest to make in the country. Then she rides for exercise to accompany him". The diary closes the episode with :"I heard with dismay from old Colonel Fraser that Lerrier Godfray has run away with Jane Cuppage. I was shocked, but not surprised. It was the talk of St. Helier. Just as I was coming away, the General gave me a letter of resignation as A.D.C. from Lerrier Godfray, which confirmed his villainy". Cuppage seems to have had no luck at all. In 1865 he had the passing gratification of presenting a Royal Humane Society medal to his only son, aged sixteen, for rescuing a soldier from drowning, but the poor boy died soon afterwards. Then Gardner, the Governor's secretary, a civil servant with long and blameless record, was found to have been embezzling £36 per annum over the past five years from the militia accounts. Advocate Vickery defended him for six hours before the full Court, the Attorney General replying for the Crown in 55 minutes. Gardner

---

1. In Great Union Road.

was found guilty and imprisoned in Jersey, being later moved to Millbank.

The unhappy Cuppage governorship closed in 1868, when Major General Guy took over. After the traditional arguments about furniture, it became clear that the new Lieutenant Governor was not interested in his farm and garden, and intended to let them both. His wife, a daughter of Admiral Plumridge, was much younger than he. But the diaries tell us little of them. By now Sir John was too old to take an active part or interest in what went on at Government House. The same applies to Guy's successor, General Norcott, but at least he had the distinction of being the last of a round dozen of Lieutenant Governors under whom Sir John served. This must surely be a record, and Norcott may have realised it, for he often deferred to Sir John in discussion of local affairs, and treated him as the father figure which by then he had become. There are photographs of Generals Cuppage and Norcott, if the labels are correct, at the Museum of La Société Jersiaise, but they bear an uncanny likeness, and their identification awaits further research.

Throughout history it has been the fate of Jersey, largely for geographical reasons, to be a haven for political refugees from many different lands, and plenty of them appear in these papers. In 1826, for example: "Sir Colin and Touzel specious and cautious about General Buriel the Spaniard. Commenced a collection for him": and again: "making a collection for General Buriel who commanded at Cadiz in 1823 and who is now here a banished man". During this period the fair land of France was rent by constant revolutions counter-revolutions and coups d'état, and Jersey heard about them at first hand from the refugees. In February 1848 Louis Philippe, the Citizen King, abdicated, and in conversation with a military friend Sir John had anticipated this. "We agreed that the Duc de Montpensier's folly in signing the order to assemble the artillery at Vincennes . . . . would be the downfall of Louis Philippe's dynasty, and that he might yet be seen living in retirement in England". Then: "Sad news from Paris. A fresh revolution. Louis Philippe is said to have abdicated on Tuesday. The Tuileries and Palace Royal sacked, and much bloodshed . . . . Everybody anxious about the exciting news from Paris. It is clear to me that the Phantom King, Le Comte de Paris, will never suit them. A republic will be their aim". This Comte de Paris was the grandson and heir of Louis Philippe. That same day, "as we were returning home last evening about 5, we saw a tall Frenchman with a night bag and small desk in his hand, who had just landed from the small Le Seelleur's cutter. He announced that a republic had been proclaimed but declined to give his name". The news was conveyed to the Lieutenant Governor through the Constable, and the next day it transpired that the stranger was General Le Fèvre, who was accompanied by another, younger man. "He told us that they had escaped on the morning the King had quitted the Tuileries. He has witnessed some fighting. The regular troops had behaved well; so did the municipal guards; but the national guards interposing between the two, and crying reform, destroyed the unity of action. I said he was extremely fortunate to have escaped, especially with a lady and children, whom the papers called 'illustrious'. He then asked me 'mon avis' on the safety of getting to England, whether the Wonder was safe . . . . 'But Sir', I said, 'since you ask my advice, as A.D.C. to the Queen of England, I feel that if these are really part of the royal children, the Queen of England herself would be deeply interested in their welfare; and as there is a man of war steamer in this station, if the Governor would spare her, she would be the vessel to take them over. Her Captain is my relative, and he would be proud to take them over if Sir James Reynett advised it . . . .' He said they were two gentlemen of La maison du Roi, who had confided these two precious children to their care, with their gouvernante, and it was of the highest concern that they should reach England in safety". The party turned out to be the Duc de Montpensier, fifth son of Louis Philippe, with the Duchesse de Nemours, wife of the second son, and her children.

Sir John offered them all aid, and invited them to Belle Vue where he said his wife would take the greatest care of the children. The Duchesse declined the invitation, but Montpensier, with the Comte Aymé, accepted. It was arranged that Captain Dumaresq of H.M.S. Cuckoo would take them from Gorey at midnight next day or at 2 a.m. the following morning. Sir John visited the royal lady and saw her two little boys, the Duc d'Alençon and the Comte d'Eu, aged 5 and 3, found playing in a basket at Polychinelle[1]. "She is a lovely young creature, about 22, with regular aquiline features, rather Roman, fine teeth, a very sweet smile, speaks slowly and very distinctly; large hazel eyes of great expression; light brown hair; fine taper hands; gentle yet royal manner". She thanked him for all his attentions and said she felt "quite happy at being in such a hospitable country and in such security". She told him of their journey from Dreux, where they left the King, to Granville where the Mayor had given them all passports. There they found passages on Captain Le Seelleur's boat. Sir John apologised for presuming to invite them to his house, not knowing their royal estate, and explained how he had discussed with the Governor who these royal visitors might be. A portrait of the Duc having been found, he was identified, and Sir John then realised that he had been talking to the son of a king in this familiar manner. This much amused the Duc and Duchesse. They were naturally most anxious for news of the King from England, but there was a fierce gale blowing and the packet was delayed. News came that Belgium was now in revolt, that King Leopold had escaped and gone to his house at Cleremont in Surrey. Speaking of the disorders, which of course were uppermost in their minds, the Duc said that his father saw it would take a civil war for him to retain his throne, and decided not to be responsible for shedding French blood. He had been the King of their choice, and the moment he ceased to be that he abdicated. They all felt they would infinitely rather become simple citizens than remain Princes at the price of blood. Sir John said the time would come when France would regret this change, the Duc replying that at the moment only a republic would satisfy France, essentially republican in spirit. They asked if such troubles were likely in England, and he replied that the English were not republican because they were liberals, even the radicals; although, he added, Lord John Russell's income tax had caused much discontent among the manufacturers of Birmingham and Manchester.

The royal visitors were staying at the Royal Yacht Hotel. As soon as Sir John heard of the safe arrival of the Duc de Nemours in England, he went to the hotel to inform the Duchesse, who ran to tell her boys that "dear Papa" was safe. On the night of their departure they dined with Captain Henry Dumaresq on board ship. Sir John was there, and took his butler William to help with the waiting. The two small boys were at table, and behaved "perfectly". There was roast beef and plum pudding, and the company "dined heartily in excellent spirits". The Duc said he had left his entire fortune behind, as a good citizen should, and that had his wife had no money they would have been on "le pavé". He thought Guizot[2] a wonderful man but uncompromising and stern, the finest orator in France.

1. Merry Andrew, or puppets.   2. François Guizot (1787-1874), Louis Philippe's Prime Minister.

He also spoke of Monsieur de Salvandy as "an able counsellor and friend of the King, Minister of Public Instruction". All ministers, he said, would have been sacrificed if the mob had got hold of them. At 3.30 they embarked, with the Governor, Sir John and Salvandy to see them off. Next day a vessel arrived from Granville reporting that all was quiet there, and that in future the suffrage was to be "anyone who can write". The day after the Courier came in with the news that the ex King and Queen and arrived safe in England, the King with the words: "Thank God I am safe on British soil": while "the honest John Bull farmers warmly congratulated him on his escape". Henry Dumaresq, on his return, reported that he had safely landed his passengers at Gosport, where the Admiral sent a state barge for them, and that they had "rewarded the sailors and servants in a princely manner".

Comte Narcisse Achille de Salvandy (1795-1856) was a distinguished politician and man of letters, who had held the posts of Ministre de l'Instruction Publique and Ambassador to Madrid. He did not follow Louis Philippe to England but settled for a time in Jersey, renting the house at No. 1 Caesarean Terrace in St. Saviour's Road, now known as Monaco. Salvandy Terrace in Springfield Road nearby is named after him. Sir John became very friendly with him and found him "a very interesting and able man". He recorded many of his opinions, for example: "He considers the dynasty of the Orleans defunct": and many of his statements about European events and personalities. Of Prince von Metternich, Austrian statesman (1773-1859) he said his "prevoyance was marvellous. In the year 1812, two years before Bonaparte's invasion of Russia, Metternich was sent to Paris as a special ambassador. He had a long conversation with the Emperor in private, and wrote to the Emperor of Austria stating that he did not consider the French empire would exist two years longer. It was not on a 'fondation stable'. He foresaw the elements of its dissolution . . . . I stated that it was known to us that Thiers[1] in 1840 or 1841 had meditated an attack on this Island. Though of course he could not acknowledge it, if he had known it officially, he did not deny it, and said that 'M. Thiers was a very able man, equal to any great combination . . . .' The pamphlet of the Prince de Joinville was very much disliked by the Government. It had given England alarm and made it arm. It had gained the Prince much popularity . . . . Madame de Salvandy would probably have to return to Paris to secure his property from being confiscated if possible. He did not intend to expatriate himself, but hoped for better times".

A few days later there was news of more unrest in Europe, and Salvandy considered "the news from Vienna as a revolution throughout the world; Austria paralysed in Italy; and the reaction to reach Russia, where the Nobles will rise". A little later he thought there would be "a reaction and a call for the monarchy from the Provinces". In spite of the disorder in France, his son Paul Salvandy was returning to the Collège Henri IV. In 1849 Salvandy was still in Jersey but "in very low spirits . . . .; sees little hope for a settlement in France . . . . His friends are to propose him as Deputy for the Seine Inférieure". In 1850 he gave a brief address to the Jersey Chamber of Commerce, expressing his gratitude for the Island's cordiality, kindness and hospitality, and saying that he would at all times be happy to render any service to Jersey, a place of safety and a refuge to the unfortunate. Dining at Belle Vue in this year, "he was very communicative. He thinks the socialist party very strong, and dangerous, because the two royalist parties will not unite". He

1. Louis Thiers, statesman (1797-1877).

continued cryptically that "the President is prudent and firm, but a liaison with an English woman is highly prejudicial to him. Lord N. visits her". In 1851 Sir John mused: "I wonder what Salvandy will say to my letter to him a month ago, that the people of France would stand by Louis Napoleon in preference to those who have never served them as he has done. What have the two branches of the Bourbons done since Louis Philippe's dethronement? Nothing but quarrel among themselves without a thought for France; and if they had been patriots, the younger should have given way for the elder branch, and their fusion would have re-established legitimacy. They deserve to perish; yet it is hard upon the little Comte de Paris".

In 1864, sixteen years after he had befriended the French royal family, he received a summons to visit the Duc de Montpensier in London, on the day before the wedding of the Duc's son, Le Comte de Paris. He found Kingston and Esher bedecked with flags and arches, and forty or fifty carriages on the lawn by the house. The house was Cleremont[1], originally built for Clive in about 1770 by Holland and Capability Brown. In 1816 it had been bought by the Crown for Princess Charlotte of Wales, who died there the following year, and it remained in possession of her husband Leopold, uncle of Queen Victoria and future King of the Belgians, until his death in 1865. He married the daughter of Louis Philippe, who lived at Cleremont from 1848 until his death in 1850. His widow and family, as we see, were still there in 1864.

The Duc came out and greeted Sir John in the most friendly manner: "Je n'ai pas oublié les services que vous m'avez rendus ainsi qu'à ma famille . . . . Votre charmante île, prospère t'elle toujours? C'était au Mont Orgueil que je vous ai quitté". He then led Sir John to an inner room "full of elegantly dressed ladies, standing in a crescent from the door to where the venerable Queen[2] was seated in an arm chair. The Queen graciously said: 'Je suis charmée de vous reçevoir ici, Monsieur le Colonel, et de vous témoigner ma reconnaissance pour les services essentiels que vous avez rendus à mes enfants lors qu'ils étaient a Jersey'". He replied with an elegant speech in French, and was then presented to the Duc de Nemours[3], who was still mourning the sudden death of his beautiful Duchesse, whom Sir John had met in Jersey. The two little boys he remembered, the Duc d'Alençon and Comte d'Eu, who by then were "fine young men", also conversed with him. Montpensier then presented him to the Infanta his wife. She was the Infante Marie Luisa, sister of the Queen of Spain, who between them created "the Spanish Marriage Question". "She is a pretty, slight person, a brunette. The Duc also introduced me to his very pretty daughter. She is only sixteen, to be married to the Comte de Paris tomorrow. Her figure is slight and elegant. On my offering my felicitations on her approaching marriage she curtsied and thanked me with a sweet smile. The Prince de Joinville also came and thanked me for my attentions to 'sa famille' ". They invited him to the wedding breakfast next day, and when he asked if he should wear uniform he was told: "Non, non, en habit noir, costume du soir, pantalons noir".

Next day he left London in the morning and "when I got near Kingston the road was thronged with vehicles . . . . At Kingston Chapel (Roman Catholic) the crowd of

1. "Henry Holland, his life and architecture", by Dorothy Stroud and "Georgian Houses" by Christopher Hussey.
2. Marie Amélie, daughter of Ferdinand of the Two Sicilies, widow of Louis Philippe.
3. Nemours, Joinville and Montpensier were the second, third and fifth sons of Louis Philippe.

people was amazing . . . . ; flags, arches, decorations ; Vive le Comte de Paris et la Comtesse
. . . . ; the school children, some hundreds of them, were marching with flags and a band . . . .
The lawn at Cleremont was literally covered with carriages; the hall full of expectant
gentry, Sir Edward Cust there ready to aid in marshalling the noblesse. When the royal
ceremony was over, the firing of cannon at Kingston announced that the bridal pair would
soon arrive . . . . The bride . . . . came up the steps under a salute of artillery, bands playing,
flowers strewn in her path and great cheering. She looked very pale, pretty, lovely I should
say, only sweet sixteen, her handsome tall husband six and twenty. About a quarter of
an hour later the Prince and Princess of Wales arrived, coming up under a salute and God
save the Queen. The Duc de Nemours brought in the Princess of Wales, who was most
becomingly attired in pale pink. The Duke of Cambridge with Princess Mary and other
grandees came in . . . . ; the great élite all went into the inner salon where the venerable
Queen Amélie received me yesterday . . . . At 2 o'clock the doors (of the banqueting hall)
were thrown open . . . . ; the Prince of Wales came with Queen Amélie leaning on his arm,
the Grand Duke of Mecklenburg led the Princess of Wales, then the bride and bridegroom,
followed by all the grande monde". A little later Sir John found himself in a huge marquee,
"splendidly decorated, with the table laid for 120, covered with superb plate, Sèvres porcel-
ain etc . . . . ; an enormous wedding cake in the middle of the table, in front of Queen
Marie Amélie. The Prince of Wales sat to her right. I placed myself just behind, so that
I had a capital view of the august party and could hear them converse. The Grand Duke
sat on the Queen's left, with our lovely Princess next to him; then came the Duc de Montpensier with the Princess Mary of Cambridge. Opposite to the Queen was the lovely youthful
bride with her orange blossom wreath, and her happy looking bridegroom beside her.
Then sat the Infanta of Spain in a yellow striped dress, evidently national, of Spanish
fabrique, the Duc de Nemours and Princess Alice on their right. It was a grand and glorious
sight to behold the real heirs to three great thrones of England, France and Spain so seated.
The Mayor of Kingston, whom I took for a Frenchman, asked me to have some refresh-
ment at a side table, which I gladly accepted, with a laugh at taking each other for French-
men . . . .

"I resumed my observations of the elegant party, all of whom seemed to be enjoying
the delicate creature comforts with plebeian gusto. The Princess Mary is what the young
guardsmen call her, a right jolly girl. She was laughing and chattering with her neighbours in
a lively spirit". When the toasts were proposed, one over-zealous Frenchman shouted
"Vive le Roi", whereupon the Duc de Nemours, with great tact, called out "Vive la Comtesse
de Paris". Noticing Sir John, the Duc de Montpensier went over to speak to him, inviting
him to visit them at Seville, to the manifest surprise of the Duke of Cambridge and the
Princess Mary, who heard the invitation. After the royal party had retired, the rest of the
company sat down to a delicious meal, with wonderful claret. "The plate and china ornaments all over the table were really superb, the finest thing of the sort I ever witnessed".
On his way back, Sir John, ever an opportunist, stopped at Veitch's nurseries and much
admired the wonderful display of Chinese plants, but as they were priced at half a guinea
each he felt he could not afford any for Belle Vue.

Not all refugees to Jersey were French. In 1848 a Hungarian nobleman[1], captain
in the Imperial bodyguard, was living here: "a very intelligent man, a friend of Esparterre[2],

---

1. Unnamed in the diary.   2. Possibly the Spanish General Espartero (1792-1879).

who says he is a noble character. He considers that Austria must make concessions in favour of the press, trial by jury etc., or she may be shaken. Germany, under the double headed eagle, as a confederate, would be invincible and a barrier between rational monarchy and republicanism. Very useful to England". There was also a Count de Brody Zabrocki, who published "An epitome of the History of Poland" in Guernsey in 1845. This is not mentioned in the surviving diaries, but the book is dedicated to Sir John with a profuse eulogy.

In 1850 there was an official French visit[1] to Jersey. "A large party from France. The Mayors of Avranches and Granville, the Commandant and a number of National Guards come over to visit their friends here. Lt. Col. Sullivan and the officers of the South West Regiment were the persons to invite them. The crowds on the pier to receive them were immense. The Band and troopers of the Town Regiment marched them into the town in a sort of procession . . . . There was a grand fraternity dinner given to the French party of 400 or 500. It went off very well". Next day: "Assise d'Héritage. The French travellers came into Court. Mons. Bouvattier, the Mayor of Avranches and a member of the French Chamber of Deputies, is a fine looking man, the others pretty well, only two or three having the bearing of what we call gentlemen . . . ." The day after: "The fraternising National Guard party left at eleven, parading among a rabble in the Royal Square. Everything has gone off very well and cordially, which is very pleasing".

Not long after this, Victor Hugo arrived in Jersey, and became the acknowledged leader of his fellow refugees of all nations, called Les Proscrits. They published the newspaper "L'Homme", which made a venomous attack on Queen Victoria when she paid her state visit to Napoleon III. The diary for October 1855 records: "The General showed me the declaration of the French Republicans who have resented the expulsion by the General of Riberolles, Piancine and Thomas, three red rascals who had published the libel on the Queen. It is a savage attack on the Emperor which should be instantly punished, as he has been the fast friend of England. The General seems determined to be firm and will march them off, I expect. It is signed by Victor Hugo and 35 more, and is pasted all about the town". A week later: "The General informed me that he had sent notice to those refugees who signed the protest, or the attack on the Emperor of the French, to leave the Island in the course of a week. It is strange that such a man as Victor Hugo should not have had sufficient good sense, if not a sense of gratitude toward the English government, that gave him and his fellow outlaws protection and comfort, not to attack their ally, without whom he well knows we could not carry on the war. As to Riberolles and the other red republicans, they would probably murder Bonaparte if they could. Disorder and confusion might be their time of harvest . . . . They are to leave this on or before Nov. 2nd". On that day: "Those republicans have all left by today's packet. They had proposed to go off with colours flying, but they got a hint not to do so. A few called out 'Vive la République' as they embarked, but they were hissed by the crowd". Victor Hugo went to Guernsey, where he stayed for many years. In discussion of French refugees with Lord Hardinge, Sir John said: "I thought, with General Love, that when foreigners chose to criticise our laws and not to obey them, they should be removed. Indeed, instead of allowing the 2000 socialists and red republicans to be publishing manifestos from their own press in

---

1. See Bulletin of La Société Jersiaise, 1965, p.55.

Jersey, they should all be sent away, and the Channel Islands considered as close fortresses. Lord Hardinge . . . . quite agreed with me".

A French friend whom Sir John made late in life was the French Consul in Jersey, Baron Charles de Chazal. At a Government House soirée in 1867 the diary says that the Baronne "was the most striking person there, prettily dressed in the true Parisian style, which sets off women to better advantage than any other but a Greek costume. I played whist with the Consul, who plays a fair game". In 1870 they had a conversation which, in the light of history, is somewhat ironical. "I saw . . . . Baron Chazal yesterday, calling to offer my sympathy to him on the disasters of his beautiful country. He expects the Republic to last for a while, and then the Comte de Paris to come in. Thinks the Prussians will not take Paris. Nor do I, unless by a rush or coup de main, according to their practice". In September of that year much sympathy was expressed for the wounded, and a meeting was held in the Prince of Wales Assembly Room "for the wounded of the two armies, a goodly meeting for Jersey. The General, the Bailiff, the Dean and myself addressed the meeting. £50 collected". At Belle Vue Harriet organized a team to prepare comforts for the troops, and one day seventeen ladies assembled and worked all the morning. "When I went down to the dining room it was in a litter of bandages, rollers, lint, caps etc".

Monsieur Drouin de l'Huys and his wife also spent some time in Jersey. He had been Ambassador in London, and Minister of Foreign Affairs to Napoleon III, and was opposed to the cession of Alsace and Lorraine, on which his comment was: "All die first". He was present with the official party at the opening of the railway from St. Helier to St. Aubin. Soon afterwards Sir John invited Chazal and l'Huys to dinner at Belle Vue and they "sat a long time after the ladies left, having an exciting chat over French affairs. The Baron said it was 'un diner exquis . . . .' I gave them the best wines. I observed to M. Drouin de l'Huys that the rash saying of Napoleon, 'L'Empire c'est la paix', which he ought to have held to against the opinion of his ministers: and the saying of the King of Prussia that he 'made war on the Emperor, not on the French people'; were equally false". They had a wonderful meal: vermicelli soup; very fine John Dorey; croquettes; hare; mutton cutlets, mushrooms and tomatoes; turkey; ham; tongue; grouse; cheese; apricot tart and pears. Like many another sojourner in the Island, they had sampled the hospitality and friendship which Jerseymen have shown through the centuries to men and women who have sought their shores, for whatever reason, and for however short a time.

CHAPTER ELEVEN

LA DEFENSE DE L'ILE

Until the dawn of the Atomic Age, defence was one of the greatest preoccupations of mankind, and man-hours incalculable were spent in erecting fortresses of one kind or another to keep the invader at bay. This was particularly true of Jersey, a fragment of the British Isles, but far removed from the protection of the mother country, and perilously near the shores of a country which, until comparatively recent times, was as often as not a declared enemy. To England the Islands had immense importance as an outpost, a refuge for shipping and a base for operations; and military considerations loom large in the chronicles of their past. So it is with these diaries. When the history of the Royal Jersey Militia comes to be written, as written it must be, its author would do well to study the Le Couteur archives, for in them he will find a boundless store of authentic material. Indeed, the indexing of the item "militia" was well nigh impossible, as there are comparatively few pages on which it does not feature in some form.

In 1821, when only twenty-seven years of age, Sir John was appointed A.D.C. to the Lieutenant Governor of Jersey, with the militia rank of Lieutenant Colonel, and two years later was given command of the 1st or North West Regiment. In 1842 he moved to the command of the 5th or South West Regiment, and in 1850 to the 4th or South. Letters to his son, then serving in India, tell of the disappointment which other officers felt at his preferment. Sir John's daughter Mary wrote to her brother: "I dare say you were somewhat surprised to hear that dear Papa was actually in command of the Town Regiment. On the whole his appointment has been received better than I should have anticipated. Clem Hemery is sadly disappointed as, on dit, that Sir Thomas had promised him the command, but I hope he will come round and work under him. Papa had seventeen of the officers to breakfast with him last Thursday". Papa himself wrote: "You will necessarily be very anxious to learn how I have got on with the Town Regiment. It could not be expected that such an appointment could take place without vexing some who fancied they could command it better than anyone else. Brevet Major Godfray, the Captain of Grenadiers, intimated this to the Governor . . . . I told them . . . . I hoped to see all the corps out on Her Majesty's birthday. I gave each three sovereigns, including the band and drums as a separate company, to drink the Queen's health . . . . The S.W. officers have presented me with a most flattering address, exceedingly à propos to demolish any stupid feeling of jealousy".

In 1853 he became Adjutant General to the Militia, holding this post until 1872. He had wished in 1857 to effect a complete retirement from all military activity, but received such a pressing letter from the Lieutenant Governor, General Mundy, that he said "I could not with propriety decline". He put heart and soul into the training of the militia, as an essential part of the framework of island defence, and imparted his enthusiam to those who served under him to a point where military training, which was unpaid and interrupted the work of all who took part in it, came to be regarded as a patriotic duty which could be enjoyable. He was a popular leader, and in 1846, after a review with which the General had been greatly pleased, the officers "did me the honour to invite me to sit to Mr. Stonehouse, the portrait painter, to be placed for them in our Mess room; a very kind and flattering compliment which I could not decline". C. Stonehouse exhibited thirty-five pictures at the Royal Academy, including one entitled "Jersey peasant girl at fountain". The portrait of Sir John, now in the possession of the States of Jersey, had become badly damaged during the Occupation years, but was recently restored and looks very fine. It shows him three-quarter length, in militia uniform, with the compelling blue eyes which have already been mentioned. The arms of Jersey are on the frame. An embossed card was at the same time given to his wife, inscribed: "This portrait has been painted by the unanimous desire of the Officers of the said Regiment, and placed in this Arsenal as a token of the high esteem and respect which they entertain for their gallant Colonel. 2nd November 1846".

As early as 1830 his inventive mind had evolved for militia use a belt buckle with a slide action, to avoid piercing the leather. This he showed to Colonel FitzClarence, who pronounced it "a capital idea . . . .: he thought . . . . it would do for the whole army. He said they had long thought of it, but could never invent anything that could do". He then "took the belt and buckle to General Macdonald and to FitzClarence, and tried them on a man of the Guards before them, and they both approved of it fully. General M. told me not to hurry it through the board, as it must be proved practically before it could be ordered for the army. He would show it to Lord Hill, and would pledge himself that it would go to the board recommended by him. However FitzClarence, who is all heart and very kind to me, said: 'Go from me, and enquire when the board will sit' ". The board happened to be sitting at that moment and Sir John was invited in. "General Fuller sat as President of a committee of five, to whom I explained my plan. They very politely and handsomely said that they would meet again the day after tomorrow, as I wished to return to Jersey". On hearing all this, General Macdonald was "a little impatient at being hurried and said: 'If I was to repeat it fifty times, I should not recommend precipitation. It must be tried practically, though you see there is every disposition to forward your views' ". We hear no more. But one wonders how much the slide-buckle, in use today in civil and military costume, owes to a Le Couteur prototype.

In 1851 he was badly injured during a review. "Left home at 7.30 . . . . The men were tolerably punctual, the flank company about 28 files. Told them off into two battalions, Colonel Simonet to the right wing and Major de Ste. Croix in charge of the left wing, the band with the former, and drums and fifes with the latter. Told them off into fours, and tried them in wheelings myself, and passed the church at $\frac{1}{4}$ past ten. When passing the detachment of the 15th Foot, which was under the command of Captain Colborne, Lord Seaton's son, he, on my ordering the Brigade to carry arms, opened his ranks and presented arms, which compliment I rode to acknowledge and thank him for. He was struck with the close steady march of the Regiment, which did not shake a step while they passed the *Regulars*, and thought us very strong. When I got to the Tower, the sands being heavy, I marched the men on the road, for which I paid dearly. On passing La Folie[1] . . . . where the road is wide, I left the head of the Brigade to reconnoitre the ground at the common, where the St. Lawrence Regiment was in line. As I passed the troopers,

1. At Millbrook.

one of their horses kicked at my mare and struck me above the ankle, a most violent blow that nearly unseated me. I almost fainted from pain, but rode on to keep the blood in circulation. The Le Couteurs (of La Hougue Boëte), to whom I related my accident and suffering, said I must not go home, or the drill would be ended if I did. I rode it out on that, and mentioned the hurt to no one of the corps, and the movements were really very well performed. Firing in line behind the edge of the sandhills: close columns: in rear of right Divisions: advance in direct échelon of columns at deploying distance: the right or leading column covered by skirmishers, which the St. Lawrence Light Company did very well but too slowly, as Fraser said . . . .: Officers and colors to the front for a General Salute . . . . I was suffering severely and acutely at times, but all went off very well, considering it was our first drill. The St. L. Light Company were slow, and Major Le Geyt made the officers shift at the wrong point, which I corrected in time. Simonet blundered in some of his repeats. Ste. Croix did not repeat the cautions but gave the words of movement only. Machon lost his distance . . . ., and I was obliged to move the left battalion, not to move two. In coming in, the Town Light Company were confused, because they had not been cautioned to act as I had drilled them, and in marching out with the advance guard, went on the road instead of keeping the sands. However, the officers and men were very intelligent and steady, while Sir James Reynett, Touzel and other old soldiers were pleased and applauded our first assay. The Commandant of the Republique at Granville and some of his officers were on the ground in uniform, with some five hundred spectators. It was a lovely day, and we got back at half past one''. However little one may comprehend the above manoeuvres, they have been repeated here in detail to show how seriously the drilling was taken by those participating in it, and by the community as a whole. One may also salute the officer commanding the parade for his close attention to every phase of it, though his leg was hurting him abominably.

His narrative continues: "The officers were surprised to hear that I had met with a severe accident, for I could not alight, but hurried off to Dr. Dickson, who could not tell from the inflammation whether the fibula was broken or not. He ordered me to apply a dozen leeches to the part, and to go home in a cab, to take a strong dose as soon as possible, and let the leech bites run in hot water as much as they might. All of which I did in great suffering, and helpless on the right foot". The doctor's orders may seem harsh to us, but accorded with the state of medical knowledge at the time. Purges were prescribed for all ills, and leeches were the only agent then available to doctors for reducing inflammation. The leech, it appears, knows his own business and is able to ensure that his bite continues to bleed by reducing the clotting potential of his victim's blood. Sir John on one occasion obtained temporary relief for a rheumatic shoulder through leeches, and eased the sufferings of a Mr. de Boursier, who had broken his arm, by applying fifteen leeches, after the doctors had failed with a lesser number. And, it used to be said of Dr. Dickson:

> "Oh, Doctor Joe Dickson
> is the man I would fix on
> to put new wicks on
> the lamps of life".

Having assured his patient that the fibula was not broken, Dickson diagnosed that the leg was badly bruised and cut by the horse's shoe, and prescribed cold applications for several days, followed by linseed poultices every six hours. But the leg continued raw and painful, the patient became increasingly fractious, the wound went septic and developed boils, and Sir John went to England for a second opinion, consulting Sir Benjamin Brodie, who seems to have treated the matter lightly. He said the wound had not healed owing to a debilitated system, and prescribed lead ointment, wine and good living. The experts of the time were evidently only on the fringes of Sir John's problem, for nothing they did was much help, and the injury gave him discomfort and pain for many years. But this is a personal interlude, and we must return to the militia and Island defences.

In 1852 Field Marshal Lord Hardinge, Commander in Chief and a Peninsula veteran, arrived in Jersey by the steamer Sprightly. He was greeted by a salute of 19 guns and proceeded to Bree's Hotel[1]. Later in the morning he was found at Havre des Pas "attended by a numerous suite", and had a chat with Sir John. "How do your experiments get on?" "Very satisfactorily, my Lord. I have adapted a ball for the regimental rifle your Lordship was so good as to give me[2], which ranges 1500 yards". "A heavier ball than the Minié?" "Yes, my Lord, over an ounce and a half". "Well, Colonel Le Couteur, I shall send you six arms of two patterns. One only weighs eight pounds with the sword or bayonet; the other is heavier. You will try them, and report to me through the Lieutenant Governor; and if you approve of them, I will let your men have which they like best of the two". "Which", says Sir John to his diary, "was very liberal and handsome to our militia". This was the climax of many interviews with Lord Hardinge and letters to him, about a ball cartridge which Sir John had evolved, and which retained its shape after impact. Hardinge was "very much surprised at the perfect form of the ball when compared with the rest", and thought it would suit the Brunswick rifle. He arranged for Sir John to go to Woolwich for trials, as we shall see in a later chapter.

The "numerous suite" attending His Lordship in 1852 were Sir John Burgoyne (Inspector General of Fortifications): General Love (Lieutenant Governor): Admiral Sir Thomas Hastings (Surveyor of the Ordnance): Colonel Sir Frederick Smith, M.P. (Chief Engineer at Chatham): Colonel Wood (commanding the Cavalry Depot at Maidstone) and other persons of consequence. This shows how seriously Whitehall took the defences of Jersey. After inspecting the ground at Havre des Pas and approving a plan of defence, they all got into carriages and drove to Elizabeth Castle, where two mortars on the upper battery were condemned. At this point Sir John was informed that the party were going to have lunch at his house, and he sent off a bombardier with an urgent note to his wife. Hardinge "told me by all means to go on and prepare a biscuit and a glass of wine for them, as he wished to see the cartridges, and also my cattle". In those days, evidently, high ranking officers were under no illusions as to their own importance. On arrival at Belle Vue Sir John's heart sank, for Harriet was out at a school committee, the faithful housekeeper Ann Luce was in town and there was a new cook. Her name was Wallace, she rose splendidly to the emergency and promised a good lunch. A maid was sent hot-foot to fetch Harriet home, and Sir John hurried down to the bay to meet the great men. When he returned home with them a fine lunch was ready. Hardinge examined the cows and calves and went round the garden, where he admired the Australian plants. "He told me there was every wish to do justice to Jersey, to defend the island in the best manner and to arm the militia . . . . We should have the new rifle grooves to the percussion musket to carry ounce and a half balls,

---

1. In David Place.   2. See Chapter 17.

V   Colonel JOHN LE COUTEUR
as Commandant of the 5th (South-West) Regiment of Royal Jersey Militia, 1846
(*portrait by C. Stonehouse*)

VI   THE QUAY, St. Helier, with Collins' Old London Hotel, and Lowe's Royal Yacht Club London Hotel, and Fort Regent behind.

40 instead of 60. As the Jersey militia will have no packs to carry, they can carry a heavier ball". The party then proceeded along the northern parishes to Bouley Bay where Hardinge "Saw what scarping would do, looked over the Jardin d'Olivet, then drove to the Arsenal of the North Regiment (between Trinity and St. Martin). It was in fair order, the worst of any I have seen, but he thought it a very capital arrangement". By the end of the day they had driven 26 miles. There was a dinner for twenty at Government House, where the butler had been "tasting the punch so freely that he offered port with the sweets".

Next day His Lordship, becoming impatient at delays, went off on his own to inspect Gallows Hill, which he considered very important. "I told him how anxious I was to have proper arsenal and drill ground for the Town Regiment under Gallows Hill . . . . I was in uniform and waiting in the arsenal yard, where the artillery were assembling in a very steady manner, and staid there till half past ten, when I had to quit in order to tell off the Regiment, which was assembling in the cattle market. There were but 300 of the best men, very clean and steady. We marched out at 11, and just as I formed them into open column, with the advance guard of riflemen, the whole cavalcade came up. His Lordship sent me a message by Colonel Hemery to say he would inspect my Regiment before the Artillery, if I thought proper. I begged to be allowed to march to my camp colors, when he rode close in rear of the Regiment, which was marching beautifully. I joined His Lordship, who said: 'I wish our eighty thousand militia in England could move in that style. That is capital marching' ". The new English Militia Bill, just out, recommended calling men out for 28 days, which Sir John thought would unsettle their domestic habits and displease the masters. "I fancied our system, with a drill once a fortnight if practicable, would keep up the drill better and satisfy both parties more agreeably". The narrative continues: "I rode back to the Regiment, wheeled into line, opened ranks and received His Lordship. The men marched past admirably both in slow and quick time, wheeled into line, advanced in line very well and saluted. His Lordship desired me to inform the officers, non-commissioned officers and men that he had derived the greatest satisfaction from witnessing the soldierlike bearing, smartness and steadiness of this fine regiment. From the accuracy with which he perceived they had moved for his inspection, he could judge how well they might manoeuvre. He was anxious for the moment when the militia force in England should be able to move with the same discipline. He had been very much gratified, and should not fail to report it to Her Majesty". After inspecting the Artillery they went to Mont Orgueil Castle: "Saw its weaknesses. Entered his name and thinks, I suspect, of not exacting the sixpences".

In 1853 "our grand Brigade review" took place before Lord Raglan. They again had the rendez-vous in the cattle market and "marched to our position near the Volunteer Redoubt, formed the Brigade, the St. Lawrence, Town, Rifles and East into a mass of column . . . . and my twelve guns on the sandy road to the left. They moved down remarkably well, though Le Geyt threw his points out . . . . exactly where they were not wanted . . . . The 1st Brigade, the 58th and 73rd[1] were engaged, and the second Brigade moved down, when I formed a line of contiguous columns and marched up in that order to my supporting distance . . . . The tide would not allow the East regiment to deploy, so it remained in column in support . . . . Lord Raglan asked me how it came that so many arms missed fire, even among the rifles. I said that it was so owing to the men having no means

---

1. The Northamptonshires and Black Watch.

K

or aids to clean their arms properly. Many got rusty in the winter. They should be given into store in the winter and re-issued in the spring. . . . The Master General quite agreed with me".

After considerable manoeuvring, the salute was due to take place, but "Lord Raglan says I must not march past himself, as the Lieutenant Governor represents the Sovereign . . . . : that I must command the whole and march past at their head . . . . I galloped to the right flank and ordered 'Open order and general salute'. At shoulder arms, an A.D.C. of the Line rode up and said: 'Sir, the General says you are to go on'. 'Go on? What does he mean?' 'He says you are to go on, that is all I know'. Well, I was going to slope arms and stand at ease till Lord Raglan and himself should have arrived at the flank of each corps . . . . But to 'go on' signifies to move, so I thought time would not allow them to ride along the line, and gave the word to break into open column. The General came up: 'No, no, not that. Reform line. We have to ride along the line'. 'Sir, your A.D.C. brought me word to go on'. Lord Raglan heard this and saw the mistake was not mine. He admired the Rifles as smart, and the North Regiment as big men . . . . I then marched past at the head of twenty-four guns and ten Battalions, eleven with the Rifles. The troopers with Captain Godfray at their head made some absurd charges. The march past was pretty good. The three bands of each militia brigade were formed into one. The men were very irregular in firing off their arms as they marched home, shooting from the ranks, exhibiting their want of discipline to the public at large. It is but a raw militia at present". That evening there was a grand dinner with the Lieutenant Governor as guest to 160 militia officers. It was a merry party, but the company "were vexed not to have had the big wigs who had not stayed to be entertained". Next day Sir John was appointed Adjutant General for the Militia.

The militia drilling was by no means always a matter for congratulation. The Town Regiment was "wonderfully unsteady" one day, we read, and Sir John freely criticises where necessary, and complains about absenteeism, and the petty quarrels of officers, particularly over promotions. But he seems to have got on well with the men, and often the Band would march up to Belle Vue to wish the Colonel a merry Christmas and play him some tunes, being rewarded with a good meal and drink, and much bonhomie shown on both sides. In December 1853 there was a large militia dinner at Belle Vue, with twenty-eight at table. Harriet told her boy in India all about it. "We managed to lodge them at the table very comfortably by placing it cornerwise, closing the usual entrance door . . . . and extending the table towards the window; thus making two entrances, one towards the hall, the other through the study by the verandah, which we enclosed as a sort of porch, placing your dog-cart lamps to shed their lustre through the window. The dinner was therefore served up both ways, three servants on one side and three on the other . . . . Colonel Simonet sat with me at the top, Clement Hemery on my left, who was useful in carving . . . . They paid us the compliment in coming here in full dress, having had black trousers with red stripes on purpose for Regimental dinners. You do not know how smart your father looks in his blue militia drill coat, looped with braid and frogs".

Sir John's success and popularity inevitably aroused envy in certain quarters. There is among the La Haule papers a neatly bound manuscript book, unsigned and undated, which opens with a description of the island and its defences, illustrated with exquisitely drawn plans. The writer goes into minute detail about militia clothing and severely criticises Sir John and his father for their management of militia affairs, mocking at their lack of ability and even imputing dishonesty in keeping the accounts. This might be the anonymous "communication" which the Lieutenant Governor, General Cuppage, submitted to Sir John, who commented that "it is an ignorant and scandalous libel, built upon a slight basis of truth, as are all libels. Had such a document been addressed to myself, I should have declined to reply to it. As it is a charge against a system, I shall show how it is erroneous". This was in 1866. A possible author of this attack is Gardner, the Governor's secretary, who was convicted for embezzlement of militia funds. Whoever it was, he can scarcely have been telling the truth, in view of the tributes Sir John received from officers and men, and the confidence he enjoyed from his superiors.

Inventive himself, Sir John encouraged enterprise in others. One example of this was an invention by Lieutenant Chevalier of the 1st West India Regiment. "Saw Lieut. Chevalier yesterday. He had just come from Hythe, where his electric self-recording target had electrified General Hay and all the instructors of musketry". It was decided "to ask the Committee of the States on Friday at Crabbé to order one. It would be an honour to a Jerseyman to have the first established here". Next year there was a tragedy in the family, for Chevalier's father, the Harbour Master, was drowned with three other men while laying down sailing marks. It was proposed to send his son back to the West Indies, but Sir John interceded for him: "no one wished to go there", he said, and the young man did "not wish to leave his family, who are almost destitute since the father's death; and Sir James Scarlet, Adjutant General, advised him to get an exchange or get an unattached company".

Much of Sir John's abundant energy was devoted to establishing drill sheds for the militia regiments, and arsenals to house the 24 guns of the field batteries, and the arms and uniforms. In 1829, when he began to work on this, the guns were kept in parish churches, militia equipment deteriorated from lack of proper storage, and there was no place where the men could drill under cover in bad weather. Those in St. Mary and St. Peter are most often mentioned, and caused a good deal of discussion as to the best site, and acquisition of the land. Sir John advanced the money for St. Mary's drill shed himself, and had to petition the Governor to get it eventually refunded. In 1844 a law governing the arsenals was framed, and he proposed a clause to settle the question of supplying horses for militia use, which caused constant friction and discontent. It ran: "Any person rated as a Principal de Paroisse who claims exemption to carry arms in the ranks, who keeps a horse, shall furnish the horse for the guns if so appointed by the Colonel; or shall pay ten shillings annually for his exemption. Any person paying the rate of a Principal de Paroisse, or paying a house rent of thirty pounds a year or more, or the owner of two horses, who may claim exemption from carrying arms, may be named by the Colonel to furnish such horses for the service of the artillery, or otherwise shall pay one pound annually as a commutation".

He was also concerned with coastal towers, as an integral part of island defences. All but the northern coast of Jersey is ringed with so-called Martello Towers, though they predate towers of that name in England by at least twenty years. They are also of different pattern, akin to towers in the Mediterranean but not identical with them, nor with those in Guernsey. Many still remain, but several which Sir John knew have disappeared. In 1846 he wrote: "Went . . . . to St. Ouen's Bay in the storm. Found that the slip at La Pulente was destroyed last night, the sea having gained eight or ten feet on the back in the south-east angle. Several feet of the banks all along had slipped, and the south tower will be in danger of falling this night, the abutting wall all round it having given way in three

*The vanishing MARTELLO TOWERS
of St Ouen's Bay, Jersey.
(from an unfinished Le Couteur sketch
of about 1840).
Three of these five have disappeared.*

places. The cracks in it have enlarged, and it has a heel to the south-east. Tower 2 has a crack in it also, St. Ouen's Bay is likely soon to be bounded by the hills. The first inroad will be below the two above towers, if not at the Pond". Had no sea wall been built his prophecy would no doubt have been fulfilled. Indeed on driving down there in 1851 he said: "The sea has gained greatly inside the ruined martello, which is three parts down". By 1860 he was writing: "Iron martello towers will, I think, be impregnable, and supersede stone walls or earthworks".

It may be a surprise to some readers to learn that a tunnel under Fort Regent was thought of as long ago as 1843, by a railway engineer who was conferring with Sir John. The diary says: "Returned by Fort Regent and the pier, where the engineer would like a tunnel below the road between the garrison hospital and the south Hill. I do not think the Ordnance would allow a tunnel anywhere near Fort Regent". The British Government expected a French attack sooner or later, and the Island defences in general, and Fort Regent in particular, were of great importance to them. This was made quite clear to Sir John by the Duke of Wellington himself in the same year, 1843, when they met at a levée. The Duke asked how things were in Jersey, a place which he said was very interesting to him, and enquired about the militia, with the warning: "You know, it should be kept in an efficient state. There is no knowing when it may be wanted". Jersey was anxious about her defences, Sir John told him, the Duke replying: "So are we". They also needed a breakwater as protection for a steam fleet, he was told. "That", said the Duke, "will be considered. We are always alive to everything the French do". But he said he had not heard the report that the French were then assembling a camp of exercise at Rennes with 40,000 men, who might assail Jersey or Ireland. "I shall run over to see that army, if it be true", said Sir John.

"You had better", replied the Duke; and continued: "You know it has ever been my opinion that this country will never have a little war. It will be a great contest whenever it comes .... Your defences are under the consideration of the Government. I have already paid attention to them". Two years later they met again, at Apsley House, to discuss a report Sir John had submitted on defence, accompanied by a model of the Island. The conversation lasted an hour and a quarter, and at the end of it the Duke said: "You see, Colonel, I agree with you in every part of this report". And then, "the venerable old hero shook my hand most kindly, as if I had been an old friend". In 1852 Sir John was moved to write to him to ask to be considered for "the office of Lieutenant Governor, which is about to be vacant", on the grounds that "the present state of France places the Island of Jersey in the most critical state of its history .... I expect the first blow may be struck at Jersey". We do not have Wellington's reply, but Sir John did not fill the vacancy.

Railways and Harbours are bound to feature prominently in an island's defences. Today Jersey has no railway, and her harbours are not very different from what they were a century and a half ago. But a great deal was written and done about both in the intervening years, and Sir John played an active part in it all. The curtain rises in 1840, when he wrote to an unknown correspondent, probably someone in the Home Office, about the harbours in St. Aubin's Bay. At this stage he was concerned solely with commerce. His defence schemes come later. He explained that there were two harbours in the bay, the major port of St Helier, on the east, exposed to south-westerly storms, and recently damaged in a gale. A pier built only twenty years before had been breached, and another had developed a dangerous bulge, "owing to the jobbing that is winked at in our public works". A powerful consortium of St. Helier's merchants had lately induced the States to vote £103,000 to build a new pier on the basis of plans prepared by Mr. Walker. On the western side of the bay, "in perfect shelter", was the small harbour of St. Aubin, and 500 yards away the "Tower Port", to which a patent of King Charles II granted "a share of harbour dues, and all the petty customs for ever". Farmers in the west of the island needed a port from which to ship their produce, and asked for the modest sum of £10,000 to link the harbour to the Tower Port, but the eastern consortium were so jealous of rivalry that "they prevent our having a doit".[1] Unfortunately most States members either lived in St. Helier or had shipping and business interests there, and there was no hope of getting the St. Aubin's claim through the assembly; though it was obvious that St. Helier would always remain the capital, and more prosperous than her poor relation across the bay. £62,000 had already been voted by act of the States to commence work at St. Helier, and the letter proposes that a caveat be entered against it. The western farmers would gladly build their harbour extension at their own expense in return for certain concessions from the States. "Do you conceive Government would oppose us?", he asks. "It appears to me not. I am truly sorry thus to oppose all my mercantile friends and near relations, but (do) it in defence of .... an undoubted right which a powerful body wish to trample on". The powerful body need not have feared. St. Aubin was never a threat to their prosperity, and the controversy is long since forgotten.

We now move on five years to the summer of 1845, and over to the east coast of the Island. "A Mr. Prow(le) called on me .... to say that a railway company, in concert with the Government, were going to establish a breakwater either at Bouley, or at St. Cath-

---

1. A mite, or coin of negligible value.

erine's Bay, with railways to St. Aubin and St. Helier and some across the bay: that Mr. Stevens, Sir Robert Peel's solicitor and one of his nephews, was coming here to make arrangements. As the de Lisles recommended him to me I can scarcely think the whole scheme a romance. He pretends that they have had conferences with the Master General of the Ordnance . . . . The General thinks it all humbug". Sir John was already hoping "to move the Government to build a Harbour of Refuge at St. Catherine's Bay, and a Breakwater at Noirmont, which being connected by a railway would form a girdle of protection to the weaker points, and enable us to move any force at great speed all along that line . . . . We did not view it as a speculation, but as an admirable accessory to our means of defence". He really preferred Noirmont, if a choice lay between the two, and twenty-five years later was still hoping for a harbour there. In a letter to the Rev. J. C. C. Pipon of Noirmont Manor he said: "I have never lost sight of your interests in . . . . a breakwater at Noirmont, opposite the Pignonnet and Grune du Port rocks. When Mr Pickering came here first I . . . . recommended (him to purchase Noirmont) so as to be master of the quarries for the building of a breakwater . . . . Later he, being afraid of the States and the unstableness of their proceedings, did not close with you . . . . There are influential men planning a railway to Gorey and St. Catherine's Bay with an ulterior view of a harbour in that quarter, which would give a steam run of only six hours direct to Portland. But that would answer only for passengers and light goods traffic. A breakwater at Noirmont would be serviceable for the larger trade of St. Helier, and for defence". But the breakwater was never built. . Nor was another suggestion followed, for a "snug little port" to be created by running a jetty from Gorey to l'Equerrière rock.

Meanwhile another company came on stage, only ten days after Mr Prowle's visit. "A deputation from the Great Western Railway . . . . about a proposal to place a rail between St. Helier and St. Aubin. 1 told them of the former company, and how . . . . I had consented to place my name as a member of the provisional committee. They begged me to recommend them a solicitor. I named Mr. Hugh Godfray". The G.W.R. seem now to have faded out, leaving the stage to Messrs. Prowle, Stevens and a civil engineer named Hudson, who accompanied Sir John and Captain Martin White to Noirmont Point. "The tide was out, $38\frac{1}{2}$ feet spring which enabled them to see the Grune du Port and Pignonnet rocks very distinctly", ... and "the capability of establishing a breakwater at small cost. The means of making a railway out to Noirmont were easy, by cutting into a bank. They all dined with me". At dinner he realised that the company's aims were purely speculative (and the diary entry is rounded off with "in vino veritas") but added: "If, however, they spend a large portion in adding to the defences of Jersey, I shall have gained my end". He had already made exhaustive enquiries in London as to the bona fides of the visitors. He insisted that a railway act should be passed by the States before any local persons would take part, and in autumn 1845 such an act was prepared. He attended "the first meeting for the establishment of a railway in Jersey, at Lozey's Hotel. The large room was crowded, upwards of five hundred of the principal men and merchants being present. The Dean, Mr Lemprière and Mr Godfray came to speak against it. The Dean fortunately remained silent. I was called to the chair, and explained that the deputation would develop the plan and reply to any questions". The Dean, as was explained later, was "much displeased with the railway prospectus. £20,000 a year would go to England . . . . The States should build it, if it is required for the defence of Jersey". Sir John also had a "very long conference with the Marshal (Lord Beresford) about the railway defences. He considers that Noirmont peninsula should have a strong fort or redoubt on it, and a line of outworks over St. Aubin: that heavy bodies of troops should be stationed at St. Aubin, St. Helier and Grouville: that a line of defence should be established in Grouville Bay: that a harbour over at Gorey or St. Catherine's would be useful: but does not see how the railway will pay, though it would certainly keep men fresh if moved on it: only of value till a landing is effected". In reply to the question how many men were required to defend Jersey against attack, Beresford was told: "The district of Grouville should always be 3000 strong: 5000 at St. Helier and 3000 more at St. Aubin: that is I calculate on 7000 from England and 5000 militia. A thousand men would guard the small bays on the north coast". But in spite of all these negotiations the plan came to nothing, and it was many years before Jersey saw her first railway train.

Out of all these varied projects, the only one which still plodded on was the Harbour of Refuge at St. Catherine's. There is page after page about it, far more than could be reflected here, including the knotty problem of compulsory purchase of land. In 1847 the Earl of Auckland[1], First Lord of the Admiralty, came over to visit the works. Welcomed at Belle Vue, he "complained of the magnificent lunches we give in Jersey .... He was very courteous to my wife and admired her pretty rooms and furniture .... We then drove on to Noirmont Point, which became a source of long investigation and decided approval." In October 1847 "they were within fifty or sixty yards of Archirondel Tower and will reach it by Xmas". On the Verclut side there was spectacular progress: "the rock comes away capitally: they rose nine tons at one blast last week ....: 300 men at work .... Saw Dingle in their hospital. He bears the loss of his leg well very. A rock rolled onto it and smashed it. It is a wonder that so great a drunkard escaped so well. He declares he will be a reformed man". The gangs were a headache to authority: "The General spoke again of the St. Catherine's Bay workmen, whether it would not be well to have the two superintendents and special constables over their own men, to act as Police officers". Later that year the work was so far advanced "that in the opinion of Captain Martin White it is 'already useful for shelter' ". It was then said that 200 men were advancing at the rate of 1000 cubic feet in a month, or a front of 17 feet of masonry.

In 1849 a formidable party arrived: Sir Francis Baring[2] and Admiral Dundas, Lords of the Admiralty; and Sir C. Wood, Chancellor of the Exchequer. They made for Belle Vue, and when Sir John got home he found them all there admiring his farm. After discussing sundry matters with them he steered conversation to St. Catherine's, and said that Captain White "urged the completion of the north arm to the Pierre Mouillée; then to forward the south arm as much as possible, so as to cover the north arm, when it would be a fine harbour. If not, the south-east winds would run along from the Pierre Mouillée to the Couperon and silt up a deposit all along the curve." Indicating the Chancellor "as the purse-bearer, Sir Francis said: 'We are willing, if he will give us the supplies', and the Chancellor replied: 'Keep going on as at present. It is capital work, done quickly and cheaply' ". It was suggested that there should be a strong battery on the Pierre Mouillée and another on the Ecréhous, but "any sudden demonstration of defence or great outlay of money .... would lead to a similar result on the other side of the water". Divers were

1. George Eden, Earl of Auckland (1784-1849).
2. Sir Francis Baring (1796-1866), First Lord of the Admiralty (1849-1852).

employed on the work, receiving 7s. to 10s. per tide, with extra flannels and waterproof clothing.

In 1860 the work was still dragging on, with doubts as to whether the south-eastern arm would ever be finished. But the fear of France was the stimulus, and "as the Ariel French war steamer came from Carteret to St. Catherine's in fifty-eight minutes last week, it points to whence an invasion could be most quickly made; in fact in as short a time as the East and North Regiments could assemble to resist landing. In peace time this communication will be most advantageous .... In war time, most dangerous, if the harbour at Verclut is not completed, and protected at its entrance by iron towers and six hundred pound guns, with a powerful steam turretted ram off its mouth". Sir John expected that quite a town would spring up round the area. It never did. For a decade the Harbour of Refuge and its future were a mystery, and it was not till 1873 that it was admitted that the project had been dropped. The application of steam to large vessels, no longer dependent on wind or in need of shelter, had rendered it superfluous, redundant, obsolete: and with it the railway which would have served it. St. Catherine's Harbour was as extinct as the dodo, and all the thought, paper and effort expended on it had been in vain. It is fashionable to regard it as a folly which should never have occurred. That is unfair. At the time it was done in good faith. What killed it was changing conditions. What has not changed is the breakwater itself, a superb example of craftsmanship in granite. A monument, one might say, to the quarrymen and masons who toiled there, and the earnest men whose minds were focussed on the Defence of the Island, and sought to ensure it in the best way they could. One of them was undoubtedly Sir John Le Couteur. Another had been the Duke of Wellington.

The story of the Alderney breakwater is similar. The first glimpse we have of the island is in the 1831 diary, when "Captain Babot went through the Swinge and took us into the bay at Alderney. It was fortunately very calm and most favourable for steam, otherwise the scene on deck would have been bad, as it was already marvellously disgusting. 'Steward', and 'a basin' were echoed from a hundred sickly voices, in tones from G sharp to double bass". In 1848 work on the breakwater was under way, and Sir John went over in H.M.S Cuckoo with the engineers to examine it. Stone was being brought from a quarry $2\frac{1}{2}$ miles away, overland or by small steam tug, at the rate of 1000 tons daily. In 1850 there was despondency, and somebody forecast that it would take eighty years to finish the work. Six divers were being employed for four hours a day each to place the line in 40 feet of water. In 1852 the diary tells us that "the breakwater already affords great shelter. It is 1130 feet long, and is to be carried out in a direct line a thousand feet further". But like St. Catherine's the enterprise gradually faltered and died, and this valiant feat of masonry now lies unfinished and much damaged.

It is plain from the diaries that in those days Jersey's importance lay not only in its strategic position, but in the volume of its shipping. Sir John estimated that whereas in 1800 the Island had only 5000 tons of shipping, in 1823 no less than 138,000 tons cleared in and out, making Jersey "the fifth port in the Kingdom",[1] and in 1830, Jersey-owned shipping amounted to 20,000 tons. The commerce of the Island "had increased astonishingly". In 1850 he claimed that "Jersey possesses more shipping than Bristol, and carries on trade with thirty different parts of the world. There are but twelve ports larger".

Since the Le Couteur archives were written, the problem of defence has changed out

1. As he told King William in 1830.

of recognition. The Island militia no longer exists, and its guns have vanished. Forts, batteries and Martello towers are no longer manned with soldiery. The Arsenals have been converted into residences. Sir John would be quite bewildered at what has taken place. The changes have rendered much of what he wrote quite obsolete, but his papers remain a valuable and interesting record of an episode in British history, and a testimony to his own dedication to the defence of his native Island. He and his contemporaries pursued this object continually and consistently, by direct and oblique methods. Almost every new enterprise was assessed by its relevance or otherwise to the paramount needs of defence. The Rifle Clubs, for example, which sprang up during this period, were widely popular not only on account of the conviviality of their meetings, but because they trained their members as marksmen. We have seen Sir John himself encouraging a speculative railway company to build a line, and as they faced each other across his table the visitors were thinking of profits, he of moving his troops swiftly in their trains. He positively excelled himself, and as early as 1837, in justifying his support of horse-racing on defence grounds. He wrote: "There was a secondary consideration of great importance to the defence of the Island, in my view as a military man, which induced me to give them my support and countenance. The introduction of a more powerful race of horses, to enable us to horse our Island artillery of twenty-four guns in a more efficient manner, indeed in a perfect way, in the event of a future war with France: an object which I could not avow openly, but which I was sure to effect silently by popular means". One wonders if race-horses were really harnessed to the parish guns, and whether the severe critic to whom he was writing accepted his explanation. Very likely not. The critic was Elizabeth Fry.

CHAPTER TWELVE

A.D.C. TO THE QUEEN

There is no diary describing the death of William IV, the accession of Queen Victoria, nor her confirmation of Sir John's position as Sovereign's A.D.C. in Jersey, but a letter of 1840, enquiring whether he, as A.D.C., would be required to attend the "approaching joyful occasion, as I had the honour to assist in Her Majesty's coronation" shows a continuance of that office.

The real highlight from every point of view was Her Majesty's visit to Jersey on September 3rd, 1846. It was really the first state visit of a monarch; true, we had received Charles II on two occasions, but both were when he was exiled from England, and other monarchs who had visited us had done so in times of stress. This was a pleasant change, a spontaneous and care-free visit, which evoked immense enthusiasm and loyalty. Only a few days' notice was given, not the many months of preparation which now precede royal visits. In fact on the previous Thursday Sir John said: "The Bailly requested me to go to Sir Edward Gibbs to ascertain whether the Queen would really arrive here on Monday. He had given private notice to the States to meet for an address. Sir Edward knew nothing of the Queen's movements, but had given orders for a good look-out to be kept at Noirmont and La Moie signal stations, and if two steamers were seen approaching the Island on Monday, a private signal would lead the Castle to fire two heavy guns, when all preparations would be made . . . . Sir John [1] arranged that he and I were to go on board to know the pleasure of Her Majesty and to offer our horses, houses, etc. It is a great pity that the Queen does not announce her intention officially that she might see how loyal Jerseymen are." Then there was a gap with no news, and on August 28th: "Wrote to Lord Adolphus FitzClarence[2] to try to learn whether the Queen was coming here. He replied that he has had orders to prepare to leave on the Wednesday following, but for what place he knew not. We at once decided, on knowing that Captain Goodridge had been taken from our Island steamer, that it was for Jersey." Every preparation was accordingly voted by the States and parishes; ". . . . (Monday); All Jersey at work, triumphal arches etc., cleaning streets. (Tuesday); Yesterday there was a hot discussion about changing the programme. I urged it being left as the police wished, that they must be the proper judges of the arrangements they had to guard . . . . Much discussion too, about precedence, and who were to be the ladies to receive the Queen. I was told that my wife was proposed as one, but that a certain party leader was violently opposed to it. I assured Sir J. that it little mattered, as I could present my wife when I pleased. This morning on arriving at the office I found a note announcing that Mrs Lemprière,[3] having declined to attend at the landing of Her Majesty, owing to the state of her health, my daughter Harriet had been named to replace her. I accordingly sent a message on horse back to have her prepared for this distinguished

---

1. i.e. Sir John de Veulle, the Bailiff.
2. Naval A.D.C. to the Queen, fourth son of William IV and Mrs Jordan.
3. Wife of Rev. William Lemprière, Seigneur of Rozel.

honour, and she soon came in and wrote to Miss Le Maistre to know where to meet her."
In view of the very short notice given one wonders if the group of ladies could all have been
attired in uniform white, as shown in pictures of the event.

The narrative continues, "I had Atkinson out at Belle Vue with the four state horses
for the Queen's carriage, and fired several shots over their heads; they were quite steady
and brought me to town nicely, walking steadily through the noisy streets, full of leaves,
branches, flowers and garlands. I had Noel's[1] set for the Lords in Waiting out this morning also, which were equally quiet under fire. A third set were in reserve from Collins[2]
in case of accident to the Queen's set . . . . (Wednesday); All Jersey busy, very pretty arches
in many places, the town arrangements quite superb. We were all in town all day.

"Three o'clock came . . . . my trooper arrived from Crabbé, stating that he had seen
four steamers coming towards Jersey by Grosnez, and the signal for them ran up. Shouts
of joy were heard about the town. Cleaners and sweepers all at work. At half past five the
two guns announced the Royal Squadron, the Victoria and Albert. Le Breton and I
dressed in uniform and went for the Bailly. Chevalier, the active and energetic harbour
master had prepared a fine boat and crew for us . . . . he piloted us out as the salute was
fired from Elizabeth Castle. It was a lovely afternoon and bright sun and smooth water.
We laid on our oars, close to the Royal Yacht, which had just come in grandly, followed
by three smaller steamers, the Black Eagle, the Fairy and Garland, and as soon as Colonel
Dixon[3], the Governor's Deputy, and Colonel Fraser were on board, we stepped on deck.
On being announced, Lord Palmerston, the Foreign Secretary, attended by Sir James
Clarke, and another gentleman, Mr Anson, came to receive us, and were introduced by
Lord Spencer. Colonel Dixon came to receive orders, Sir John to hand in the programme,
Le Breton to be allowed to present the Militia address, and I to say the horses were ready
for the Queen, and with Ouless' book. Lord Palmerston settled all these matters by ref-
erence to the Sovereign, while we waited, looking at the Prince of Wales and the Princess
Alice[4] who were in the glass rotunda watching us. Presently out came Prince Albert, to
whom we were severally presented. He asked where they were to land and what to do.
I said Sir John had a programme, which he handed to the Prince, who went in to the Queen
with it, came out and asked when the tide would serve . . . . Chevalier came forward . . . .
and said if she should draw three feet, at nine or eleven . . . 'Could the Fairy come in at 11?'
'Hardly to the stairs, but the barge could' . . . . 'Then Her Majesty would land in the barge.'
. . . . I said to Prince Albert that the people of the western district of Jersey had made great
preparations and hoped to be honoured by seeing Her Majesty. He asked how far it was
to Mont Orgueil, and how long that drive would take." He was told it would take three
hours, and a visit to the west would take another two or three hours. He replied: "Then
it would be more than would be good for the Queen." He asked what was to be seen at
Mont Orgueil, and was told, "a beautiful old Castle built by the Romans[5] in a high state
of preservation." The programme settled and the landing time fixed for 11 o'clock next
morning, Her Majesty came on deck, and the party was presented to her. She remarked
to Sir John that she was looking forward to seeing the beauties of Jersey, about which
she had heard so much.

1. Noel of Upper Don Street.   2. Collins of Beresford Street.
3. The Lieutenant Governor, Sir Edward Gibbs, was not well enough to attend.
4. Aged five and three respectively.   5. Archaeological knowledge has advanced since then.

On the great day the Queen's A.D.C. got up at 4.30, dressed in full uniform and "sent my horses on to the Black Rocks where the Regiment was to assemble at nine; got there and told them off and equalised them; urged them to be as steady as rocks while the Queen passed them; the Major then came up and I handed over the Regiment to him. At 9.30 I took the royal horses, three sets of four, Atkinson's beautifully dressed in red ribbons as on state occasions in London, himself and the man in the Royal livery, down through the countless multitude to the pier, where I saw the royal carriage with the Queen's own footman. I asked him what fancies or likings the Queen had about getting into her carriage; he said 'Her Majesty always likes to get in on the near side, so that the Prince may not step over her dress . . . . Why, Sir, what fine horses, this is just like home, just as in London, the Queen's livery too' . . . . When I had placed the horses I went to the ladies, then all was in confusion. They would stand as they were; I told them to drill into a line for the Queen to pass through. . . . then the States wished to be presented severally; Sir John was en désespoir. I said that Lord Spencer had arranged with Prince Albert that they should present the address as at Court, that I would do so as acting equerry . . . at last they agreed . . . . to present the address, the Jurats, the Clergy, the Constables, then the Colonels. Just then the Queen's close arrival was announced. Down the stairs Colonel Dixon and I went. The landing box with a crimson cloth covering it and a rich rug was at foot; we launched it as the royal barge approached, and I told the Jack Tars to haul it steadily on to the gunwale of the boat. 'What is this Colonel?' said Prince Albert, 'is it safe?' 'I will show Your Royal Highness.' I walked over it and back. Instantly the Queen stepped on to it and came up gracefully, biting her lip with emotion at the thundering cheers of twenty thousand voices. I presented Lady de Veulle[1], Mrs Simmonds, Miss Le Maistre and MISS LE COUTEUR to Her Majesty, and then back stepped to her chair of state under the Pavilion." The loyal addresses were then presented, by Sir John de Veulle for the States, and by Colonel Le Breton for the Militia. The latter knelt to present his address and the Queen instantly rose to receive it. "I whispered to Lord Spencer that Mr Le Sueur wished to present an address for the Town parish, but Lord Spencer said that it had not been notified, 'However', he said, 'I will name it to the Queen' who graciously agreed to receive it, but Le Sueur was off. Then we conducted the Queen to her carriage while the guard of honour presented arms, 81st[2] depot and Flank companies of the Town regiment, commanded by Major Creagh. The young ladies strewed flowers in the Queen's path. After the Queen was seated Prince Albert said to me, 'What a fine Grenadier company.' . . . . I then took my post at Her Majesty's right hand, with Lady Jocelyn facing her, and Miss Carr opposite to Prince Albert. The Queen was visibly struck at the grandeur of the scene in a small unknown (to her) island. The vast elegantly dressed throng to her right and left, the hills and front covered with living souls, the masts and yards of the shipping dotted with men among the gay flags, the Fort and South Hill standing boldly before her, the triumphal arch as she approached it. As each bend was reached I named the corps to Her Majesty. 'What a great force of artillery' the Queen said to me . . . . she immediately called the attention of Prince Albert to it, who questioned Major Creagh. Mr Nicolle's[3]

1. These ladies were: the wife of the Bailiff; the daughter of the late Sir Thomas Le Breton, late Bailiff, and sister of the future Bailiff; Mary Le Maistre, daughter of the Seigneur of St Ouen; and his own daughter Harriet.
2. The Loyal North Lancashires.
3. He lived in what is now the Museum, 9 Pier Road and his shipyard was nearby.

large ship the Iris, particularly struck her attention; it was a mass of living beings, the yards manned and an immense gallery being laid over the deck, a most imposing sight. The shouting and waving of hats from it was electrical. Then on turning to the Esplanade the coup d'oeil was grand, multitudes all along it on both sides. When at the corner of Gloucester Street, 1 named our Regiment to Her Majesty, and at the prison . . . the hospital, when I said: 'I beg your pardon, but poor as well as rich have come to greet Your Majesty. These are the poor inmates of the infirmary' . . . . she graciously bowed to them.

*'And the little children too,
please Your Majesty'.*

'And the little children too, please your Majesty,' and she repeatedly bowed to the charity children. At the Parade the effect was grand, the arches at Gloucester Street and here attracted her attention . . . . when in the Royal Square Chevalier pointed out the statue to her, I said: 'Please Your Majesty, this is the Square in which the gallant Major Peirson fell in the capture of the Marquis de Rullecourt and the whole French invading force.' The Queen stood up to look at the Square, in which a dense multitude were sending their voices to the sky, windows, house tops, all crowded. At the market place I pointed it out, adding that there were four other markets. 'How very gay and tasteful,' she said." The Prince enquired how large the population was, and was told it was about 30,000. Then a group of Frenchwomen was seen, in Norman and Breton Costumes, which the Queen much admired. They passed St. Mark's church, and she was told that it had been consecrated but a month before. "When the Queen saw the cortège turn the corner and witnessed the poor States trotting rather than walking, she exclaimed; 'Dear me, Colonel Le Couteur, have those gentlemen been walking all this way? How very fatigued they must be. Do go and tell them I am very much obliged for their attendance, but that I beg to dispense with their pursuing it further.' I instantly went to Sir John, and the States drew up on the footpath. At Government House the old veterans being drawn up, Atkinson drove in." This was a mistake, but the Queen said it did not matter, as long as there was a turn, and she was told that the Governor, Sir Edward Gibbs, with a fine military record, was not well enough to attend her in person, but that the drive past his house would be "a most gratifying compliment."; to which she replied "I am very happy at it." She enquired about the veterans drawn up on guard, and said: "What fine looking soldiers", with tears in her eyes. The Governor's sister, Miss Gibbs, was then presented and they drove on, past General Touzel's house, d'Hautrée. At this point the Queen dispensed with the police escort. At St. Saviour's they passed Saunders' nurseries[1], and Sir John explained that "we have an excellent climate for acclimatising exotics." Colonel Dixon wondered if the Queen was going to alight at Mont Orgueil, and Sir John rode round to the other side of the carriage to ask the Prince, who said "What is to be seen?" and the reply was :"One of the most perfect of the ancient castles in the Queen's dominions, built by the Romans in the time of Caesar, and King Charles inhabited it: on which the Queen said she wished to see it . . . . The States and three or four carriages were kicking up a vile dust in front of the Queen, so I thought a manoeuvre would be fair. I called to the troopers to go the short way by the Queen's Farm, on which all the carriages went off to the right, while I gave them the dodge by taking the road to the left by St. Martins, and the Queen could breathe freely in the shady native arch, more triumphal after all than that of man. 'What a pretty rich country this is, so quiet', she said"; to which he replied that it was so as everyone had gone to town that day, which made her laugh. She enquired about the potato crop, and he replied, " 'the tops are almost withered and almost generally so, but I am happy to say that although vegetation was necessarily stopped by this check, the bulbs, though small, are excellent and by no means as bad as last year. Mine are as good as can be.' 'Do you hear what Colonel Le Couteur says about the potatoes, Albert?' 'Yes, I am glad to know that, for in some parts of England there is a total failure.' " This, it may be recalled, was the period of the great Irish potato famine.

On going down Gorey Hill Sir John stopped the carriage and "ordered the boys to stop and put the shoe on . . . . as it would not be safe otherwise." At Mont Orgueil the Acting Governor presented the keys to the Queen, who returned them. At the second gate it was decided that it would be safer for the Queen to alight. The Prince and Earl Spencer went all the way up to the Keep, leaving the Queen with her proud A.D.C. to follow as far as she chose, and they actually climbed as far as the Grand Battery where, after an interval (one supposes) to regain her breath, she questioned him closely[2]. He explained that although, as she had said, our coast was protected by rocks, " 'steam power has deprived us of much of our protection, because sailing vessels were not safe in these rapid tides among the rocks.' 'Well I consider that steam can always be met by steam; we have a greater steam power than any other people, and at the outbreak of any war we should have a great advantage.' 'Very true . . . . there is now a discussion in Your Majesty's government, which is still very secret, as to whether it would be best to have a harbour of refuge for a steam fleet, running out from that pretty point, Greencliff, off Verclut, out in this direction over these rocks, or to have one at Noirmont Point, running out from the land, which would entirely protect Your Majesty's Yacht where it now lies. As a means of general defence the Duke of Wellington is of opinion that Noirmont would be the most proper point.' "

1. Opposite the entrance to Grainville Manor.
2. Ouless' account says that the Queen asked for a telescope, and that Sir John "immediately set off and returned with one."

They then passed on to the matter of language, and Sir John told her, of the local dialect, " '. . . . the old Norman, it is NOT French. A Frenchman of rank once said to a market-woman that he did not understand English, when she had spoken Jersey to him:' " to which the Queen replied, " 'Well I respect those old attachments to language. There is something pleasing to see the Welsh for instance retaining their ancient tongue. Those national habits and manners are always interesting, and I should not like to see a people deprived of them. I noticed that the Police spoke in Jersey French to each other, though they spoke to me in English!' 'They always converse in their vernacular tongue, Your Majesty, but can all speak in English, so does everyone in the Town. In the country they do not, but there are English schools in every parish. The Court and States speak French.' " Prince Albert then returned and after Lord Spencer had signed the book recording Her Majesty's visit, they drove back very fast. The Queen said: " 'Colonel Le Couteur you must be very warm'. She saw the perspiration streaming from my face, as my hat was off. 'Rather so, Your Majesty, but it belongs to our climate to be so.' " She then asked for the carriages to go a little more slowly. She asked him to acquaint everyone concerned with her pleasure at the arrangements and the reception she had received. As soon as they regained the town the noise of cheering met them. "Near half way up the quay poor Sorel's horse fell, and the Queen, seeing it, rose and held up her hands and said, 'Oh, Colonel, I hope that young officer has not been seriously hurt. Pray let me know presently and whether any other person was not hurt.' " This enquiry the kind hearted Queen repeated, and she then proceeded to her barge "and the cheering was deafening as the Queen went to the Fairy".

And so ended a visit of only three hours, but a landmark in the history of Jersey. No apology is offered for quoting this account almost in extenso, for although there are many printed accounts of the visit, there cannot be many personal memoirs from someone who was at the Queen's side for the whole time she was on Jersey soil.

The Crystal Palace Exhibition of 1851 was one of the excitements of the century, and Sir John visited it so many times that even his enthusiasm waned eventually. His first source of interest was the fact that he was actually an exhibitor, showing wheat specimens, as we shall see later, and because of this he was involved in the preparatory arrangements. One of the main anxieties of the organisers seems to have been shortage of space, and he suggested; "my idea would be to increase the space by having a second place of exhibition for all the implements, articles of hardware, and those not liable to injury from wet, and to leave Hyde Park for all the elegant works of art and fashion; the interest would be divided and so would the risk and the crowd. Then in order to remove any feeling of jealousy at the foreign competition, to put the idea of triennial periodical shows in the great manufacturing districts . . . . which would stimulate them to view the foreign works . . . . as patterns to be excelled." This was because there was some uneasiness, it seems, "against the great show of industry of all nations . . . . some persons fear a riot, fire, destruction of foreign property, and there is indeed some cause for alarm when you invite every adventurer to come to your capital." In March 1851 Sir John sent off his "case of classified wheats for the Great Exhibition" and in April he went over and "went to the Glass Palace for a season ticket; 15,000 had been sold . . . . the Austrians will show the French and English both are backward in the fine arts as far as furniture goes; their suite of apartments is unrivalled for beauty of design and execution. Gillow may hide his hand or take a copy out to vie. The confusion, yet withal order, which prevails in this fairy palace is truly wonderful." On May 1st he arrived early in the morning, and found that the ladies were required to go in first, "which raised no small alarm amongst them, but off they went leaving their loves behind them . . . . The Queen and Prince were admirably received, so was the old Duke. The Chinese Commissioner, Kianli, was the greatest curiosity in the procession, which was a failure as such. The silence, after the cheering, while the choruses and prayers were going on, was very imposing, the quiet of 30,000 persons. While the chorus was being chanted a singular occurrence took place. The Mandarin walked round the circle of diplomats, bowing to them gracefully. While the world looked on wondering, he walked quickly up to the throne and prostrated himself at the feet of the Queen, rose, bowed, and retired, receiving the gracious acknowledgement of Her Majesty. His homage before the nations, paid for the first time by a Mandarin to a European monarch . . . . He was loudly cheered for it . . . ."

"England holds her place in all but some of the finer arts, the Italians in their cameos, paintings and velvets, the Germans in some iron fancy articles from casts, the Austrians in some furniture, because it was at the Imperial charge; the French in laces and dresses, but in all that constitutes the wealth and real power of a people surely England is pre-eminent. The United States' contributions are pitiful, all others curious and varied . . . . It was no Babel of confusion, order prevailed everywhere. The policemen were earnest but civil, no disobedience to their orders was attempted . . . . except one act of standing on a platform to have a peep at the Queen. The sight from the gallery above the dais was quite astounding, an immense anthill of intellectual beings humming to and fro . . . . like a swarm of bees." A few days later he visited the exhibition again, with the Bishop of Winchester and a family party, and "The Queen, Prince Albert, the Prince of Wales, Princess Royal, Prince and Princess of Prussia were there, and passed close by us. Prince Albert recognised me and gave me a gracious salute . . . . the Queen seemed in thorough good spirits, and the royal children delighted the exhibitors with their earnest questions." He then repeated his impressions of the various countries' exhibits thus; "In the most refined arts Italy and India. The most useful and refined England, Austria, Belgium, China, Prussia. Russia exhibits half a dozen specimens of coming greatness. The Swiss, Greeks, Turks, Americans, Brazilians, rudest as you go westwards." On another occasion he visited the Palace with his sister in law, Louisa Janvrin, and his daughter Harriet, and "although it was a shilling day the people behaved quite as well as their superiors, not their betters, in behaviour at all events." And again; "The half crown gentry not so polite as the people on Wednesday . . . . met the Queen and Prince Albert in one carriage and the two Princes in another, just returning . . . . The company more select and more rude to each other. The high fashion came at 3, their style is quite a part de son genre,—there is no mistaking it. The police told me . . . they could accommodate fifteen hundred carriages."

Then one day he went to see the Jersey butter being made, trying out various churns. "We had twelve of the Sappers to turn for us and were at work from 10.30 to 6.30. One churn made 21 lb. 2 ozs. of Jersey cream into butter in two minutes, and another 28lbs. in $4\frac{1}{2}$ minutes. We sent the 28 lbs. to the Queen." The next day he called at the Palace to make sure the butter had been received. By July he said: "Visited the Crystal Palace for the fifteenth time. The novelty has worn off and it has now become a matter of business to examine it." In 1867 when he visited it again, the exhibition had been moved to Syden-

VII   PRINCE'S TOWER, or La Hougue Bie, past which the Queen drove on her return journey to St. Helier,
2nd September, 1846.

(from lithograph by W. Gauci of sketch by T. Neel).

VIII   The MARKET and HALKETT PLACE, St. Helier, with Fort Regent behind, c.1840.
(from a lithograph of a drawing by P. Le Lievre).

28.   QUEEN VICTORIA reading despatches
(*from a drawing by Sir William C. Ross, R.A.*, 1841)

29.   QUEEN VICTORIA landing in Jersey, 2nd September, 1846
(from the painting by P. J. Ouless)

30. 'Instantly the Queen stepped on it (the landing box) and came up gracefully', her Jersey A.D.C.,
Colonel John Le Couteur, being among the first to greet her.
(*Detail from the picture by Lieutenant E. P. Bedwell, R.N.*)

31. 'A harbour of refuge running out from that pretty point Verclut.'
(St. Catherine's Breakwater, Jersey)

ham, "where the new object which most astonished me was the *Wellingtonia gigantica*[1] from California." In June of that year; "Went to the Crystal Palace to the Handel commemoration, 2000 voices and 500 musicians did honour to the immortal composer's divine music. 'Judas Maccabeus' was never so grandly brought forth. The 'Sound and Alarm' and 'See the conquering hero comes' were thrilling and sublime; 'Oh lovely peace and liberty' thrilling and exquisite. Then the National Anthem and the old 100th Psalm were never more nobly sung. The Queen entered thoroughly into the joy of her subjects. The grand waters played for an hour after the Oratorio, and the view from the west angle of the terrace below was most enchanting."

What other glimpses do these diaries give us of the Queen and the Prince Consort? Many. As Q.A.D.C. Sir John was often present at royal levées and balls, though the duty was taken in rotation, and he was always told when his turn of duty would be, and on occasion asked if it were possible to change the dates when they were for some reason inconvenient. Let us take a few of the many royal occasions recorded, and through his eyes, view the contemporary scene.

In 1850 he was able to take his son, Halkett, to a Prince of Wales' Levée, and said that the Prince "has grown quite stout." But three years later there was a better impression, for at a levée which the Prince was conducting for the Queen, "he looked very well and young in his Rifleman's dress as Colonel of the Rifle Brigade." A week later there was another levée where "gentlemen kiss hands, as to the Queen. Colonel Neville of Gentlemen Pensioners, who is there to keep order, said he would require the police . . . . as they were pushing us as in a mob. I have seen peeresses do so at a drawing room. Lord Dinorben told me he had heard of the Jersey Republican funerals, and that the Government ought to put them down." This refers to the French refugee proscrits who always made the occasion of the death of one of their members an excuse for propaganda and oratory. In May of that year there was a Queen's ball, and Sir John attended with his friend the Guernsey Q.A.D.C. Colonel Priaulx. "The King[2] and Queen of Hanover, the Prince of Prussia, Lucien Bonaparte[3] etc., were there with two thousand more. The King of H is a very intelligent and interesting looking man; his sightless eyeballs seem to seek for vision, yet he is very cheerful. Our Queen is sweetly attentive to him. The Queen of Hanover[4] is not handsome, but she has the brilliant reputation of being a most excellent lady. It was a crush to get a peep at the two Queens dancing in a quadrille, with the Princess Mary, the Duke of Cambridge with our Queen, Prince Albert with the Queen of H. No one dances more lightly than our Queen. . . . I took Major Ainslie and Major Banner to see L. Bonaparte, who was the lion of the evening. He was very richly and handsomely dressed, very quiet in his manner and like his immortal uncle."

In 1854 Sir John again took his son to a Queen's ball; "We had time to walk through all the five drawing rooms before the Queen appeared . . . . she looked very bright and handsome in green and diamonds. The King of Portugal[5] looks like a jolly English farmer's son, and the Duke of Oporto a nice looking boy. The Prince seemed in high spirits. Dancing

---

1. *Sequoia gigantica* or Giant Redwood.
2. Prince George of Cumberland, grandson of George III (1819-1878), deposed 1866.
3. Prince Louis Lucien Bonaparte (1813-1891), fourth son of Lucien, brother of Napoleon. A Philologist, he visited Jersey in 1862 to study Jersey-French.
4. Mary of Saxe Altenburg (1823-1907).
5. Probably Dom Ferdinand II and his son ,the future Dom Pedro V.

L

commenced soon after. I went round the second time the Queen took the haut pas. The Prince Albert did me the honour to shake hands with me . . . . I was not a little amused to find that Johnny was dancing in the Queen's quadrille with the Countess of Limerick . . . . It was half past three before I turned in by day light."

In 1857 there was a Waterloo day parade of Chelsea pensioners, when Sir John's son had just become a Lieutenant Colonel in the Coldstreams. "It was a most crowded levée with 657 presentations, and though the Queen must have been tired she must have felt gratified at such extended homage. The Prince of Prussia[1] seems a quiet, gentlemanly, unassuming young man, very observant of all things. He stood next to Prince Albert . . . . The Queen bowed and the Prince graciously offered me his hand." The proud father was bursting with happiness at seeing his son present at such occasions. That same year his newly married daughter-in-law, Mai, was presented at a drawing room at St James' Palace and "she was very becomingly dressed in white moiré with a green silk train and looked quite a belle . . . . I took her in by the entrée as my privilege, so that she saw all the grandees and had a snug seat for an hour . . . . she went through her obeisance with much grace . . . . The Archduke of Austria seems to have more hauteur (than the Prince of Prussia), is buttoned up in the Austrian mode, the Prussian wears his coat open with his ribbands concealed in part. The Princess Royal seems young yet to marry, but she is very précoce and clever it is said. The Queen looked quite pretty . . . . The Court were in black, not the Princess Royal nor the Princess Mary; what a fine head this Princess possesses." At another ball in 1859 he observed that "The Queen danced as lightly as ever; Princess Alice seems very sweet and agreeable." The next year the novelty had, perhaps, worn off, for he said: "Few of my old habitués were there . . . . a long affair. It seemed to me that there was a dearth of beauty. Was I evil eyed at the time?" However at the levée the next year he met many friends who were all most hospitable, including Sir Harry Jones, Admiral Sir George Sartorius and the ex-Governor of Jersey, Sir Frederick Love. He said that now that Wellington and Talleyrand were dead the most striking looking person there was the Persian Ambassador, ". . . . a venerable bearded Artaxerxes looking face, long hooked nose and patriarchial, with a Persian sheep skin cap and a rich dressing gown with jewelled orders." After the death of the Prince Consort in 1861, the Prince of Wales conducted levées and drawing rooms for his mother, the first one being in 1863, by which time Sir John was the senior A.D.C. in attendance, and therefore had his place on the right, next to the gentlemen in waiting, and he said: "The Prince has filled out, is about 5 foot 8, seemed to be in the highest spirits, very courteous to all his acquaintances . . . . he is a nice looking young man of pleasant manner. The Duke of Cambridge seems to be on the most friendly terms with the P. There were 1000 presentations, an immense levée, the largest I have witnessed this reign."

In March 1863 the future Princess of Wales arrived in England and "all London is beside itself. The streets in the city yesterday were crowded beyond all my experience, a dense crowd moving, creeping, amongst carpenters, joiners, hammering and cloth spreading, red cloth, wreaths of flowers, evergreens, triumphal arches, lighting of gas in Prince of Wales' feathers and all sorts of A-E-A and stars and garters . . . . Windsor is wild with excitement . . . . The glass continues to fall after this lovely week, and the weather is overcast. Oh, Lord, grant an auspicious day for the entry of the Danish Princess to her new

1. Shortly to marry the Princess Royal.

home." Sir John had been offered a seat in a house overlooking London Bridge, and started out with friends at 7 a.m. and away they went "over Westminster's magnificent new bridge . . . . London Bridge and its adjuncts had been entrusted to the city architect for its decoration, and nothing could be in better taste or finer. The compliment was wholly paid to the lovely Dane, Danish Kings and Vikings in large medallions, gilt columns surmounted by the Raven and the Elephant, bearing the flags of Denmark . . . . In order to clear the crowd good humouredly, from the bridge, a strong body of police, unarmed, in a solid column, followed by a fine band and the Royal Horse Artillery, cleared the space . . . . The Lord Mayor, Aldermen, Common Council, all in their state carriages, all the companies with their flags and banners borne by men in costume . . . . Six carriages preceded the hope of England. She was seated on the right of the Prince's carriage, her mother on her left, the Prince of Wales opposite to his chère amie, and her father[1], a princely looking man, by our Prince, her sweet bright face, full of joy, beaming with pleasure, under a pretty white bonnet and roses. When she found they were halted, she rose like an honest girl to admire and enjoy the noble scene, when such a roar of cheers and waving of handkerchiefs greeted her as made the Prince seem almost uneasy and anxious. An equerry came to inform him of the cause of delay, at which he laughed and told his father-in-law, 'London big wig mobs are as difficult to move as other mobs.' " The wedding day arrived on March 10th, and poor Sir John was stricken with flu, and wrote: "It is a great mortification to be deprived of seeing the marriage cortège and ceremony, and my son in command of the Queen's guard of honour." Unfortunately there was a thick London fog that day, but in the evening, ". . . . at Trafalgar Square among the countless throngs. The crush was so great that in that direction after watching the Drummond light[2], flashing from the Duke of York's monument on to Nelson's statue, looking truly white and ghastly like the ghost of the hero, I crept through the crowd."

The new Princess of Wales conducted a drawing room in 1863 and "she is considerably slighter and thinner than I had fancied when seeing her in her bonnet and shawl . . . . she is the slight figure my wife was when we married, such as I could take under my arm and run away with[3]. The Princess has a noble as well as a sweet expression, when in repose looks grave and very full of mind. Her smile of welcome to the ladies she honoured by shaking hands was very sweet. Her laugh was honest when the Vice Chamberlain dropped his staff of office on a lady, also when another entangled her dress with my neighbour, Colonel Vyse's spurs, which I had to kneel to disentangle. The Princess Alice of Hesse stood next to the Princess of W. When she first came in there was a cloud of gloom over her sweet countenance; the last time she stood there her mother and beloved father were there. She almost fell into tears, but the announcement of the Ambassador by Sir E. Cust soon caused her to regain composure. The Princess Mary of Cambridge with her noble brow, was looking so well,—she is remarkably popular." This particular entry in the diary is headed 'A remarkable drawing room' and the account explains why this is so.

"Act I. The Prince of Wales was next to her in his new garb as Colonel of the 10th Hussars, which becomes him much better than the red uniform of a General. After about one thousand ladies had been named, and four o'clock had come, we all thought

1. King Christian IX of Denmark.
2. A calcium light invented in 1825 by Thomas Drummond (1797-1840).
3. He never did.

the affair was over. The Princess turned to follow the Lord Chamberlain, Lord Sydney. In rushed one of the Chamberlains to say that there was a delay, 500 ladies were assembled and waiting to come in. Open, Sesame. The tired Princess had to resume her position. 500 more ladies came by. A halt. No one coming. Doors shut again.

Act II. What was it now? Ponsonby came in to say that hundreds were yet coming, the line of carriages reached to Harley Street. The Duke of Cambridge and the Lord Chamberlain had a conference, and agreed with the Prince that the doors should be kept closed for a quarter of an hour; seats were got for the three Princesses who sat down to have a little real rest, after having stood and curtsied from 2 till 5.

Act III. It was a very pretty and gorgeous scene, what one has seen in a grand theatrical scene, but here was realised. The ladies in waiting and maids of honour all grouped round the throne, as a background in black, with the three Princesses in white with glittering diamond tiaras, seated in front. To the right of these the Lord Chamberlain and Gold Stick in splendid uniforms; to the left of them the Princes of Wales, Louis of Hesse, the Duke of Cambridge, Prince Frederick of Holstein, while some thirty of us A.D.C.s and other military attachés, who remained, were looking on and admiring this remarkable occurrence. All the formality was gone and the Princes chattered to the Princesses, while we did the same in groups. This lasted until a quarter past 5 when the doors were reopened, and 300 or 400 more ladies came hurrying by, till 5 minutes to 6 when the dear little Princess seemed thoroughly wearied, made her graceful curtsey to our homage, and retired. . . . It was a most remarkably complimentary drawing room, loyalty and curiosity combined to see the new Princess. A great number of old dowagers were of the curious."

In 1867 there was a ball given by the East India Government to Sultan Abdul Aziz of Turkey. When he arrived in London he rode with the Prince of Wales on his left, and a guard of honour of the Blues . . . . "a fine countenance with a very dark beard, evidently pleased and even surprised at the uproarious greeting which thousands and thousands of Englishmen were giving him." Two days later there was a command concert given in the Sultan's honour at the Crystal Palace, which Sir John attended with his daughter-in-law, and the Sultan was "habited in plain black with a bright red fez . . . . though impassive as a Turk should be, he smiled on several occasions, seemed greatly pleased with the tremendous cheers with which he was assailed . . . . (we) viewed the splendid fireworks. The electric balloons were new to me and lovely." A few days later the East India Government gave a ball for the Sultan, to which Sir John went, in uniform, with Mai "in half mourning with diamonds in her hair, looking her best . . . . we got to Downing St at 10, carpenters were yet hammering and nailing, flowers and shrubs coming in. Sir William Russell was in a great fuss, asked Hal to act as an assistant steward. The ante rooms were bare of chairs or furniture . . . . the ballroom was 150 feet long, 120 feet wide and 60 or 70 feet high, gorgeous in red and gold, columns in alabaster support the galleries. It was a courtyard covered in . . . . We saw every magnate pass by, Duchesses, Marquises, Countesses and every esses . . . . Lord Derby and the ministers came at about 11, then the state procession . . . . The Prince of Wales, the Duke of Cambridge, Duchess of C, Princess Alice, handed by the Sultan in a Turkey General's uniform. The scene was gorgeous and most imposing." Dancing then took place, a quadrille, with the Sultan chatting to the royal Princesses on the dais, through an interpreter. Sir John was introduced to Sir Digby Wyatt[1], "the architect of the whole building, whom I complimented on his success." At midnight supper was "indistinctly announced," and tables for eight were arranged. In the room prepared for the Sultan and magnates, "the Queen's and other gorgeous plate was displayed, a king's ransom." But there was a tragedy to follow, for "at about 10 o'clock we were horrified at hearing that Madame Masurus, the Turkish Ambassador's wife, had been stricken with paralysis. Her daughter, in an agony of tears, rushed past us, and we heard the sad intelligence that she was dead. This cast a damper over the whole scene of festivity."

In 1853 there was a splendid military review at Virginia Water, and during the preparations for it Sir John mentioned that the 38th, that is the South Staffordshire Regiment, "marched best off the ground in open column." The Queen attended but was later than usual, "her habit being exact punctuality." A bridge was made by Sappers, men crossed a river in guttapercha boats, they skirmished and attacked from the woods, "the sight of the troops and crowds magnificent on a delicious day."

In 1856 we have a naval review. "Found the royal carriages at the George (at Weymouth) waiting for Prince Albert and Prince Frederick of Prussia, who is going to pay his devoir to his lady love . . . . Went on board the gun boat where Tom Saumarez . . . . told us to order lunch till he returned from the Victory . . . . Went over the Erebus floating battery, a terrible iron coffin, with walls of iron six inches thick. When set off rolling, I should fancy most alarming; brave indeed would be the men who would cross the ocean in such a vessel. While we were at lunch on board the Lapwing, the Fairy and Elfin crossed us with the Princes en route for Osborne, when the salutes made us run up. The roar increased to a cannonade when the shipping took it up at Spithead and all the yards were manned". At another review that year he commented, "It was a magnificent spectacle and a more glorious reflexion that between two and three million people, including the Queen, her family, her guests, her Lords and Commons, had been together witnessing the peace rejoicings without bayonets, police or guards to keep order."

Sir John found the Prince Consort friendly and approachable. In 1852 he was given an interview on the subject of getting promotion for his son, and the Prince promised help, saying, on the offer of testimonials; "Thank you, that is quite unnecessary Colonel Le Couteur; I know you and that is sufficient, you are the Queen's A.D.C. and we know who you are. How are you getting on in Jersey?" That same day he attended another of the many drawing rooms, and noted: "Her Majesty was looking remarkably well, she wore a profusion of brilliants. As I stood third from opposite to her I could notice the very kind greeting she always gives to her old friends . . . Lord Derby[2] and his Aide stood now where Lord John[3] did when I last was there. Johnny came by, and was civilly greeted by the Queen and the Prince shook hands with him. The Rajah of Coorg[4] made his salaam with his gold jewelled cap and golden slippers. Lady Constance Grosvenor looked the fair constellation of the aristocrat, a very love, simple in attire, gorgeous in beauty."

In 1843 Sir William Symonds had given him a ticket to see the new Royal steam yacht, the Albert and Victoria. It is described as being very spacious and comfortable, except

---

1. Sir Mathew Digby Wyatt (1820-77), brother of Thomas Henry Wyatt. No relation to James Wyatt.
2. Lord Derby (1799-1869), Premier on three occasions.
3. Lord John Russell (1792-1878), Prime Minister (1846-53).
4. Coorg or Karg, a province in India, annexed in 1834.

the nursery which is "dark and dingy". Also there is "one peculiarity, that the paddles can be thrown off work in a gale or when immersed, by a small crank wheel . . . . which shifts them six inches in or out of gear. She is to steam 12 knots per hour they hope . . . . Will it every see Jersey?" Ten years later a visit to another royal yacht, the old Royal George, was recorded. Sir John, with his wife, daughters, and son-in-law went to Portsmouth to visit their relative Tom Saumarez, who was rather an anxiety to them, on the yacht. They had a nice lunch with a concert from the Master of the Band and "four lads who sang some glees and catches very nicely." The Captain's cabin was said to be finely decorated with drawings and sketches by Prince Albert. In that same year there was a fire not generally known about, but recorded thus; "Heard to my horror that the Queen had been burnt out of Windsor Castle last night. The Prince took her to Frogmore, but she had the presence of mind to send for the London Fire Brigade, which reached the fire, with two engines, in an hour. The loss is named at eighty thousand pounds."

In 1861 Sir John took his family to the opening of the new Horticultural Society's gardens, where there was a wonderful show of fruit and flowers, "such as no country in the world could elsewhere produce." The Prince Consort and the Royal family arrived, the Prince planting a *Wellingtonia gigantica*. In walking round he recognised Sir John and greeted him. A few months later the Prince died, and the news was received by his admirer, then away on the continent, on December 16th 1861; "The Aigle gave the saddest news I have heard for a long while, the death of the excellent Prince Albert on Saturday night last. What a dreadful affliction for the poor Queen, sorrow for the whole nation. Never had so worthy a Prince been so near a throne, a calm honest adviser. In this crisis too! How wonderful are thy ways, Oh, Lord."

Of Her Majesty's second visit to Jersey we have very little detail. This is particularly sad, but it comes during one of those unaccountable gaps in the series of the diaries. It is, however, known from other sources that this was an unexpected visit, in the course of a sea trip[1] on board her yacht, and she decided on impulse to see the college to which she had given her name. This she did, having a boisterous welcome in town, after which she returned to her yacht. But she landed again later in the day at St. Aubin, and her ever attentive A.D.C. took her for a drive up St. Peter's Valley, which he rightly considered to be one of the most beautiful spots in the Island, and round by the northern parishes to St. Catherine's Bay, where she re-embarked. About a week later he wrote to her equerry, Sir Charles Phipps, acknowledging a cheque sent "to be distributed amongst the coachmen and servants of the gentlemen whose equipages were made use of for the Queen's service, after paying Mr Gregory's bill. This commission has perplexed me greatly, because no private carriage but my own was used by the Queen's suite. To be certain of this I went to Mr Gregory who supplied the carriages for Her Majesty . . . . and he assured me not . . . . Those three carriages with the horses and jockies were ordered to be fitted and prepared by the President and States of Jersey for the Queen's reception, as State carriages at the public expense." Sir John wondered what he was to do with the cheque for £21.18.0d. He suggested that "if Her Majesty will permit me to give a guinea to my coachman for having had the honour of showing the way from St. Aubins to St. Catherines, he will esteem it a very great honour and unexpected boon." He went on to ask Sir Charles Phipps if it would be in order to allocate the balance towards the National School in St. Aubin, ex-

---

1. Suggested by Prince Albert, after difficulties with the Cabinet.

plaining that "in 1815 when the late Mrs General Le Couteur established a Sunday School to teach English to the Jersey children, there probably were not a dozen in the school who could read English. Now in our National School, of which I am Secretary there are about 60 boys and 49 girls who read English well." A bazaar recently organised for this object had raised £285, and "as Her Majesty landed on St. Aubin's pier and admired our pretty little town . . . ". he suggested that this would be a worthy object for the Queen's cheque. This was evidently approved, for shortly afterwards an acknowledgement was sent to Sir Charles Phipps for "a cheque for £20, gift to the school."

It is nice to think that when the poor Queen was feeling worried by politics, bedevilled as ever by party disputes, she was able to come to our Island, and enjoy the peace of a day driving through our valleys.

CHAPTER THIRTEEN

PATER FAMILIAS

Despite the glitter of these exciting occasions in London, Sir John's heart remained always in Jersey, at his home Belle Vue, referred to then, as it still is by his descendants, as B.V. What a contrast there was between these two compartments of his life, a house in a small island, and the English Court in all the brilliance of mid-Victorian affluence; when almost every European royalty had some relationship to the Queen of England, and England was the most stable of European kingdoms, and at the forefront of scientific and industrial expansion and productiveness.

Each time he returned home, by the Atalanta, the Wonder, the Ariadne, the Lord Beresford, the Calpe, or any other of the brave little vessels which ploughed back and forth over the Channel, maintaining our link with England, he was once more immersed in home and Island affairs. What an active life he led. There were days devoted to militia work when he rode long distances on horseback to drill the men, often in inclement weather; and others with divers duties in Court, whether as Constable, Jurat or Vicomte. Nor were these voluntary functions entirely sedentary. He was always moving to and fro, inspecting road and harbour works, checking weights and measures, visiting the prison, and attending numerous committees connected with the work of the States, agriculture, education and the church. As a private person he had other duties as executor, trustee or family confidant, and responsibility for various properties. At home there was gardening, the elaborate experiments with wheat, and a great deal of entertaining. With no telephones, and transport only by horse or carriage, one cannot comprehend how these Victorians managed to pack so much into a day.

Although his wife Harriet, like all members of the family, managed to find time for painting, of which she was very fond, most of her life must have been occupied with housekeeping, and catering for the large dinner parties which were so often given at Belle Vue. It was not extraordinary to have thirty to dine and twelve was commonplace. In addition, it was quite usual for some of the guests to stay the night, and for friends and relatives to make visits of several days or weeks, coming out from town for a change of air and holiday. With such a fine garden, large quantities of preserves were made, and there are records of jam made from raspberries, strawberries, black, red and white currants, plum and gooseberry; and orange and apricot marmalade, damson cheese, blackcurrant jelly and raspberry vinegar. On Harriet's birthday, in 1850 Sir John wrote in his diary: "Dear old wife 52. Mrs Pipon,[1] the old lady of Noirmont . . . . said to me she looked quite well and had grown fat. 'Yes, and saucy too', which amused the fine old lady". There were always large parties at Belle Vue for Christmas with twenty or more sitting down to dinner, and for years Sir John enjoyed this as much as anyone. But one day he complained to his diary that, being sixty and his wife but four years younger, he found the social whirl too tiring, and intended to have fewer and smaller parties. There was no noticeable reduction, how-

1. Probably Elizabeth Hodges, wife of James Pipon, who died 1854.

ever, after this resolve. Quite often they gave wedding dinners in honour of a bride. One such was the wedding of the Solicitor General, Robert Pipon Marett, who was later Bailiff, to his distant cousin Julia, youngest of five daughters, of Philippe Marett of La Haule. The menu was mock turtle, fish, turkey, ham, roast mutton, vol au vent, mutton cutlets, curried eggs, prairie hens (grouse), sweetbreads, cabinet pudding, velvet cream, jelly pears. In reading these menus one must assume that some of the earlier courses were alternatives. To partake of them all would have been asking too much. At that party there were sixteen diners. A fortnight later a similar meal was placed before eighteen guests, when Sir John was over seventy years old. With such lavish fare it is perhaps not surprising to find Harriet in discomfort and complaining of cramp at night. Sir John told her "she had been living much too well all the time Fred and Jane were here, champagne extra two or four times a week, because of course we drank remains from parties . . . . At breakfast this morning nevertheless she ate buttered cake and a large petitoe[1]. At lunch I said nothing. She ate a good slice of roast pork. Yesterday for dinner she ate a rich curry of roasted duck; very nice, for I tasted it as there was no plain meat to be had, neither chop nor joint. If such a diet may not cause stomach complaints and cramp, I am no quack . . . . My dear wife complained of cramp at dinner. Boiled fish and roast veal might not create cramp but, as I told her, curds and cream with a bumper of port wine just afterwards might disorder a stomach. I could not touch such. She is 63, I 67. Frederick, she says, will outlive us many years but, as I reminded her, he takes walks of ten or fifteen miles daily by himself, then eats, drinks and sleeps well. Idlers who get up at 7, take no exercise, but eat breakfast, lunch, dinner and tea, must have cramp or dyspepsia". In those days there was everything in the butchers' and fishmongers' shops to tempt the housewife, particularly the latter. Passing through the market in 1825, Sir John counted twenty-two kinds of fish on sale. Home-grown oysters were readily available. The Jersey oyster dredging industry was flourishing, as one diary entry alone, in 1847 shows: "Drove to Gorey. Went to the oyster beds with Dumaresq on board the Seaflower. A very good haul for a boat is about twenty tubs a day".

From time to time the accommodation at Belle Vue must have been stretched to the limit; when, for example, the daughter Mary, with husband, seven children and a bevy of nurses and maids, all came to stay. It was even worse when the Bishop came. On one visit he preached a "beautiful discourse" in All Saints' Church "in aid of its external embellishments", and left the next day. His host got "up at 5, to make arrangements for the departure of the Bishop and party, consisting of: Emily Sumner, now nearly nineteen, a lovely girl: John and Mary, and sweet little Harry: Mary: another nurse: Emma, Emily's maid: Hagget or Higgett, His Lordship's valet: Thomas, his footman: and Alfred, John's servant: ten in number, who have been with us since August 31st". That was a stay of three weeks or more. The standard of living at Farnham Castle, the Bishop's residence, and at Winchester House, where he lived when in London, was sumptuous. A Farnham menu of 26th July 1866 offered soup, three types of fish, five entrées, five meats and seven sweets. There must have been some wonderful cooks, butlers, kitchen maids and housemaids in service then, and many of them, but the papers tell us little of what went on behind the green baize doors. Good living was taken for granted by those who could afford it, and a thing which should not lightly be surrendered. We find Sir John, for example, reminding Emily Sumner

1. Pig's trotter.

that she "has lived in a palace from her birth, with carriages, horses, servants, splendour at her command; more like a Duke's daughter than a private gentlewoman". He advised her never to marry unless her suitor had at least £800 a year, though she assured him she would be content with a moderate life such as her sisters had. In the event she married Canon Milford. There is a delightful pencil drawing of her and her brother George, known as "the handsome Sumners", at Farnham when they were children, with effective highlight in white chalk.

There were also quite a number of Clubs,—the Union, the Turkey and the Thursday Clubs appearing in the papers, and others for playing whist, and also for shooting, which was usually at Noirmont or near St. Ouen's Pond. The 1853 diary relates that "the General dined with our new Victoria Club, 58 in number, very hilarious". But in 1866 General Cuppage was "very much excited about de Carteret's row at the Victoria Club with Mr Thrashy". He had not so much minded about being called "an old fool", but found it mortifying that the Committee, his friends Clem Hemery and Charles Robin, had not taken the matter out of de Carteret's hands. They should have intervened on their Patron's behalf. He was inclined to cancel his New Year's Day reception. "I observed that to give up that annual levée would be attaching an importance to a vulgar transaction below his notice. Why cut out all Jersey for such a trifle?"

There were picnics, races and regattas. Then, as now, Jersey families entertaining visitors took them on picnics to La Corbière, Bouley Bay or Mont Orgueil: the only difference being that then they went by carriage, not car, and the paint brush and sketch book have given way to the camera. What fun those outings were. One day they all raced up to the top of La Corbière rock, before there was a lighthouse there. On another day: "went

Belle Vue from the foreshore.
from an unsigned sketch c. 1840.

in the cart with Punch to a shrimping frolic with Dan Janvrin, Jimmy Pipon and Beaumont Pipon. It was fun for the boys, but a bad tide". While the men thus disported themselves, the girls ardently collected seaweeds, which they took home to dry and mount in albums, some of which were sold for considerable sums in aid of charity. There was bathing too, but less than there is today.

The papers first mention the Jersey Races in 1836, when Sir John wrote to Sir Harry Wheatley at St. James' Palace, accepting for the Society for the Promotion of Races a King's Plate, similar to that granted to Guernsey. The plate was to be competed for by Jersey horses only, "meaning all those dropped in the Island". For some reason the King's Plate never came, and two years later he had to write to Sir Harry and Lord Albemarle that its non-delivery was unfortunate. "Several persons were put to considerable expense in training their horses" for it, and the winner, "a respectable young farmer, feels greatly disappointed that he has not received it". This award of an invisible trophy was naturally damping "the spirit which is now manifesting itself for improving the breed of horses here", and Sir John hoped His Lordship would use his influence "in the proper quarter, that it may yet be granted as the late King's plate". By 1841 the King's Plate had become the Queen's Plate, and a suggestion had been made for transferring it from the Race Course authorities to the Agricultural Society, and he wrote again to Sir Harry. He felt, on the one hand, that "nothing like an ungracious act should even appear to proceed from Her Majesty, by the transfer of a grant made by a former sovereign". On the other hand, he agreed locally bred race-horses had not proved to be what was wanted for the militia guns, which was part of the raison d'être of the Race Course organisation. There was the further complication that "several of our leading gentry have set their faces against races, in this small place where liquor is so cheap". The only strong demand for races was from "English or Irish gentlemen, birds of passage, or officers of the garrison, for whom we can always get up a race". On balance, he favoured the transfer of the Queen's Plate from the context of race-meetings, with their drawbacks, conducted under the guise of training of militia horses, to an Agricultural Society award for two year old colts and fillies, in alternate years. In 1849 there was a two-day race meeting and all Sir John's clerks were "off to the races". A man named Baker won the Queen's Plate, but wanted a monetary prize of £25 instead. "I saw Baker and explained to him the nature of the gift; that if he refused it, it might be transferred to the Agricultural Society. It would be an affront to Her Majesty. Lord Limerick wished it to be exhibited from the stand, and finding no one who would go for it, I drove to town for it, when it was exhibitited to the admiring gaze of the public. Baker took it after the races, which were very good, but requested me to take charge of it for him. Renouf came round by Faldouet to make a saisie of one Nicolle, who escaped on seeing us, scaling a wall and dashing into some corn". This is a reminder that the races took place on Grouville Common at that time. The 1853 diary says: "Went to the races to see the Queen's Cup won, the only good race. The ground is most dangerous, as they allow booths to be erected on each side. The north side being open, two horses bolted into the crowd and a boy was nearly killed, and two other persons hurt. The booths should all be at the top behind the winning post". We hear no more of the Queen's Plate or Cup, but are left with the feeling that horse-racing is an uncertain area into which Sir John should never have intruded. He only did so in the first place in order to secure a flow of horses to the militia artillery. But the racing enthusiasts of his day had very different motives.

A regatta was an irresistible part of the Victorian way of life. In 1849 several of the voyeurs[1] on the Grande Vue des Chemins in St. Ouens were members of the Grève de

1. Those sworn in to point out to the Court the worst roads in the parish, on the occasion of a Visite Royale.

Lecq Regatta Committee, and "did not loiter in taking us through 'les plus mauvais sentiers'. The scene in the little bay was very gay, the Cuckoo and Seaflower decked out, with a band on board the former, and clouds of fishing boats made a very pretty display. There must have been several thousand people on the hills. The Court dined in the Barracks, and Judge Winter Nicolle brought a dozen of old wine to treat them". There was another wonderful regatta at St. Aubins in 1863. "A lovely day and bright scene. The people came in crowds from St. Helier by steamer, canoe, sail and row boats, omnibus, gigs, cabs, cars, phaetons, four-in-hand, horseback and on foot; a very pretty gay scene. The bay looked most beautiful".

It was important to a man like Sir John to be correctly attired for each occasion, and to this end he spent a good deal of time and money. Some of the items seem very expensive, even allowing for the altered value of money. In 1827 he was charged £30.6.6. for an overcoat, but deducted 10s. from the bill "for a velvet collar .... I never have worn a velvet collar to a black coat". Mr Woolf, Military and Court tailor, to whom this admonition was addressed, was later asked to send 1 frock coat, 1 silk waistcoat, 1 pr. black trousers, 1 pr. grey trousers, 1 light pr. grey trousers and 1 pr. drab trousers for riding, "and to make the coat an inch wider in chest and shoulders". In another order the same firm were asked to supply 1 pr. black doeskin pantaloons, a double-breasted loose wrapper in green lined with silk and a brown plush waistcoat. In 1851 he arranged for Woolfs to send him "four suits of clothes annually for twenty-two pounds, and no extras". In Jersey, Messrs. de Gruchy were asked to "have the cricketing flannel washed in hot water for my flannel waistcoats". A complete inventory of his clothes appears in 1870, and includes among many other things: a Crimean greatcoat, a total of six cloaks, five frock-coats, one Bishop's jacket, a Q.A.D.C.'s full dress and undress uniform and sash, and plenty of waistcoats, one of which was "velvet flowered". From Swan and Edgar he bought "a rich silk dress" for six guineas for Harriet.

There are detailed housekeeping accounts for the last few years of his life, kept by his daughter, which give an interesting picture of expenses at the time. The servants were apparently paid by the quarter, and their annual wages amounted to: £17 for Ann Luce (the faithful housekeeper): £16 and £10 for the maids: £19 for the coachman and £20 for the gardener. Potatoes then cost 4s, for two cabots: a telegram, 1s: dog tax for two dogs was 7s.6d: tuning a piano cost a guinea. A woman named Martha was employed at 1s. a day for milking. A "bottle of phosphorus for destroying mice" was only 4½d. How uneven it all seems to us now. A top hat, or a uniform sword could cost £10 each; yet Seville oranges were only 1s.6d. a dozen and a chicken 2s.9d. The identity of some articles is obscure. Cod sounds, which are mentioned, were a delicacy which the Newfoundland cod fishers used to bring home, being the fish's air bladder. But what is sponge oil?

Repairs to the houses Belle Vue and Le Bocage were undertaken at intervals by Mr. Dart and Mr. Boniface of St. Aubins. Thatching at Le Bocage and Dell Farm was done by Mr. Le Marquand, and in the case of the latter was quoted at £6.16.6. There are not many mentions of furniture, apart from purchases made just after marriage, but no details are given of these. A local cabinet maker appears in 1837, in a letter which says that young McDermott, son of General Le Couteur's butler, "built a vessel as master carpenter last year at Newfoundland for Mr. Perrée, and is therefore quite au fait, having had the further advantage of some years' tuition in cabinet making with old Carrel[1] of St. Aubins". Years later Sir John was writing on behalf of Carrel's son Josué who wished to become a ship's carpenter at Portsmouth. In 1849 "Mr. Hotton engaged to make me nineteen mahogany dining room chairs, similar to the pattern chair made by Gillow in London, with the top of the back less sharp, covered with the best sheep's skin morocco leather, for twenty-eight shillings a piece, Jersey currency, of the best wood and work; to be completed in three months; payment at Xmas. N.B. stuffed with horsehair. As I wish the framing to be all of oak, I have agreed to give one shilling British more on each chair, rather than have beech".

We have already heard of the purchase of the proud new phaeton. In 1833 an order was placed for "a car . . . . for which I will give you, with patent axletrees, fifty-nine pounds. It is intended for one horse, but put a couple of eyes to the ends of the shafts, in case we should require a leader occasionally. I have lamps to a carriage and phaeton. You need not therefore send any; only place holdfasts for them in the body of the car. Do not omit (to) make the back and seat cushions as soft and easy as possible, as well as the springs. My crest is on the seal. Send it over by Capt. Bazin[2] when ready". There was then correspondence about the harness, which was to cost eight guineas, with 3s.6d. extra for crest. One is surprised to find the word "tiger" in use as late as 1870, when "Fred Cheal, fifteen years old, left by the steamer for Weymouth in charge of Captain Falle, en route for London as tiger for Hal and Mai. A very good sturdy lad, well up in English and French. Gave him a black cloak of mine, neck ties, six shirts and five shillings, with plenty of caution against mixing with London waifs".

In 1831 he bought a turkey carpet, 22 by 17 feet, at the India House for under twenty pounds, "which I think cheap. The broker told me the company allowed £500 a year for cats' meat, each cat being allowed a penny a day[3]. In 1859 he bought a safe with two drawers from Chubbs, of St. Paul's Churchyard, for £18.5s. Always interested in new inventions, he saw a sewing machine in 1860 belonging to Clara de Lisle, and ten years later he evidently gave one to a deserving woman: "Miss Burlton came to return my gift of a sewing machine for Mrs Amy, which her donkey-proud sister will not allow her to accept, although she has three starving children. I refused to have it back". In 1872 he bought another, for seven guineas, to present to Mrs. Paul, the mistress of the infant school at St. Aubin. In 1865 he was telling the proprietor of a French hotel how much he would benefit, especially with English guests, if he installed a water-closet. "What he has is beastly, a hundred years behind England". Belle Vue had this modern convenience by 1871 if not earlier. It is therefore all the more surprising that he wrote in 1865 to Mr. Baker, his tenant at Le Bocage, who had asked for a water cistern to be built: "another tenant required a water-closet in the house, which I declined to place, such not being in the lease". The tenant was then given advice on sanitation: "Before and during the period of the cholera I caused to be used chloride of lime, which removed any smell . . . ., renewing it when necessary. This I do here occasionally in hot weather. I recommend you to have thrown in a load of straw, with any weeds you may cause be to drawn . . . . This will supply you with excellent and cheap manure biennially . . . . I send you a bottle of Sir W. Burnett's[4]

1. Later Carrel, the cabinet maker, was in La Motte Street.
2. Whose ship was the Ariadne.
3. There must have been 329 cats on the pay-roll.
4. He also invented a cure for dry rot in 1836.

disinfectant liquid which I use in this house". Eventually a compromise was reached whereby landlord and tenant shared the cost of a more modern installation. In his own household Sir John issued written instructions for cleanliness.

"1. use clean water, soap and a nail brush or scrubbing brush to clean your hands well by rubbing them with the brush.
2. empty that water which is foul, take fresh water and rinse your hands and the brush.
3. wash your face.
4. never leave the foul water which you have used in the vessel for the next person to empty or to use. It would be piggish.
5. the towel will not appear much soiled with such cleanly care".

It is difficult to assess what income Sir John had. In 1830 he said his private income was but £400 a year, but he may not have included his wife's income. About ten years later, when writing to the Royal Military Academy at Woolwich for entrance for his son, he said that as the boy was his only son he would inherit £600 to £700 a year. He himself drew army half-pay as a Captain, and as Vicomte may have drawn some perquisites, rather than a fixed salary as now. It would probably be correct to say he was comfortably off but never rich.

A number of servants were employed inside the house, and there were farm employees as well. Many of them are mentioned by name, but none with more affection than the steadfast Ann Luce. She was born in 1798, the daughter of Edouard Luce and Suzanne Le Marquand of either St. Mary or St. Ouen. As a young girl she came as nurse to the children at Le Bocage, and remained with the family for 55 years, retiring on half pay in 1874. In her will she left "un louis ancien cours de Jersey" to the poor of St. Mary's parish, and after dividing her personal effects between her brothers and sisters, she left "aux enfants du Colonel Le Couteur de Belle Vue, à John Halkett, deux cueillers à soupe: à Henriette, deux cueillers à desserte: à Marie, six cueillers à thé: et à Sophie, les pincettes à sucre, toute en argent. A Madame Henriette Le Couteur ma broach, en mémoire de moi. Je nomme Jean Le Couteur Ecr. mon exécuteur, et je lui lègue deux louis pour acheter une bague en mémoire de moi". So much a member of the family was she that she was buried in their private vault, and they erected a mural tablet to her in St. Brelade's Church in which she is called "a faithful and attached nurse". Pixley's charge for the tablet was £9.16s., and the family also paid £6.18.3. to the undertaker, £2.8s. for the grave, and the account of the doctor who attended her. A portrait, by Berteau, shows her holding her knitting in the Jersey manner.

When the family went for a trip to France in 1822 Ann Luce accompanied them as a nurse, saw a theatre for the first time, and was enchanted. When taken to the Tivoli Gardens in Paris she said she had never seen anything so beautiful. When the General was so ill in England it was Ann who went over to nurse him, and again travelled with her mistress to Buriton to nurse Mary when she was poorly. In 1854 the son, Halkett, came home "with a moustache according to new regulations", and "was much moved when his old nurse Ann kissed him, whom she brought into the world". She knitted socks for him in the Crimea, and at his wedding she rode in a carriage with the grandson Harry Sumner. By this time she was called "old Ann Luce" or "dear old Ann", though in fact she was exactly the same age as her mistress. A spinster, she was formally referred to as Mrs. Luce, a traditional compliment to the senior member of the staff. In 1864 she left for Dinan in a gale with Harriet, but the diary has no misgivings: "the old Atalanta is a thoroughly safe boat". A few years later, when unwell, she was sent on a visit to one of her sisters, the diary commenting: "wrong, I think, she will not be so comfortable there as here". In her latter years she saved over £1000, and Sir John acted as her adviser, investing it for her and conducting all the correspondence. The eldest representative of her family was W. G. Aubin, a solicitor, who "conducted the affairs of the great bankruptcy of the Joint Stock Company". Her life was one of complete devotion to duty, and the mutual respect between her employers and herself constituted an ideal relationship.

The life of Harriet, the daughter, through these years was that of a typical Victorian lady. Close in age to the Queen, she was the epitome of Victorianism, exhibiting its virtues and its limitations. She played the piano, but perhaps not very well. She painted, and took lessons from a Mr. Poulet in England. Her father was anxious that she should work hard to improve her drawing and painting. Her own diaries show that a great deal of time was taken up with paying visits and shopping, and that she was an ardent worker for the St. Aubin's schools and Bible classes. Quite early on she was considered a confirmed old maid. Her father's diary on 19th April 1848 reads: "Harriet's birthday. Heard the cuckoo as usual . . . . The 'dear old girl' (as Mary calls her) is a very good one, with amazing self-denial on many points. She will never marry, I think. She is too independent and frank to please men, though she seems to be a great favourite among her friends." An 1860 diary discloses that both she and her mother were unpunctual. "Some years back, on good Mrs Sumner, the Bishop's wife's plan, my wife wrote cards for regular hours of meeting by call or bell; prayers at 8, breakfast; lunch, dinner and gave me a card on punctuality, printed. It is now on the old book of morning prayers. She or Tit have scarcely ever been punctual since. Carriage ordered at a given hour, ten or twenty minutes late. Gloves to put on, shawl forgotten, orders to give just after I had got into the phaeton. Servants all unpunctual in consequence . . . . This morning ordered the phaeton at half past nine. She left with Edward at a quarter to ten. I shall hereafter note which of us is unpunctual." It is an age-old privilege of Pater Familias to be irritable on occasion. But it does seem that Sir John had a lot to put up with from his ladies.

He was devoted to his daughter Mary and admired her. At the age of twenty one, it will be remembered, she met the son of the Bishop of Winchester, and was married to him at Farnham Castle on 15th November 1843. Buriton, near Petersfield, where they lived, is a pretty little village. The ancient church contains a Norman font, and the thirteenth century chancel contains a piscina and three sedilia. On Speed's map the village is written Beryton, and so it is pronounced to this day. The vicarage appears to be an old house with Georgian additions. Exposed in the stucco of the side facing the road is a feature which could be a piscina, or a window, removed at some time from the church. On 26th December 1845 Mary had a son, named Harry Le Couteur Sumner. He would eventually have been the heir to Belle Vue and all its contents, but he did not live to enjoy his inheritance, which passed to his son. He was the grandfather of the present representative of the family. On Mary's birthday soon after the birth of her son, her father wrote "Dear Mary's birthday; an old Mamma already, and a very nice tender one she will prove". Thereafter Harry became one of the main interests in Sir John's life. If he attributed exaggerated intelligence to the child, it is no more than most grandfathers have done. In 1847, delighted that the little

BURITON RECTORY, 7. August 1845.
from a sketch by J. Le C.

boy had recognised him, he went on a shopping expedition in Regent Street to order a riding habit for Mary, who said of her outfit: "I sport a black wide-awake, which is much more comfortable than a hat". She must have looked pretty in it. Harry was with him, and he wrote: "I took Harry in my arms, 16 months old, and showed him a lay figure handsomely dressed in a hat and feathers and riding habit. He looked at it several times, and then at me. 'What is it, my sweet fellow?' said I . . . . He looked at me, sighed deeply . . . ., a long sigh still looking at the figure . . . . He sighed deeply again and looked at his Mamma . . . ., evidently showing in his own expressive language, without sound, that he perceived the figure had not the power of breathing. May not this indicate a great early power of observation?"

When at Buriton, Sir John used to walk and drive about the beautiful Hampshire countryside, visiting local families, and keenly noticing everything connected with farming: and always comparing it, as Jerseymen do, with conditions at home. He took great interest in his son-in-law's garden, and examined minutely the crops he grew in land attached to the living. There is an old photograph of the domestic staff of the vicarage, showing three women for house-work and three men for the garden and land. Mary had a large family. Soon after Harry's birth she had another child, a girl, who died in infancy, and in 1851 another daughter Eveline, known as Evie, who was to be the joy of her grandfather's heart to the end of his days. The Buriton household spent many happy holidays at Belle Vue. John Sumner, and later his son Harry, often preached at St. Aubin's Chapel.

There is, of course, a great deal in these papers about Sir John's only son, John Halkett Le Couteur at the various stages of his career. Much of it reflects his father's efforts to obtain commissions and promotion for him. In those days, a man who wanted either had

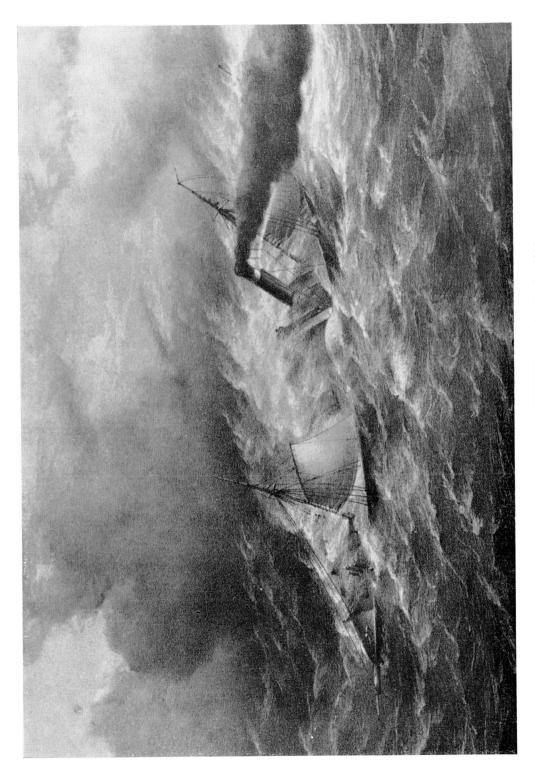

32.   The Paddle-Steamer WONDER in a gale, October 1846.

33. ANN LUCE
'Dear old Ann'
Nurse to the Le Couteurs for 55 years.
(*from the pencil portrait by Thomas Berteau*, 1848)

34.   HARRIET LE COUTEUR
(1819-1894)
(*from the pencil portrait by Thomas Berteau*, 1846)

35. Rev. JOHN MAUNOIR
SUMNER and his wife
MARY (née LE COUTEUR),
at Buriton, Hampshire.

36. JOHN HALKETT
LE COUTEUR and his wife
MAI (née LOW), at the time of
their marriage in 1857.

to ask for it, and only got it if he had strings to pull and could pay the exorbitant sums demanded. This extraordinary system was at its worst during this period, and was not changed till 1870. We have seen Johnny (Halkett, or Hal: he was called by various names) at boarding school and with tutors in England, and left him with his Regiment, the 87th, at Newport in Wales. While there he was ill and his father went over to stay with him in October 1846 and again in June 1847. On his way there Sir John fell into conversation with a Corporal, who said: "There was not an officer better liked in the corps, nor a smarter drill for so young an officer. He never spoke roughly to anyone, though he was strict in his duty. Nice praise from a soldier", Sir John proudly recorded. When he met the commanding officer, Colonel Majenis, he was told that his son "was a most amiable youth, everything that could be wished and a most excellent officer". In the mess he met a future Lieutenant Governor of Jersey, Colonel Love, and described the evening thus: "The mess room looked very handsome, a fine carpet £50, the centrepiece £500, lots of plate of all sorts, very rich, a good dinner, well cooked, quiet waiting, no pressing, all very nice . . . . I sat next to Col. Love, who told me all his adventures at Cephalonia, in Canada and here; one long succession of triumphs and honours. Would he come to Jersey?"

While at Newport Sir John attended every military exercise, commented freely upon them and had the time of his life in the company of military men. When he left he reflected: "They are a nice set of young men, very gentlemanly and friendly to each other, addicted only to those foibles which are almost inseparable from youth, if greater vices do not take the place of them . . . . Jack seems very steady now; when marching at the head of the leading company, no. 8, the men moved like a wall, admirably, much better than other companies, I fancied to please me. Their kits and barracks are in excellent order. It is very strange to see them so sickly, of a low typhus fever, 11 deaths last month and 4 dying in hospital. Dr. Johnson did not know what to prescribe: all his resources fail him". In 1847 Johnny came of age and was already in "command of a detachment at Northampton, on his own resources". When he came home on leave in 1849 he brought his own horse, and while at home he often helped his father with making maps and surveys, as well as with the garden. At the end of leave he returned to Sandhurst "taking his grey with him. Old Considine would wish him to have a stronger horse, but this one is perfectly quiet now". He was on leave again in 1850, and on New Year's Day "the regimental band came as usual to play martial airs in full uniform, and partake of dinner. High life below stairs for 36 persons. Johnny was surprised at their military appearance and accuracy of time. Johnson takes great pains with them".

In 1850 Johnny was under orders for India, and the day before he left was a busy one. "Johnny and I transplanted the Cedar of Lebanon in the east slope . . . . We walked to the Vendue des Froments dinner at Pitons[1] near the church . . . . We were about 35, a very young party, I being the third eldest. All the old Principaux are dropping off fast. The Froments du Trésor sold for 20 livres, those of La Charité for 24, very low indeed. We had a capital dinner for 5s. a head with a bottle of marsala. Captain Morgan, R.N. sat next to me . . . . He was the individual who informed the Government of the enormous frauds which took place three or four years ago in the silk and spirits trades, by which some of the excise officers made immense fortunes . . . . The parishioners drank Johnny's health on his expected departure for India in a very friendly manner. He answered very nicely".

1. Either at Le Marais du Val or La Valleuse. Both were owned by Mr J. Piton on Godfray's Map of 1849.

M

seen on the voyage to India, 1850.

He left England on 20th April 1850 on board the Ripon. His parents and John Sumner saw him off. He wrote long letters home describing every detail of the voyage and the places they stopped at, illustrated with some water colours of very fine quality. Everyone in the family was devoted to him. His sister Mary wrote to him in June: "That nice little Berteau's sketch is over the piano . . . . It is so nice to sit and sing to you there". At Gibraltar Johnny and two friends set out on horseback and went up the Rock. He describes the wonderful panorama, "which made me feel I still stood upon soil which England may ever be praised for having taken. . . . They have provisions there for seven years, besides being able to procure water from the hills". The people were "a small race of men, very quick and active, running alongside of the horses uphill when at full trot". In Malta he met "Pipon and his nice wife and chicks". At Alexandria they left the ship and travelled a short distance by canal, changing from tug to horses after a while. There were several changes of boat, by

MOCHA, in the Red Sea, 14. May, 1850.
from a water-colour by J.H. Le Couteur.

the end of which they "were all filled with fleas". They proceeded by horse to Suez and embarked in the steamer Haddington, rather superior to the Ripon, and in this ship they continued by way of Ceylon to Calcutta. He travelled up country at a leisurely pace to Ferozepore, on the way making contact at Cawnpore with Dick (Dr. Richard Valpy) de Lisle, a contemporary and close friend. He was Sir John's godson and, after his retirement to Jersey, his doctor and executor. He lived at the house Le Coin at the top of La Haule Hill, built in 1762 by Brelade Janvrin, father of Dick's mother Elizabeth. The closest friendship was maintained between the two families, and Sir John was devoted to Dick and his sweet wife Clara. Johnny said that in India Dick always wore "a pith hat of Charlie Napier's shape".

Johnny had a wonderful time in India, with much social gaiety, and was extremely popular. Among the papers there is a tiny envelope of filigree, containing a poem of seventeen verses, dated at Allahabad on 17th August 1850. It seems to have been composed by some lively young ladies who had enjoyed his company at a ball, and were familiar with Longfellow's "Excelsior", published in 1841. They may have been the daughters of Mrs. Lowther, with whom he was staying. Here are a few of the verses:

"Who came to live in this hot clime?
Who stay'd with Mrs. L. a time?
Who made the ladies here write rhyme?
                    Le Couteur.
Who met us at a Ball one night,
when we were deck'd in Lilies white,
and who descried them at first sight?
                    Le Couteur.
When sleep forsakes you, and you lie
with throbbing head and heavy eye,
think of the Lily. Will you sigh,
                    Le Couteur?
A merry, happy day we spent,
for all agreed too soon it went,
and to its joys your aid you lent,
                    Le Couteur.
And when 'twas o'er, I tell you true,
we lik'd you, though we "bullied" you:
and that we'd say to very few,
                    Le Couteur."

He was a most conscientious correspondent, and sent home all sorts of seeds to be tried in the garden at Belle Vue. Every item of home news interested him, and he and his father exchanged long letters on military detail. He was already speaking of trying to exchange into the Guards, but Lord FitzRoy Somerset's advice to his father was: "Wait till he gets his company before you take any step". In 1853 Sir John confided to his diary: "After six weeks of steady application I have succeeded in obtaining dear Johnny's exchange into the Coldstream Regiment of Foot Guards, whether for weal or woe depends upon himself. His principles are no doubt fixed . . . . He got his company without purchase on the 15th March last . . . .": and then the remarkable statement of cost: "I paid £2156

. . . ., including all the fees for Guards Club, £31.10s.: Regimental Mess, £10.10s.: Presentation fees, £10.10s.: Plate fund, £2.2s.: stamp on Commission, £1.10s. . . . for the exchange with Captain Chichester: making Johnny's commission worth £4500 . . . . with a pound a day a man may live elegantly anywhere, so the agent tells me". When he called on Lord Strafford, previously Sir John Byng, he was told that "any officer recommended by Lord Raglan was sure to be well received". He found that Johnny was posted to the second battalion to which he was to report himself immediately upon landing. His bearskin cost £18.2s., and his father, generous as always, paid the bill.

Johnny's time in the Crimea is described in the following chapter, but it will be convenient here to mention his marriage, which took place after it, in 1857. The year before, while staying with his uncle Frederick Janvrin at Bath, he met Miss Mai Low. Sir John described her as "a very sweet looking young person, light hair, blue-grey eyes, soft looking, a very fair complexion, tall and embonpoint, a very nice figure and carriage . . . . Mrs. Low, her mother, is daughter of the late Professor Nichols of Glasgow University . . . . Mr. Low is an old gentleman who has had an apoplectic seizure, but his intellect is quite clear. He is a fine ruin . . . . ; very courteous". A marriage settlement was arranged between the families, and "I said they would be nearly thrice as well off as their mother and I were at starting in life". That night there was a ball, but "the girls generally were not dressed as in our ball-rooms in Jersey. Johnny and Mai were as smart a couple as were there, and very good dancers too".

For the wedding on 2nd April 1857 the bridesmaids wore cherry-coloured tarlatans[1], white scarves trimmed with fringe, and white tulle bonnets with red roses and cherry-coloured ribbons. As to the bride: "Sweet Mai looked very lovely. She was habited in a white moiré antique rich silk dress, with a pretty wreath of orange blossoms and narcissus, over which hung a superb Honiton lace veil . . . . Johnny, or Halkett, as his benedict name better becomes him, looked very well in a blue frock coatee, white waistcoat and light grey trousers; pretty much the pattern we all followed". The procession drove to Wolcot Church, where the Rector was assisted by John Sumner, who "read the service very impressively". There followed an "elegant déjeuner à la fourchette for thirty-two guests, and John Sumner made "a pretty speech in reference to his alliance to the Le Couteur family, and his love for Mary after thirteen years of marriage . . . . Duckworth made an elegant speech in proposing the health of the four bridesmaids, 'fortresses as impregnable as Sebastopol, if not carried by fair approaches'. I replied to the toast of the parents, and afterwards proposed Colonel Low's[2] health, a hero of Balaclava . . . . At half past one, sweet Mai had changed her dress to a beautiful lilac and black fringe woven into the dress, and a sweetly pretty white gauze bonnet with feathers, and a black velvet mantle . . . . A handsome chariot with four greys and postillions received them. Mr. Bowen flung in a bouquet and a shoe for luck, and off they dashed, cheered by us all, with old Ann and a footman in the rumble[3]. "Soon afterwards Johnny brought Mai home to Belle Vue, where "the dear new daughter was welcomed to her future home by every soul in the house". There is no portrait of Johnny between the Crimea and his wedding except one of a man beside a chess table, which is believed to be of him. Who else could it be? In 1850 his father had

---

1. Muslin.
2. The bride's brother.
3. Back seat, like a dickey.

written to him in India: "The very beautiful sets of chessmen too arrived in safety . . . . The large set are the finest I ever saw out(side) of the Chinese collection in London . . . . They go well with your grandfather's Indian chess table. So two generations have supplied ornaments for the drawing room from India, within three quarters of a century".

Johnny and Mai returned to Farnham, where Sir John visited them, being met at the station "with their nice little wicker phaeton and pretty little mare . . . . Drove to the Camp, where I had the satisfaction of seeing Halkett in command of the Coldstream Guards . . . . Marched them to Church where the minister, a Crimean, gave them a pungent sermon . . . . on prayer . . . . It was an earnest, appropriate but rather coarse sermon, unfit for ears polite".

In 1858 Sir John went with his son and son-in-law to Cherbourg, to attend a ball at the invitation of the Mayor. On arrival they found "nine line of battle ships and a large gun frigate were drawn up in order of battle behind the 'Digue'. The Captain placed our steamer admirably, after taking us all round the French fleet. We had a lively dinner on deck, the noble men of war in front and a lovely coup d'oeuil of 300 or 400 English yachts, gaily dressed, astern . . . . About six, the hour appointed, the Royal Yacht with the standard at the main having the lead, steamed grandly round the head of the breakwater, when such a roar of fire from seventeen hundred guns burst forth as I had never heard. The French four-decker Bretagne gave the one gun signal to the thunder which followed. The French fire their guns in steady succession, very finely. The Royal Albert, our noble three-decker, drew up at her moorings close by the Queen's yacht; the Renown, a beautiful 90-gun ship a little astern. The Emperor and Empress visited the Queen at 8 p.m." Next day there was a regatta, with three bands entertaining the vast crowds, and the Queen "drove round the town and forts meanwhile with her Imperial hosts, under endless salutes from ships and forts". Sir John called on the General Comte du Moncel, who was most hospitable and had the Emperor's A.D.C. and the Minister of Agriculture as his guests. He and Johnny explored the new wonder dockyard, which was 20 acres in area with 30 feet of water at low spring tides. "What is it all for?", Sir John asked his diary. "The railway which is now open from Paris might convey any force in a few days, to be embarked in these basins, secure from apparent attack. But are all these Members of the House of Commons in their yachts not wide awake as to what they are inspecting? Do not those lovely little pleasure boats, manned by the flower of our seamen, each represent a line of battle ship or a frigate, ready to defend our sea-girt Isle? I smile at the danger, for danger there is none. The Emperor must be sincere, or his imperial diadem will fall from his brow. The British are his true friends, who wish him to consolidate his power by peace and commerce . . . . There was a rumour that he would be shot at . . . The streets had been covered with sand six inches deep in order to prevent the explosion of any infernal machine". At a grand dinner with the Comte du Moncel Sir John was told that he was "a gentleman of the olden school"; and also that the "bon ton" do not dance at balls, merely look on. There were fireworks that evening, including a set piece of the blowing up of the Malakoff. Next day the ceremony of opening the dockyard was performed by the Emperor. The ball that evening was too crowded for enjoyment, and Sir William Williams of Kars said to him that "I should have my uniform torn off if I attempted to go on: he had given it up. The ladies called my uniform 'bien riche', and took me for a General, and Halkett for my A.D.C. The Empress is very lovely and sweet looking, but not beautiful: quite courteous and smiling when speaking, but relapsing at once into an air of intense anxiety. While the Empress put on her wraps, the Emperor chatted to a man of rank near me, yet he also wore an aspect of care".

This vivid narrative, and others in these papers, are naturally full of adjectives. Sir John, who must have been extremely well taught, had a rich store of these at his command, and drew upon them energetically to convey his meaning. If a word did not come readily to hand, he was not above inventing one, as we saw in the case of the dancical governess and Temple Bar citically decorated. A student of word usage will find interesting examples here of words which have changed their meanings in the past century, in some cases meaning almost the opposite. "Genteel" had not then its modern pejorative sense, but meant cultured and well behaved. "Honest" often meant natural, unaffected, straight-forward. "Off-hand", so far from meaning stand-offish, indicated a friendly and forthcoming personality. "Subordinate conduct" meant obedient and becoming behaviour. "Laborious" meant hard-working. And there are many more.

There are hints here and there that Sir John did not approve of smoking. When in France he referred to it as "a bad custom, taken from us": and when his tenant at Le Bocage, David de Quetteville, asked to have the dining-room re-papered, "I positively refused . . . ., because I objected to smoking in a dining room". Still less, one imagines, would he have countenanced the chewing of tobacco, thinking it a dangerous habit, and noted in his diary: "Halkett poisoned our house dog Neptune with tobacco taken inwardly yesterday, and is wondering why the dog is ill today". On the subject of drink, being the wise man he was, he made a distinction between drinking and drunkenness. He said, of a regiment about to be stationed in Jersey: "when composed of young recruits, as this second battalion is, (it) should not be sent to Jersey, where spirits are so cheap, and where numbers of low women lead the inexperienced into constant troubles. None but old, well trained corps should be sent here. It causes the British Army to be a by-word in France for drunkenness. During four months that I was at Pau, I think I saw only one French soldier intoxicated". Only a few days later the Governor received a letter from the Commanding Officer, Colonel Chapman, complaining that his men were maddened from debauchery and intoxication, by liquor obtained at the Devonshire Arms Tavern in Hill Street . . . ., and the Bull Tavern, corner of Wharf Street, "I got samples of brandy and gin from both these disreputable houses". But wine, as a complement to good living, he enjoyed greatly, and in speaking of a dinner he always mentioned the quality of the wine. He also believed that wine should be purchased with care, and tasted, to make sure of its merit.

He does not seem to have made any pronouncement on divorce, which was practically unknown, treating the problem of incompatibility in a common-sense way. When a relative, Margaret Houghton, wished to divorce her husband, he thought it folly, "as your husband is neither a drunkard nor a libertine, and he has never maltreated you by beating you". A dignified separation was the answer: "Come and reside here under the protection of your sister and brother, and under the eye of your connections, who will sympathise with you, and afford you sufficient retired society to enable you to bear your lot with resignation, if not with cheerfulness". Though a man of high principle, he was not so straight-laced as many of his contemporaries. He described himself once as having been a ladies' man in his youth. He was not averse to a little gossip, but some of the tit-bits he records are cloaked in riddles and the meaning is obscure. When somebody he knew was straying from the straight and narrow path, and concealing the fact successfully, he tolerantly remarked

"The devil has his own way at times". Nor did he express exaggerated horror at lapses from good taste, though this does not mean he condoned them. At a large London party in 1866 "Mr. Quentin Twiss sang a most amusing and vulgar song, which quite electrified some of the elders, quite in the slang taste of the age. It would have horrified Addison or Sir Richard Steele. What is to be expected when the young men are to be seen *in the Row* by their mothers and sisters, either riding or walking with their improprieties?"

World events, as they occurred, were reflected in a greater or less degree in the diaries. With Johnny in the Crimea, he was deeply concerned with the progress of that campaign and wrote him many letters, and made many diary entries. When news of the Indian Mutiny reached Jersey there was great consternation. A relief fund was at once organised, and for the inaugural meeting Miss Westaway gave her rooms free of charge, and £156 was collected. Harriet Le Couteur formed a ladies' committee, which collected £75 in a short space of time. A month later the total Island collection was £1455, an enormous sum for those days. There is a good deal in the papers about the financial crisis in Jersey in 1873, when first the Mercantile Union Bank and then others stopped payment. Sir John wrote: "Great alarm at the stoppage of the Mercantile Bank. Moses Gibaut of Mainland and many others nearly ruined". The next year he wrote to the local paper on the subject, deploring that the unstable conditions at home were causing "some amount of exodus out of the Island of its early manhood and strength". One night, after dining with the Gibauts he returned home to find the young maid Amelia "very poorly from a bilious fever", and here we see him as the real Pater Familias, the head of a family which included not only his own kith and kin, but all who dwelt beneath his roof. He gave Amelia medicine, and in the morning consulted Dr. Low, who however, "treated her as he had done poor little Sophy, lightly, and gave her a bottle of mixture which had no effect whatever". For ten days the girl was nursed, the family taking it in turns to sit with her, Sir John himself taking her pulse and preparing hot drinks for her. This degree of kindness and attention was exceptional in those days, and few men in Sir John's position would have known their way around the kitchen well enough to make a cup of cocoa. It is by simple acts of humanity like this that he earns a special place among the father figures of the Victorian age.

CHAPTER FOURTEEN

BONO JOHNNY

At a quarter past seven on a November morning in 1854, a column of the Coldstream Guards moved off from Portman Street Barracks for Waterloo Station, en route to the Crimea. At their head were six horse-cabs, decorated with banners: then the band, drums and fifes: and immediately behind marched the young Captain commanding the troops. He was Johnny Le Couteur. They halted for a minute or two in the Strand to allow an artillery train to pass and, after exchanging pleasantries with the gunners, resumed their march. An enormous cheering crowd followed, and all along the route window-sashes squealed up, hands clapped and handkerchiefs fluttered. At the station 700 men entrained, including the Grenadiers and Fusiliers: three bands played "God save the Queen", and in half an hour the train pulled out. Johnny was away for 20 months, during which he wrote 92 long letters home. What follows is culled from them. In his kit were 20 pocket prayer-books, in which he wrote the names of the sergeants and corporals of his company, and handed each man his book. The deep religious sense which prompted this act is apparent in every letter he wrote. He believed that he, his family and his men were in the hands of the Almighty.

Portsmouth gave them a boisterous reception. "Our men were offered pots of beer and ale which made them reel again . . . ., and I had trouble forbidding it . . . .; the mob here shouted: 'Let them have a drink, poor chaps, they'll deserve it' ". They embarked on the Royal Albert, "a most noble vessel; every deck is filled; . . . . we have 30 tons of shell on board and 50 tons of powder". On the 9th December they spoke with the Spiteful and Sampson, on their way to Malta for repairs: "the former's masts were spliced, the latter lost her main mast, figure-head gone. Sevastopol still holds out". It was a tricky voyage: "We have not a single good Sergeant or Corporal, and obliged to borrow . . . . of the Grenadiers . . . . I am termed 'the Sergeant' by all, having done the duty of one till I am perfectly sick of it". On the 14th they passed through the Dardanelles, reaching Constantinople on the 15th. Next day they lay off the Crimea.

The great engagements of Alma, Balaklava and Inkerman had already taken place, and the siege of Sebastopol was in its fourth month. The British had chosen Balaklava Harbour as their base; the French, Kamiesh Bay. The Allied siege works lay in a semicircle south of the town, the French at either end, the British in the centre. Their respective camps lay between the bases and the trenches. The map of the Crimea does not pretend to accuracy, being merely a diagram to elucidate what Johnny seeems to describe. From

Balaklava Harbour to the defences of Sebastopol was about 7 miles, and a rough track ran for part of the way. "It is an incline from Balaklava for a couple of miles", he explained, and half way up it was the village of Kadikoi. On the hills above this village he was in "Camp, Balaklava Heights" from 1st April to 5th July 1855, overlooking the "valley of the shadow of death . . . ., where the charge took place," and one day he went out to locate the battery which Lord Cardigan had attacked, and the embrasure through which he had

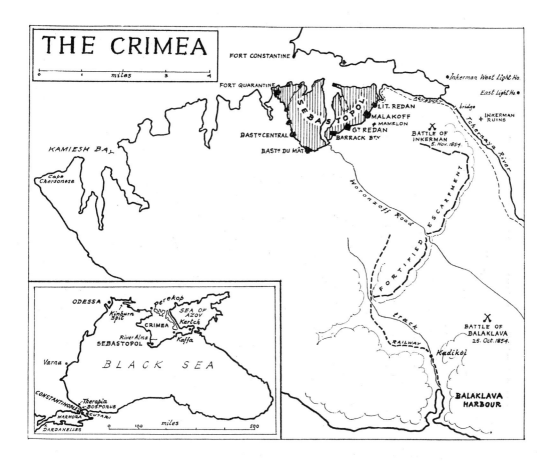

galloped. After the Kadikoi incline "comes a very steep ascent . . . . to the top of the hills . . . . You ask whether (it) is like Bouley Bay . . . .; it is like that up our valley, though rocky, but a little longer". Somewhere on this escarpment he was in "Camp before Sevastopol" from 1st January to 8th March, and 25th July 1855, to 20th January 1856. The gradient was almost too much for his servant when bringing up a heavy box from Jersey, and he asked Belle Vue for more consideration: "It is a mistake to suppose that a soldier with his full pack, 50 rounds, Minié and firelock, could also carry that box".

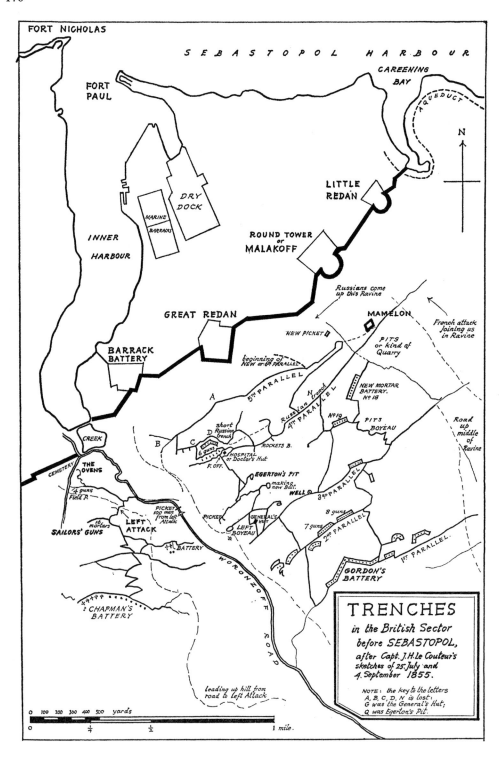

FORT NICHOLAS

SEBASTOPOL HARBOUR

CAREENING BAY

FORT PAUL

AQUEDUCT

N

DRY DOCK

MARINE BARRACKS

LITTLE REDAN

INNER HARBOUR

ROUND TOWER or MALAKOFF

Russians come up this Ravine

MAMELON

French attack joining us in Ravine

GREAT REDAN

NEW PICKET

PITS or kind of Quarry

BARRACK BATTERY

beginning of NEW or 6th PARALLEL

Road up middle of Ravine

A

5th PARALLEL

Russian 4th PARALLEL trench

N. trench

NEW MORTAR BATTERY. Nº 18

Nº 19

PITS

short Russian trench

Nº 19

BOYEAU

D

CREEK

B

C

ROCKETS B.

6 guns

HOSPITAL or Doctor's Hut

CEMETERY

THE OVENS

F. OFF.

EGERTON'S PIT

making new Batt.

WELL

3RD PARALLEL

4 guns Field P.

8 guns

PICKET 100 men from Left Attack

PICKET

GENERAL'S HUT

7 guns

2ND PARALLEL

16 mortars

LEFT ATTACK

LEFT BOYEAU

1ST PARALLEL

SAILORS' GUNS

BATTERY

GORDON'S BATTERY

WORONZOFF ROAD

CHAPMAN'S BATTERY

TRENCHES

in the British Sector
before SEBASTOPOL,
after Capt. J. H. Le Couteur's
sketches of 25 July and
4 September 1855.

NOTE: the key to the letters
A, B, C, D, N is lost;
G was the General's Hut;
Q was Egerton's Pit.

leading up hill from road to Left Attack

0   100 200 300 400 500   yards

0   ¼   ½   1 mile.

Still less authoritative is our plan of the Trenches. Johnny drew such a plan, we know, and his friends gratefully borrowed it to avoid getting lost in the labyrinth, but it has vanished and its contents can only be guessed from four hurried drawings in his letters, and a sketch or two. One such sketch, reproduced here, is of "this beautiful town of Sevastopol . . . . It (the sketch) was taken under occasionally a shower of bullets . . . ., many a ping, many a bob, as well as very heavy shells . . . . bursting in the air . . . . The Church at top stands out a little over the sea, a white and green roof. The oblong over the Battery (Redan)[1] is like the Pantheon[2] and is the Governor's House, a beautiful building".

In his off-duty hours he was a keen explorer, and before long was in the ravine where Inkerman was fought. It was "impregnated with horrid smells" from several hundred dead horses, and the bodies of fallen soldiers lightly covered with heaps of earth. "The shot and shell lie in every direction . . . . Never was any battle fought with such undaunted pluck . . . ., nor is it on record of so much ammunition being expended . . . . Many men fired 200 rounds that day, and even then were seen pelting the Russians with stones". But "it is most inconceivable to me how they came up those steep . . . . ravines . . . ., got their guns in position, without our pickets being aware of their approach". On the other hand the area was covered with scrub, and "our poor fellows say they could not see them until quite close". Johnny again mentioned the battle, apparently in reply to a paternal comment that officers should only use swords: "It is absurd in you old hands supposing officers ought not to fire on ye[3] Russians. At Inkerman our officers fired away as well as the men: and so did Goodlake at the Tchernaya (river) . . . ., dressed in a shooting coat, and kept the Russians at bay . . . . Now he is laid in a vineyard".

North of the Tchernaya were the Inkerman ruins, "of very ancient date, said to be Genoese": south of it was the Aqueduct, of seven arches and 160 paces long, and beyond that some "curious excavations like those at Gibraltar" where he followed a tunnel through solid rock for 324 paces. Near by were the Quarries from which the town was built, "a pure white sandstone, very soft and like that at Malta", and here one day he found a Zouave expertly trimming a tombstone for a fallen comrade.

Johnny lost no time in writing home for things he needed, and the incoming Crimean mail often meant a day of hectic packing at Belle Vue, especially when he said: "You must make no delay about all this". Much of it, he feared, he might never receive, for "hundreds have lost everything that was sent out, all from the bad management of government; baggage, blankets etc. laying in the wet, saturated, and no one to look after it". Some of his items are echoes of a bygone age, while others have a surprisingly modern ring. Listen. "Long Jersey waterproof boots . . . ., and get some . . . . paste to rub into the seams". They came, but were "a mile too big" and he asked for others: "let nails be in them . . . ., a pair of sabbots or French wooden ones, with a slipper to wear inside . . . ., are most useful in very muddy weather, or in a hurry". The men needed boots as well: "If Ching sent out his sons and workmen . . . ., and bring out . . . . lots of heavy boots . . . ., they would make a fortune . . . .; the men would give any amount; and so would the French". For waterproof coats, "Emary in the City is a good man". Once he ordered dresses and a couple of irons for "two poor soldiers' wives who have always followed the Regiment"; but there

---

1. Redan, more correctly redent, is a word applied to any tooth-shaped or triangular bastion with its point towards attackers. 2. Or, ? Parthenon.
3. In these letters Johnny uses "ye" for "the" when he is being jocular or slightly impertinent.

was delay, and he enquired: "When does Mrs Patrick's dress intend being sent?" When invaded by mosquitoes and flies he wrote: "Try and send me some green or blue net like that on your cups, to place at the door of the tent": then, "we are tormented by .... immense centepedes. I hope you will send me my Musquito curtains". Ann Luce, "dear old creature", knitted him socks, which he promised to wear at once.

Foodstuffs sent to him included a barrel of brawn which went bad in transit and made a stench so noisome that it was ejected from camp. The Jersey butter was "pronounced A.1 ...., but the crock was smashed to atoms", so next time, "put me up a small barrel of that exquisite butter": and, "try and place me some marmalade, which I am very fond of". As to potted meats, "Fortnum & Mason is the cheapest way of getting those kind of things ...., their beefsteaks are excellent. The small pots they have for breakfasts, of potted game ...., would be quite invaluable". Among priority items were four 6 lb. cases of short candles, and "Arnica plaister ...., it is excellent to heal cuts .... with". His mother sent medicines but he had little faith in them: "as if all of them would save one. We are in Higher hands". He much enjoyed his pipe: "then I should wish you to go to Hudson and buy me ... 4 lbs. of best Birdeye tobacco". Also, "a good spirit lamp and Etna[1]": just as well, for "my cook never came ...., consequently I am my own cuisiner": and, "my Soyer stove, complete with spirits of wine, 4 bottles". But in the end he secured some culinary help: "I may be a capital M.Soyer; however, it is owing to my faithful servant, the Duchess of Sutherland's footman".

There was much else: American moccasins: a patrol tent from Eglinton of Charing Cross: a Policeman's dark lantern: a small cooking canteen ("The utensils should fit into one another, as they have in Bombay"): "my spy-glass .... pocket sextant .... a small pocket filter from Hill & Millard .... pocket compass .... my pocket sun-dial, which is very accurate in .... sunny weather ...., in lieu of a watch: a small pen-knife, quill pen and ink ....: taper matches, not wooden ones, the damp plays old Harry with them". And: "Do me a favor. Go to Wilkinson and order me a straight sword ...., sharp both sides to a little past the centre of percussion, then it .... would resist a good blow. The hilt is also a great protection .... Let it be a steel scabbard". Just before his second Crimean Christmas: "I wish you to order me out a Letts' diary for 1856 at once".

At intervals he sent clothes home for re-furbishing, and after the fall of the citadel some trophies of war were consigned to Belle Vue by the ship Robert Lowe, including a brass helmet, "the shell I picked up in the Redan, the sword from our attack". He acquired a splendid tray painted with the scene of Cleopatra's death, but it was too large to send and is probably still somewhere in the Crimea. So, no doubt, is the "curious old three-pounder piece of ancient date" which he picked up in Kertch, hoping one day it would be "mounted in old Belle Vue". But it is not there today.

One gets the feeling that by degrees Belle Vue grew weary of Crimean demands, from a note headed "Johnnie's Orders", with "Mother's Answers and Questions" in a column opposite. It closes with a Parthian shot from Mother: "Specify all clearly, either for Peace or War; and think of every thing you may require, that all may be conveyed at one time". There were few if any more requisitions.

We will now try to follow in chronological order the events and experiences which

---

1. A conical water-heater of tin with flat lid, mounted point downwards in a saucer to contain spirit: long since obsolete.

Johnny describes. At Christmas 1854 Balaklava Harbour was crowded with shipping, and he visited young Jersey friends on various vessels, Malet on the Firebrand and Armstrong on the Vesuvius, which was "almost a wreck," having lost a gun, and only her mizzen standing. Others he met later were Philip Pipon[1], Dick de Lisle, Le Mesurier, Tunny James[2], Chevalier, and Hamilton of Gorey.

By New Year's Day 1855 he was clamped to a harsh routine of pickets, working-parties (apparently a euphemism for trench-digging), and Trenches (manning the trenches thus dug). The day after arrival he was placed on advanced picket, came off next morning and "was in the act of having a wash when I was told the working-party had fallen in and were waiting for me". That evening "I read prayers to my picket, seating them round a fire"; and at night was "tolerably snug in my Indian resigh[3]", which he found a godsend. There was a daily parade, "such a curious turn-out: some men and officers have hardly trousers to their names, torn and patched in every direction". A new hazard now beset the pickets, for Russian vessels in harbour had begun to throw shells right over two valleys into the British trenches. There was also much illness, and this devout man could be found at a patient's bedside reading the service for Visitation of the Sick. He was himself far from downcast. "I am far jollier here than in London. This strange life suits a wanderer better than a walk in the Park". For greater warmth he had his tent floor dug two down feet by Zouaves. Then he went aboard Imperatrice to invite Stepney to join their mess, the other members being "Rose, Whitshed and . . . .Le Couteur (Head Cook)".

At this time Russian and Allied pickets were often within earshot of each other, and exchanged fraternal cries of "Bono, Inglis" and "Bono, Muscov". Up in Gordon's Battery in January Johnny remarked that the Russians "call out to our men . . . ., who reply 'Bono, Johnny'. Curious, this", he added. The explanation is that Turkish soldiers, it seems, thought every Englishman's name was John, and the polite way to greet him on the path was "Bono, Johnny" (good Johnny). So assiduous were the Turks in this courtesy that they became known themselves as the Bono-Johnnies, and finally the phrase was an esperanto used on both sides, meaning little more than "Hullo, there".

His first impression of the battlefield was "Mud. Mud is what is so beastly . . . . We have to carry our own things in mud up to one's knees. I have bought boots up to my thigh". Worse than mud was the incompetence of headquarters, particularly over roads and transport. "The arrangements are as bad as they can well be . . . . Our delays and failures have been disgusting . . . . Our wonderful mismanagement". Things were at their worst in January: "there is no means of getting anything up to Camp . . . ., no mules or even carts . . . . The men are now employed as beasts of burden for any and everything . . . . The French are sending 6000 men to carry our shells up". At the quayside "bales over bales are allowed to lay on shore in the wet; clothing, hay, in fact everything . . . ." What animals we had "are so fagged they drop and die on the road". He reckoned that within 100 yards of his tent he could find enough dead horses to build a strong redoubt. "As to the huts, they are a farce, for did they arrive they could not be taken . . . . up". The small arms also "are in shameful condition; . . . . instead of having armourers to look after them as they came in, they have been allowed to rust". In any case they were of inferior pattern: "the Enfield is a far better arm".

1. Philip Gosset Pipon (1824-1904), who became Colonel Commandant in the Royal Artillery, a C.B. and a General.   2. Captain Henry James of the 20th Foot.
3. A thick, heavy quilt, filled with wool.

Other shortcomings of British headquarters are revealed up and down these letters, and when grouped together they make sorry reading. There was lack of liaison in the field: "There is no system whatever . . . . you come here", he wrote in the trenches, "walking over awful ground, shot and shell . . . . as thick as peas", and no one to guide you to your post. "The Field Officer this morning was not aware we were coming with our 100 men". Nor were all officers efficient on parade. Some, who were rebuked by Lord Rokeby, "really know nothing, only creating confusion with wrong words of command". Sheer stupidity was shown; one day when the thermometer stood at 112° and "our Brigade goes out for drill in Bearskins and Red. The heat outside is fearful". Many of the men, of course, fell out. The enemy were sometimes more resourceful than we: "No wonder (they) are able to carry off their guns, when every Cossack has attached to his equipment a pair of traces". A Russian soldier's kit also included two pieces of leather for mending his boots. At one stage officers were apparently ordered to get pack-horses at their own expense to transport their provisions to the front, and Johnny acquired three for £29.10s., but one of them was stolen. "It is placed in the Hue and Cry, but I shall never see him again". In all he lost three ponies by theft. As regards the conduct of the siege, he thought the overall strategy far too flabby. "The place might have fallen twice over, had they had a good Engineer instead of an old Molly Coddle to advise . . . .: I wish a Napoleon or a W(ellington) would turn up, for we might harass the enemy in many quarters at the same moment: Odessa, Kertch, Perekop, Sea of Azof . . . ." Lord Raglan inevitably came in for reproach. He "never is seen in Camp, and great complaints prevail . . . .: never goes out of his house and knows nothing of his men"; though one day he did ride over to the Coldstreams' position, where he said to a Corporal: "Oh! That's the Russian Fort, is it not?" "Oh, no, My Lord", the man replied, "that's the French redoubt. That (pointing to the one opposite our pickets) is the Russian one". "We have signally failed", Johnny wrote, "owing to Lord Raglan having taken up more ground than his troops could manage properly to hold. Consequently the men were worn out by fatigue . . . ." But as time went on he shifted the blame on to equally culpable shoulders: ". . . . the papers are abusing Lord Raglan, and deservedly too. However, I blame his aids and heads more particularly. Not worth a farthing, any one of them". These men may have been responsible for "our disgust with Lord Raglan . . . ., as they have again ceased fire after having silenced most all of the batteries . . . ., and we hoped a few days more would have seen us within the stronghold . . . . But No, we having lost 603 men and officers . . . . so affected old Rags, he now intends to go regularly by sapping up to the works, and thereby lose daily a great number of men". Then, in June: "poor Rags has been much struck at Estcourt's death and is seriously ill"; and on the 28th, "poor Lord Raglan is no more". Later, "with all his faults, he was greatly tried by the French always. He died of a broken heart. All his arrangements were knocked in the head on the 18th by Pellissier. No wonder he failed . . . . Poor, good-hearted, gentlemanly Raglan, the true English gentleman at all times". To this testimonial the diary of Johnny's father adds that, after Alma, Raglan was for carrying Sebastopol from the north, but the French commander refused as his casualites had been so great. Johnny was also convinced that owing to appalling losses we had insufficient men to take the city. Of the 54,000 who came out originally, "How many", he asked, "remain? Not 20,000 . . . . We have 150 men of the Regiment left . . . . Thirty of our Brigade and more have been buried a week". From Gordon's Battery he wrote: "Mark me all, their 21 guns in this battery could be spiked for want of sufficient men". Surviving troops he considered "a melancholy wreck of a noble army". On 20th January 1855 he met six men and a few convalescents, sole survivors of a regiment, going south with their colours, and wrote: "the 63rd are extinct". Of one unit he recorded that of 350 men who came out, 50 had been invalided home and 240 had "died of Trenches, or disease".

But of all the evils of this miserable campaign there is none he stresses more than the sufferings of the rank and file who manned the trenches. "The work is awful; all mud up to one's knees . . . .; poor fellows, you know what it is to be frostbitten, which many of them are now laid up from, their feet perfectly raw . . . . Some of their boots hardly hold together . . . . They are living skeletons". One working party said to him: "We have had nothing since breakfast . . . ., and five nights out of six out of bed". "Query", he commented: "can any man stand, that long? . . . . I regret to say many die of cold, after sitting, and sleep overcoming them".

He was impressed with the cheerful efficiency of the French. Under Arctic conditions they were "wonderful fellows in all this. They come up, clear away the snow, have tents up, cook their meals and are like . . . . bees at work, making their usual row, vivandières etc." A visit to their base confirmed this impression: "If I saw one 'Equipages Militaires' I saw at least 50: ditto Ambulances, all with 8 or 10 mules. On our side we have not one . . . . They are a pattern to us". In siegecraft they were our superiors: they "strengthen their pickets very differently to ourselves, always en force, and by night strong advance ones". At Constantinople he found them "an astonishing, rising people. A police is established here, and 700 assassins or thieves have been siezed, besides . . . . 3000 rogues have gone off to America". In October 1855 he witnessed a march-past of the French Imperial Guard in the Crimea, which was "most painful to my feelings. With each Battalion, following the Band, was the Cantinière. Now this force was organised in 18 months, perfect in every branch . . . . I felt so small, and rode away . . . . To think that England cannot adopt a system similar".

PARIS, 17. July 1848.

a naval 'Mobile' on sentry, and a Vivandière in Mobile uniform.
after sketches by J. le C.

Having thus summarised Johnny's main criticisms of the handling of the campaign, we pass on to his record of events and impressions in each succeeding month. January 1855, as we have seen, told a tale of cold, mud and incompetence. One day in February he reported for duty in the front line with 170 Guards, and was politely requested to take some to the Second Parallel, others to the Ovens (see plan). "The Russians lay just underneath . . . ., one could hear them talking all through the night . . . ." Forward of the trench he placed 14 double sentries, so close to the enemy that "I do not think they could have taken us prisoners, as they did with the 50th at this spot . . . .: which occasioned the joke of the Russians relieving the 50th, and the Rifles relieved the Russians". At this time the Round Tower in the French Sector, known later as the Malakoff, and to the Russians as the Korniloff Redoubt, seemed impregnable: "on that's falling, I think the remainder will go". A French Engineer, newly arrived, also perceived that it was the key to the citadel. "Où est Sevastopol?", he enquired. "Mais, Monsieur, le voilà, en face". "Monsieur, mais non", rejoined the Engineer: then, pointing to the Round Tower, "Voilà Sevastopol". The crocus was now appearing all over the battle area, and Johnny sent his mother some bulbs, so that Belle Vue might display "something growing from ye Crimea". But it was still bitterly cold, and one day he returned from foraging with his moustaches frozen hard. When he bought underclothes at an auction, a bystander warned him: " 'They don't wash'. 'No', I said, 'but I only want them for a month in severe nights' ". He continued: "We have been served out with capital sheepskin coats . . . . From the embroidery on the back you would take me for some grandee . . . ." In spite of a pair of Turkish slippers, two pairs of socks, long stockings and the long boots he often had cold feet all day. Lord Rokeby had read " . . . . most flattering letters from the Queen" asking that articles she had worked be given to the campaigners. "If any remain over we are to get one each, either mitts or muffetees".[1] By the end of February "the tents inside and out have been crusted quite thick". Suddenly the winter ended. The first week of March was "very, very warm".

A letter from Balaklava to Jersey took about a fortnight. The sender paid 3d, somebody scored a large "3" in ink on the front and the postmark "Post Office, British Army" was franked on the back. The letters always came to hand, but hardly deserved to as they

copy of postmarks on a letter posted in the Crimea by J. H. Le Couteur on the day Sebastopol fell.

were so small and flimsy. Mrs. Le Couteur must have guessed that they would look more important with stamps affixed, and sent some to Johnny, for he wrote: "It was a capital idea of yours . . . . so like you. Stamps are not to be got for love or money . . . ."

Ever alive to home news, he congratulated his father on his successful experiment in early planting of potatoes, and on acquiring another carriage: but "Is it round in front, as I advised?" The old retainers were remembered: "I am glad to think our faithful old

---

1. Wrist-bands of worsted.

William[1] is closing his life so quietly . . . ." Johnny owed some bills in Jersey, but not many, and sent instalments, while grumbling: "Those rascally tailors are the deuce". For news of the progress of the war the Camp relied on newspapers, but those from home were so slow in coming that their contents were stale. Nor did Johnny find them reliable: "You must not be at (all) guided by the accounts of the Times and other papers. Bad it has been: however, all is now in a flourishing state of amendment, and England will yet come up well at the last".

By this time, March 1855, the railway from Balaklava to Headquarters was forging ahead, and "will . . . . save the poor troops coming so far for their rations", which in any case were only salt pork and a little beef: but they did get a daily tot of rum, considered "very good". Milk was not on the menu, and Johnny had seen none since he left home: "nor do I consider the potted stuff good for anyone; it's unwholesome". He sent home the resign for servicing in the Indian fashion, which meant picking it all to pieces and re-building it. He was doing his own darning: ". . . . the needles do admirably. I can sew famously with them, and thread them also". Rigid economy in note-paper was achieved by cross-writing: "My Father will say[2]: 'Bother him, why does he cross his letters?'"

Considering the conditions, he was keeping remarkably fit. There was an attack of jaundice and "though still very yellow, I feel my appetite returning with the aid of a bottle of calf's-foot jelly": and bouts of dysentery "which all get touches of occasionally; . . . . I find rice . . . . with cups of arrowroot a capital method" of dealing with it. There may well have been malaria, for "I have cured myself of languor . . . . by taking your quinine with lime juice when I feel so". During March he had 18 days sick leave at Constantinople, embarking on the ship Brandon with 108 other invalids, each of whom as they came aboard surrendered his blanket and clothes, had a warm bath and was given a new suit of blue flannel. He lodged in the Hotel d'Angleterrre at Therapia, half way down the Bosporus. "My window is all but washed by the water . . . ., and steamers . . . . pass here within a stone's thrown". He took long walks in the countryside, which was ablaze with wild flowers. He then moved to Messirier's Hotel, Constantinople, and went across to Scutari "to see the burial ground, the largest in the world". He also saw the Hospital, which was "beautifully clean and in very nice order". At the Valley of Sweet Waters he saw Turkish belles, "beautifully dressed, sitting in their carriages . . . ., loaded with diamonds and jewels over their foreheads". But he disliked Constantinople: "I will be glad to get away from this filthy, dirty place of nasty smells".

On 1st April 1855 he was back on Balaklava Heights in "a jolly Maltese hut". Three miles of railway had been completed, and quantities of ammunition, stores and hay had gone up to Headquarters. A room had been adapted as a Church, with a Sergeant leading the hymns. "The Camp is a regular farmyard now, with innumerable fowls, turkeys, geese . . . . they make a fearful row of a morning". On Easter Monday, 9th April, the Allied guns were "pounding away at a great rate" and an assault was expected to follow, yet none was made. But the advance continued and the French were close to Quarantine Bay. "I still hope we may be a reserve at the assault . . . ." and be able "to sport 'Sevastopol' on our Colors . . . ., which we shall not do if stuck down to do fatigues and dirty duty in Balaklava . . . ." On the 26th, Lord Strafford de Redcliffe arrived out, with Lady Paget and

---

1. William McDermott.
2. So did the transcriber.

two Miss Cannings, who visited the Marines' Heights. Johnny strongly objected to female sight-seers in the battle zone, and wondered how they would react when they visited the Tchernaya River and saw thousands of soldiers of all nations bathing in its waters. "I cannot imagine women coming out here for curiosity. It must brutalize the delicate, well-organised feelings of a gentlewoman".

In May the limelight fell upon other Allies. "We saw about 20,000 Turcos in the plain, ... an immense long line extending for three miles . . . ." Then, "some of the Sardines came into Harbor . . . ., a very nice gentlemanlike set of fellows . . . . a beautifully constituted army". They had a picturesque uniform, and glazed wide-awake caps with feathers on the side, as well as a splendid band, "and the airs likewise were very pretty". Heat had now become a problem: "my turban I find of great service riding out during the heat". Somebody gave him a two-gallon water-bag in the shape of a half-moon, "a wonderful comfort in action". Their diet was enriched by a new fish, like turbot but with "spikes all over". Meanwhile, in London, Johnny's father attended a presentation of Crimea medals by the Queen, and pinned that of Sir De Lacy Evans "to his honoured breast, and also that of my friend General Arthur Torrens." On 21st May Johnny wrote that huts were being built near Balaklava as a sanatorium, and there "the men recover better than if at Scutari": and added: "Poor Miss Nightingale is still very ill with fever. She will have to be sent home, or sent to sea for a time, although even after that, fever returns when exposed to the sun". On the 27th news came of the capture of Kertch, with 53 guns, a foundry, magazine and 2000 head of cattle, without the loss of a single man.

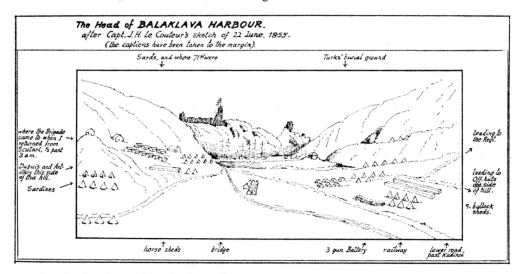

By the 7th June 1855 the French on the right seemed to have success within their grasp. "The Mamelon and Pits were taken . . . . The whole place must have fallen that night". But it did not. A very determined attack was launched early in the morning of the 18th, but was a disaster. "We were repulsed three times by heavy discharges of grape and canister. We have lost Sir J. Campbell, Colonel Shirley 88th . . . ., near upon 1000 men and officers . . . . a second Badajos . . . . a complete reverse . . . . this will damp the spirits of the Army amazingly . . . . we are now to give up all hopes of assaulting, and must sap up to the Redan by regular work". In a letter to his godmother Mrs. Le Couteur, Dick de Lisle wrote: ". . . . at early dawn (I) would have shaken hands with my worst enemy. By 6 o'clock I would have kicked my dearest friend, for then I knew we had failed . . . .I believe you might have heard a pin drop in any one of the camps . . . .": and Johnny added glumly: "Sevastopol is doomed not to fall . . . . We shall get nothing when we do take it, but simply walk over dead bodies; that's what they (the Russians) say". His father, deploring this reverse, thought it folly to attack, by daylight, defenders armed with Minié rifles: the assault should have been by night, with the bayonet. He had also heard that some of the men engaged had only received their rifles the previous night, with ammunition of the wrong calibre.

Johnny was having ups and downs with various batmen. "I am again parting with my servant, as I have to put up with many inconveniences, such as coming home, finding no dinner . . . ., wet blankets . . . .: not liking to say much or be savage, it puts one out". Finally he had to admonish him "about being so fond of rum. It will do for him if he is not careful. The sun here will not permit of drink".

The July letters give a grisly picture of trenches slowly creeping forward, and severely chastised by the defenders. "In the pits lately taken, a constant fire of grape and canister is kept, together with small arms. This accounts for our lists of casualties . . . . Though we are 40 yards only from the Redan[1], I do not see how the place can be taken without an enormous sacrifice. They (the Russians) are making second lines within now, and are famous fellows . . . ." On 25th July he wrote from the Old Advance Trench: "We were shelled amazingly last evening, as well as graped . . . . You have no idea how the pieces of shells fly through the air. You hear them a long way off, then comes the pat on the ground. They are nasty customers. . . . All the trenches are a mass of filth, and the stench abominable. I come to the conclusion, a siege is decidedly unsatisfactory".

In August 1855 things were even more wretched. "You never experienced trench work for any space of time . . . . you can have no conception of the misery of 24 hours continual . . . . wet in those trenches . . . . One of our finest men had his arm taken off the other day. My servant went to see him . . . . 'Well, Moore, how was he?' 'Quite well, Sir; I should say very happy, Sir'. 'What, happy at losing his arm, poor fellow?' 'Yes, Sir. I should willingly lose my leg or an arm to get home, rather than suffer as I did last winter . . . . Often, Sir, for 48 hours I have only had my raw ration of pork, raw coffee: no boots: one shirt, Sir, for a couple of months, and covered with vermin: and in the bargain my foot frostbitten.' " On the 10th August Johnny wrote: "Just returned very fatigued after my 30 hours in Trenches. They gave us a warming during the night . . . .: four Fusiliers' heads taken off by one round shot and 14 more wounded. A jolly fire was opened and nobly returned by Johnny Russ . . . . You cannot show your nose but a bullet whizzes past. . . . I fired two shots at an embrasure, and they gave me two round shot with a dozen of small arms in return". Two days later Dick de Lisle was recording his own impressions in the following words: "An attack was expected this morning . . . . However it was a false alarm . . . . I dread another 18th affair . . . . Since that event the Russians have risen much in my estimation; for they get licked week after week and come on as gaily as ever . . . . they never presume to decide that they have been beaten until the fact is made known to them by their officers, and that I fancy it very seldom is". He then described how the enemy had begun to fire

1. He means the Malakoff: the Redan was 300 yards from our front line: he paced it on 10th September.

180

round shot to such high altitude that it sank four feet into hard clay soil. "I don't like the shells, for when they burst, the pieces may hurt some of my men. But I care little for the round shot. They may hit one man, but as they fall vertically they can scarcely hurt more. There", the letter ends, "goes another shell close to us". On the 31st August, when Johnny was on working-parties near Egerton's Pit, the enemy made a sortie on the Sixth Parallel and we suffered heavily. "It is a pity employing young men . . . . to those very advanced works, as they are too hot for . . . . young soldiers, who cannot at first help bobbing . . . ."

Sebastopol held out for the first seven days of September 1855 and Johnny wrote a great deal about them. But it is not always easy to determine exactly where he was or what was happening. One can only read what he wrote and record it in part, in the apparent order of events. On Saturday 1st September he visited the White Works on the right and

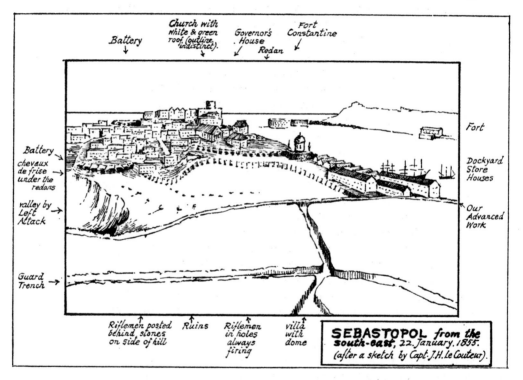

found the French in possession of Careening Bay, and up under the very walls of the Malakoff. In the citadel opposite was "a pretty villa with a dome (see sketch) . . . .; ladies are seen walking about there"; and the groups of Russians moving about their camp were as visible as "a Regiment at drill at the valley from Le Couteur field . . . . The Harbour . . . . was a pretty sight . . . . boats sailing, rowers, etc . . . .". By Tuesday, the 4th, the final assault was at hand, and on the back of a stop-press sketch of the trenches Johnny scribbled: "By this you will remark . . . . a new Battery making in rear of Egerton's Pit . . . .; dotted line shows the New or 6th Parallel, where we are daily losing an immense number of men and officers: a warm nest". That day he was in action in the 5th Parallel, and "enfiladed one spot most beautifully". All next day he was in the same place, his men keeping up "a capital fire; some fired upwards of 200 rounds . . . . Just as I was leaving the trenches I saw a frigate . . . . burnt to the water's edge". The French were "so near the Malakoff they can get no further". That morning a three-days' bombardment of the town had begun, as a prelude to the attack.

On 7th September the Generals met in Council and "a most effective and fearful fire" was maintained. "Never was such a roar . . . . heard . . . . It is necessary to be *at* something, and have done. Nick or nothing is the toss . . . . The whole Army are ready for anything". The final assault was planned for noon next day. "Our men, poor fellows, remain in again tonight, come out in the morning . . . ., form a reserve in the Woronzoff Road, and come in for the grand finish". He had been watching a Russian "two-decker on fire . . . .; the flames through the ports were splendid".

At noon on Saturday, 8th September, the combined assault began, the main objectives being the Malakoff for the French, the Great Redan for ourselves. The storming of the Malakoff "was done in a few seconds, and held". Johnny learned later from Russian officers that what happened was this: the outgoing guard on the Malakoff left before the arrival of their relief, who were delayed by losing their way. They also inadvertently left a couple of planks over a ditch. "Francis found this out", wrote Johnny, swarmed in over the planks and engaged the relief as it came up the hill. "*Thus* did they get the key, and then fell Sevastopol". The Redan was to be stormed by "the Second Divsion under Markham, supported by the Light division . . . . They fought well and got in . . . ., but the supports did not come up in time, and . . . . they were driven back with awful slaughter . . . . It is an army of boys". Had they been more experienced, "The English assault would have succeeded . . . . At about 11 a fearful explosion took place, and they went on during the night. The Russians had evacuated the place, set fire to everything . . . ." The day's events, he considered, were "a great victory, due more to the French than ourselves . . . ."

On the 9th September we had planned a further assault to make good our failure, but the Russian evacuation made this unnecessary. That morning Havilland John de Carteret[1], who had been in with the Highland Brigade, was passing Johnny's quarters "complètement épuisé[2]. Je pouvais à peine marcher avec mon régiment . . . ., si je n'avais heureusement rencontré Le Couteur, des Gardes, qui . . . . me fit déjeuner avec lui, et me prêta ensuite son Pony . . . ." "I managed to fish (him) out", was Johnny's version, "and gave him some breakfast. He was ordered into the Redan at 5 a.m. . . ., he says it was a fearful scene. The thousands lying killed and wounded . . . ." There were "caves, furnished beautifully", some with leather upholstery. At this moment Johnny received a message that Russians were advancing from over the hill. He went to see, and there they were, marching to the water's edge and embarking in steamers. He had no idea of their destination. "As we had not one gun ready for them, I felt rather nervous, with only 200 of the Brigade to protect a landing, and went to the Field Officer in the Redan for orders". But it all passed off, and no landing was attempted. That night was one of conflagration: "the . . . . flames were fearful. Imagine the whole of St. Helier's in a blaze, the College, and flames issuing from every window . . . .: it was grand beyond . . . . description, only fit for poor old Turner's style . . ."

On his way to the trenches next morning, 10th September, he scribbled a note home:

1. Of the Trinity branch of the Carteret family.   2. From "La Nouvelle Chronique de Jersey", 29th September, 1855.

"Glorious news. The whole place in a blaze last night . . . ." He paced the distance from the 6th Parallel to the angle of the Redan, and found it "at least 300 yards", an important figure in assessing the causes of our failure and the success of the French, who were far closer to their objective. "The abattis[1] was not as bad as the ditch to pass, but it's an awful place . . . ." During that day and night, it seems, he was on Main Guard on the Esplanade overlooking the Creek at the head of the Inner Harbour, and he and Lambton got into an upturned sentry-box, using it as their Guard Room for the night. The buildings opposite were burning "with the greatest fury and blaze", the flames reflected in the water. The Guards lighted an "immense bivouac fire" from timber in the ruins. In this area he found cookhouses, artificers' shops and holes in the solid rock in which the defenders had lived: further on, the Marine Barracks, crammed with a medley of weapons and equipment; and finally the "building creek, which is . . . . even finer than Portsmouth".

During the next three days, 11-13th September, he roamed over the centre, right and left of the battlefield, finding in the centre a 21-gun battery from which "I have had some narrow squeaks . . . . I never saw anything with its strength, and once in, 'twas impossible to get up or down. In front were large trous-de-loup[2], then came the abattis, then the chevaux-de-frise[3]". The protection of the magazines was amazing, enormous baulks of timber one above the other, covered with sandbags and earth: and the shot-proof treble-rope collars on projecting gun-muzzles were admirable. "Just as I got on my poney I observed a tremendous smoke . . . . a mine, and sure enough up went Fort Alexander". That night, 11th September, he said the Russians fired and sank all their steamers.

On the 12th he found many bodies still lying as they fell in the Redan and Malakoff, the latter being "a most fearful work of immense extent". Returning along the Marine Dock he found our men bringing out the Russian dead. There were 300 bodies or more which had lain there for a week, "some perfectly decomposed . . . . and the sight and smell was enough to turn the stoutest heart".

On the 14th September he examined the French left, where the defences were even stronger than the Malakoff, especially the Bastion du Mât, or Flagstaff Battery and, most formidable of all, the Bastion Central. The defenders' guns were badly mauled, some with muzzles gone, and one with a shot straight down the bore. He noticed some of his "dear old friends the Bouquets, about 50 shell in one case . . . .". Compared with the French, he found our trenches "shamefully constructed". He ended this pilgrimage with: "May I never see the fall of another great Town, it's most saddening . . . not a door or window seemed untouched . . . . the main streets must have been very beautiful". A few days later Lord Rokeby distributed medals, but Johnny decided to sport the ribbon only, unless they gave a clasp "for the Trenches, which were worse than 20 general actions". Later he ordered a miniature, "the size of a 4d bit, from Hunt & Roskells, as they got the die cast".

Peace had not yet been declared, and Russian units fired sporadically at any inviting target, including one day "our band, which was playing ye British Grenadiers along the Esplanade". By the end of September "the greater part of the Army are now employed making drains each side of the rail, and a good 30 feet military road"; and soon Johnny found himself acting as road superintendent to the entire force. He became dedicated to

---

1. From French, abattre (to fell): a barricade of felled tree-trunks, embedded in front of a trench, with sharpened points towards the attacker.
2. (Wolf-holes): covered pits containing sharpened stakes.   3. (Frisian horses): lines of timber or metal spikes erected to discourage attack.

this task: "I am throwing my whole mind, body .... and soul on this new road .... I'll show the Guards do and can work". He hoped that his enthusiasm might secure him some senior post, one created specially for him perhaps, from which he could improve roads and commissariat and thereby lessen the sufferings of the ordinary soldier. He was quietly firm with everybody, whatever their rank. "Brigades .... send their men down .... without breakfast or dinner, and how can I expect 500 men to work .... with bellies empty ....? I will insist on having what I consider best for the men .... The 33rd is the one I bully, but not much". One day he had encounters with "all these swells", as he called them. "Rokeby .... came up, shook hands with me: 'How do ye do. I wish to say a word ...., my dear Le Couteur ...., nothing could be better than the way you are doing your work' " .... "Then, up rides General Barnard: 'Captain Le Couteur, how is this, Sir? There is General Simpson and Airey both complaining that their Regiment's idle'. 'Sir, I refer you to my report .... I have a certain system I shall and will have carried out ....' I then turned my horse's tail on Barnard and .... effectually stopped his jaw". Johnny was on top of the world. "I am the happiest and most contented fellow going .... The dear old Duke is my example .... (He), I find, knew .... every branch of the service."

On 18th October 1855 he reported our successful naval action off Kinbourne Spit, and sent home a letter from a young friend in H.M.S. Leopard about it, "to prove what young British stuff is made of". On the 15th, we read, "our mortar boats were towed into possistion and began firing ...., making very good practise." On the 17th they joined Admiral Stewart's division and steamed past the three forts on the spit "firing away to our hearts' content"; then anchoring to watch "the line of Battle ships go in and give their broadside .... They had seaced firing, and we asked if they had surrendered, when they had the cheek to want to march out with all the honours of war. 'No, no,' we said: 'if that is the case we will give you another turn of it, so you better think it over again.' We took 1160 prisoners. The place was fearfully nocked about .... They did not seem over sorry at leavihg, except the old Governor, who seemed quite broken-hearted".

By November 1855 Johnny had a government hut, but it was a bugbear, leaking so

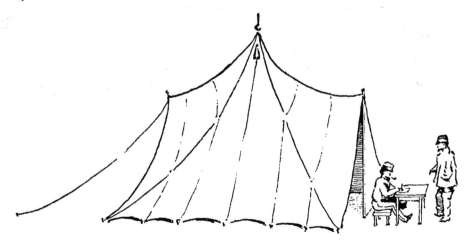

Johnny's Crimea tent.

badly that he pitched his patrol tent inside it. This was no surprise. He had already sampled one at Balaklava and "it was a jolly sieve for . . . rain". It got colder and colder. "My ink freezes as I write . . . .; I have been forced to warm it". One morning he awoke with a chill, having left off the nightcap his mother insisted he should wear: "Mama came over the . . . . experienced soldier this time, and no mistake". He now took on a companion: "Here I am . . . . with my Russian kitten . . . . playing with the quill as I write—(Puss, be quiet with my pen!)—". He had begun to sign himself as Major. He sent home a sketch of the interior of his tent, by Darling "son of the old General, a peculiar little fish, but good fellow. . . . . It gives me a little more space than I really have".

On 21st January 1856 he was transferred to Kertch as Instructor to the Turkish contingent in handling the Minié Rifle, and was there till the 5th of May. It was a beautiful place, with some magnificent houses. He was soon out exploring, made a plan of the defences and examined the Tomb of Mithridates and the many domed tumuli near Kertch, some of which had recently been opened and yielded coins and pottery. Others had been disturbed by modern entrenchments, and "the destruction of noble old vases on the glacis is sad to behold; bones, sculls &c are visible at every step". The Straits froze solid, and as late as 21st March "I have been able to walk on the Sea for several days . . . ., an arctic scene, vessels blocked in with ice . . . ." There were other phenomena: "The bituminous springs are excessively curious . . . ., a small hillock is formed a few feet high, on the top of which bubbles from a spring rise, ... to 4 and 5 inches . . . ., of a deep blue similar in color to . . . . Mother's Cashmeer cloak". Father must have mentioned that the caper grew at Kertch, for Johnny promised to get him seeds of it. Now and again there was bird-shooting on the shores of the Sea of Azov, where "the enormous bustard, immense hares, partridges, quail, plover and duck" abounded. There was a Race Meeting, "but as I am not a racing character I did not attend".

He worked daily from 10 to 4. "You will perceive I have a good deal to do, to . . .. instruct 16,000 men . . . . I place each man in position for firing myself . . . ." He had to interpret everything, and go through the motions himself. "I find my work very tiresome and laborious, on my legs from 6 to 7 hours daily". But the Turks were "wonderfully apt in picking up the loading the new arm, which they are much pleased with". The first consignment of Minié were "in a shameful, filthy state" and he sent 39 away for replacement; 6000 more, with two million of ammunition, were soon on their way to him. But he never really liked the Minié which, with the Brunswick, "I would keep for . . . . arming men in Martello Towers . . . ." Our new Enfield arm was "a beautiful little weapon for troops".

The family asked him what the soldiers thought of the War. "They know nothing and care less, I think, except those who have been out the whole time or have ties to take them home. That new "Order of Valour" [1] will be worth more than the Bath for soldiers and sailors . . . . The Army generally will be much pleased with the distinction".

A steamer with flags flying brought the news of Peace to Kertch on 4th April 1856. "The bells ring and all seem joyous, except the Tartar population, who say they will be hung or sent to Siberia. Many deserve it, for the crimes they committed were awful, as the Russians left". He sent home sketches of Kertch, and £12 worth of "photographic drawings, some of which when magnified are intensely interesting". But this unusual material was not at Belle Vue. Nor was the journal of Vicars, "a devoted soldier . . . . sad loss to the

---

1. The Victoria Cross.

whole Regiment", who died from loss of blood after combat in the Trenches, no tourniquet being at hand.

There was friction with the French, who "insult us on every occasion . . . .; there are few who from their hearts would not like to give them a right good drubbing". The Russians were far more friendly. At the end of April Johnny took a trip through Kaffa, Karasu Bazar, Simferopol and Batch Serai to Sebastopol, where Russians showed him over their fortifications. Russians troops moving north were most respectful to the travellers, raising their caps as they passed. At Simferopol he noticed a lady wearing her late husband's uniform, other widows wearing crosses, and many more with two medals. He met with the utmost civility everywhere, and at Kaffa was sumptuously entertained by the Russian commandant.

On 5th May 1856 his post as Instructor lapsed and he was recalled to Balaklava. On 2nd June, having visited the field of Alma, he was at Sebastopol, about to sail home in the Agamemnon. The Grenadiers went in the Acre, the Fusiliers in the Princess Royal. It was a good passage, "but the accommodation execrable . . . ., a disgrace sending us on board Men of War with no accommodation". But he made himself comfortable "on the Poop, in a cot slung to the spanker boom". Arrived in England, they were not dispersed, but obliged to wait until it was convenient to make their ceremonial entry into London. From Farnham Castle he wrote: "The whole thing is a farce . . . ., the poor men feel it, having been on English soil some days. I say, like many of our privates: 'But when are we to get leave?' " On 4th July he was in London "to provide myself with a Hat, the sign of a civilized being . . . . We go to the Tower, ... the 2nd Battalion, Windsor".

This Crimean chapter would be incomplete if one failed to quote an enthusiastic message, in rather wild handwriting, on a scrap of blue paper enclosed in Le Couteur's letter of 9th March 1855, without explanation. It is evidently addressed by a French Sergeant to a Senior officer who enjoyed his complete confidence. We read:

"Générale, je vous an voie la carabine, les balle et les capsssule de Mr. Nigon.

Mon Général, je suis desvoué au tout et pour tout pour vous de aux jourdhuis.

Si je puis vous être uttile, ninporte au que ce soit, faite mois l'honneur de me prevenir.

Jaie l'honneur, Mon Générale, de vous saluer de coeur.

—Sarchand.

P.S. pour vous epreuvent, demandes moi, je suis tout à vous".

Most of us would be glad to have a document of this kind amongst our testimonials.

Here this remarkable series of letters ends. His father's diary of the 9th July rounds it off to perfection with a glimpse of the grand review in Hyde Park. The Guards marched in and formed line, leaving intervals for the Crimea battalions who, having been showered with bouquets as they strode through Westminster, "came in very grandly" at 2 o'clock and slid into their vacant positions. The Queen then arrived with a glittering staff, received the salute and drove past. When she had done so, the entire Brigade advanced in line of seven battalion columns, led by the Duke of Cambridge, halted, and gave "three times three tremendous cheers".

"It was the finest thing I ever saw", said Sir John.

CHAPTER FIFTEEN

LE VICOMTE DE JERSEY

Sir John was Vicomte de Jersey from 1842-1875, and during that time he had as Deputy Vicomtes Jean Philippe de Ste. Croix, George Helier Horman, Mathieu Gallichan, Helier Simon and Thomas Simon.

In explaining this position to people in England, Sir John used to liken it to a Sheriff and Coroner. By Jerseymen it is regarded as an office of immense antiquity and dignity. When the appointment was announced by Sir James Graham, the Home Secretary, he stipulated that ". . . . I should hold it for the present as my predecessor had done, subject after the death of Lord Beresford to such regulations as the Crown may then see fit to be included in my patent: . . . . that for the present he entrusted the office entirely to my discretion . . . . that I might say that great interest had been made to give the appointment to an Englishman, Irishman or Scotchman, but that he had resisted every such interest so as to give it to a Jerseyman, as he now had given the Bailiwick of Guernsey to a Guernsey-man, Mr. Guille: . . . . that Lord Beresford's recommendation had had great weight with him, but that I had been backed by the very greatest of all interests, that of the Duke of Wellington, who was most anxious that I should have the appointment. I exclaimed 'Indeed, how grateful I am to His Grace' . . . . 'So you see you enjoy the unlimited confidence of the Government and I am persuaded that you will act in it with judgment and prudence.'" An echo of contemporary absenteeism is found in the next question which was; "You will reside in Jersey and attend to the duties yourself?", to which he replied ". . . . every superior duty I will discharge in person, all the inferior duties such as sales and arrests, by my deputies, and in proportion to their activities will be the efficiency of the office and the mortification of those who will oppose me." The actual wording of Sir James Graham's letter was as follows:

"I contemplate making the following changes in the office of the Viscount of Jersey. I propose,

1. That the appointment shall be during the pleasure of the Crown.
2. That the Viscount shall be constantly a resident in the Island and that the duties shall not be done by Deputy except in cases of unavoidable necessity.
3. That the fees shall continue to be exacted as at present, but they shall be paid into the Public Treasury instead of to the Viscount.
4. That the Viscount shall receive a fixed salary not to exceed £500 a year.

I am now taking steps to carry this plan into effect, and your acknowledged high character, your station and connexions in the Island of Jersey, induce me to ask your cooperation. To ensure success to these new measures the hearty concurrence of the holder of this office is absolutely necessary, and provided you will be willing to use your endeavours in furtherance of the plan which I have propounded, I am prepared to recommend to Her Majesty's favourable consideration your claims to the appointment." Sir John has noted by this letter "Given me unconditionally eventually as my predecessor held it."

It would not have been possible for him to conduct the office without the aid of deputies, as well as his military duties, and frequent absences in England on Court duty as A.D.C. and so he was permitted to have two Deputy Viscounts to carry on much of the routine work of the office.

For the ensuing thirty odd years, the prison, one of his main responsibilities, took up a great deal of Sir John's time. In 1835 the great reformer, Mrs Elizabeth Fry was in Jersey, and produced a report on the local prison. While it could not be said to be complimentary, conditions were probably no worse than in any other prison at that period. He wrote to her, ". . . . the only hitch is now with Lord Beresford. I enclose you a copy of the act of the committee, on which I told them that I thought they asked too much of His Lordship in common fairness; it is true the population of the town is increasing, and unhappily crime may increase in the same ratio, but I think if they had asked the last year's expenses which may amount to £300, it would have been sufficient . . . . I am persuaded the States would instantly set about building a House of Correction, for if the Committee did not then propose it, I will engage to do so. If Lord Beresford does not move in the matter, I am sure the States will not either . . . . I read them extracts from your letter, and the Committee unanimously decided to recommend the alteration from the present system to that of Guernsey, with the amendments suggested by you . . . . so that, my dear Madam, your valuable labours will not have been in vain."

In 1849 Joseph Hume[1], M.P. for Montrose, visited the Island, incidentally somewhat alarming Monsieur de Rozel, as he disapproved of the current works at St. Catherine's Bay. Sir John met him and, "had a long and very interesting chat with the great reformer, Harriet chatting to his younger daughter, a nice, lively girl. He considered our Prison . . . . very good. Hospital or poor house very good also, schools large, might accommodate a hundred or more children each, boys and girls, desirable to take them out of the streets for education . . . . Court for the recovery of small debts very useful . . . . happy state of the Island, self government so good, though it might be better, great wealth generally diffused . . . . had seen Clarke the shipbuilder, timber from England, not from the New Forrest, he knew of peculation in the sale of timber . . . . Clarke told him why we can build more cheaply than the Liverpool shipwrights, Jerseymen sober, frugal and industrious, work six days, no Unions to strike, no idlers to maintain . . . . George Ennis gave him information about iron, the foundries etc., Chevalier about the harbours, revenues and shipping. Went on board Mr. de Ste. Croix' new vessel, very strong, excellently formed. I was exceedingly pleased with the very entertaining conversation of this remarkable man, whose questions made to the Government in the House of Commons a fortnight since, have sent the Lords of the Admiralty and the Chancellor of the Exchequer on a voyage of discovery to St. Catherine's Bay, Alderney and Portland, in a word, to see their own works. He avoided speaking to me on the subject, though Captain White heard he did not like the works at St. Catherine's. Greatly admired the beauty and fertility of Jersey."

Sir John was much opposed to corporal punishment, where it could be avoided, though he felt that in certain circumstances it could not. As a very young officer in 1813, in Canada, he had fainted when seeing a man receive three hundred lashes, and said: "The officers laughed at me but the men did not," and in 1840 when his son was at an "academy" at

---

1. Joseph Hume, (1777-1855), Philanthropist and enlightened reformer.

Woolwich, he wrote to the Headmaster asking that corporal punishment might be withheld, saying "I must confess to you I utterly abhor corporal punishment, except for the lowest vices. I have seen it so cruelly put into action in the army, and once at school, where it created a mutiny, that I have never laid my hands on my boy, though for a lie or a disgraceful act I should certainly have flogged him, as I know the army could not exist on foreign service without it." He added that the boy's mother and grandmother were deeply distressed at the possibility, for rumours of the headmaster, Mr Barry's extreme severity had reached them, though he conceded that Johnny was "a spoiled only boy".

He felt strongly that offenders were entitled to privacy, and in a letter to the Bishop of Oxford, he said: "One of the first steps I took on being made the Sheriff here was to establish a prison van in order to seclude offenders from public gaze. Previously they were marched through the town, twice a day, when on trial, surrounded with crowds, some of whom clandestinely offered means of escape or liquor. It seems to me that a public execution is almost as great an evil as that public mode of transport was. Comparative privacy, with due authenticity and severity being all that is necessary." Another letter to the same Bishop, in 1856, said ".... relating to removing executions from Gallow's Hill to within the walls of the prison in Jersey.... so as to get rid of the dismal procession and the terrible display on Gallow's Hill". In 1866 Jersey was horrified by the murder, by a youth named Bradley, of an old lady living alone on the borders of St. Peter's and St. Brelade's parishes. On July 12th of that year Sir John said: "Left a bell at the gaol with Le Rossignol as an aid to the sentries over François Bradley, the assassin of Miss Le Brun," and the next day, "The goaler reported to me that two French debtors had been talking to the condemned murderer François Bradley, in defiance of his order to have no communication with him, (and) that he had therefore locked him up, which I quite approved." Bradley was therefore removed to a double cell in the House of Correction, where he was apart from all other prisoners, and then "the villain was more calm, but was indifferent, if not insolent, to General Cuppage, who did not comprehend what he said. He says he will not live to be executed."

Sir John took great care over every detail of these arrangements, that all should be as proper and merciful as possible, and the sentence was carried out at the corner of Patriotic Street and Newgate Street, within the prison walls, and not in public. He visited the condemned man to tell him the verdict and said: "I could not avoid shedding tears on seeing a youth so near his doom; he was calm and shook hands with me in a grateful tone. Though rude to others, he never was to me." On the day, he arranged for the police to "urge the people to be perfectly silent while an unhappy man was hurried before his Maker, and to have mercy on him, which they did."

There had been trouble about prison maintenance in 1830, when Sir John called on Lord Beresford in London, and discussed Island affairs .... "He had represented to Lord Bathurst that the King's revenue had been improperly attacked by the States who charged the maintenance of prisoners against the Crown revenues, when a House of Correction had been expressly mentioned in the Patent .... The States had caused a jail, which had been originally estimated at £5000, to be constructed, which eventually had cost £2000, he believed, and Lord Chatham had generously given £1000 towards building it, in discharge of further charges, but it was the States who had built it, and now they wished to charge the Government with its repairs. Then the dinners for the roads committee, they had no right to charge against him. I explained the nature of them. The Receiver's dinners he said were all very right. I explained how far I thought the Governor had been liable by custom to bear the expenses of maintaining the prisoners in the jail, which had originally been so few in number that thirty or forty years back it could not have been a matter of moment to the Governor to pay for their maintenance, but now that the population had vastly increased that a great number of English or Irish had come to the Island, the prison was always full of vagabonds, and it certainly was a hardship on the Governor."

There used to be a treadmill in the prison, and it is now in the local Museum. An entry for the diary in 1827 is illuminating; "Reading a treatise on the treadmill and prison discipline: de Veulle wishes me to support a proposal for one in the hospital. There I could not, in the prison I will. A hospital is not intended for punishment but for charity." In 1844 the treadmill was in use, and a further entry reads; "four Jersey and four English and Irish girls all promised to be quiet. General Touzel agreed to my suggestion to have the large mill repaired in order to have beans and oats ground. Idle and dissolute women should break stones." When the mill was in order again it could grind 40 lbs. pepper in an hour, but he found "three turns in a minute too fast," and so a crushing mill as well as the oat mill was installed. On one occasion, in 1847, there were "eight convicts on the tread-mill."

A great deal of time and ink were expended over the case of one, Carus Wilson, a prisoner who was a thoroughly difficult person, and perhaps of unsound mind. This was a delicate and technical legal affair, the point at issue being whether or not a writ of Habea s Corpus from England could run in Jersey, and it was decided by the Court of the Queen's Bench: ". . . . Lord Denman[1] observed that the Sol. Gen. did not contend, and indeed it was not possible to contend, that a Habeas Corpus could not issue out of this court into Jersey . . . . The liberty of the subject is guarded by a superior power from any possibility of illegal detention, while the legal power of the Court here is untouched." Again some years later this question arose and in 1850 he noted; "The Royal Court met in full assembly to receive the order of Her Majesty in Council authorising the writ of Habeas Corpus issued by the Lord High Chancellor of England to run here . . . . Smash, No. 1 of our Charters!"

Much time was taken up with the duties of coroner, and in addressing the Lieutenant Governor, Sir James Reynett, about one such case in 1848, he wrote; ". . . . I am led by a sense of duty to call your attention to the fact that though the jury are sworn, the witnesses are not. It may thus happen that a person who, under the obligation of an oath would disclose 'the truth, the whole truth and nothing but the truth', might be led on mere parole evidence either to conceal or distort it. A law to remedy this evil has been lodged au greffe about two years, and I trust Your Excellency may consider the subject sufficiently important to lead you to invite its early discussion."

Sir John was again ahead of his times in considering that lunatics and prisoners should be kept apart, in the interests of both groups. As early as 1827 he said: ". . . . I go to town about putting poor Falle, who is of sound mind, out of the maniacs' cells in the hospital. He is lying on the bare stones without fire or comfort of any kind. Under such circumstances, and surrounded by the yells of the maniacs, it is a wonder he does not become one of them. If he has offended the laws as a thief, let the law judge him, but his merciless relatives shall not detain him there if I have the power to prevent it." The situation for the lunatics continued far from satisfactory and in 1847 he noted: "Sir John de

---

1. Thomas Denman, first Baron. (1779-1854), Jurist.

Veulle showed me a long correspondence from the Home Office calling on the States, very properly, to build a lunatic asylum. He fancies they will object. Why?, say I. They have had their own way so long and have turned their ideas solely to money-making projects that it is time they should begin to reflect, and work for humanity occasionally, without regard for profit." In spite of all, Sir James Reynett, when newly arrived in the Island, ". . visited the prison and hospital and was pleased with both." Mr Joseph Hume reappeared on the scene with "letters and books . . . . which he has in a kindly and humane spirit offered to our Island library for the use of the National Hospital. I quite concur with the honourable gentleman in the propriety of having a separate asylum for the reception of the unfortunate persons who are afflicted with derangement of intellect." The books concerned were parliamentary papers and reports, strange reading matter for the "unfortunate persons" in question. In 1857 Sir John was still urging the building of an asylum, particularly to the then Lieutenant Governor, General Mundy, who was found contemplating the situation "at a signal post, gazing at the misty, beautiful quiet scene before him, the town a mystery and the calm sea ruffled by a single steamer coming in. He told me he sometimes stood there to meditate by the hour, the view was so charming." By then the affair of the asylum had been recognised as urgent, and the President of the Committee, Judge Nicolle[1], had been to see three possible sites, and "that at St. Lawrence, near Patrimoine, they preferred. One proposal was made by a Captain of Militia, whom he had seen when out riding, which the General played off against another . . . . I told General Mundy that he would be sure to carry every measure if he would take the trouble to show an interest in what the Committee were about. The presence and friendly intercourse of the Lt. Governor had invariably great weight; they liked one who mixed with them cordially." The situation became tense, and in 1861 a note said: "At a meeting of the Gov., B. and Jurats. The vexed question of a lunatic asylum. The Hammond party, which is supported by the recommendation of the Doctors, would vote for Hammond's cottage at Samarès[2], just to leeward of the S.W. winds under the miasma of the canal and marsh. The Nicolle party for the place close by Patrimoine. Browning declares if they treat for it he will overbid the States, in order to prevent a madhouse being next to him. The Godfray party wish to give the lunatics 'au rabais' to Pothecary at Patrimoine, to save Frank Godfray from a partial stroke of ruin with Pothecary. However the meeting remembered that the Home Secretary has tabooed Pothecary as an unfit person to have charge of lunatics. The General suggested whether the Queen's Farm would not reconcile all parties . . . . (it was) of 70 vergées, rents for £80 a year, would be cheap, airy, fertile and healthful. All seemed to agree and I reminded the General that the States would be the safest tenant the Crown could have . . . . The States asked G.B. and J.[3] to lend them £5000; the G.B. and J will do so on condition that the States name the site, the cost and plans and submit them to this body previous to having the money. Very wisely too." Later that year it would seem that the matter was still not decided, because "The General (Sir Percy Douglas) seemed very much vexed that the States decided yesterday to send the lunatics to Pothecary's establishment, setting aside the engagement to build the lunatic asylum for the present. Threatens to place his veto on the act." There was further discussion, and a site at Bagatelle was mentioned, but eventually the Queen's Farm

1. Philip Winter Nicolle, Jurat 1837-1866.
2. Perhaps Samarès Cottage, now demolished.
3. G.B. J. indicates Governor, Bailiff and Jurats, not "Great Britain, Jersey" as on the back of a car.

site was chosen, and that is where the asylum building now stands. During this period of discussion, Le Patrimoine in St. Lawrence was owned by a Dr. Ducat, a close friend of Sir John's, whose "services in India have led to the sad misfortune of almost total loss of sight, with greatly debilitated health." The two men first met in Canada during the 1812-1814 war with America, and Dr. Ducat had subsequently gone to India. It is not clear just which was Pothecary's house.

Postal services were in their early days, and in 1829 there is an entry: "Called on Mr Louis the Post Office Surveyor at Sir James Saumarez' desire, and asked him to dinner on Saturday. He imparted his plan to me which I think will answer very well." Elsewhere Sir John recorded that in 1839 he "asked Lord John Russell to include the Channel Islands in the penny postage bill." But two years later, in 1841, he wrote to a friend: ". . . . I find many letters are lost since the introduction of our very accommodating system of penny postage": and in 1845 he wrote: "Went to the Treasury where I had a long interview with Mr Trevelyan, who conducts the arrangements with the Treasury for adoption, in connexion with the Admiralty and Post Office, to forward the mails from Southampton to Jersey and Guernsey. He gave me numerous documents to read, then entrusted a packet of papers and the conditions or articles of agreement to me, to draw up a memorandum to him on the subject, as I showed him that Government had omitted to claim power over the days of sailing and arrival, having only reserved the hours. Also that the time for transport was not limited, which it should be, as time would involve efficiency of power and vessel". In 1855 he met the famous Rowland Hill, "about the new stamp act affecting Jersey papers . . . . I showed him that before the act came into play on the 29th (June) I could send Jersey papers to the Crimea for a penny; after that I should not without a stamp, and that was a real loss of privilege. He saw it at once". In 1859 a certain Mr Gregory was applying for the position of Post Master in Jersey, and Sir John forwarded a petition saying, "Mr Gregory is a worthy and respectable man who carries on his business in a very creditable manner. He attended the Queen in the tours Her Majesty took in Jersey without desiring any personal reward. I do not believe that the honour which he solicits will stand in the way of any person, because he has by far the best establishment here". However it would seem that the petition was unsuccessful, as three months later a letter was addressed to "Arthur Forrest Esq., Postmaster, St. Helier."

Correctness of weights and measures is a subject which naturally appealed to Sir John's meticulous mind, and in 1842, he "examined weights and measures and found the standards all false. Charged by the States to produce correct standards . .": and in 1843 he "went at own expense to Rouen to examine standard pound weight of Charlemagne; found it corresponded with Jersey's. Fixed the standard pound at 7561 grains . . Drafted a law for the better government of markets". These he considered to be far too crowded. In a letter to the Lieutenant Governor of the time he wrote: ". . . . at the time that I made an examination of the measures for liquid last year I was not aware that they were derived from the ancient brass standard cabot measure, which is thus referred to in the code law of 1771; 'a certain vessel of brass containing one quart according to the standard at the Castle which contains ten pots, and stamped by the Viscount conformably to the regulations established at the Court of Heritage[1] the 2nd May 1754, shall serve hereafter as the standard for liquid measures'. I am informed that the above brass quart having been lost, and an

---

1. Heritage division of the Royal Court.

act of the States which was passed on the 12th January 1828 declared that, as 'the standard quart no longer exists', a comparison of the brass standard cabot with the liquid measures then in use was instituted; when, in order not to disturb the measures then existing, the standard was declared to contain nine pots two pints and a half, or one pint and a half less than ten pots, which was its standard denomination by law confirmed. The Viscount was authorised to have a set of copper measures made on this modern computation". The minutiae of this discussion are rather lengthy, but it seems that the net result was: "since the year 1828, or in 16 years, the change has occasioned a loss to the Impôt of £6,000". In 1845 he was working on "an official comparison of the Jersey and English weights". In England that year he went to see de Grave, who had made some standard weights; ". . . . with his fine balances he found the difference between the pound in pieces and the single pound still greater than I had. He will adjust them accurately and make me an iron 26 and 52 lbs. Jersey. The cabot he tried with water and a syphon and glass dropping tube, when it was found to contain one half bushel of water, one quart and three gills. He is not to touch or file it, merely to level up the two ends where we had placed putty, and make me a quart standard one twentieth of the contents".

In the matter of market jurisdiction he seems to have had a stiff row, and ". . . . told them I had nothing to do with the States Committee as their officer. I was the Officer of the Crown. As they had deprived me of the right of speech[1] I could no longer feel myself in the enjoyment of the common rights of a citizen of Jersey in the States, that I should communicate privately what I pleased to the Government. Some members of the Government had done me the honour to confer with me, and I had frankly told them my opinion. I would not answer irrelevant questions from Mr. Godfray. If he chose to put them through the President, I might then reply to them. In point of law the Committee had no business in the interior of the markets, they were a legislative body and I, as Viscount, the Executive. I had taken great pains to meet their views, (and) had gone to Rouen at my own expense to execute them. The Préfet of the Seine had sent me an elaborate report on the weights and measures, which I laid before the Com. in July last, and it had been reported to the Secy. of State, that delay occurred owing to want of my report . . . . I expected to be thanked rather than blamed, and left them in wrath".

In his official capacity Sir John made many many visits to markets, and shops, to examine weights, and they usually seem to have been faulty. Let us take a few examples. "Examined all the weights in the shops in St. Aubins. Mr. P. Laf. the worst in Jersey; confiscated them all." . . . . "On a complaint from Mr Gautier de Ste. Croix that the gauger rod is not stamped and that it is incorrect as a measure. I went to verify some casks which I found did not agree with the gauger, but as there is a doubt I determined to measure it again to-morrow". . . . "Eighteen half pounds, light weight, of butter, in the hands of a Frenchwoman . . . . confiscated. I directed it to be sent to the hospital . . . ." . . . . . "From 11 to 6 p.m. at Gorey, examining the weights; found many using false weight, stones, lead and brass, all of which I confiscated, some scales false. Le Breton's in excellent order and very clean. Saw seventeen shops". . . . . "Visited all the shops round St. Catherine's Bay, and by Fliquet to Archirondel and La Croix de Bois[2]. Confiscated a good many false weights". . . . "Visited the butcher's weights in the meat market . . . . the richest are the greatest rogues. I confiscated weights from most of them. Le Sueur told the Att. General, who

1. An Act of 1842 denied to the Viscount the right to speak in the States.
2. Five Oaks.

happened to come by to buy meat at 5 p.m.: 'Les boulangers vendent les pains de quatre livres qui ne pesent que trois livres et demi. Monsieur Le Vicomte dit qu'il n'y a pas de loi qui les en empêchent; quand il sera notre Bailli cela sera corrigé'. Dupré looked glum and muted. What a speech to make to him and me". And so it went on through the years, with constant testing of weights, dry and liquid, as well as the strength of spirits. The weigh-bridges came in for testing and scrutiny too, first in 1827, and then being modernised in 1854, when: "went to de Grave about counter poises for our weighbridges . . . . (he) had one put up to show me its construction. They make the counterpoises *from* the machine by placing a ton weighed accurately in detail, upon the bridge, then the counterpoise to that is the *unit* from which to subdivide or to increase. If the bridge is kept clean and the beds bright, which should be done by a competent person every six or twelve months, the bridge must work truly".

There was still a town crier in 1852, for he recorded: "Put off the drill for the morning yesterday by the town crier, as I had secret intimation that the men had determined not to turn out in numbers, so took the initiative".

In 1846 a Royal Commission visited Jersey to report on the criminal laws, the members being Messrs. Ellis and Bros. The latter was a Governor of the Bank of England, and lived at Upper Clapton, where Sir John often visited him, He became very friendly with them both though when he heard of their appointment he described them as "lawyers of no public eminence to enquire into our criminal laws, the best portion of our system, with power to hear upon oath". However as soon as he met them he found them to be "very gentle-manly amiable men. Thanked me for the courtesy of my answers and the very interesting historical sketch I have given them of the criminal law. Told them I was not a lawyer, but having had all my grandfather's papers and precedents, with a quarter of a century of experience, I had endeavoured to study the law of my country . . . . I said that if they would forgive me for suggesting it privately, if they could make it be understood that no intention was manifested to examine the Jurats, a great deal of soreness would at once be got rid of . . . . they were not men learned in the law, but they had all been Constables and practically conversant with it; they had been elected by a majority of their countrymen and enjoyed their confidence, and however they might be run down, they were honest and upright men and gave their judgment to the best of their abilities. I had sat as a Jurat for two years, and could declare how anxious my then colleagues always were to give a right judgment . . They wished to know what the last commission had done . . . . That commission (I said) had made a great mistake in not urging the return to our real constitution; it was prophetic however . . . . I left them, much pleased with their courteous demeanour and perfectly pure intentions I believe". The following day Sir John, in his capacity as Viscount, intro-duced them to the States, and this only a very few days before the Queen's visit. Once that was over, "All the time in daily attendance on the Commissioners, who are very able men, and conduct their examinations with great judgment and ability . . . . they left us on Sunday for Guernsey, where I followed them on Friday morning with a view to follow up the en-quiry and to compare the institutions of Guernsey with ours". He left Jersey a day late, as the Wonder had been delayed by storm, and attended the Guernsey Court, where several well known Jurats were to be seen; Mr. Le Marchant, Colonel de Havilland, Mr. Andros, Mr. Métivier and Mr. McCullock, as well as General Napier the Lieutenant Governor. But he thought poorly of the Guernsey Court and said: "The Court possesses enormous

O

power. It makes laws, it makes ordinances which are laws, it directs the prosecution of the infractions, it judges them secretly, then decides on them publickly, it is Judge, and jury, it is the coroner, in a word it is universal in its jurisdiction. Venice under its Doges and Magnates was not more arbitary. Yet, the Guernsey folks think it perfection. Let them have it, say I".

Some days later, "Left Guernsey with the Royal Commissioners, on their kind invitation, in the Princess Royal steamer, for which they pay forty five pounds for one week. We started at ¼ past 10 a.m. and after a beautiful passage got to Alderney . . . . the steamer bowsprit was almost ashore behind the small pier at Braye harbour . . . . Disappointed at Alderney cows, they are generally small and very inferior to our best, price £10. Horses punchy and good . . . . The Court is composed by the Judge and six Jurats, men of substance whom Ellis referred to as the learned judges with such gravity that I thought I should choke to suppress laughter . . . . Longy Castle would be a good site for a pharos to look into Cherbourg from, the whole island should be one great fort, which it could easily be made. The soil is poor, ill cultivated; the town St. Anne's is very clean with 1,000 or 1,100 inhabitants".

The party then went on to Sark, and on the Sunday they all attended church, where "the clergyman, a Swiss, preached an interminable sermon about Jonah . . . . Land is sold at two quarters and let at £2 the vergée, cows worth £10, coarser than ours". The party had considerable difficulty in leaving Sark, owing to the bad weather, and were indeed delayed for twenty four hours, and then had a very bad passage to Guernsey. Two days later when Sir John crossed back to Jersey the journey took him seven hours, in the steamer Drake.

The next year, when on a visit to London, he visited Mr. Ellis, living at Bedford Place, and there he met, "Macaulay the M.P. a lion[1] . . . . Miss Ellis is an elegant highly cultivated young person. Macaulay was making dignified love to her in language most sublime; it was real fun to see her shrink from the embrace of Jupiter. Without being a beauty, she is an enchanting girl. What a nice mother she will make with her fine discriminating mind".

In July of 1847, he attended the States: "to hear report of the Royal Commissioners which the gallery received with much applause. There were some long faces among the judges". And a few months later: "States; letter from Sir G. Grey cautiously worded, expects the States to second his wishes and to meet the report of the Royal Commissioners. Le Sueur and Godfray talking all the while". This Commission advised the abolition of the Royal Court and its replacement by three Crown appointed paid judges, proposals which go against the grain for a Jerseyman. In spite of this there is a lengthy report, by Sir John, dated 1864, and proposing just this. Referring back to the report of the commissioners of 1811, whose recommendations about the election of Jurats were not adopted, he said: "It will be in the recollection of many that in the years 1835 to 1836 the lawyers had adopted a most damaging mode of challenging the Jurats, and on referring to no. 5145 of the last Commissioners' report, it will be seen that the proceedings of the court were entirely suspended by this insane mode. It had the first great effect in lowering the dignity which a Court of Justice should maintain, and made it ridiculous in public estimation. This essentially led to the resignation of the writer from the office of Jurat". One had

1. Apparently Lord Macaulay the historian.

wondered if it was really ill health alone. The position was that in the early days the men of wealth and property were the only ones with the education to fit them for the post of Jurat, but that as time passed, and education improved there was a wider choice, and men with no legal knowledge at all were being chosen to sit in judgement on their fellows. The Commissioners, Ellis and Bros, said that they felt party politics were playing far too large a part in the selection of men for the office of Jurat, and that " . . . . the functions which the Jurats were called on to discharge in the States necessarily operate in keeping party feelings alive. The result is that this tribunal does not possess the confidence of the inhabitants and we think does not deserve it". Sir John himself continued: "I became so convinced of the unsuitableness of the system to the age of intelligence and development to which the Island has arrived, from its population, wealth and vast enterprise . . . . that I urged upon successive Secretaries of State the absolute necessity there was for an enquiry into the civil and municipal laws of Jersey". In 1852 three Orders in Council were issued, and these were revoked the following year. They provided for Courts of summary Jurisdiction, Petty Courts and a Police system. It was not the recommendations of the Orders which caused the trouble, but the question whether there existed the power for the Crown to legislate for the States. When the case came up in 1853, Sir Frederick Thesiger, who had been Solicitor and Attorney General of England, pleaded for Jersey, presenting petitions from the States, from forty nine inhabitants, and another from over four thousand ratepayers. Some persons were found to have signed both the latter petitions, though their objects were contradictory. Sir Frederick's speech occupies 169 pages of manuscript, and it is not proposed to consider the details contained in it, but only to examine Sir John's opinions in the matter. On Friday March 4th he said "The case for the States of Jersey was pleaded before the Privy Council. The late Conservative Att. General Sir Frederick Thesiger opened the case, by going over their printed case seriatim. He advanced so freely that the people or States of Jersey had an inherent right of legislating for themselves that Dr. Lushington asked, 'Do you deny the right of the Crown to enact laws for Jersey?' Except for taxes he insisted that there was no instance in which the Crown had enacted a law without the intervention of the States . . . . As he found he had gone too far, he recanted so far as to start from 1771 and called the Code of laws the Charter of the Jersey People . . . . Sir Fred made a very sorry speech for the States. He was thinking of the Jew question which he was to discuss the next night . . . . Roundell Palmer M.P.[1] began a fine speech by contending that Jersey had a right to frame its own laws . . . it would be beyond common sense, beyond belief if when the principle obtained in 1853 that self-government was proper for all our colonial possessions, the Island of Jersey should now be deprived of its ancient privilege of self-government". Finally, as already said, the Orders in Council were revoked, because doubts existed as to their legality in the circumstances.

Yet another Royal Commission came over in 1859, and Sir John was questioned by them about the prison, and "they were much pleased however with the cleanliness and appearance of the establishment, all but the lunatic department". They were invited to attend a Visite des Chemins in Trinity and St. Mary, Sir John Awdry "observing that it came legitimately into the spirit of their commission to see and examine the parochial usages". The night before producing their findings the Commissioners gave "a private dinner to those who had been hospitable towards them . . . . 18 in all . . . . a very good and

---

1. Roundell Palmer, first Earl of Selborne (1812-1895), Jurist and hymnologist.

pleasant dinner, no toasts, not one word of politics, local I mean".

The dinner customarily given after a sitting of the Cour d'Heritage, by the Sovereign, unfortunately caused some heart searchings. One vexed question was whether the Lieutenant Governor should notify, or invite, those who, from custom, had the right to attend. General Cuppage wrote for advice to Sir Robert Peel, saying; "whilst fully acknowledging that, diverted as they were from their former use, the expenses of these dinners should give way before more essential wants, I am still of the opinion that it would be for the dignity of the Crown that these old and cherished habits should, in their ancienty, be maintained; and that the Seigneurs of the Island and Officers of the Court, who by right are entitled to be present, together with a deputation to represent their body from other ranks of the court, should be invited by the Lieutenant Governor, in the name of the Queen, to express on these occasions their homage and loyalty to Her Majesty". In reply to this very lengthy sentence, Sir Robert, for the Lords of the Treasury, said that in spite of the "very limited amount of the Crown funds available for such useful purpose . . . . their Lordships will not object". Sir John reminds us of the original reason for such dinners in a note which said; "The good General little knows what trouble he will give himself. Sir Percy Douglas had taken the odium of getting rid of these dinners, required in the olden time before there were carriage roads in the Island, and they were a real boon; now they are a political mischief". However, he felt that if the dinner were to take place, the Colonels of Militia and the Adjutant General of Militia should also be invited. The latter stipulation did not in fact affect him, as he was included in any case as Viscount.

The Fenians, an extremist Irish movement, gave some trouble, and in 1866 Sir John forwarded to the Lieutenant Governor, "the enclosed Fenian treasonable paper . . . . found under the door of the St. Aubin's weighbridge, probably placed there by some Irish person, not so wickedly inclined as the treacherous writer hoped he might prove. It shows plainly that there may be Fenians in the Island, and that efforts are being made to convert all Irishmen to that detestable conspiracy. May it not be prudent to take precautions with regard to the arms in the central arsenals which are only guarded by a storekeeper?" The letter in question said:"My dear Irish brothers. I am informed that you are all well drilled soldiers in Jersey and also in those Channel Islands. We call in the name of our country upon you, for I can assure you that all Ireland was never so ready to rebel for her rights as she is upon the present time. I assure you since the year '98 there was not the excitment known in Ireland this many years as there is this many days. Dear brethren, you must not fret for arms. We have arms for millions ready upon this day, there is many Catholics country ready upon this day to free us from the Saxton (sic) yoke. We hope the day will come when Ireland will be a free republic". A confidential letter was sent to the seven colonels commanding the detachments of militia saying: "Care to be specially taken at the present period against any Fenian move. To place themselves in communication with the Constables of the parishes if necessary. Arsenals guarded . . . ."

Sad as it is, there is no doubt that Sir John's opinion of local politicians at the time was very poor. In fact when the Lieutenant Governor, Sir Frederick Love, suggested recommending him as Bailiff, he recorded that " . . . . I told him I did not consider myself sufficiently qualified, nor did I wish to be mixed up with the very low persons who rule the court. I should be at constant war with them". He seemed to consider Mr. Carey of Guernsey the most proper person to succeed Sir Thomas Le Breton, "Guernsey being only worth

£400 a year and this worth a thousand". And referring to a certain bankruptcy case he said: ".... it is now in the lawyer's hands. Lord have mercy on it".

As a Deputy for (as opposed to 'of') the States, Sir John had acted as early as 1835, when he received a vote of thanks on parchment, and from the Guernsey States a "piece of plate worth fifty guineas"[1] for his work with the House of Commons against a bill affecting the Channel Islands corn trade.

Deputies of the States first sat in that assembly in 1857, and on January 12th that year he recorded; "The town in a ferment about the election of new Deputies to-morrow. Rumour gives it to Sorel, Dallain and Vickery. Hemery is said to have damaged himself by refusing Eraut's brother a commission in the town, saying: 'Oh, he is a shopkeeper, I cannot give him a commission'. All the shopkeepers will vote against him .... It did nearly lose his election as he was at the foot of the town list and only beat Wellman by about 20". Then on January 29th; "The States with the fourteen new Deputies, held their first sitting. I was told yesterday that Deputy Dallain was to propose that the Treasurer Godfray should offer security sufficient as Treasurer of the States, but neither he nor others had the courage to bell the cat".

To Colonel James Godfray, a most distinguished member of another branch of the family, and who was later to hold his own position of Q.A.D.C. he wrote rather peremptorily, under instructions from the Lieutenant Governor in 1868, concerning a Queen's birthday review, at which the Lieutenant Governor had noticed that the troopers under Godfray's command were not in the position that had been ordered; and "General Cuppage desires to know by what authority the troopers neglected to perform the required duty?" The letter containing these orders had been refused by Godfray, being under-stamped, although under H.M.S. cover; but Sir John said he had paid the excess postage so as to be sure the letter of orders was duly received.

The feud with various members of the Godfray family was so intense that clearly nothing the one did could possibly be right in the eyes of the other. It is epitomised in the word Devilfray, always used to refer to any member of the family. This first arose from an unfortunate incident, when the Deputy Viscount, under orders from Sir John, had put the official Viscount's seals on the property of a certain person under distraint, and Godfray, a Dénonciateur of the Court, had broken these official seals, and even attacked the Deputy Viscount in the performance of his duties. For this Sir John could never forgive him and the resulting controversy covers many many pages of manuscript. When the tempestuous Advocate François Godfray died suddenly, he wrote: "I heard him pleading an appeal case before the full Court yesterday, apparently in full power of voice. He has wasted fine abilities in violent party measures, and I believe dies a ruined man". It is ironical that these two lifelong enemies should both have gone blind, and that François Godfray's son, Charles was one of the doctors in attendance on Sir John in his last illness. But there were no hard feelings towards the son, for Harriet wrote a few days before her father's death; "Dr. Godfray performed a very successful operation, one of the first tried in Europe. I was most grateful, and then Father was blessed with a good night's sleep". Seldom can a bitter family quarrel have ended on such a note of mercy.

Hugh Godfray's wonderful map, published in 1849, naturally comes in for praise only, and reference to it is often made. In 1856 he recorded; "Called on Sir G. Seymour on board

---

1. Decribed in his will as an 'epergne and stand'.

the Black Eagle. He took me into her beautiful cabin to look at Godfray's map of Jersey which I took for his inspection. He saw our line of travel and the line of defence which I propose for Noirmont. The General and I took the party round the markets and to the Court House, to see Sir George's uncle's portrait of Field Marshal Conway. He is much pleased with it. Young Seymour is very much like it". This refers to the Gainsborough portrait of Field Marshal Henry Seymour Conway, Governor from 1772-1795. It was painted at the request and expense of the States of Jersey. It was on the occasion of this visit that Sir George Seymour quoted to Sir John an anecdote about Lord Nelson, which must be preserved for posterity. It happened when "Sir George was a middy on board the Victory, and was dining with Lord Nelson, when a scientific captain said to him: 'My Lord, I wish you would see my winch; with my winch I can weigh the brig's anchor with half the men I would otherwise require'. 'Aye, hang your winch; with these mechanical aids the time will come when our navy will be all machinery, and seamanship worth nothing. Then your spaniards and your French will be just as good as ourselves'. ". In 1861 in a letter to the Lieutenant Governor Sir John said; "Constable of St. Brelade's reports that the road leading towards the Common and La Cotte tower[1] is private. If he refers to Godfray's map it ends in a trapezoid at Lamberts. General Don once opened a temporary road down from there, a war precaution".

In his various official capacities he naturally had a great deal to do with the Attorney General, and of Mr. Dupré he thought well as a lawyer. But there was a embarrassing situation in a case of debt in 1860, when a Madame Ramié claimed that he owed her some money, and as Viscount it was Sir John's painful duty to intervene in the matter. He wrote her a letter recommending mercy and forgiveness and said: "Poverty may drive a creditor to incarcerate a debtor, where there is a chance of obtaining money, but where there are good means to live, and no chance of obtaining by means of imprisonment, how can we expect forgiveness hereafter? . . . . If for filthy lucre's sake we should cause absolute ruin with no chance of success . . . . I never intend to deprive a being of his liberty for any debt due to myself". A few months later he wrote to her again saying that he had been delighted to hear that she had decided to accept £150 in settlement. So perhaps alleged friendship with the French proscrits was not the only reason why Dupré was passed over for the Bailifship, as has been suggested, in spite of his unquestioned legal ability.

The next Attorney General was Robert Pipon Marett, later Bailiff. For him Sir John entertained the highest possible regard, officially and personally, and there was a close friendship between all members of the families.

Another colleague, officially and in connexion with the militia, was Helier Touzel, who was a first cousin once removed. He was a Lieutenant General, and held the office of Receiver General, sometimes with a co-Receiver, from 1814-1863. In spite of considerable difference in age the two men had much in common and often met and discussed affairs of mutual interest.

Sir John's Baton of office as Vicomte is still in the possession of his descendants. It is silver, surmounted with a crown, and engraved: "J. Le Couteur Esq. Viscount. 1842".
On the base he had engraved his arms, quartered, curiously, not with those of his wife, but with those of his mother's family, the Dumaresqs. He held this office for over thirty years, and conducted it throughout with a deep sense of duty and consciousness of its dignity.

1. Presumably meaning the Martello tower at Ouaisné.

CHAPTER SIXTEEN

THE AGRICULTURIST

To Sir John all branches of agriculture and horticulture were deeply interesting and important, but it was as an early experimenter with wheat that he gained some modest fame. Indeed it was for this that he was elected a Fellow of the Royal Society. The citation for that election, bearing the signatures of thirteen famous men, sets out his qualifications, and they almost all concern wheat. In the first place he was author of five monographs:

a Work on the varieties, properties and classification of wheat, 1836.

a Paper on "Hoeing wheat", printed by the Society of Arts, 1837.

a Prize essay on "Pure and improved varieties of wheat lately introduced into England" 1839.

a Paper on "The culture of the Parsnip", 1840.

a Paper on the "Jersey Trench Plough", 1841.

(the last three being published in the Journal of the Royal Agricultural Society of England).

In addition he was cited as:

an Improver of the culture of wheat.

Distinguished for his acquaintance with the science of agriculture and collateral branches of enquiry.

Eminent as a promoter of the informed systems of modern agriculture.

How does his reputation as an agriculturist stand today? Outside Jersey he is largely unknown: and science has made such rapid strides since his day that the results of much of his work have been superseded. He had never heard of the theory of Mendelism. The conditions under which he worked, the climate and soil of Jersey, the early land on his home farm were all conducive to success. But that success was his own. He was the sort of man who would have succeeded anywhere, through his own exertions, his meticulous attention to detail, and above all his imagination. He had the imaginative power to see that crop selection and purity of seed were needed in order to improve yields, and thereby to improve man's lot. This power, combined with the practical knowledge of a real farmer, showed him the way to go, and that the improvements he had in mind were no theorist's pipe dream, but things which any intelligent farmer could actually do. No longer famous, he is still recognised in the textbooks as a pioneer, innovator and stimulator of thought in the early development of new varieties of wheat, and of novel ideas on a wide range of aspects in its cultivation. As such, he was a benefactor to his fellow men, and that above all is what he wanted to be. In another chapter we have noticed an identical ambition in his son, but in a different field, the bettering of the lot of the ordinary soldier.

In the early 1830s the political hazards on the continent brought to Jersey an eminent refugee, Professor La Gasca, Curator of the Royal Gardens at Madrid. In 1835 the Royal Jersey Agricultural and Horticultural Society presented him with a copy of Hooper's Botanical Miscellany as a "trifling yet sincere memorial of their esteem and respect": and four years later, when Sir John was their President, the Society printed the results of La Gasca's botanical observations in Jersey in a list of twenty-six plants. All but nine of these plants can still be found in the Island. The list is given in Babington's[1] "Primitiae Florae Sarnicae" of 1839, but L. V. Lester Garland in his "A Flora of the Island of Jersey", 1903, dismissed La Gasca's work as "absolutely valueless". Today La Gasca's records are accepted, with the reservation that he included some garden plants which were not truly native. Sir John related that he saw about eighty distinct sorts of wheat growing in La Gasca's nursery garden, and that the Professor had classified over nine hundred varieties in Madrid. He invited La Gasca to inspect his own crops, which he then considered to be pure, but to his dismay "he drew from three fields three and twenty sorts, some white, some red, some liver-coloured, some spring wheat, some dead ripe . . . ., some ripe, some half so, some in a milky state and some green . . . . I reflected on the subject, and immediately became convinced that no crop in that state could either produce the greatest weight of corn, give the largest quantity of flour, or make the best or lightest bread, such as would be produced from a field in an equal and perfect state of ripeness . . . . I requested Professor La Gasca to show me those which he considered the best and most productive. He pointed out fourteen sorts . . . . These I grew with extreme care".

One sees here the practical application by Sir John of the theoretical knowledge imparted to him by La Gasca, and from this partnership there sprang an advance in the science of this subject. It was carefully geared by Sir John, to whom every detail of husbandry was familiar, from having taken part in it himself, to what was attainable by his farmer friends, and kept within practical bounds by his own common sense. In his experimental work he did not attempt to evolve new types of wheat, but contented himself with selecting, though in the case of his Belle Vue Talavera (*Talavera Bellevuensis*)[2] he selected with such care that it became a variety of its own, almost identical with *Richelle de Naples*. It has, of course, been superseded long since, but was important in its day. The botanical name allotted to it was *Triticum aestivum var. albidum*, indicating that it was white grained, white chaffed and awnless. Writing of it in 1880, Vilmorin[3] considered it an exceptionally fine and productive type, its only fault being some sensitivity to cold.

At the Crystal Palace Exhibition Sir John exhibited 104 varieties of wheat, all classified, and seven of them bearing the name Jersey. The Belle Vue Talavera was described as Colonel Le Couteur's seedling, taking 52 bushels to the acre, with 27 pounds of flour, producing 35 pounds 14 ounces of the finest bread. Another specimen was described as: "Mummy. Tombs of the Kings of Thebes. Sir Gardner Wilkinson. Raised at Belle Vue from one ear sent by M. Tupper Esq., 1846: 27 pounds of flour produced 35 pounds bread, very light, white superior". The exhibits were divided into seven varieties:

> white winter wheat
> winter compact varieties
> elongated winter wheat
> downy or hoary wheat
> red wheats
> spring wheats
> bearded.

1. Professor C. C. Babington, (1808-1895).
2. Not to be confused with a variety named Belle Vue, introduced in 1940 by a French breeder, Tourneur.
3. Vilmorin started as a Paris florist. He and Sir John were exchanging wheat samples as early as 1835.

The claim to have germinated mummy wheat, I am informed, is not possible in fact, though clearly he thought he had achieved this. He spent a great deal of time preparing the exhibits, noting one day: "Very busy all the afternoon arranging and poisoning my select wheats. All the best varieties have been attacked by insects": and on another: "all day occupied with Adams the engraver, writing the names of 104 varieties of wheat to be exhibited at the World's show; and wrote to Mr. Wyatt the Secretary to announce them for entry". In March 1851 he made special arrangements with the Customs officials at Shoreham to pass them through the excise. At the Crystal Palace he met a Colonel Reid, special Commissioner, who was interested in Jersey Militia law as well as the wheat exhibit. He wished to introduce the former into Bermuda, and had already cultivated new grasses there, "and made hay where none had ever previously been seen. But many grasses were shy bearers of seed; indeed some would not grow beyond the 32nd degree of latitude . . . . He came to see my case of wheat . . . . Very important, I ought to have it printed and engraved just as it is. A man who wishes to diffuse and serve mankind must publish, not place in a newspaper, matter of his own, bear the loss, and let the world judge his purpose. He had disseminated my work on wheat wherever he had commanded". The Crystal Palace exhibits which Sir John had prepared formed part of two special collections in the Bethnal Green Museum when it opened in 1872, but after a lapse of time they perished and no longer exist.

The book referred to by Colonel Reid was entitled: "On the varieties, properties and classification of wheat", and was published in 1836 by Robert Shearsmith, of Catherine Street, Strand. Sir John had trouble with the stationer, who failed to deliver the requisite paper to the engraver: and with the publisher, who was tardy in advertising and circulating the book, with the result that people who had heard of it complained that they could not obtain it. He considered printing a thousand copies of it, translated into French, but so far as is known this never came about. He sent a copy to the Duke of Sussex, F.R.S., the sixth son of George III and the only one of them with scientific interests, to whom he had been presented by the Duke's son, Sir Augustus d'Este. A second edition was printed in 1872, and a copy sent to the Queen, "for the use of your Majesty's farms".

In 1839 the Royal Agricultural Society of England published his prize essay on varieties of wheat, and the following year he attended the Society's show in Cambridge. On entering the show yard he met Lord Spencer who told him "they had decided I was to speak on wheat at the dinner *today* in Trinity Hall. Said I was unprepared. 'Never mind, speak on the impulse; you will do it very well' . . . . Duke of Richmond saw me in his room; told me I must speak; hoped he would allow me to say something about an experimental farm. 'Certainly, he would support it also'. The dinner in Trinity Hall, for 430, was very grand. I was greatly pleased to hear I had got the prize for wheat . . . . Breakfasted with Mr. Babbage.[1] There were Mr. Corelli, Mr. Lusi of Greece and other savants, besides Martin and I. After breakfast he explained to us and showed us the wonderful calculating engine, and wonderful it is . . . . He does not look as clever as he is". Next day there was a grand assembly with 2700 men present. Sir Robert Peel "was admirably received and spoke well. So did the American Minister Stevenson[2]; Lord Hardwicke also. The rest were scarcely heard".

The correspondence Sir John conducted about wheat was immense, and he supplied

---

1. Charles Babbage (1792-1871), mathematician and astronomer: chiefly known for his calculating machine.
2. Andrew Stevenson (1784-1857), United States Minister in Great Britain 1836-41.

classified samples of grain to enquirers all over Great Britain. The activities of Customs officials infuriated him. They used to turn out the wheat to examine it, and he feared they would mix the types he had taken such care to keep distinct and pack separately. One wrong grain tossed into a sack by an ignorant official could upset the purity of a sample and invalidate months of experiment. Carelessness in sweeping barns and cleaning winnowing machines might have the same effect, and he used to urge recipents of his parcels to choose one, or at most two, types suitable to their soil and climate and concentrate on them alone, so as to keep them pure. Let us take a cross-section of the many people to whom he wrote. Among others we find:

Thomas Knight[1] of Downton, President of the Royal Horticultural Society.
Sir John Sinclair, President of the Board of Agriculture.
The Hon. Mrs. Pomeroy of Dublin.
Monsieur Donker à Coetbo par Phélan.
Robert Brown, Secretary to the Central Society of Great Britain and Ireland.
The Earle of Albemarle.
William Hamilton of Plymouth.
The Rev. Gwilt of Suffolk.
J. Cloudon of Bayswater.
J. White of Plymouth.
Robert Barker of Lincolnshire.
John McConnell of Gaspé.
Sir George Mackenzie of Coal, Dingwall.
Bailiff de Lisle Brock of Guernsey.
Henry Handley, M.P.
Lady Webster of Battle Abbey.

A letter to Captain Stoddart in Persia said that the sender had selected several varieties of wheat which he hoped would be found suitable for the climate of Persia, which was "contiguous to, if not the original one, in which the plant was first presented to the human race". Detailed instructions follow as to the planting and cultivation of this wheat, but one wonders if Stoddart was able to comply with them, for a letter note on this letter adds: "Doctor Woolf, who went to Persia in search of poor Stoddart, dined with us here afterwards . . . . He was inhumanely mutilated and murdered". This was in 1842.

Sir John's great attention to detail is manifest in tables in his wheat book, showing the produce of fourteen varieties grown under controlled experiment, with a further table giving the return in weight of corn. Modern farmers, accustomed to mechanical spreading of pre-fabricated manures, will marvel at the toil endured by their predecessors in achieving similar ends. Page 108 of the book announces: "It should be an invariable rule to mix nitrate of soda with salt, when it is to be used as a top dressing for wheat. Nitrate of soda and salt are best adapted to stiffish soils in good condition, and a specially prepared mixed mineral and nitrogenised manure to the soils which possess rather a lighter character. On light land I would recommend the following mixture which, I know from experience, answers exceedingly well in an economical point of view: $1\frac{1}{2}$ cwt. of nitrate of soda: 3 cwt. of common salt: 2 cwt. of Peruvian guano: and 40 bushels of soot. The guano should first be passed through a fine sieve, and all hard lumps broken up, a work which will be much

1. Thomas Andrew Knight (1759-1838), horticulturist and botanist.

facilitated by the addition of some sharp siliceous sand to the lumps. When sharp sand is not at hand, perfectly dry and sifted coal ashes or burnt clay may be used instead. The nitrate of soda and salt should be passed in like manner through a fine sieve, and these salts are always more or less damp and therefore difficult to sift, it is well to mix them previously with a dry substance in the same manner as guano. The next step is to mix these sifted and finely powdered manures with a sufficient quantity of burnt clay or coal ashes to make up twenty bushels. These are finely mixed with forty bushels of soot. Thus we obtain sixty bushels of a manure which will suffice for three acres. The twenty bushels which will have to be used per acre will cost about 25s. and, I have no doubt, will be found a very economical and useful top-dressing for wheat". We do not doubt it either, but as we visualise the regiment of men required to sieve, mix, bring sand and coal ash, burn clay, cart the soda and salt from harbour, measure out the bushels, load them and drive them to the land, sow them by hand from buckets, drive home again, unload, unharness, stall and feed the horses, we are bound to wonder how it was all done for 11s.1d. per vergée, (of which there are $2\frac{1}{4}$ to an acre). The answer, in a nutshell, is the cost of labour. Sir John's formula for top-dressing would be quite uneconomic today. The same explanation applies to the figures he gives for an experimental farm in England which had won a prize. There the wheat was "all hand-hoed twice in the spring, at a cost of 3s.6d. per acre each time. It is cut with a fagging-hook, at an average cost of 11s.0$\frac{1}{2}$d. per acre, which included tying and shocking". He was extremely anxious to see experimental farms established in order that work could be done in them for the benefit of the farmer, and would have rejoiced at the prospect of one in Jersey; but it was many years before the Howard Davis Experimental Farm at Trinity was established.

In 1845 the Farmers' Magazine wrote to him: "We propose to give your portrait in the Farmers' Magazine, after the style of those of the Duke of Richmond, Mr. Pusey and others. Have you a painting from which we can take an engraving, and if so shall how we get it?" Their issue of March 1846 carries an article entitled "Colonel Le Couteur", with an engraving by J. B. Hunt "from a painting by J. Bertean". In fact this was a drawing by T. Berteau, a Jersey artist several of whose works appear in this book. The Magazine describes Sir John as "an eminent British farmer, an high and enviable character . . . . purity of purpose, perseverance in action or excellence in exposition; we beg leave to introduce Colonel Le Couteur". The article is highly eulogistic.

In 1848 Sir John was told that he was to receive a presentation from the Royal Jersey Agricultural and Horticultural Society. It had been founded in 1833, five years before the English "Royal", and he was its first Secretary, and four times President, in 1839, 1847, 1853 and 1868. The customary "piece of plate" having been suggested for the presentation, he asked it he might consult his with wife. The result was—a telescope. But it sounds as if he did not quite approve of the supplier: "Marett told me that General T. had consulted Le Roy about the telescope: a man named Mills had been written to instead of Dollond". On the 27th February 1850 the diary recorded: "Presentation of a lunar telescope to me by the Jersey Ag. and H.S. The President, Mr. Bertram of Beaulieu, attended". Thirteen members came, and "staid to dinner at half past two, and left at 7, mutually pleased I hope". The newspaper account, while not relating that they all staid to dinner, gives full coverage of the presentation and the speeches. Mr. J. B. Le Roy, Optician, of Mulcaster Street, was in charge of the testimonial, that is to say the telescope. At the close of his address of thanks,

Sir John said, "I urge the necessity of taking due advantage of our position, to raise the best, most pure and above all earliest crops of every sort, garden seeds as well as grain, in order to establish for Jersey a name as being a propitious, true and sure seed market. This is practically within the reach of every farmer and gardener, either by his own intelligence and industry, or by that combination, which is so well understood through our French[1] Plough system".

When the Seigneur of Rozel resigned the Presidency in 1868 there was an unfortunate incident. "I was called to the chair. Messrs. Marett, du Heaume and others opposed the vote of thanks to the late President, when proposed by old Ph. Le Feuvre. I addressed them to show that the ill humour of last Saturday should not make them forget the long services to the society; when the vote passed unanimously". The matter in dispute was very trivial, fourteen instead of fifteen days' notice having been given of some item, which was consequently ruled out of order by the President. The next week Sir John was again chosen as President, and at first declined of account of age. He was then seventy-four: "however, my old friends and the farmers urging, I consented. At the annual dinner that year at the Imperial Hotel there were forty present, with the new Governor, General Guy and the French consul, Baron de Chazal, as guests of honour. "I gave them an outline of the successes of our Society since its formation in 1833 to now, when our cows have risen in value from £12 to £100.

Sir John took an immense interest in the cows and the betterment of the breed. In 1849 a committee was named to examine points for judging the animals, and he "proposed the alteration from 28 to 34 or 36 points". Invited to Belle Vue to discuss it, the committee arrived at 7 a.m. before morning milking: "General Touzel our President and his daughter came first; then Patriarche, Marett, Mourant, Gibaut and Le Feuvre of St. P. Hume sent a fine cow of his, and Gibaut sent two. Hume's cow gave nine quarts, one pint and two gills; a fine milker, a large cow. My Belle, which they thought the handsomest of the lot, gave seven quarts and a pint[2]. After breakfast we worked till 12, and fixed 36 instead of the old 28 points". The next day he "took a sketch of Belle before breakfast in order to draw the points all round her". A sketch was also made of a prize-winning bull belonging to Mr. Bowerman; the two drawings were approved by the Board of the Society, and Sir John was asked to "write to Mr. Hudson to know the charge for lithographing them". Soon afterwards a lithographer named Standridge of Old Jewry in London was asked to provide mere outline drawings, 750 of the cow and 250 of the bull, at 30s. for each drawing, and the prints at 2s.9d. per hundred.

Then, as now, the parochial and Island Agricultural Shows were important annual events, and these papers mention and comment upon many of them. There was a sad tale to be told about the show of 1842. Madelon Morlee the milkmaid, it appears, rose at 5 a.m. on the day of the show, and left at 7 a.m. to take her cattle there, having had no time to eat any breakfast. She tended her cows on the show ground till after midday and milked several of them, and began to feel hungry and tired. Somebody persuaded her to take some milk and eau de vie, which refreshed her considerably, but to a point where she appropriated some of the prize ribbons, and when these were found on her she explained that she thought her cows deserved them. Heads wagged and the solemn voices of authority dis-

---

1. Probably a printer's error for Trench Plough.
2. These would not be considered particularly high yields nowadays.

cussed her offence, and things might have gone ill for her had not Monsieur and Madame Le Couteur testified that that poor Madelon was "une honnête fille" who had worked for them for two years and that they were happy to keep her in their service. One hopes that her zeal for her employer's herd was rewarded at another show with a prize ribbon. From time immemorial country girls have expected to return from the fair or the show-ground with coloured ribbons and baskets of posies.

Sir John regularly appeared at cattle shows, as exhibitor or judge, and at the inevitable dinners after them, and kept records of it all. In 1847, for example, a hundred head were exhibited at the St. Peter's show but there were only "some good ones" amongst them. At the Island show that year there was "a great improvement in the eastern district, very nice cattle, some beautiful ones. The servants were greatly elated to find that Beauty's heifer, Bella, had got the first prize, and Julia our old cow the second, while the two others were decorated". A distinguished newcomer to the Island, Lord Limerick, who for a time rented Trinity Manor, was also a cattle enthusiast. By 1857, in one of the eastern sections, there were 249 cows and heifers on show and the standard had much improved. At the western Three-Parish show that year there were 300 head exhibited at the St. Mary's Arsenal ground: "Gibaut, James Godfray and I were the judges in the last resort of 48 beautiful animals in yearlings, two year olds, three to five year olds and old cows. £36 were offered, and refused, for a two year old. 130 men afterwards sat down to a very handsome cold dinner. Halkett returned thanks for the army, very well. Dupré made a good speech, and I urged them to have clubs in every parish, and to contribute to the parent society". How delighted he would have been at the flourishing state of the central and parish societies today.

In June 1847 a two year old heifer (bought from Mr. Thomas Filleul for £23), and a yearling bull (given by Sir John), with another heifer, were presented to the Prince Consort. The diary tells us: "Took a mail train from Paddington to Slough, got there and on to Windsor by 10. Called to see Lord Spencer, the Lord Chamberlain, ... who obligingly sought for Colonel Phipps. He being away, the Earl referred me to General Wemyss at the home farm, where the appointment was made, and there I repaired. Unluckily for me the Queen had just driven to see the cattle . . . . and had just left, otherwise I should have explained matters to herself in person unattended, for Her Majesty happened to be in her pony chaise. I sent my card to the Prince, who sent for the cattle to show them to the Duchess of Kent at Frogmore. There we found the Grand Duke Constantine of Russia, the Prince of Saxe Weimar, the Prince of Saxe Leningen, Prince George of Cambridge and a host of attendants. All the royalty came out with Prince Albert, who spoke to me in the most kind and affable manner, even so much so as to reach out his hand, then to recollect etiquette: and very kindly and politely expressed his sense of the compliment, a very acceptable one, of the very beautiful cattle which the Jersey Agricultural Society had made to him: and desired me to make suitable thanks to the society in the most gracious terms. The animals were greatly admired. The Grand Duke asked the Prince what were their valuable points beyond their beauty. The Prince of Saxe Weimar put me the same question, which I explained. The Prince then handed Tocque and I to General Wemyss and charged him, as he afterwards told me, to show us every civility and attention. The kind General then took us all over the royal aviary, dairy farms etc., where everything is nearly 'comme il faut'. His farming is really good, and real improvements have taken place since old K., the late King's farmer, had them". At the Windsor show in 1851 this staunch Jerseyman recorded: "Guernsey beat us by a visible Jersey cross. Lord Egremont's Jersey bull excellent. Our blue mark along the white. My pet stock".

Breeders to whom Jersey cattle were being exported in those days make an impressive list. To take but a few:

The Rev. Gwilt, of Suffolk.
Mr. Lane, of St. Alban's Place.
Richard Nicklin, of the Isle of Man.
General D'Evereux, of London.
Charles McNiven of Godstone, Surrey.
Thomas Alcock, M.P., of Ewell.
Sir Walter James, of Sandwich.
The Marquis of Tweeddale.
Mr. Barker, of Basingstoke.
Mr. B. Johnson, of Albany, New York.
Captain Wood, M.P., Q.A.D.C.
William Harris, of Massachusetts.
James Pedder, of Boston.
The Viscount Enfield.
Monsieur Sigismond de Thaly, of Austria.
Lord Hardinge's son-in-law.
Mr. Weld, F.R.S.
Lady Cavendish.
Mr. Motley, of Boston.
Thomas Moore, of New Zealand.

The total value of the animals sent to Lord Enfield was £205, and of them Sir John said: "I do not believe that eleven such young cows either for beauty or quality ever left Jersey in one lot".

In early days Jersey cows were often referred to as Alderneys, and various explanations have been offered for the misnomer. Sir John's explanation, given in a letter to a Hungarian enquirer, was that his grandfather Sir John Dumaresq had sent to his father-in-law John Le Mesurier, Governor of Alderney, some Jersey cows which were much admired, and came to be known in England as Alderneys in consequence. Those in Alderney at that time, he said, "were very small and much degenerated, while those of Guernsey were larger, stronger, heavier and more bony and more predisposed to fat". In the same letter he says that his grandfather sent cattle to Scotland "qui ont formé le type de la belle race dite 'Ayrshire'". On the subject of prohibition of import of foreign cattle to Jersey, he wrote: "In the year 1789 an act of our legislature was passed by which the importation into Jersey of cows, heifers, calves or bulls was prohibited, under the penalty of 200 livres, with forfeiture of boat and tackle; and a fine of 50 livres was also imposed on every sailor on board who did not inform of the attempt. The animal too was decreed to be immediately slaughtered and its flesh given to the poor. Later laws are equally stringent. No foreign cows are ever allowed to come to Jersey, but as butcher's meat". This was in a letter to two American breeders, in Boston and Bronxville. It goes on to mention that Guernsey cattle are "large and considered too coarse, though famous milkers. Our judges at our cattle shows have discarded both them and their progeny". But "there are scarcely ever a dozen of that breed in our Island".

The letter goes on to discuss the true Jerseys. "The origin of the breed we know nothing of, beyond what you will see in the essay which will I send you. The late Earl Spencer, once Chancellor of the Exchequer, who bore the noble sobriquet of 'honest John Spencer', when President of the Royal Agricultural Society of England . . . ., counselled me to advise our farmers never to risk a cross, even with the shorthorn or Devon, or any other breed. They had a character established for milking and butyraceous[1] qualities . . . . I had informed the Earl how the bulls reared on the north and north-westerly coast of our island, which was rocky and elevated, and exposed to south-west storms, were hardy and enduring: and that cows bred on the southern and eastern coast, which was low, warm and alluvial and richer in pasture, were large bodied, of fine form, though rather more delicate than those from the hills. Lord Spencer recommended to cross bulls from the northern hills with cows in the southern low pastures and vice versa; by which means, if adhered to, our stock might be kept select and superior for ages. This in a great measure is so adhered to. Hence, as our stock had continued pure these past eighty years, I see reason to hope that with our present jealous care our herd book may tell the same honest tale eighty years hence. I may add that owing to the sea breezes wafting saline matter over our Island, it is believed that it conduces to the health of the breed. There was no instance of cattle plague[2] when it raged in England".

The Jersey Herd Book, a department of the parent Society, was formed in 1866, largely at Sir John's instigation, its object being to ensure that the true parentage of every animal recorded should be known. There were at that time over 1200 head of cattle in the Island. It was not a new idea, for the 1851 diary says: "I am working at points for English cattle. The herd book will be a great aid". He was delighted to find that "the young farmers seem to come into the idea".

The American breeders already mentioned now come into the picture in a rewarding way. Mr. Swain of Bronxville wrote a letter about cattle bred of Jersey stock in New York, which the committee published: and Mr. Motley of Boston, "who bought £500 worth of our Jersey cattle last year, has come again to purchase stock here. He attended our Board Room Committee. Stated that it was affirmed in Massachusetts that Jersey had imported 700 Guernsey cows to improve our breed. The members assured him that there were not a dozen in Jersey, never had been at any time. He was much interested in our herd book, and stated that they had begun a Jersey herd book, of which he was on the committee". In 1869 Sir John wrote: "Is it not a great triumph for our small island to have awakened those clever and enterprising agriculturists to the value of our breed of crumpled horned cattle; to have led them to establish a herd book distinctive of our pure breed of Jersey cows? The high and remunerating prices which American gentlemen have given for our cattle in the last few years are an earnest of the value with which Jerseys are held in the United States, and should lead our farmers to be doubly jealous as to the care with which they prohibit the breed from intermixture".

On the colour of Jersey cows, he wrote: "the favourite colours are brown and white, with a grey edge about an inch wide around the brown: fawn and white: or grey and white.

1. Rich in butter-fat.
2. Rinderpest.

The pure Jersey is rarely of one colour, though at this moment I have a fine heifer quite black, the first I ever had". As to their shape, he wrote to Lord Spencer: "All my cattle five years ago had the old Jersey defect, that of being cat hammed, or falling away from the hip to the tail. Now, from having been constantly careful to breed from straight backed, wide chested, small headed bulls, I have removed the defects greatly". He constantly impressed on local farmers that the choice of sire was as important as that of dam, and great was his fury one day when he found his cowman had taken a cow to the La Haule bull to save trouble, when he had expressly stated that she should be bred at another farm. It was not so much that the man had disobeyed orders, or a reflection on that bull, but that the owner always made careful plans for crossing particular bulls with individual cows, and in this case his employee had brought them to naught.

A major problem on a dairy farm is how to maintain milk production in the winter months, January to March, when the grass has ceased to grow, and some substitute diet must be found. Sir John's solution was this: "Winter food for cows, to cause them to give as much milk as in summer. Take a bushel of potatoes, break them whilst raw, place them in a barrel standing up, putting in successively a layer of potatoes and a layer of bran: and a small quantity of yeast in the middle of the mess, which is then left to ferment during a whole week: and when the vinous taste has pervaded the whole mixture, it is given to the cows, who eat it greedily". Probably an excellent recipe, given the labour to prepare it. He had an answer to many of the other difficulties which may arise in a herd of milking cows, and his remarks upon them show that he approached them not from the safety of the armchair, but from practical personal experience in the stable. He well knew that some, not many, cows tend to kick when being milked, a habit which, if not checked, can become a thorough nuisance, and waste the dairyman's time. What he used to do was this. The moment the cow kicked, her bucket of food was removed until she was quiet, and the process was repeated until she had grasped the law of cause and effect. There is only one reference to a milking machine in these papers, in a letter of 1863 to the Lactal Works in Birmingham, complaining that the cow milking machine which had been ordered had been so long in coming that it was now no longer wanted: an early example of the loss of export orders through lagging deliveries. Careful tests of the quality of milk were made at Belle Vue, and Sir John possessed a lactometer, which he mentioned when the Marquis of Tweeddale asked him to buy two cows on his behalf. He replied: "As they are intended for the Marchioness' own dairy, I would not wish to be closely limited to price, because I shall insist on having them brought to Belle Vue on trial by my lactometers before I purchase them. I should say if I am allowed to go as high as £15 to £20 a piece, I shall get what will be sure to please Her Ladyship . . . . I think that for a lady's dairy, beauty, and very deep giving cream and yellow butter is required". Butter making was once of prime importance in Jersey, and quantities were exported. In a previous chapter it has been mentioned as arriving at the siege of Sebastopol. At Belle Vue it was made for home use and also, as one might guess, as a controlled experiment. Sir John had his own cure for foot and mouth disease, which he recorded in 1875 as follows: to add one tablespoonful of permanganate of potash to half a pint of water, to be used night and morning to sponge out the mouth; and a teaspoonful to half a pint of water for internal use.

Other animals come under dicussion in these papers, of course, pigs, sheep and horses in particular. It has been said that the Russians who were stationed in Jersey from 1799-

37. Silver gilt Baton of the office of VICOMTE DE JERSEY,
belonging to Colonel John Le Couteur, and inscribed
with the date 1842, when he assumed that office. (*see page 198*)

Triticum Hybridum.
Cobœrianum à Compactum,
of La Gasca.

Talavera.   *Belvoensis.*

I. Le Couteur (after Nature).

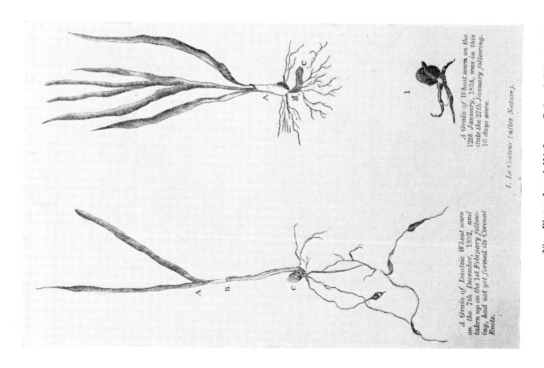

*A Grain of Dantzic Wheat sown
on the 7th December, 1832, and
taken up on the 1st February following, had not yet formed its Coronal
Roots.*

*A Grain of Wheat sown on the
12th January, 1834, was in this
state the 27th January following.
15 days sown.*

I. Le Couteur (after Nature).

38.   Plates I and IV from Colonel John Le Couteur's book 'On the Varieties, Properties and Classification of Wheat', 1836. (*see page 201*)

39. 'Have you a painting from which we can take an engraving?'

Thomas Berteau's pencil drawing of 1845, engraved by J. B. Hunt for an article entitled
'COLONEL LE COUTEUR' in the Farmers' Magazine of March 1846.

40. JERSEY COW and JERSEY BULL, with the agreed points for judging in the show-ring.
(*Drawn by Colonel John Le Couteur*, 1849)

1800 left some of their horses behind them, which affected the local breed, and this is confirmed in a letter Sir John wrote to the Marquis of Tweeddale about a trench plough which he had sent. "I should like", he said, "to see one of your Clydesdale teams of four horses walking away with it, as eight of our little Jersey cossacks do, frequently turning 18 inches of clean soil on the manure and 3 inches in turf". In another letter to the Marquis he said: "Has Your Lordship forgotten the Jersey Trench Plough? I am still convinced that for certain and speedy work it is the finest instrument in the world". Having in the course of his life ridden hundreds of miles on horseback and driven in horse carriages, he must have known a good deal about horses. In 1839 we find him consulting Professor Coleman of London about a sick horse who "would prove valuable if I could recover him"; having apparently no confidence in the local veterinary surgeons of the time, he expresses himself rather venomously about them: "We have such complete quacks here that I would almost as soon allow the horse to be shot as place him in their hands".

In the fifteenth century there were large flocks of sheep in Jersey. By Sir John's time they had dwindled, but did still exist, for in 1830 he wrote: "the grass on the Quainvais (sic) is miserably short, and sheep require vetch or some other good grass to fatten them .... I do not know by what right Orange monopolises to himself so large a portion of the common as 97 sheep must eat, which the poorer people certainly have a right to. He is a curious personage at best". In 1839 he ordered a ram and twelve ewes from England, and his instructions for their transportation were: "Have them sheltered and secured in the paddle-boxes, or as well as possible, during the passage in this stormy season".

In 1838 Jean Le Boutillier, a young blacksmith, invented a new plough, and Sir John made enquiries on his behalf about obtaining a patent. Later he wrote to the Secretary of State for the Home Department with a petition from Le Boutillier to this end. He said: "He is in a humble walk of life, but of extremely industrious habits and unusually intelligent. He has at considerable expense devised a plough which works paddles and prongs that revolve, and take potatoes out of the ground with astonishing rapidity and much saving of labour. It will also be of great value for comminuting[1] a stiff soil, and for mixing all sorts of light or powdered manures with it". The next year it must have been on exhibition at the English Agricultural Show at Oxford, for Sir John noted: "I offered to go and

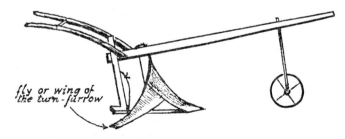

Le Boutillier's JERSEY POTATOE-SETTING PLOUGH, 1835.

approximate scale in feet.

---

1. Breaking up into small particles.

make arrangements to have Le Boutillier's plough tried". His article in the Journal of the English Royal Agricultural Society describes it as being invented by Le Boutillier at his own instigation. It is evidently an early form of horse-drawn potato-spinner. One wonders what happened about the patent, and what is the relationship, genealogically, between Le Boutillier's "paddle or potatoe-digging plough" and the horse-drawn potato-spinner, still in use in the Island twenty years ago and known as the Jersey Lily: and the various tractor-driven spinners which succeeded it. Le Boutiller also invented the Jersey Potatoe-setting Plough shown in the illustration, designed to be drawn by one or two horses. To all appearance it is the direct ancestor of the Jersey Planting Plough, which is still in use and still horse-drawn, and a number of farmers prefer it to more up-to-date alternatives. Sir John's article in the Agricultural Society Journal also describes and figures the Great or Jersey Trench Plough, and in writing of the Grande Charrue, when neighbours co-operated to do the annual deep ploughing, he said that it was "sometimes drawn by 14 horses, in an old luzerne ley, turning 18 inches of soil".

In Sir John's youth Jersey's early potato industry was in its infancy, but the potato was being grown, and considered important. Harriet Le Couteur's album of exquisite water-colours of fruit includes one page of potatoes entitled: "Seedling potatoes of 1832 raised from one apple[1]". To the modern eye they are a strange assortment, four small tubers of differing shapes and colours. Another picture shows: "Phillip's red potato, given me by Mr. Isaac Gosset in 1822: grown at Belle Vue 1833: weighed 11 pounds, 7 ounces, 6 gr. (Jersey) . . . . A capital sort in 1855". Sir John carried on a brisk correspondence with Thomas Knight, President of the Horticultural Society of London, who sent him various potato seeds and tubers to try. On one occasion he wrote: "I have been successful in raising some very good seedling varieties; one, a rose-coloured potato, from a red potato grown among white ones, promises to be first rate. I have also had some good black ones, but they are so much the colour of earth that they are more difficult to clear . . . ., which for the following wheat crop is very inconvenient". To another correspondent he said: "I have now forwarded two sorts to you, a white 'broad eye' and the red Pelham, both being considered excellent of their kinds. My mode of boiling much improves them. It is (and here we see Sir John again in his kitchen), when they are half boiled, to pour off their hot water and add cold, and set them to on boil again. . . . Should they suit you, I wish to know what you will offer for twelve tons of the White and about eighteen tons of the Red, delivered to your agent, as high up below London Bridge as the cutter can conveniently and usually go. My object is to endeavour to improve the name of the Jersey potatoes in the market, and I would grow more next year if I succeed". He was writing to a merchant in Hungerford Market.

In writing to Dr. Mackenzie of Dingwall, he gave a comprehensive account of the mode of raising potatoes in Jersey, and the following is the gist of it: "Old grass is broken up in the summer and left to rot . . . . A trench is opened in one or two places in the field, a foot or 18 inches deep, and the earth is thrown off on each side with the spade[2]. The land is dressed with twenty tons of dung to the acre, spread on the turf. A plough drawn by two horses[3], which takes the same width of furrow as the trench plough, then . . . . skims the upper turf as thinly as possible, together with the manure, and turns both into

---

1. The seed-pod not the tuber.   2. It is much easier to "spread the furrow" with a stable fork.
3. Known latterly as a "breezing plough", and usually drawn by a single horse.

the bottom of the trench. The trench plough then immediately follows the skim plough, drawn by four or six horses, and turns twelve to twenty inches of clean earth on the turf and manure, so that not a particle of grass or dung is seen. This plough will perform two Scotch acres in a day . . . . This is also the practice for carrots and parsnips . . . . Mr. Knight wrote me: 'Your mode of culture appears to be admirable, much better than ours, and your great plough, when the soils are deep and rich, must be an excellent instrument, never used in England, I believe'. By this culture from 20 to 28 tons of potatoes per acre have been raised". This last is a difficult figure to digest. Allowing for the fact that at that time Jersey potatoes were grown for weight, not earliness, and that the ton has meant many different things in different times and places, the yield is phenomenal. There may be a mistake in arithmetic, or in the conversion of vergées and cabots to acres and hundredweights. But that is what he said, and on more than one occasion.

He was acutely aware of the Irish potato famine, and wrote: "It is conclusively admitted that the repeated culture of the potato in Ireland for a long succession of years with, in many cases, little intermixture of crops, has so indisposed the soil to produce it, and likewise unfitted it for the proper nourishment of the root, that . . . . a mutual distaste may have been established between the root and the soil. We have the authority of Sinclair[1], Knight and Liebig[2] that . . . . plants will not thrive when grown in constant succession in the same soil . . . . Indeed it may be questioned whether the potato disease may not have been generated by the continued growth of the plant in one spot: its first injury being a decrease in quantity . . . .; the second, a manifest decrease in the size of the root: and third, incipient disorder, and perhaps finally the seeds of an epidemic spread far and wide". Jersey did not entirely escape the descent of the great potato disease or blight of 1845. In that year Sir John "visited the farms . . . . One third of the potato crop found to be injured by this new disease. A fungus round the plants, stems and leaves". There is much more about the Jersey potato in these papers. Here one can but offer an hors d'oeuvre, to whet the appetite of those who desire a fuller meal. But after reading it all, one comes once again to the conclusion that in this field, as in almost everything he touched, Sir John was ahead of his time, and this is one of the elements from which the amalgam of genius is forged. He seems to have known that long after he was dead the potato would become the king-pin of the Island's prosperity. And with the same unerring judgment, he foresaw a time when, in order to survive, his potatoes would have to appear on the London stalls a week or more ahead of foreign competitors. Whether it was he or someone else who first put abroad the idea that the Jersey was an "early", one cannot be sure without deeper research. But was it not he who was congratulated in 1855, in a letter written by Johnny Le Couteur in the trenches before Sebastopol, on his successful experiment in planting his potatoes earlier than was customary?

In his lifetime root crops were more widely grown than they are today. The parsnip was a favourite in Jersey, for men and animals alike, and he used to tell enquirers, in letters of conscientious detail, how best to grow it, and send its seeds to friends in England and Ireland. No other root, in his opinion, compared with it for fattening cattle, which explained "the predilection which Jersey farmers for nearly a century have constantly asserted in favour of the parsnip over all other roots". The white carrot was also "an admirable root".

---

1. Sir John Sinclair (1754-1835), agriculturist. 2. Baron Justus van Liebig (1803-1873), German Professor of Chemistry.

In 1834 he ordered grass seed in quantity, of eight types, and told the seedsman, in the rather severe phraseology of the time, that as this would be "the first trial of artificial grasses on upland in Jersey, I shall thank you to keep them quite separate, parcelled in bags". He knew all about lucerne. "I have cultivated it upwards of eighteen year myself, and my father nearer to thirty years. I consider it to be one of the most valuable products imaginable, and I have recommended it to our farmers in the strongest manner, especially during the last two or three seasons of drought: as it preserved its verdure and vegetation when all other grasses were burnt up . . . . Gypsum is among the best manures for lucerne".

Then, as now, haymaking was a vital episode in the farming year, tiring, time-consuming and bedevilled by the vagaries of the weather. Once the hay is down, the farmer's mind is never at rest until it is made, and up, and this canon of husbandry recurs again and again in the Le Couteur diaries. By 1860 he realised the practical value of a mowing machine for the hay, and Messrs. Burgess and Key offered him one for £30, but before closing with them there was much he wanted to know. Will it pass through a five-foot gate? Will it cut an acre an hour? Will it perform on sloping ground? Will it mow the aftermath in September without injury to the knives? Can it be repaired by an ordinary smith?

By 1835 he had studied cider, and was considering rules for making it which would be "clearly comprehensible to our ordinary farmers, whose principal staple commodity is cyder, which they make execrably. I have some which has continued eight weeks in a state of fermentation, and which I am waiting to draw off the moment it ceases; manufactured from one variety of apple, the Romeril, a favourite cyder apple here; which has the peculiar property of flowering late and being a great bearer, but its cyder discolours if left open".

This remarkable man was a frequent prize-winner with his flowers, fruit and vegetables at the shows of the Agricultural Society, often held at the Imperial Hotel now the Hotel de France. After perusing one of the books in this collection, the late Mr. H. G. Shepard, himself the author of the R.J.A. & H.S. centenary publication, remarked: "There is material here for a book on the agriculture and horticulture at Belle Vue".

He was, in fact, following in his father's footsteps, as these archives show, for they include the detailed records kept by General Le Couteur of how he handled the lands and gardens of Belle Vue. By English standards, which consider acres by the hundred, the area is minute, but if you live in a small island there is no room for extravagance and every square yard is of importance. The General's notebooks cover the years 1803 to 1809 and 1817 to 1820. There cannot be many farm records of so early a date, and such as survive could scarcely be more meticulous. We find here an enthusiastic panorama of potatoes, turnips, mangel-wurzels, parsnips, wheat, oats, beans, vetches, lucerne: grass and hay: fruit: forest trees: thorns: hedgeing: cabbages and asparagus: cattle, pigs, poultry: application of salt: and a chronicle of work done around the farm. There must be something in the retired warrior, father and son, perhaps discipline, which attracts him to a rural wilderness where he can reduce chaos to order in his old age, as once upon a time he used to do, in the garrison, the camp and the field. It is an admirable combination. Nature is disorderly if left to herself, but under trained hands can yield an hundredfold. But there was something else these old Le Couteurs had, and you cannot have failed to notice it in father, son and grandson. They had a thirst for knowledge of every arena in which they performed and, what is more uncommon, a sense of obligation to record that knowledge, in the hope that it might one day be of service to others. One could not speak more highly of anybody.

CHAPTER SEVENTEEN

THE INQUIRING MIND

Sir John was in no way a genius, but it is the diversity of his interests which impresses one. There was no aspect of learning in which he did not take an interest, and he was the first to greet new inventions, and to see in them benefit for mankind. It was thus that he welcomed the power of steam, anticipated the power of electricity, and showed himself to be what is now termed "forward looking"; always allowing that the subject in question was, in his opinion, for the betterment of the human race, for its advancement in the pursuit of goodness, and not of material gain as an objective in itself.

Let us consider a few of the many interests which reveal themselves in the diaries. They are, also, a reminder that he lived in an age teeming with energy and confidence and bursting with inventiveness.

On many occasions, when in London, he went to the British Museum or the Record Office, to look up matters of Jersey history, and in 1846 he said: "At the British Museum all day, looking up the ancient manuscripts relating to Jersey; took notes of several which are highly interesting. Colonel Legge's is the most valuable to a soldier[1], one which 'belonged to King James and was given to me by Colonel Grahame' is very interesting. It speaks of rams with six horns, Vittoé and Boscher, strong native liquors, of half a hundred pouquelayes, of the Eskerhos rocks and the Priory on them". A few days later he returned and "All day at the British Museum . . . . gave me leave to copy anything but not to trace . . . I worked at the view of Jersey in the Hon. Col. Legge's report till dusk". A few years later, again at the British Museum, he found someone copying the same sort of material for Guernsey, and said: "an everlasting job he has, which will give him bread for many years; the Guernsey folks would build a pier for the money. They are liberal in literature, happy to have a learned Bailiff. Saw and copied a letter of Sir Walter Ralegh from Jersey, 1602; July 3rd he reached it, a wilderness he calls it". On another occasion he copied out a further letter from Sir Walter, dated September 21st 1601, which he stated was "in the possession of Mr. Le Cornu of Vinchelez de Haut". The dates given are not in fact contradictory, for Sir Walter did not visit the Island for some time after his appointment as Governor. The letter quoted cannot, alas, be found, though many Vinchelez papers have been preserved in the Le Cornu family.

Sir John often said "went geologising" or "went botanising". In 1830 he said; "Up at 6, and off to La Pulente in the expectation of seeing the tide quite high up the slip; not at all. It only rose about as high as the third oak, though a 42 foot tide. Rode to L'Etacq and went out to a rock called 'le chesne' or 'quesne' to try and see the oak roots that are said to be there[2], but without success. The high tide had uncovered some of the peat, several pieces of which I obtained". There is a surprising entry in 1871, when Helier Simon made an agreement with Sir John, as Seigneur of the fiefs of Orville and du Prieur en St.

---

1. See Bulletin Société Jersiaise 1968. p 325. The account was dated 1679.
2. He was right. There is a submerged prehistoric forest there.

Pierre, for permission to quarry and mine for lead or any other metal substance on the said fiefs, for which he had to pay the Seigneur 6% on any metals so obtained. There is no further reference to this project and one may assume that it was not successful.

He was deeply interested in meteorology, recorded exceptional climatic incidents during the years, and in late life took detailed account of the clouds he observed each day, and the wind direction. Of a tide in 1847 he said "the 36 foot tide last night washed down three yards of the bank near Mr. Nicolle's wall[1] in the bay, besides rather less in many other places," and shortly afterwards; "The base of the second Martello tower[2] in St. Aubin's Bay is just eleven yards from the edge of the bank; the sea has gained several yards on the beach all along this portion of the bay in these last four or five years. Query? Has the new pier assisted in this operation?" In 1869 in February: "A raging storm blowing from the S.W. High water at 9.8. Yesterday at 8 a.m. the waves were driving over the N.W. wall of the tower in sheets . . . . whole waves washed over the pier on the S.E. angle against the little doorway of the tower[3] . . . . At 2 o'clock I drove along the banks to see what the sea had done. Two or three of the old elms and the rough wall washed down, pathway broken up. Near the third tower[4] several hundred feet of wall down, the banks washed away 20 or 30 feet near the steam and wind mill[5], the walls washed down. At the blacksmiths, outhouses washed down. His house will be in danger tonight. Clarke's yard blown open, all the sheds blown down, the slip by the Alexandra Hotel[6] filled up with stones, shingle and sand and more than one hundred yards of the parapet wall broken down and levelled to the main road by the Alexandra". Then in December of the same year ". . . . a large barque seems to have pulled up close to, if not on, the Diamond rock . . . . The tug came out at about 2 o'clock to tow the large American barque into the Grand roads; it blew so hard at 3, that she could not draw her ahead . . . . so finally tugged her into St. Aubin's tower where she anchored . . . . (Friday.) The American is lying over on her larboard side, snug in the tower".

His interest in tides was deepened by his lifelong friendship with Captain, later Admiral, Martin White, who surveyed the surrounding waters for the Admiralty, with his ship H.M.S. Shamrock, after which the rock, Shamrock Bank, north of Frémont, may have been named. White was appointed her Commander in 1825, but had already produced Admiralty charts in 1821, which formed the basis of later revisions. He published sailing directions for which the States thanked him, and made recommendations for a port at Noirmont, for which the parish of St. Brelade thanked him. In 1827 Sir John wrote to the then Lieutenant Governor, Sir Colin Halkett, saying: "I have this day received a letter from Captain White of H.M.S. Shamrock, which I have the honour to transmit to Your Excellency, rather than to the Committee of Harbours, the end to be obtained being the advantage to H.M. service, your recommendation may ensure the application. As the Committee of Harbours have already allowed a deviation, perhaps I ought rather to say winked at a deviation, from the existing law in favour of the steam vessels, I imagine they may be induced to yield to the justness of Captain White's observations". On White's work on tides he said; "With Captain White, who lent me his new work on the tides, explaining and accounting for their causes. His line of contact runs from a point in South America, near Curaçoa, up

1. Perhaps Jurat E. Nicolle, living just beside the wind mill at Bel Royal.
2. At Bel Royal.
3. At St. Aubin's Fort.   4. At Beaumont.   5. At Bel Royal.   6. Site of present Grand Hotel.

to the Western Isles to Feroe (sic), where he considers the three great tides meet, the greatest from the South Pole, the next from the North. It will create much discussion in the nautical and philosophical world". In 1865, when away on the continent after his wife's death, he said: "Heard that my beloved old friend Admiral White is at death's door". In after years Sir John worked vigorously, even writing direct to the Queen, to obtain a pension for Miss Ellen White, who had been left in great poverty. He stressed that she had always acted as her father's secretary and translator in all his work, particularly with the Hydrographical Office in France. He added: "I have in many seasons in summer and in the storms of winter witnessed his untiring devotion to his arduous and dangerous duty in an open boat, along the rocky coast of Jersey, around which spring tides run with alarming velocity". He felt that Miss White deserved some compensation for her assistance, but it does not seem as if the plea was successful, although she had been given hopes of a pension by Lord Palmerston, but "his decease destroyed these hopes".

She was not the only lady in need whom he helped, for amongst others, there was the sad story of the Misses Parker, for whom he again intervened with the Queen through the Keeper of the Privy Purse. These ladies had been left by their father with a house and a modest income, but the trustees had gambled with their property, unsuccessfully, and they were reduced to penury. One died of grief, it was stated, and another became stone deaf in one night from the shock. They took to collecting seaweeds and lichens, from which they contrived ornaments, and they felt that if Her Majesty would purchase one of their confections, it would permit them to say so, and other orders would then follow and "secure them a patronage and means to live". The plight of middle aged women, utterly untrained for employment, was indeed sad at this period, and they really were "in sad destitution . . . . almost in a state of starvation".

In 1858 Sir John was in correspondence with Admiral Fitzroy[1], F.R.S. and he said: ". . . . though I have not followed up the science 'en savant' I have bestowed much time and consideration on the weather and its effects on agriculture". Some detailed observations on local weather conditions followed. Then in a further letter he said: "The instrument I had in use when (the barometer) fell to 28.45 on the 23/24 February 1838, was a mercurial marine barometer by Ramsden. It was left to me by my late uncle Captain Dumaresq of the Victory, flag Captain to the (then) Sir James Saumarez commanding the Baltic Fleet in 1812. It was so fine an instrument that my uncle used to signal the fleet to make *snug sail* of an evening when all seemed clear, but the faithful monitor foretold a coming squall. He was laughed at at the outset, but the glass was of infinite use in that stormy water . . . . I have frequently saved a crop of hay or corn by watching that marine barometer. On one occasion I noticed the barometer rising on a Saturday evening whilst pouring. I ordered my men to have their scythes ready for daybreak on Monday, and there was a bright week in which I saved my hay. The following week it began to pour and the season was so snatchy that a vast quantity of hay was lost. My neighbours trusted in my barometer afterwards".

In 1839, when discussing harbour plans with officials in England, he met Captain Beaufort, probably the future Sir Francis Beaufort, hydrographer to the navy, and discussed the matter with him thoroughly.

Sir John also possessed an aneroid barometer[2] in which he had great faith, and

1. Probably Robert Fitzroy, (1805-1865).
2. An instrument for recording atmospheric pressure without the use of mercury or other fluid.

which he used to take away with him when going abroad. Up until a year before his death and in spite of blindness, he was receiving publications from the Meteorological Society of London, and he continued all the time to record such events as seemed unusual, even to the following, in 1870, when there was a storm which "lasted from half past six to eight . . . . the small cottage next to the house occupied by Mrs. Messervy on the road to town was struck by lightning this morning; the chimney top was rent in half, the electric fluid flew down and scattered the grate below, in the room where two children were sound asleep, unhurt. I was sure that the last crash was indicative of harm". This extract is interesting in showing the current belief that electricity was a fluid.

He also had a clinometer, an instrument for measuring slopes, and ordered from England an olophon, an instrument that has not been identified. In 1830 he wrote to Messrs. Pointer of Camden Town, saying: "I had the satisfaction of seeing one of your admirable flexible tubes . . . . in the possession of a gentleman who experienced the greatest comfort from it. It was a neat little one, sufficiently long to hold a conversation with at a dinner table". He ordered a similar one for his aunt, not saying which of his many aunts was concerned, for three guineas, with the extremities of the tube in ivory, and went on to ask ": . . . . if you make cheap unornamented tubes, as a poor country farmer, a neighbour of mine, who is a worthy clever person, and very deaf, would find one an invaluable comfort".

This was so much an age of discovery that one forgets that objects that are now commonplace to us, were matters of wonderment to his generation. In 1830, in London, he "went to see Carpenter's Gigantic acromatic solar microscope, 24 Regent Street. It is the most magnificent and interesting spectacle I have ever beheld, which the liveliest imagination of description cannot convey a full idea of. To my utter astonishment I saw objects invisible as forms, contained in a single drop of water, magnified three thousand two hundred and fifty times. They are represented on a highly polished white opaque slightly concave circular surface, nine feet in diameter, perfectly and sharply delineated, little fish as large as a good sized whiting or mackerel, invisible eels as large as a quill, and other aquatic insects floating about in the drop of water appear as monsters of the most varied horrible forms, like tigers and lions unceasingly warring on the invisible people (to us) with unrelenting ferocity . . . . It was inexpressibly beautiful . . . . I went on to Guy's[1] hospital, which Dr. Beauvoir de Lisle showed me over, a beautiful institution which owed its origin to woman's disobedience, as Mr. Guy would have married his maid if she had not ordered a pavoir to lay a stone more in front of his door than he had desired . . . . (fortunately for four hundred in-patients, and two thousand out-patients ever since 1721) she contradicted him and proved more useful to society than she ever contemplated. The arrangements, cleanliness and appearance of comfort, even of cheerfulness among the patients, was most gratifying. There is a nice little museum, a dissecting room, a surgery and apothecaries shop, all attached to it".

He was much interested in the science of astronomy, and in 1850 wrote "Reading Nichol's[2] architecture of the heavens. He is a Professor of Astronomy at Glasgow, a fine writer. The wonders disclosed by Lord Ross' telescope are truly astonishing, and all we formerly knew of astronomical research is only like standing on the shore of a boundless ocean, so mighty and past finding out are the wonderful works of God". The telescope

1. Thomas Guy (1645-1724), Bookseller and philanthropist. Founded Guy's Hospital 1722.
2. John Nichol (1804-1858), Scottish astonomer. This book was published in 1838.

given to him by the local agricultural society has already been alluded to, and it gave him immense pleasure through the years; with it he could see what was happening on Gallow's Hill, at Elizabeth Castle, and, he claimed, at Coutances. One day, "Rev. Mr. King, a capital astronomer, came to see us in the evening and amused us greatly with the telescope. Showed us the planet Saturn with his beautiful ring and the double stars in Ursa Major, from the roof of the house". On Wednesday 29th September 1858 he recorded, "Donate's[1] comet was most brilliant, reaching far above the star which was in the edge of its tail last week". In 1866 an entry said, "Up at 2 and at 4. No falling stars". He had evidently expected some heavenly event which failed to occur.

Telegraphy was greeted with enthusiasm, and in 1827, Sir John, then in France, went to see an exhibition, being given a ticket by M. Chappe, son of the inventor.[2] A trial message was sent to Calais, and the reply came back in five minutes. He was told by the man there that "(he) was at the telegraph in 1814 and 1815 when the Allies took Paris. He saw the whole advance, the actions, in short everything that took place. He had suffered agonies in seeing where his countrymen were about to be ambushed, and could not warn them". There is no further mention of the word telegraphy in the diaries until 1858, and then: "The electric telegraph was opened this day. After a more or less ridiculous procession, because only the Bailiff and three Jurats, Le Bailly, Le Quesne and Lerrier (attended). The Dean and Mr. Le Sueur, with Dupré and myself were the only members of the States, I believe, there. Hundreds of others, with two bands, perambulated the town, which was gaily decorated with flags and triumphal arches. Then we halted at the telegraph office and a message (was) dispatched to the Queen. At five, 112 men sat down to a very good dinner at the Pomme d'Or. Speeches were made by the General, Bailli etc., but not published. Reams of champagne drunk. A great, and I have no doubt, highly useful and peace working agent duly inaugurated". In 1863 there was a further advance, and: "The General desired Gardner to read to me his letter to the Home Secretary regarding the £12,000 for the submarine telegraph, to impinge on the Isle of Wight, or Swanage, or Isle of Purbeck, starting from the north coast of Jersey, to Alderney and on. To me he suggests that the house of da Silva, on receiving £1400 yearly, will guarantee the safety of the subm. cable 20 years. I said I thought war would be a bar to the agreement. We should accept the offer as Govt. allow us £1800 a year; there would be a profit of £400 without the working". On consulting Admiral White, who "though past eighty is very clear on many points . . . . (he is) quite of opinion that the submarine cable should start from a point near Bouley Bay to Alderney, thence to Swanage. The bottom is sandy. An enemy's flying steamer might run out from Dielette[3] with creepers and dredge for the cable, in war time, almost impossible to prevent her. I suggested to Sir P. Douglas that if Guernsey does not contribute in proportion to Jersey towards the cable, Guernsey should pay us for the use of it". The completion of the project seems to have been somewhat delayed, for in 1870 he said: "Invitation to attend luncheon from Mr. Le Feuvre, chairman, on opening of Jersey and Guernsey telegraph to the world". This was in December, but the direct link had in fact come into working order in the previous September.

The first mention of gas was for illuminations for the King's birthday in 1830 when "the most brilliant by far were those of gas". The same year there was a fear that "the pos-

---

1. Giovanni Donate (1826-1873). Discovered the comet named after him in June 1858.
2. Charles Chappe (1763-1805). Inventor of the first, simple, telegraph.   3. North of Carteret.

sibility of the gas pipes being cut, and several streets being enveloped in darkness suddenly, when thieves would make a harvest . . . . I thought an act of parliament should be passed, obliging all persons in such a case to place a candle in each of their windows, which they both thought a very proper idea". 'They' in this case were Colonel Frederick and Captain Adolphus FitzClarence. Another entry on the subject of gas said: "Professor Bachhoffner selected a freezing machine and a bottle or apparatus for aerating water or liquids with soda powders, both invented by Masters, the pastrycook. The inventions have cost him £20,000 to perfect. Advised me to see de Fries gas apparatus for boiling and cooking. It will altogether supersede coal he thinks".

But this was London, and naturally Jersey was somewhat behind, though in 1849, "Mr. Edge called to engage me to support the lighting with gas all along the road from St. Helier to St. Aubin, which I did". But gas also had its disadvantages, and in 1861 there was "an elegant ball and supper to 300 fashionables. I did not know six families in the room. The odour of gas was dreadful and the heat melted the wax lights to the discomfiture of coats and dresses. The General left before supper". In 1864 he wrote to Josué Brayn, the Constable of St. Brelade, to recommend as gaslighter John Nolais who had an "industrious wife, weakly, six children".

Electricity was very new and exciting, and in 1854, when on a trip to the continent, Sir John noted: "Some experiment was in progress here; there were small houses for an electric telegraph keeper, in which a bell rang as the train flew by". And again: "Officials are placing lines of high poles (pine trees) about 20 feet long, at every 70 paces for an electric wire to telegraph from Cologne to Wiesbaden". Many are the experiments he comments upon, and galvanic batteries were mentioned. But more interesting is the subject of table turning, and this because he did not see it as having any connection with occult forces, but as being a matter of electricity. His prophesy at the end of this excerpt is worth noticing. This was in 1853, when he went down to Portsmouth with his son-in-law, noting on the way that the Connaught Rangers at drill were "rather unsteady", but that the band of the 38th[1] played very nicely. They met Tom Saumarez, described as "a rattle" and went to lunch on board the Royal George; "we went on board of the famous America which beat all the yacht fleet, a beautiful sloop schooner with two enormous masts; she reminded me of the 'Lady of the Lake', Commodore Chauney's scout schooner on Lake Ontario, which beat all our fleet. Saumarez gave me his berth for the night, and illuminated it with four candles while I dressed for dinner. We found Captain Halsted of the unfortunate 'Dauntless' which lost 15 officers and 86 men by yellow fever caught at Barbadoes . . . . We had a very nice dinner, and good wines, some of which the officers provided. The Captain gave us some dry port of 1822 to taste, old enough, but different and superior in taste to the sweet wines of the present day. After coffee we agreed to try the electric chain on the table, a two leaved mahogany table on six legs. Six of us sat round it . . . . in twelve minutes our table began to move, and on my blowing on it, it moved round with velocity, till Saumarez was thrown down". The experiments continued for some time, with the incredulous members of the party trying unsuccessfully to stop the motion of the table, which was always maintained if those around it kept a continuous touch with each other's fingers, until, ". . . . the whole of us complained of tingling in the extremities of the fingers, or of darting pains up the elbows to the armpits, like sparks or shocks from an electric machine. All but myself had

1. The South Staffordshire Regiment.

headaches, but altogether it was the most interesting experiment of the kind I ever witnessed. At first we talked and laughed much so as to arrest or delay the action of the magnetic or electric fluid, but when we applied ourselves resolutely to the work it was amazing to see how quickly success attended our efforts. There is much exhaustion after continued experiment, and the following day I had a severe headache, besides feeling very much fatigued. I question the propriety or safety of frequently practising these experiments. Captain Halsted, who took a very philosophical view of the trials, was thoroughly convinced of their truth, and meant to see Dr. Darling experiment on electric biology, as connected with his secret and strange agency, destined, I think, to take the place of steam, by means I do not pretend to account for". The year before Dr. Darling had evidently been to Jersey, for an entry said; "Harriet, Tit and I went to hear Dr. Darling, the electric biologist, lecture and perform. His mesmeric power over seven young men was awful".

Sir John had some faith in phrenology, but only as a guide to assist in correcting one's faults, or in educating one's children to best advantage. He went himself, with his daughter Harriet, then aged seventeen, to a Mr. de Ville, to be examined, and was most impressed, and left a record of Mr. de Ville's findings.

In 1851 a fountain pen appeared, but the sample letter he wrote with it is so faint and hard to read, that one may wonder what initial success the invention had. It said: "The ancient prophet said: 'Ah, that he might write with a pen of iron.' He never thought of writing with a tool as hard, but far more brittle, which I am now doing, while one single dip would carry me through the whole of this letter . . . . as I saw it at the exhibition at the Glass Palace . . . . no mending, no dipping, no soiling after the one first dip; you fill your pen of glass, a small bottle with an aperture at foot as fine as the eye, or even point of a needle, wipe it clean, and might write all day as I am now performing".

As the art of photography advanced, so likenesses of members of the family multiplied, and while there is no extant portrait of Sir John's father, the General, photographs of his grandchildren abound. These pictures bear on the back the names of many of the Jersey photographers of the time. The standard is excellent, and in most cases there has been no fading, though some must be a century old.

One is surprised to hear that in 1869, when on a visit to England, he "drove to Moorpark, Mr. Bateman's[1], the proposer of the tunnel between Dover and Cape Grisnez". And on another journey, in Lancashire, he said: "At Preston we had the good fortune to see Mr. Green ascend in a balloon; it was a most beautiful ascent, and the balloon passed just over our heads. We distinctly saw him let a pigeon fly, which scarcely seemed to know where it was".

Natural history was not ignored in these diaries either. The birds about Belle Vue were noted and remarked upon. Sir John's interest in botany may have started from his friendship with La Gasca, or in any case been accentuated by it. In 1857 he went to the botanical gardens in Florence and met Professor Filipo Parlatore[2] and "he showed me the beautiful and extensive library left to the Museum by an Englishman, Mr. Webb, who had made a most superb collection of ancient and modern works on botany, some of very rare and very beautiful execution". In London at a horticultural show, he said: "Mr. Blenkins introduced me to Mr. Fortune, a great explorer of botany in China". Back at home, in

1. An engineer who reported to the Royal Society on the work at Suez. The Canal was opened in 1869.
2. A noted Italian botanist, expert in cotton.

1861 he noted: "Mr. Larbalestier came to breakfast; he is preparing for the Church. His relaxation is in the study of lichens and botany, in which he is greatly aided by the two Babingtons, who are of his college at Cambridge". On one occasion, when some of his grandchildren were on a visit he said: "Took Evie and Maudie to the Mouriers through the lovely Fern Valley of St. Mary's. Talked to the young Mahiers[1] and Mr. Richardson[2] on Les Huriaux by Crabbé . . . down to Le Creux Terrible[3], where Maudie's frisking made me frightened, in vulgar parlance. She saw two excursionists sliding into it, and would have done so too if allowed. She has no fear and fed the horses and cows. I found the 'white heath' on the hill for the first time, though I had sought it all my life time in Jersey. Mrs. Hamilton had seen it in St. Peter's Valley. We collected several varieties of ferns and planted them round our pond". Our modern botanists will wish he had described more exactly the place where he found the white heather.

When staying at Buriton Sir John met a Mr. and Mrs. Darwin, friends of his daughter's, and indeed Mrs. Darwin stood proxy for Harriet as godmother to Mary Sumner's baby Charles, in 1857. The relationship to the great Darwin has not been ascertained, but his works were studied at Belle Vue and one entry says: "Returned Dr. Cleave Darwin's work 'The variation of animals and plants under domestication', a very clever book of vast range. He does me the honour to quote my work on wheat. I have ordered one from Le Feuvre". In a letter to Darwin, admiring his work, and thanking him for a letter which he said "belongs to the gems of literature, a very few of which I possess from authors", he continued; "I must beg you to pardon me for frankly expressing my disbelief in your view of 'The Descent of Man'. I cannot by any train of thought or even of prayer through Divine aid, bring myself to comprehend how the writer of these sublime works would have had apes for his original parents. I more easily and readily accept that Adam, who was formed in the image of his Maker, with a spark of Divine intelligence, was the grandparent of such a writer . . . . Pardon me for troubling your valuable time with idle speculation . . . . In the year 1837, when I was endeavouring to farm with care, I was led from having a fine breed of pigs, to breed in and in. After doing so for a year or two, and particularly twice through a sister and brother, nearly all the progeny, when under a year old, were siezed with fits, stood up on their hind legs, whirled round and round, and died suddenly . . . I also bred in and in with poultry during two or three years, the result was lamentable. The fowls ceased to lay eggs, or very few, and in the last year the chickens were miserable . . . . (better) to cross a sow with various boars almost yearly, even a cross with an inferior boar . . . . (is) preferable to breeding in and in. This I have found to be correct and in consquence I have given more little pigs to our Rector than any man in his parish[4] . . . . I am sorry to add that the breeding in consanguinity in this Island has led to much distressing deformity and decrepitude. Many years back, as Secretary to our Agricultural Society I constantly urged our young men at Committees to avoid marrying cousins or even natives, but to seek wives from the British Islands or even France. I believe that my suggestions in the past forty years have led to many alliances, more safe to the constitution than was anciently the case, when it was thought to be strange in a Jerseyman if he could not find a wife within the circle of his parish or its vicinity".

1. Either Les Hougues, or the mill opposite, in Les Mouriers Valley.   2. At La Falaise.   3. Usually now known as the Devil's Hole.
4. This is a reference to the ancient right of the parish Rector to one piglet from every litter.

Railway travel appealed to Sir John's practical frame of mind, but always to the fore-front was his thought of whether it would prove a help or a hindrance in time of war. Nursery rhymes, which he quoted in 1853, show a more frivolous attitude to this new invention.

"Little Bo peep
Is fast asleep,
    In the excursion train you'll find him.
Oh, its ten to one,
If he ever comes home,
    For a 'special' is close behind him."

"Fly by steam force the country across,
Faster than jockey outride a race horse,
With time bells mismanaged, fast trains after slow,
You shall have danger wherever you go."

"Smashery, smashery, crash,
Into the 'goods' we dash,
    The 'Express' we find,
    Is just behind,
Smashery, smashery, crash."

As already described in the chapter on defence, there had been a early attempt to found a railway in Jersey, from 1845 onwards, which came to absolutely nothing, and it was not until 1860 that the subject reappeared in the diaries, when an entry said: "The Atty. Genl. and I called on the General, as part of a deputation to request his support in aid of the Railway. He said that when the papers were laid before him, and that it should be made clear that it would be useful to Jersey, and to the defence of the Island, he would give it his support". Four years passed without further reference and then, "Captain Richards, the Surveyor of the Channel in succession to my laborious old friend Admiral Martin White, called at my office with a railway speculating amateur engineer, Mr. Wood, and took me to Havre des Pas, where he showed me the beautiful work he is completing of the present survey. He urges the breakwater to be at St. Brelade's Bay, enclosed by two arms. He is unaware of the mighty waves which the Atlantic throws in there. Mr. Wood proposes to have a railway from the slaughter houses under the road by Clarke's yard, inside Goose Green[1], as being cheaper than along the sealine or foreshore".

At this stage Mr. Pickering enters the arena, and in 1869 "Mr. Pickering wrote to know the price of Noirmont property". This he rented for a time, and shortly afterwards, "Mr. Pickering the railway engineer and his brother-in-law, Mr. Lloyd, a barrister, dine here to-day". And in December of that year, 1869; ". . . . a meeting of the States to learn whether (they) would accept the offer of Mr. Pickering to build a sea wall all along St. Aubin's Bay for £25,000". A hint about this man, in a different context, is contained in an entry of the next year, from London; ". . . . the Bravos and their son, a fine young lawyer about

1. At Beaumont.

24, had been in a case with Sir J. Karslake, against Pickering, our Railway contractor, who their side say is a man of straw". And in 1870 Sir John said ". . . . to the railway station at St. Aubin's where I saw Mr. Pickering and later his wife and sister. They asked me to a family dinner . . . . he said that he was getting on well with the railway; had it not been for de Quetteville's uncalled for Clameur de Haro, he could have opened it for work now". It will be recalled that this David de Quetteville caused no little disturbance at an Assise d'Heritage dinner, and he was for some time Sir John's tenant at Le Bocage, where he proved himself to be most obstructive and troublesome, attacking his wife, and constantly making scenes.

On September 29th of that year he said: "The first train of two first class carriages and two open second class carriages came from St. Helier to St. Aubin; Judge Haro de Quetteville among the passengers, much cheered". The ceremonial opening was on October 25th, and "on going to the railway station, a crowd was around it. The Rifle Company band, and band of the town soon drew up in front of it. At $\frac{1}{4}$ to 1 the General and staff with Monsieur Drouin de l'Huys came to the station. The arrangements were admirable, perfect order. In our carriage General Guy, M. de l'Huys, the Bailiff, Colonel Murray, the Dean, A.D.C. Grove and myself. The train started at one in fine clear weather, the sun smiling on the enterprise. It was the smoothest rail I ever was over. In $9\frac{1}{2}$ mins we got to St. Aubin station. Hurrahs everywhere. There was a procession of carriages, some fifty to Noirmont with the band of the 15th[1] in front. If dear old Noirmont was living they would not have photd. us there. About 3, 180 sat down to as elegant a repast as I ever saw, in a tastefully decorated shed, built, floored and carpeted for the occasion. Engineer Le Feuvre in the chair, Mr. Pickering Vice Chair. The entertainment was really superb, viands, fruit and wines. It was long, as the guests seemed hungry, doing full justice to the fête. I sat on the left of the Bailiff, Haro de Quetteville on my left, who was remarkably cordial, and asked me to come to the next committee of the lunatic asylum. The worthy Bailiff gave me a history of his son James' successes and how he might have got into Parliament if he had laid himself out for it. After dinner came some dozen or more speeches, for which see the papers. Got home at 7. Tit and all but old Ann off to see the fireworks". As the last section of this first railway was raised on piles above the sea shore it is not surprising to read, the very next day; "A very high tide. The spray is dashing over the Esplanade opposite Jewel's Hotel[2], and in some places along the railway . . . . The railway opposite Mr. Briard's and by the station was broken up by the waves last evening at $\frac{1}{2}$ past 7. There were a number of men repairing it as I came by at 10. It will never stand there without an outer sea wall as I told Mr. Pickering two months back. It was safely repaired by evening". The next year, 1872, he said: "Drove to Noirmont where Pickering has enclosed a space for a one mile race course with white railing, the skeleton of a grand stand and its surroundings, a cricket, croquet and archery grounds adjoining. What would Com. Gen. Pipon say? Yet it will add to the value of Nomt. ten years hence". An enigmatic entry suggests another side to Mr. Pickering's character. It says: "Pickering v. F. Le Couteur yesterday. £1000 damages for having harboured Pickg's wife. Poor Florence". Colonel Francis George Le Couteur of La Hougue Boëte had a daughter called Florence, of whom it is recorded that she sang well, and another, Ada. An entry of the previous year may explain it; it said:

---

1. East Yorkshire Regiment.
2. The Alexandra at West Park.

"Had a handsome lunch with Francis Le Couteur and his wife. Ada looked very handsome, so did Mrs. Pickering. They told me of his rascally behaviour".

In 1873 Sir John wrote to his friend Mr. Mourant, the Seigneur of Samarès, saying: "I congratulate you on having opened the Jersey Eastern Railway for traffic. 1 consider it to be of far greater importance now than our Western Railway. The hopes of having a deep sea harbour from Noirmont point being given up, France will hereafter, I trust, be a friend of England rather than a menace. It appears to me that the Eastern Railway should lead to the completion of the south arm already commenced at St. Catherine's harbour . . . . In a conversation with a French officer then in charge of a survey here, who is now an Admiral, he observed to me that a railway to St. Catherine's Bay would be of the highest commercial importance, because the prevailing south westerly winds in the winter season were very adverse to vessels running from St. Helier, and requiring special care as to time and tide for entering into the harbour. He had heard of colliers being detained three weeks by such an untoward occurrence".

Perhaps Jersey's railway history can best be summed up by a précis of notes in one of Sir John's letter books. He begins with steamships:

"The first steamer came to Jersey, 'navire à feu' reported to me at Bocage by a man who ran from St. Brelade's Bay to report it to me as Constable of St. Brelade. (date omitted).

1825.   Jan 27. Sir Colin Halkett received official intelligence that steam packets were to run from Weymouth to the Channel Islands.

(1830.   Sept 15th. First railway with trains drawn by engines opened at Liverpool to Manchester.)

1839.   April. I urged a railway from St. Aubin to St. Helier, and on to Gorey to Captain White.

1845.   Nov. Conference with the Duke of Wellington on my report to himself. Railway urged as an economy of force and concentration.
        Railway to St. Catherine's Bay recommended in private letter to Captain Beaufort the hydrographer.

1860.   Jersey Railway Committee met. (I was) in the chair. Crown officers and Advocate Godfray instructed to prepare a permissive bill for a railway.
        Petition of Colonel Thomas Le Breton, Colonel Le Couteur, and J. W. Dupré, Sol. Genl, to the Master Genl. of the Ordnance and the board, in favour of a railway from St. Aubin to St. Helier and Gorey, to be protected by a parapet.

1870.   Jersey railway from St. Helier to St. Aubin, constructed by Mr. Pickering, opened.

Sir John's scientific approach is also shown in military matters, and his ideas were encouraged by his old friend Lord Hardinge, who became a Field Marshal in 1855, and Sir John wrote him a letter of congratulation "on having obtained the highest rank in military annals. My very kind friend Lord Beresford used to value his title as a Field Marshal higher than his peerage". In reply Lord Hardinge said "Among the many warm greetings I have received . . . . none has given me greater pleasure that the *hearty* one that has come from you, a friend of near half a century". On various occasions Sir John procured cattle for Lord Hardinge and his son in law. On one visit to London, when considering the defence of Gallow's Hill, which he considered should have a fort with sunken ditches, he went to see both Lord Hardinge and Sir John Burgoyne about it. At Lord Hardinge's request he prepared a report on a rifle ball he had invented, and this he presented at the Office of Ordnance, and his Lordship wrote an introduction for Sir John to Colonel Gordon at Enfield and Colonel Chalmer at Woolwich, and offered to lend his own "pattern rifle as I might not find a Brunswick rifle at Enfield. How considerate". Sir John at once went to both Woolwich and Enfield to make experiments. Of the latter he said "The Government must have been at its wit's end for a locality to come to such a marsh 70 years back, in which to manufacture small arms. It is the most marshy spot in England that I know".

After two days of concentrated experiment, "Colonel Chalmer said that he should report that I had produced a very powerful ball and approved of my report to the Master General . . . . Wrote my report to Lord Hardinge which took five pages of foolscap . . . . (he) asked whether I was satisfied with the result? 'Very much so' I said. He then read it through. 'What, 11 out of 12 with the new arm?' 'Yes, My Lord, I was surprised at myself. It is the best arm I ever shot with.' His Lordship then read the report through, and said: 'There is something in this ball. I suspect there is more in the balls than in the arms? What do you think Colonel?' 'I suspect so too, my Lord. We do not yet know what is the best form of ball. I should very much like to have a new rifle musket for experiment.' 'Very well, Colonel, you shall have that one and you may try experiments with it. (to his secretary) You had better write to the respective officers of the Ordnance to offer the Colonel every facility to carry them on . . . . Here, Colonel, take that gun, I will write your name on it.'[1] Which he did". In a later conversation "I showed him George Hardinge's letter to my grandfather Sir John Dumaresq in 1788 . . . . to know if it was not from a relative . . . . because it would be a curious coincidence and show that our cattle were considered of value as far back . . . . he read the letter and laughed heartily. 'Oh, yes, that was my uncle George, he was a Welsh judge and a very clever man. Yes, it is a coincidence' ".

He invited Sir John to dine with him one day, and there he met Sir Alex Grant, whom he had previously met at Bedgebury, who said to him: "Have you a pear for every day in the year now, Colonel?" Lord Hardinge enquired after Halkett Le Couteur, saying: "Where is your son? How does he stand?", and then added: "Never mind, Colonel, he will get his company without purchase to-morrow". After dinner they had a tête à tête about Jersey affairs in which His Lordship said: "St. Catherine's a great mistake; whose? Belcher[2] and Colquhoun. Three admirals had recommended Noirmont point". When, in 1854, Lord Hardinge heard of Sir John's design for a gun rest, he sent a message, and he "approves and desires me to persevere". When next in London he "called on the Surveyor to the Ordnance, Sir Thomas Hastings . . . . after giving me half his lunch, a crust of bread and a glass of water, he walked to the Horse Guards with me, having lent me a Minié rifle which suits the rest more perfectly than the newest arm. He examined the rest and said it was the most perfect thing he had seen; saw Lord Hardinge and advised him to have one in every barracks; he quite approved it. Lord Hardinge asked the cost and said he would have one in every regiment". This gun rest was tried out and "I showed Colonel Hay that the rest which they had sent from Woolwich was altogether too clumsy and unsuited for his purposes . . . .If he would adopt my two sockets and run the musket into them, it would answer with my gun level . . . . he took me to the armourer's shop where I volunteered to have the sockets made under my eye. The armourer is a clever fellow, understood my principle at once, and set to work to produce what I require for to-morrow. Showed me

---

1. An 1851 Enfield rifle musket, now in the possession of the States of Jersey.
2. Admiral Sir Edward Belcher, (1799-1877).

41. probably JOHN HALKETT LE COUTEUR.
from a portrait by an unknown artist, c.1853.
(*see page 164*)

42. Jurat DE QUETTEVILLE raises the Clameur de Haro over the building of the railway.
An unsigned cartoon of c.1870.

43. 'Very well, Colonel, you shall have that one'.
A rifle musket inscribed:
'From Viscount Hardinge, Master General, to
Colonel Le Couteur, Q.A.D.C. 1852'.

44   'So you have mounted a moustache?'
(Viscount Hardinge to Colonel Le Couteur).
From a faded photograph of 1855.

45. Garden Party at Belle Vue.
pastel drawing by C. F. Draper, 1863.

46. 'So as to have got the sobriquet of Wellington'.
a silhouette of J. H. Le Couteur in the uniform of the 87th Regiment, c.1846.

their gun level, with a moveable water level to it, which renders it *false*. Told him he should fix it, reverse the level and arrange it so as to enter the barrel, and get rid of the parallel, a useless affair. They take out the breech of the gun to learn their levels, a folly I cannot comprehend . . . . When the first musket that came to hand was placed in the sockets, which I had covered with strips of cloth, the horizontal and vertical motions, with my gun level to fix the horizontal, became apparent . . . . Colonel Hay said that 'it was surprising that so many able men at Woolwich and at Enfield had never thought of this!' . . . . The Sergeant Major (said): 'Oh, that was what was wanted, Sir. It is capital. Now the men can be taught at once without any mistake!' "

On one of these occasions Sir James Orde came in, and shocked Sir John by keeping his hat on when the Commander in Chief had none. His Lordship's final remark was: "Good bye Colonel, you have done us a great service". And in an interview the following year he said: "Lord Hardinge approved of my tangent sight and V form of rifling barrels, desired me to write to Mr. Monsell, the Clerk of the Ordnance, and that he wished them to be tried at Enfield . . . . 'So you have mounted a moustache?' 'My General wished it, so I did so of course.' " In July of that year he noted: "Report last evening that Lord Hardinge is going to take command of the army in the Crimea; he is too old for such a heavy task".

In 1855 Sir John was able to make further experiments at the Hythe School of Musketry, trying out his tangent sight. He then noted: "It is a curious fact that in the statistics of rifle musketry I have found that 700 yards is the most deviating range for the rifle, and on examining Colonel Hay's returns we found that to be the case. The shooting at 800 is better than that at 700 yards". While at Hythe, and with agriculture always running neck and neck with military matters in his interest, he met a General King, "who is to receive an increased pension of £100 a year," to whom he promised to send "buds of best pears, or grafts, to graft onto a Marie Louise, and he is to send my wife some true Polish chickens". General King's brother, Colonel King, "was in Sir John Moore's retreat from Corunna, and the officer who blew up the bridge at Lugos after the army passed it".

Lord Hardinge died in 1856, having become paralysed after a fall, and having given up the post of Commander in Chief a few months previously. In the July Sir John said: "The Duke of Cambridge[1] has succeeded to the command of the army, in the place of my kind friend Lord Hardinge, who is doing better. A royal Prince at the head of the army is an earnest, or should be, of fair play and no favour. He need not be influenced. He is a good officer and brave soldier, very popular with the Crimean army, a great prestige". A short time before he had said "The report was that Lord Seaton[2] was to be offered the command in chief, with the understanding that he would not accept. Lord Gough[3] spoken of. The Duke of Cambridge, but the Court were averse to his nomination as he was excitable".

Sir John recorded that in 1832 he "recommended to Lord Fitzroy Somerset that officers purchasing commissions be trained at Sandhurst while awaiting gazetting. Lord F.S. and Lord Hill approved, but Sir Ed. Paget, Governor of Sandhurst, "deemed the task too troublesome". Thirty years later he noted: "General Douglas called here and had a confidential chat. He is very prudent and will help the States if they will help themselves . . . .

1. The Second Duke, grandson of George III. He had served at Alma and Inkerman and was Commander in Chief 1856-1895.   2. Sir John Colborne, (1778-1863), Created Lord Seaton. Lieutenant Governor of Guernsey 1825-1830. Field Marshal 1860.   3. Viscount Gough, (1779-1869).

I was not aware that a plan of sending candidates for commissions (which I had recomend-ed to Lord Hill) to study at Sandhurst, had been carried out. The General does not like it, but I think he is in error there. I read my lecture on 'Camps of Exercise' to a small meeting of the Royal United Services Institution. General Lindsey, the Chairman, paid me a high compliment on its practical utility, so did Colonel Adair. Captain Burgess called it an admirable paper and took charge of it for printing".

The foregoing pages give some idea of the wide variety of subjects to which Sir John applied his versatile and inventive mind, and the trouble he took to communicate his ideas to those who might appreciate them.

CHAPTER EIGHTEEN

ART AND GOOD LEARNING

Sir John was a great supporter of all branches of art and good learning, whether in the Island, in England or on the continent.

Most local artists of the period are mentioned in the diaries. Philippe Jean, the miniaturist, died in 1802, but he appears in Sir John Dumaresq's diary, in 1788, on a trip to England, when he said: "Embarked at one o'clock on board the Jersey packet Captain de Ste. Croix, for Jersey, wind west south west. Company.. nephew J. Pipon and niece Nancy[1], Miss Elizabeth Lemprière and Mr. Phil Jean the painter. Arrived same evening at Yarmouth, went on shore and supped, returned to sleep on board". A Mr. Jean, with whom he dined at George's Coffee house in 1795 is likely to be the artist too.

But to return to Sir John Le Couteur, in 1846 he wrote to Lord Spencer, then Vice Chamberlain. It will be remembered that when the Queen visited Jersey, an album of Jersey views by P. J. Ouless had been presented to her, and she then asked for the same artist to depict her landing in the Island. This letter explained the artist's difficulties, saying: ". . . . (he) has endeavoured to execute a drawing in water colours of the landing of Her Majesty in Jersey, in obedience to the gracious command of the Queen. I beg your Lordship to offer my humble and dutiful respects to the Queen, and to express to Her Majesty that Mr. Ouless felt considerable difficulty in compassing a subject so extensive to a space so confined, and that he greatly fears his attempt to convey the joyous excitement of a vast assembly may not express all he desired. The view, however, is most accurate and to Jersey deeply interesting, and should Her Majesty be so graciously inclined, will afford a beautiful engraving". Ouless need not have feared, for all Jersey knows and values his picture of this occasion. Sir John's friendship continued, and in 1861 he recommended Ouless' son, Philip Daniel, "for examination or appointment for a Master's assistant". P. D. Ouless in fact became a Captain R.N. In 1871 the annual exhibition of the Royal Academy featured pictures by three Jersey artists, Millais, Ouless (the son Walter William) and Poingdestre. Later that year the father P. J. Ouless visited Sir John, who noted: "Old Ouless the artist called to show me a photo from his son's picture which I saw at the exhibition, sold for 150 gns": and then in 1875; "Mr. Ouless, the father of the young great artist, came to have my name and subscription for a local art union. His son is doing wonders in London, and has more offers for portraits than he can perform, at 200 or 300 guineas. He has to meet many temptations and crosses". The Poingdestre mentioned above spent most of his working life in Rome, where he became President of the British Academy there, and in 1857 Sir John was touring Italy and said; "Adolphus walked with me to visit Mr. Poingdestre, a Jersey landscape illustrator of very rising merit. He has been here seven years . . . A fine sketch of Roman horses being driven in from the Campagna".

Ouless was not the only artist to have the honour of portraying the Queen's visit; Jean Le Cappelain also produced an album of views, and in 1847 Sir John said; "saw Le

---

1. His sister Esther married Jacques Pipon of La Moie.

Cappelain's paintings. The States met to send four members as a deputation with them to the Queen". Two years later he said; "Attended the Committee for the selection of the Le Cappelain pictures. Twenty were approved, some I got substituted for those which had been first chosen. Mr. Le Sueur, Mr. Le Bailly, Mr. Gabourel and I were named a committee to have custody of the selected pictures and to decide where to place them . . . . £1400 . . . . most of the sum will come in". This last remark must refer to a proposal which had been made, to found a Le Cappelain gallery, for which only £210 was subscribed, and so the project failed. A year later he noted; "Mr. Manuel called about exhibiting amateurs and other drawings with those of Le Cappelain this year".

Of his other countryman, Sir John Millais, he thought very highly, and in 1853 he said: "I went to the Royal Academy where a crowd had already assembled. Millais' 'Letter of release' is unquestionably the finest picture in the collection". And a few years later: "Went to the Royal Academy where I saw some strange pictures of Millais, very clever, but incomprehensible to me; his 'Peace' is a puzzle, a baby boy looking at his picture book is the best he has there": and later again; "Millais' picture of 'My first sermon', is a lovely little girl, a fit pendant to Sir Joshua Reynolds' beautiful little 'Samuel' ". In 1869 he visited the artist at 7, Cromwell Place, South Kensington, and "had a long chat with Millais. He was painting three pictures. One, Sir Walter Ralegh as a boy, with another lad looking over a sea shore, a big mariner in the foreground, not very historical it seemed to me. I told him I wish he had painted Sir Walter in Jersey, in our States building, Elizabeth Castle I might have added. Another, a portrait of the bride Marchioness of Huntley . . . . Wished him to paint a pendant to the Death of Peirson . . . . the Jersey States proclaiming King Charles as Charles II, when all Great Britain had forgotten him. He liked the idea . . . . He is handsome as ever, has eight children. House elegantly furnished". The next year he visited Millais again, "who showed us his six pictures for the Exhibition, Lady Huntley's lovely portrait, the Knight rescuing the Virgin, a noble picture of immortal fame . . . ." But Clara de Lisle, his neighbour and close friend at Le Coin, did not share his enthusiams, as "Clara brought me the catalogue of the Royal Society[1] Exhibition to go over; she thought little of Millais' pictures".

Draper[2] was an artist working in Jersey in the middle of the century whom Sir John evidently liked and befriended, as two delightful pastel drawings of his were hanging at Belle Vue, both showing the view over the fields to the bay, with the Fort and the Castle in the distance. One of them was almost certainly the 'Garden party' amongst pictures lent by Sir John and shown at the Channel Islands Exhibition in 1871.

It has already been suggested that Thomas Berteau may have been distantly related to the Le Couteurs. He was born in 1819 and died in 1904. He studied art in Paris under Drolingue and Richolme, engravers, and on returning to Jersey became Art Master at Victoria College. The quality of his pencil drawings can be appreciated by the exquisite work in portraits shown in this book. One of them is in pastels, and the other three are in pencil with touches of colour, the delicate fineness of the work making it easy to understand that he was also a miniaturist. He is a Jersey artist whose work has not been sufficiently appreciated. He painted at least one Lieutenant Governor, General Reynett, whose wife was herself an amateur painter of some ability, as in 1849, when Berteau would have been

1. Presumably a mistake for Royal Academy.
2. C. F. Draper, water colourist.

47.   An eighteenth-century crayon drawing, from the Le Couteur collection.
Bought on the Continent in 1819.

48. St. Brelade's Church before alteration.
a water-colour by Colonel Le Couteur, c.1845.

49. North-east entrance gate to St. Brelade's Church, built 1850.

50. VICTORIA COLLEGE, JERSEY.

51.   QUEEN VICTORIA
(*from the copy of F. Winterhalter's portrait at Victoria College.*)

but thirty years old, it was recorded; "Called at Government House to thank the General for forwarding the petition to Her Majesty from myself and the Officers of the 5th Regiment for a pair of colours. Admired Bertaut's portrait of him which is very good". The spelling of his surname varies, but he signed himself Berteau.

In 1851 the Guernsey artist Naftel[1] came over to Jersey. "Mr. Naftel called at the office. He arrived yesterday and comes to Belle Vue to-morrow. He goes to sketch at Pontac and Platte Rocque to-day". A few days later, "Mr. Naftel, the celebrated Guernsey artist, came to us for three or four days. He married a sister of our late friend Captain Robillard R.A. He is remarkably clever . . . . Took Mr. Naftel to Letac and Grève de Lecq. Heavy rain prevented his sketching St. Ouen's Bay . . . . he will become a first rate artist and is a very nice unassuming person". Harriet Le Couteur at the same time, noted in her diary: "Went to St. Ouen's Bay. Took a sketch of La Rocco Tower, a very gloomy day. Mr. Naftel took some spirited sketches in spite of the weather. The vraickers were highly amused". But at an exhibition of water colours in London, a few years later, Sir John said "my friend Naftel is heavy in his skies".

A Mr. Leitch is mentioned, but as his initials are R.P. he cannot be the well known painter William Leighton Leitch. He was here in 1859, for ". . . . Mr. Leitch arrived here last week. The weather has been forbidding, nevertheless I have taken him along the now called Victoria Road to St. Catherine's Bay, where he made a pretty sketch, and to-day I drove him where to compose his picture in St. Peter's Valley."

When in France in 1827 he met and took lessons from Gudin[2], and said of him: ". . . . Gudin's atelier, which is extremely fine. He was quite a lad when we were in Paris in June 1822, and has risen to pre-eminence rapidly. He then sketched prettily but now is the first marine painter here. I mean to study with him. Went to see Bonnington's[3] atelier, a young Scotsman who has formed a style for himself; he is extremely clever, not above five and twenty". A few days later he went with Gudin to the house of the famous poet Béranger[4], who taught him, not to compose, but to play dominoes!

When quite young, in 1816, Sir John took lessons from Fielding[5], and examination of his landscape sketches show how ardently he was trying to copy the style of his master, and at an exhibition some years later he said: "Copley Fielding keeps his place. Prout, de Wint, Cox and Gastineau next in my opinion"; and the next day he said: "What a wonderful place this city is, what wealth and riches are now rolling along this street, literally hundreds of splendid horses and carriages, full of fashion, wit, folly and beauty. It is precisely like the continued roar of a waterfall, unceasing from 10 a.m. till nearly 2 the next morning . . . . Water colour exhibition again to study their styles. Fielding's sea views are quite magical; his Nausicaa and her attendants is a beautiful composition, admirably coloured". When sketching in the lake district, he once said: "After all my work was over the sun shone and reflected the superb tints in the glassy water, but I tried to catch Dame Climate in her sighing and gloom as well as in her sunny smile. Copley Fielding has sold more pictures than any other artist from his brilliant clear colouring".

Sir John never missed an exhibition, or a visit to an art gallery, and always commented

1. Paul Jacob Naftel. (1817-1891), Water colourist who exhibited many works at the old Water Colour Society. Worked in many European countries. 2. Théodore Gudin, marine painter, (1802-1880).
3. Richard Parkes Bonnington, landscape artist, (1801-1828).
4. Pierre Jean de Béranger, poet and ballad writer, (1780-1857).
5. Anthony Vandyke Copley Fielding. (1786-1855).

upon the pictures which had attracted him. Let us take a few examples. At the Old Water Colour Exhibition in 1857 he said: "Davidson seemed to me to be the most remarkable of the young artists; Evans of Eton has a wonderfully painted snow scene, an ice pond and skaters in bright garbs. F. Taylor, Duncan, Richardson, Hunt, Gastineau, Harding are very fine"; and in the same year: "Harriet and I went to the New Society of Painters in Water Colours. There are a few very good pictures but a great number of inferior ones. The great men here are Richardson, Mole, Warren, McKewan, Haghe. There are very many of inferior note whom I thought ought scarcely be allowed to exhibit. Campion, a good bold painter, had a poor sketch of St. Brelade's Bay". Of the Louvre collection he was rather scathing, saying: "The French guide books tell us that here is the finest collection of paintings in the world. It may be one of the largest but there are a vast number of trashy productions, the French school in it. Several young persons were copying from the meritricious school of Louis 14; the whole gallery is not to be compared with those of Rome, Naples, Florence, or our National Gallery, irrespective of the noble pictures in private collections in England. There is a noble collection of drawings by Old Masters, a superb horse by Velasquez in a wonderful bold style of pencilling I never before saw; there is a noble head of Galileo worth any price, delicious funny Teniers, van Dyks, Rubens, Fra Bartolomeo . . . . those old masters had studied most severely anatomy of man and animals. What Corregios, Carraccis . . . . one of my Annibal Carracci is as fine as the best here". On passing through the low countries he saw a girl who so much reminded him of "Rubens' plump wives" that he declared that "Rubens was a wonderful painter. I'll never disbelieve him again".

In Italy he enjoyed to the full the wonders of Italian art, and recorded all his impressions, which cover many pages in his notebooks, such as ". . . . one of the Virgin and Child by Raphael, the most perfect sketch I ever beheld, a mere outline of tremendous power and truth". An intriguing entry when in Venice said: "We then took a gondola to the Martini Palace, where there are a few good and many inferior paintings. The portrait of Aristotle by Titian, which Lord Byron called the poetry of painting and painting of poetry, has been sold to an Englishman for £2000". And then again at the National Portrait Gallery in 1867 he said: "One of Hogarth's is exactly like my pencil sketch by himself . . . . Sir William Lawrence almost equal to Sir Joshua". There is among the papers a small pencil sketch with the name Hogarth written across it, but it cannot be identified as being by the Master, nor does it appear to have his quality, though one can see in it a likeness to the well-known self portrait of Hogarth. This observation brings us to the remarkable collection of pictures Sir John built up at Belle Vue, though they have naturally become somewhat dispersed through the years. There were some very fine drawings, purchased by him and Harriet on their honeymoon, and the discrimination he showed in choosing them is all the more remarkable when one considers that Italian, or indeed any other school of art, was not then studied and documented as it now is. He knew of no Berenson or Roger Fry on whose writings we can now rely for information, and indeed even Ruskin's "Stones of Venice" was not published until 1851. He mentioned at one stage owning a van der Meulen, and in codicils to his will and elsewhere, the names of Morland, Greuze, Tintoretto, Etty and Le Bailly appear. In 1861 he paid £30 for "a landscape by Galos" and £3.3. for "Fahey's[1] picture". He referred on more than one occasion to his "Charles I by Peters". There was

1. James Fahey, (1804-1885). Water colour painter.

also a "Marriage at Cana" which is considered to be by Lucca Giordano, and this is supported by an entry, made in Italy, which said "(Saw) the Marriage at Cana by Tintoretto, a fine picture but not so well arranged as ours at Belle Vue by Giordano", and once, when in Venice, ".... a fine picture by Lucca Giordano, our Belle Vue artist".

He admired the sculpture at Isola Bella on Lake Maggiore, saying ".... there are fine statues by Canova,[1] Monti, etc. The Counts Borromeo have each added to the beauties of this fairy palace, which would require twenty thousand a year to do justice to. The family only occupy one state room, they live on the upper storey, seven children. A very fine marble bust of the deceased Countess by Monti, adorned the drawing room. It is a singularly interesting creation to visit, such a legacy to a family as may become a lodestone. If all the future Borromeos who inherit it are very prudent and honest, it may exist for years". He remarked that both Napoleon and Caroline, the unhappy Queen of George IV, had stayed there.

When in Rome he went to see two English sculptors, "Wood[2], a rising man, and Gibson[3], to see his Tinted Venus, and his Pandora, the Venus of the Greeks he states. The Tinted Venus seemed to me to have the jaundice, or to be just recovering from it, a fine statue nevertheless. The Pandora is fine, but the neck seems to me to be over thick. We then drove to St. Peter's .... it seems to be smaller than St. Paul's, owing to the immense façade and the ugly Vatican, which adheres to it and is an ugly eyesore, detracting from the grand design of Michael Angelo."

Other branches of the arts were not neglected either. He was always interested in the theatre and concerts. J. Braham[4], (Abraham) was much appreciated, and at Bath in 1825 Sir John and his wife heard him and were "in raptures". In 1842 Braham visited Jersey, Mary Le Couteur recording; "Braham arrived from London. He and his son gave a concert on Wednesday". Some years before, when in Paris, she had said of Madame Cartrufo; "Her voice I can only compare to that of Braham, she has the finest sonorous bass voice I ever listened to". In Jersey, she said of a Mr. de Vos, a piano teacher, that "he played admirably to a select party .... accompanying Mr. Garott, the best singer we have had here since Braham"; and some time later she said "The Governor invited me to dinner to go to the opera with them in the evening. Braham's son is the director of the opera and has a good company here".

All the family were great readers, and there are indications that Mary Le Couteur belonged to a kind of postal library service, with the Pipons of Noirmont at least, and probably with many other members. She records what books she read, of which she enjoyed travel the most. Sir John read copiously, the classics, history, theology, and every subject that can be imagined. But he did not at all approve of Dickens, and in 1842 said, when reporting a conversation with Lord Beresford; "We quite agreed as to the evil tendency of such writers as Bulwer[5] and Dickens ...." Years later, at a dinner at the Palace, with his son, who was at the time Captain of the Queen's Guard, he said: "The conversation was very sporting, drifted into Dickens' works, which I was very sorry to hear, and which I have long since noticed captivates the taste of these fashionable young men. It exactly

1. Canova, (1757-1822). Celebrated Italian sculptor.
2. W. Wood, (1827-1886).   3. John Gibson, (1790-1866), Pupil of Canova. His Tinted Venus was famous for its introduction of colour after the Greek manner.
4. John Braham, (1774-1856) Internationally celebrated tenor.
5. Henry Bulwer, (1801-1872). Diplomatist and writer.

corresponds with the objective remarks of its style which I made last year to Sir George Clark who is gone to India in command. It is a dangerously and pleasingly vulgar style without the point and truth of Hogarth, but in a contrary sense leading to admiration of its style. All these young men, Captains and subs of the Foot Guards and Life Guards are perverted by it. The gentlemanly tones of Addison and Chatham, not to say of Chesterfield, are lost on them. Smoke and slang, with a gentlemanly but dry exterior, have taken the place of the courteous style which should ever accompany true Christian soldiers". When reading a book of Disraeli's he said: "Finished the 2nd volume of Lothair. Dizzy's aim is to damage the Jesuits, cleverly, too. Fine men and fine women he paints, gentle aristocracy, but why the fish stall? He must like fish. Fishy! it is a serene elegant work nevertheless".

Assistance was given to local writers, such as Simon, who was writing a History of Jersey, and Sullivan; "John Sullivan at my office; gave me his letter to the Queen, begging me to forward it to Her Majesty through General Cuppage; asked me to write a memoir on Sir John Dumaresq, my grandfather, for his History of Jersey which he trusts the Queen may patronise".

He set himself the task of making a translation of Wace's 'Roman de Rou' but after about 500 lines he endorsed it: "My duties left me no leisure to prosecute this translation, which I intended to arrrange as a historical romance". In 1850 he noted: "Wrote a succinct history of Jersey for Montgomery Martin's History of the Colonies". This account survives in one of the letter books, and not so very succinct either, with a covering letter saying: "I shall be very glad to see a sketch of Jersey in its true colours in your work".

D. H. Inglis' 'The Channel Islands' is one of the best of many nineteenth century guide books to have appeared, and the dedication of the last edition says: "To Colonel Le Couteur, Jersey, and Samuel Elliot Hoskins M.D. Guernsey, this volume is inscribed by the author, as a slight acknowledgement of the valuable assistance and friendly aids for which he is so largely their debtor". In 1834 Mr. Inglis, having completed his Channel Islands book, contemplated one on Ireland, and Sir John wrote to commend him to Reverend Magee in Dublin. Some years later, when he was in Sark on matters of defence, he wrote: ". . . . on the coupée and the silver mines, which are a failure . . . . they told us they have struck a vein of copper, which may be fudge . . . . the coupée which in my mother's time was two feet wide, is now six feet, and horses draw trucks over it. The scenery is grand, not finer than our Plémont or Grosnez caves—for that see Inglis with my corrections". In 1849 Mr. Inglis was apparently still resident in the Island, for we read: "Harriet and I went to Anna Inglis' wedding; the Rev. Mr. Muriel, her spouse, seems to be a nice young man. Albert D. who was a bridesman, was very officious. It was a gay affair and we left them all dancing at 11 p.m.".

The Dr. Hoskins mentioned, who was a Fellow of the Royal Society, is given descent from the Hamptonnes of La Patente in Payne's Armorial, and he was the author of "Charles II in the Channel Islands". His wife, the daughter of Sir Edgar McCulloch, Guernseyman and author of works on Guernsey folklore, was said to "assist him in his meteorological notes".

Sir John's faith was a strong element in his life, and in that of his household. It was an undying flame, ever present in his mind, a comfort in adversity, a strength when in doubt, and a source of serenity in happiness. All the family shared in this clear bright light of faith. And for him this meant Anglicanism. He did not quite approve of other branches of Christianity, and in that he was a man of his times. The Quakers he accepted through his admiration for Elizabeth Fry, but apart from her the only remark about the sect he made was in 1846 when "de Ste. Croix called with a groundless complaint from the Secretary of State relative to Lemprière, the pretended Quaker, who is in gaol for contempt of court". His mother, in talking about religion to a young girl in Paris, once described the Quakers as "très honnêtes gens". The Jews he and his mother seem to have supported. There are several references to Church collections being in favour of the Jews, and Mary Le Couteur showed in her accounts a payment of 5/5 for an annual subscription to the Jew's Society, and in 1847 Sir John noted; "Lunched with Gawler[1] .... he is very engaged with the Jewish cause for their restoration as a nation to Jewry. I like it too". One does not know how to interpret a further remark; "The House are now debating whether they will admit Baron Rothschild to take his seat, he having taken the two oaths, but stopped when it came to the words 'on the faith of a Christian', which he very properly said were not words binding to his conscience, I would as soon trust a Jew on his oath as a Roman Catholic". However, be that as it may, in 1857, when in Rome, he wrote to Monseigneur Talbot, Vatican Secretary, to ask for the honour of a presentation to the Pope[2] for himself and his son and daughter-in-law. He was passed from one official to another, and then told that the levée would be on a "Sunday if a lady came, any day of the week if only gentlemen". His brother and sister-in-law, Frederick and Jane Janvrin, and their sons Adolphus and Francis were in Rome at the time, having a "handsome britzka[3] in addition to their close carriage, for for which they pay 35 scudi[4] a month besides two to the coachman, nice horses and harness as good a turn out as any in Rome". On Christmas day, 1857, Sir John and his son both wore uniform, and with the Janvrin family, they all attended high mass at St. Peter's, in a crowd of twenty thousand. "At $10\frac{1}{2}$ the sounding of trumpets and military sacred music announced the coming of the Pope, troops, then priests, in black, in white, in snuff, in red, in purple, then a corpus of noble life guards, then a canopy under which sat the once mighty head of the Roman Catholic church .... he was borne by six or eight men who walked very gingerly beneath their precious burden .... he received the homage of all the Cardinals, the Bishops and the grandees who kissed his hand severally ... he was occasionally relieved of his mitre which seemed to be of yellow silk .... the church plate and communion service superb .... (The Pope) is a very amiable paternal looking man, of a fine presence, more benevolent than regal. They next partook of the sacrament, the wine being carried to him in the most beautifully enriched cup I ever saw, glittering with diamonds. The sacred vessels were covered with gold edged white linen when being carried to him. Lastly he returned to his throne, then administered the sacrament to the dignitaries when lo! I heard an official whisper that all the consecrated wafers were consumed, more were wanted, none at hand, so then and there the ceremony ended .... It was a grand sight, a fine pageant, but the priests and many people chattering and laughing nearly destroyed its solemnity". A few days later he recorded "News of the relief of Lucknow. Thank God". Then on New Year's Day "Halkett and myself put on our uniforms and drove to the Vatican to the Pope's levée. We had received a printed order for admittance to the Sistine gallery ....In an ante

1. George Gawler, (1796-1869). Governor of Australia. Had been at Marlowe with Sir John: after retirement devoted himself to religious and philanthropic pursuits.
2. Pius IX, (Pope 1846-1878).   3. An open carriage with calash top and space for reclining.
4. An old Italian silver coin.

room to which we were conducted by a footman in a rich antique livery of dark crimson and black . . . . we found . . . . 17 ladies and 7 gentlemen waiting for presentation . . . . When Monseigneur Talbot called me he brought us into a second waiting room and chatted with us very cordially. He said that the Pope was occupied at this season from nine in the morning to six at night . . . . I told him that I felt it a duty to pay my respects to the Pope for permitting us to have our own services here. A countryman of mine, Dr. Hue[1], from Jersey was the first clergyman who was allowed to commune and preach the Church of England service through the kind and enlightened intervention of the then Cardinal Gonsalvi[2] . . . . Monseigneur Talbot then said, "Gonsalvi did well and owed that to Englishmen, he had been very well received in England. Indeed the Pope then owed his restoration to England. The Pope and England were the only two powers who resisted Napoleon. . . . Halkett asked him whether it was true that the Pope had been in the sacred bodyguard of Nobles. 'It was a popular error. The Pope had been educated for the Church, but could not be allowed to enter, from epileptic fits. He got better, though not quite cured, and pressed the Pope to allow him to take orders. The Pope consented on the condition that a priest should constantly attend him when he administered the sacrament . . . . The present Pope had never had a fit since . . . . We were ushered in . . . . On being named I entered a long handsome room, richly carpeted, made a low bow, and walked up to His Holiness who was standing by his writing table, habited in a white dress of cloth something like our grey great coats . . . . a very benevolent amiable looking man with soft blue or grey eyes, a clear healthy fresh complexion, not much hair and a white skull cap. It was impossible not to feel a sense of veneration in standing before the representative, in the Roman Catholic belief, of St. Peter". The Pope spoke to them, asking them if they spoke French, and if they were both in the Queen's service, to which Sir John replied that he was her A.D.C. and his son a Captain in her Guards, having seen service in India and the Crimea. The Pope spoke of Englishmen he had known, some of whom had become Cardinals, and referred in kind terms to Queen Victoria.

To come a little nearer home in church affairs, there was a suggestion at one time of a Bishop for the Channel Islands, and in a conversation with Lord Beresford, the latter said that he thought the difference between the Reformed and Roman Catholic churches not so wide as to prevent their union, and that ". . . . he thought we should have a Bishop in the Islands. What will the Dean say: or rather would the Bishop of Winchester consent?" Years later a terse entry said: "At Government House at 12. General cannot take the initiative about the Ch. Isd. bishop".

Of the Deans in office during his lifetime he gives us some intimate glimpses. Of Dean Hue there is little mention, for he scarcely ever came to Jersey while holding the post. He is recorded as having been interested in education, and on the strength of this, Sir John wrote to him in 1824 asking for advice when it was found necessary to reduce the salary of the Master of the National School from £80 to £60 a year, and that of the Mistress to £40. The former refused and resigned, but the latter accepted. Sir John explaining that not only had the school income deteriorated, but provisions, so expensive in 1816, had then become cheaper and that "in order to do no injustice to either I had written to Dr. Walmsley

1. Not identified definitely. Perhaps Dean Corbet Hue (1769-1838).
2. Cardinal Gonsalvi or Consalvi (1757-1824). Secretary of State to Pius VII. Took a prominent part at the Congress of Vienna. Influential papal statesman, and bitter opponent of Napoleon. His portrait by Sir T. Lawrence hangs at Windsor, and Sir John says he had seen it.

to know what should be given to Master and Mistress, having from 100 to 150 children in their charge, and that gentleman stated the sum above named". In mitigation it may be said that the Master and Mistress were given "a lodging".

François Jeune became Dean in 1838, and the scurrilous attacks on him by some local papers are partly explained by an extract from the diary of the next year, when, in a letter to the ex-Lieutenant Governor, Sir John said; "The new Dean, a very clever person, and a man of learning and business, would have succeeded infinitely better were it not that his personal friendship with Advocate Godfray draws on him the dislike of all Godfray's enemies, who are neither few nor powerless; and Godfray being considered his adviser, he is sadly and vulgarly attacked by some of our papers". It appears that in 1851 he was concerned in choosing the first Headmaster for Victoria College and "was a highly proper person to do so".

There are few mentions of Dean Hemery, and the first reference to Dean Le Breton, father of the beautiful Lillie, was that he was unpunctual, and the next reflects on his oratory; "Attended the funeral, as a pall bearer, of my dear old revered friend James Robin of Petit Ménage. He was a man who had lived out of local politics, beyond being a steady friend of reform. He was aged ninety years and one month. His daughters Miss Robin and Mary Ann and his grand-daughter Miss O'Brien were at his grave, with his sons Charles and James[1]. There were Hammonds, Gossets, Durells as mourners. Lieutenant Governor Cuppage was there too. Mr. Bertram, 87 I believe, Captain Anley, Rozel, were the pall bearers. It was a private unostentatious burial. The Dean read so low as to lose all the effect of the grand solemn service, as he did at Miss Simmons' funeral. Does he fancy it seems pathetic? If so, it is an error". But at his own wife's funeral he said; "This was beautifully performed by my excellent friends Dean Le Breton and Mr. Falle". In 1867 there was a "grand dinner given by the clergy and laity to the Bishop of Winchester, about ninety of the leading gentry present. The Dean made a buttery speech and a lame excuse for the General's absence, who will not meet Clem Hemery. I proposed the health of the Dean and clergy". Soon afterwards; "Our Dean Le Breton preached a sermon on behalf of our schools, so eloquent as to raise £6.4.0. for us; I collected on the Marett side. The Dean lunched here and was very pleasant and amusing".

The affairs of both St. Brelade's, the parish church, and St. Aubin's, the local chapel, interested him constantly. He always attended services, and recorded a comment on the sermon, not necessarily complimentary. St. Brelade's church contains mural tablets to many members of the family, as well as a stained glass window to the memory of his son, Halkett. In the churchyard is the family vault, to which in 1845 he had rails fixed, but these have since been removed. That year, Mr. Hayward, of whom more will be heard, produced "beautiful plans for the school rooms. I invited him to come to St. Brelade's church with me on Monday, to see the Fisherman's Chapel and to take his opinion on the restoration of St. B's Church". A great deal of discussion ensued, such as "Committee of the church at 10. We were there till 12. Agreed to build the east wall and to enlarge the churchyard". . . . "Unanimous for the quay and walk to bound Captain Alexander's property[2] . . . . (he) agreed to the road being carried along it to the sands . . . . Began the work and laid down the line, given to Mr. George Jeune at ten livres the perch, only £16 in hand". By 1849 he reported;

1. See Robin pedigree, Bulletin Société Jersiaise 1907, p.170.
2. The house East of the Church.

"At an ecclesiastical parish meeting about removing the old gallery. Judge Le Gallais there. Named a Committee to treat with Captain Dean and the other proprietors of the pews there, to demolish the old one and erect a smaller . . . . Judge Le Gallais and I aided Mr. Falle to bring the Constable round to vote £50 loan on the security of the Trésor, to finish the churchyard walls and entrance pillars of granite, besides completing the slip down to the sands". By 1850; "A parish meeting . . . . to decide on the entrance to the churchyard. Proposed one in the Anglo Norman style in place of the horrid heavy Gothic performance of the schoolmaster Le Maistre; the cheapness of mine may induce the people to adopt it . . . . The model was approved, all but the symbol at top which is too elaborate. The parishioners objected to the cross as a Roman Catholic form . . . . Directed Le Sueur to set about the specifications. He thought it would be done for £80. Mr. Godfray will contribute towards the top ornament . . . . Le Sueur to alter it to meet Mr. King's views, who corrected some slight errors in its construction . . . ." In 1851 the situation was still hanging fire, and ". . . . they decided to give up the elegant design of young Le Maistre for a pair of gate posts, owing to a deficit of £25. After a two hours' discussion, in which Major Pipon and Judge Le Gallais supported my view of the inconsistency of a change after a solemn decision to carry a plan forward, for which tenders had been received through the newspapers, the Committee at length agreed unanimously to carry out the platform and base as high as the spring of the arch, which will enable us ultimately to complete the whole work. Renault was charged to employ men to carry it out by the day's work, just what he aimed at from the first, which I agreed to, not to be baulked in the building. They charged me to prepare a drawing for a lesser entrance to the westward[1]." Later that year; "Obliged to attend a Committee for the churchyard though suffering from rheumatism in my arm and shoulder. We were all very friendly. The arch is handsome and will appear light when the walls are built". A little later; "Drove by the church. The new entrance looks very well, the circular area should be paved and not be in gravel. I must send a drawing of it to the Illustrated London News[2]". In April 1852 he noted: "Consecration of St. Luke's Church by the Bishop of Winchester. The objectionable windows are in my eyes open to no objection whatever; the inscriptions are not mixed in the scroll in honour of God, but placed at the foot as acts of the donors. A very nice and pious memorial and very beautiful. The Bishop made a fine discourse. . . . we drove to the consecration of the new part of St. Brelade's churchyard". In 1852 it was decided to build the "sea wall along the cemetery to correspond with the new work".

Other churches are mentioned, and in 1826, "the ceremony of laying the foundation stone of St. James' church took place, amidst a vast concourse of orderly people. Poor Old James Hamon appeared renovated for a moment whilst performing the ceremony". In 1830 he attended "St. James' church, which is yet very cold". In August of 1846 there was the "consecration of St. Mark's church, a fine ceremony (and) the church was crowded with respectable and well dressed persons".

The establishment of a college was a matter which had been discussed for centuries before it came to fruition. Charles II, under the guidance of Sir George Carteret, recognised the need and authorised the imposition of duty on wines and spirits, some of which money was to be set aside for this object. But nothing came of it until the nineteenth century,

1. Apparently not erected, as the present entrance is modern.
2. The Illustrated London News cannot trace this.

52.   HARRIET LE COUTEUR in old age, c.1880.
(by an unknown artist)

53.   MARY SUMNER (née Le Couteur) with five of her children, 1860.

54.   EVIE   SUMNER,
c.1860

55.   HARRY and EVIE
SUMNER,
in mourning for
their grandmother,
c.1866.

56. 'Being a great grandpapa,
patriarchal honour'.

(Colonel Le Couteur,
with Rev. Ernest Utterton,
Evie and her daughter May,
1871).

57. KNIGHTED,
1872.

when it was offered as a suggestion for a memorial to the visit of the Queen in 1846. Sir John was well to the forefront in this idea, and he framed a long memorandum to the Lieutenant Governor for the rules which should govern such a college, and his diaries are full of references to this, an aim so near to his own heart. To take just a few entries; "General Touzel came yesterday and showed me that the boys in the Guernsey College pay, on average, £1.10 to each master, say a hundred of them amply pays the expenses. The ex-Dean, Dr. Jeune, finds that the Guernsey lads are more highly educated than those of Jersey, abilities being the same" . . . . "I had endeavoured to move Sir Colin Halkett to have one formed here, and that he (Sir James Reynett) would confer a lasting benefit on our Island if he succeeded in establishing one now . . . . It should be independent of any sum which might be subscribed for a monument to commemorate the Queen's visit, unless the sum subscribed was laid out to be presented to the students as exhibitions for the best essays in the English language. The General seemed to take a very warm interest in the subject . . . .". In the States shortly afterwards, ". . . . the General's letter recommending the establishment of a school or college was read and the principle adopted. Dupré spoke well on the subject after the General's neat explanation". A few months later; "States about College. Godfray's humbugging delays as usual, wouldn't let me speak, afraid of hearing the truth". A terse entry in October 1847 said: "States. College. Voted by the casting vote of the President". In fact this casting vote probably concerned the actual amount of land involved, rather than the principle of having a school. In April of the next year he said: "Saw the model of the new college which Gallichan has nearly finished . . . . The General and General Touzel think it perfect, I object to the west end which has a great hideous blank space which will do to grow ivy on to make it look venerable". An architect named Buckler was invited over at this stage, but "Le Sueur was very rude to him and talked of calling in another architect". By 1849 this had indeed occurred for the diary said; "The Greffier and I called on Mr. Hayward, the architect who built the new chapel for the hospital with the school rooms attached to it . . . . The General explained the delays in the erection of the college and gave Mr. H. all necessary information. We then went to the Victoria grounds which Mr. H. greatly admired . . . . (he thought) the building would not be seen from the harbour . . . . He stated he could hardly undertake to build a suitable building for £5600; he begged for a little latitude. He clearly understood that he was not to double the estimate". And a little later; " . . . Saw Mr. Hayward's plans which are approved, £6,500 with £500 for fittings. Went to the ground. The upper site preferred . . . . I am convinced that within five years after the college is at work, a house for the Principal will be required. He should be a first rate man". After a visit to Cheltenham College Sir John said; "I perceived that the cost was about £11,500 instead of the £6,500 they boast of. It would be impossible to erect such a building in Jersey at a cost so low". By 1850 the Committee was wondering if it would have done better to retain Mr. Buckler after all; "regular humbugs" commented Sir John. However all was well, in spite of much misgiving, as well as a visit to the Home Office to clear up a misunderstanding, and on 24th May 1850, the Queen's birthday, the college foundation stone was laid. The night before poor Sir John had acute colic, and sent for the doctor who "placed a mustard blister on my abdomen for 15 minutes . . . . and five doses of medicine". This drastic treatment was effective and in the morning, "I managed to dress in uniform though very weak. Drove in the carriage to the college ground. Saw that the platforms had caused an alteration in the deposition of the troops to be necessary. Went to the Cattle Market at 11, where the Flankers of my Regiment were to attend with the band and troopers. Inspected the band, drummers and men. The Grenadiers were sixty strong and the light company rather stronger, very clean with the exception of the edges of the belts of several, which were dirty . . . . one man in each company had his pouch belt on wrong. The band were not as clean as might be, not being used to being looked to. Gave each company three sovereigns, then band troopers and drummers one sovereign to drink the health of Her Majesty on this occasion . . . . Marched them off at four deep, with the colours, band and drums, nearly 200 men. When on the ground, the other Regt. not being up, formed the light battalion first, then told it off myself as they objected to attend to Captain Nicolle . . . . Marched four deep, about 520 men, through a dense crowd all the way. The town was gaily decorated with flags bearing mottoes in favour of education and many shops were shut. The light Battn. formed a lane for the States all the way to the Temple[1] and closed in after they had passed . . . . There must have been from 15 to 20 thousand persons in the ground. After the ceremony I formed the band in front of the Gov . . . . Not an insult or rudeness took place tho the crowd was intermixed with the band and drums. Formed both Battns. into a Brigade Column and thanked them in the name of the Lt. Govr. for their great steadiness and fine appearance and expressed my own gratification at the honour of having commanded such a fine body. Took more medicine".

The first Principal appointed was Dr. Henderson[2], and there was much discussion as to whether or not he had the right to choose his under masters. He was paid £500 a year with a house, though Sir John did not think this was enough "to be able to live up to his caste and position in society and at the same time be able to put by something annually for his family". Soon afterwards Dr. Henderson managed to get his nominations for the Composition, Latin and Mathematics masters accepted, with the French and Drawing masters to be named by a States Committee. Sir John was very critical of a decision which was taken, in appointing a Mr. Le Sueur, because he was a Jerseyman, in preference to an Englishman with superior qualifications.

On 29th September 1852 the college was finally opened. Having got a crape scarf, in mourning for the Duke of Wellington, Sir John went to the Arsenal, and organised the Militia and "told them off as soon as I had got the officers to be silent". The General arrived and was given the general salute, and inspected and praised the men. "The States met in the Temple and by Godfray's advice had decided not to wear their robes, but the General did not take the same view, and this amusing scene took place, as I was told by a performer in it. The General asked the Bailiff whether he was going to speak. No, he had nothing to say. 'Then I shall say a few words on presenting the portraits of the Queen and Prince[3].' 'It is my business to present them as President of the States'. 'They were entrusted to my care', said the General, 'and I shall present them myself. It will soon be time to proceed. Where are your robes?' 'Oh, the States never wear them, but we have the Mace'. The Lt. Govr; 'The Mace was not given for a parcel of private gentlemen in plain clothes to walk after; it was given to the Court in their official capacity, and I will not allow it to be carried before them without their robes'. The huissier was dispatched presto for them,

---

1. A 'folly' in the grounds built by a previous owner of the land.
2. William George Henderson, DCL Oxon. Principal 1852-1862.
3. Copies of portraits by F. Winterhalter (1806-1873).

and a female brought them in a bag. The Bailli and court people robed while a long silence had prevailed. The B: 'General, don't you put on your robe?' 'No, I am here in command of the troops as well as in my capacity as Lt. Govr. I do not intend to cover my uniform with a robe which I am to wear in my civil capacity. Now we can proceed'. Just as they got up the stairs the B. said: 'I am going to make a speech'. 'Why just now you said you had nothing to say.' 'Oh, I have thought better of it. I shall speak first.' 'Very well, then I shall present the portraits after the prayer.' Harriet told me that she perceived great ill humour on the countenances of both our magnates. The poor Bailli mumbled a few sentences which no one heard. The Dean's prayer was good and listened to, the Genl's short speech to the point tho he seemed nervous. It was a dull affair within and very gay without. Numbers of ladies came inside the square with tickets and lined the base of the building, while thousands stood outside in rear of the men. The salvo came upon us unexpectedly, though I had posted Captain Bailhache to give the signal to Major Holcombe . . . . The Principal was not inducted or given the keys or noticed by our ass of a Bailli".

By 1854 the college was in working order with prizes being given, to Sir John's delight, for he greatly believed in the value of competition and encouragement. He said then: "The first annual examination of youth at Victoria College. Neal, Leacock, remarkable boys. The Dean made a good introductory speech . . . . The Bailli twaddled bad English to each boy. The lads seemed highly delighted with their prizes, and the Principal and Masters very pleased with their progress. It is a glorious beginning, one which I tried to achieve in Sir Colin Halkett's time. It was instructive to see the Bailly, Godfray, and the opponents of the building of the college, the cocks of the walk, in an institution they had hindered twenty-five years, but which Sir James Reynett alone carried". By 1857 there were 170 boys there, and the Queen's medals were being given, and in 1861 "The General informed me that the Queen had granted a £10 prize for the best essay on English history . . . . the delivery of prizes was attended by all the gentry of Jersey. Young Clarke, a lad of 12 or 13, got four or five prizes, a prodigious little fellow[1] . . . . The Dean made an elaborate speech 'sentant la chandelle'[2] which he wound up by a phillipic against smoking". A few years later Clarke was still gaining prizes and Sir John went so far as to say that "The lads were more easy in their style and manner than those at Eton I saw with the Bishop of Winchester in Dr. H's time".

By 1869 Dr. Henderson had been replaced by Dr. Cleve, and an entry said: "Dr. Cleve, the Principal of the College, came to settle with me about the inkstand I offer as a prize; he agrees with me that a viva voce examination on English literature, done in my presence, and that of the Examiners on an essay written there and then, will be a capital trial of ability". This prize of an inkstand was awarded until the donor's death, and there was a set subject for the essay. In 1869 it was 'Industry' and the following year 'Athletics ancient and modern'. It was described as a candlestick inkstand, and some of the names of the winners are mentioned, Allen in 1869, Newton in 1871, Lindon in 1873, Hodges in 1874 and Johnson in 1876. It was always inscribed with the successful candidate's name and date, the engraving being done by Adams[3]. Sir John often entertained the winner at Belle Vue, and he asked that each boy should write to him a year later, and tell him of his career and success in life.

---

1. A correct assessment, as Clarke had a brilliant university career.   2. Indicates "showing off".
3. Adams of 5 Library Place.

Gymnastics, athletics and theatricals are all mentioned and so long as he was able to do so, Sir John attended all these occasions, rejoicing in the success of the college. When he was too old, his daughter Harriet used to attend in his place, and present his prize. In 1869 there was a match in which one of the great names of cricket appeared as a player, when "22 raws against south of England eleven, a lesson for the raws. Jupp[1], the best batter in England after Grace, made 170 last week in England. He, H. Jupp, made 42 and was in with eight players. He is the most cautious player I ever saw, his bat always down on guard, till he sees the ball astray, then his hits are splendid. He was caught out in the second innings by Le Cornu. Le Cornu and Newton are the two best in Jersey".[2]

An entry in 1855 said: "Sir George Sartorius[3] (asked) me: 'Who takes Elysée from Campbell?' I will put it into complete repair if the Admiral should take it on a long lease". Elysée, now demolished, was the house which Sir John had inherited from his mother, having been built by her nephew Frederick Dumaresq. Admiral Sartorius was the father of three most distinguished Victorians, all in the Army and two of them V.Cs., after whom one of the college houses has justly been named.

Sir John also took a keen interest in the Industrial School for Boys and the Orphanage for Girls, and indeed there is ground for thinking that he may have been the prime mover in the project to establish these homes. He offered prizes too, bibles, with work-boxes for the girls and sets of tools for the boys, each to be inscribed with the recipient's name. The main qualifications for these prizes was exemplary conduct, particularly truthfulness, and a thorough knowledge of the Sermon on the Mount, and one of the conditions was that "no other cause than misconduct so judged by legal decision shall ever deprive a child to whom the prize has been awarded from receiving such a prize". No surviving prizes from Sir John's lifetime have been found, but the concept continues under the title of Le Don Le Couteur, though now absorbed within the terms of the "Children's Benefit Funds (Jersey) Law 1949'. The form of the prizes has changed to conform with modern conditions, but it was sums bequeathed by Sir John which have enabled these prizes to continue to the present day. There are still a few examples of the workboxes and one, awarded to Clarisse d'Heurteaux in 1898, shows the type of box it was. It is in fine polished wood, about 12″ x 9″ x 6″, lined with silk, with a little plaque let in with the inscription. The original terms of the bequest stated that the box should have "every requisite for a domestic seamstress and materials to make up the sum", and in the case of the boys that the tools should be "the most useful working tools in his trade or calling". Sir John always attended the annual examination, with the Dean, and it was with pleasure and affection that he recorded in his diary these occasions and the good results shown by the children. What a kindly and imaginative benefactor.

The St. Aubin's school likewise afforded interest, and he, and later his daughter Harriet, were intimately connected with its administration, and in constant touch with the Master and his wife Mr. and Mrs. Paul.

An entry in 1859 records: "General and Mrs. Mundy opened the 'Jersey Soldier's and Seamen's Institute', the Bailiff and a number of ladies and gents present". On several occasions he gave lectures to the Working Men's Association. Once it was on the history

---

1. H. Jupp, twice played for England against Australia in 1876.
2. Cannot be identified with certainty, but probably either A. G. or S. C. Newton, and C. F. Le Cornu or Frederick Le Cornu. See Victoria College Register.   3. Admiral Sir George Sartorius, (1790-1885).

of music, once on 'The Rise, Progress and present state of Agriculture in Jersey', and this he proposed to have printed, giving the profits, "if there should be any" to the Association.

Museums naturally came within Sir John's scope of interest too, and indeed he was one of the founder members of La Société Jersiaise, though by the time of its inception, 1873, he was quite blind and too old to attend in any way. But we of La Société like to know that he was interested and would have approved of our aims.

The first effort to create a museum for Jersey was in 1836, and Mrs. Le Couteur recorded it in her diary; "I went to see the Museum in embrio (sic) and was much pleased with the most perfect Mummy I ever saw, with its two splendid coffins brought from the tombs at Thebes, by the late John Gosset Esq., together with other curious specimens of the early arts".

In that same year Sir John wrote to a Mr. James Hodges, offering for the "Jersey Museum several articles of North American Indian manufacture and use, collected by me while on service with the Outawa, Scioux and Five Nations tribes, on the Niagara frontier in 1813". They are detailed, but only the last item on the list is of local provenance, described as "vertebra of a mammoth found under an old hedge at Bocage in 1827". This Museum was destined to a very short life, and in 1852 there is an entry saying: "Attended a meeting of the National Gallery and Museum. Some very nice geological and botanical collections have been lent to it". This scheme was likewise of short duration. In 1865 there appears to have been a further effort, for a list survives of objects lent to "The Jersey Masonic Museum". Amongst the articles lent to this organisation is "A Magdalen by Tintoretto" which cannot now be identified, nor is anything known of it. The only exhibits of local interest in this list, which comprises largely objects of Canadian origin, are as follows;

Manuscript return of the French force which attacked Jersey under the Marquis de Rullecourt.[1]

Collection of fifty geological specimens of Jersey minerals.

Cases of white, red and spring wheat, part of a series of 104 varieties, which gained the Bronze Medal at the International Exhibition of 1851.

Heart of oak from the submarine forest below l'Etac in St. Ouen's bay.

Submarine pine and peat from Grève de Lecq.

The Channel Islands Exhibition of 1871 was largely agricultural in object, though it aimed to forward all branches of endeavour conducive to prosperity, and it achieved its aim. Though not far short of eighty, Sir John was a Vice President, and took as active a part as he could in its organisation. Its President was the then President of the Royal Jersey Agricultural and Horticultural Society, Colonel C. P. Le Cornu. He was in many ways Sir John's successor, for his interests were mainly agricultural and historical, and he later held the position of A.D.C. to the Queen. A glance at the catalogue of the Exhibition shows that Sir John lent fifteen pictures, as well as other items, and his daughter was one of the judges for classes of needlework and other handicrafts. Amongst the pictures lent were the Marriage at Cana, by Lucca Giordano, already referred to; one entitled 'Garden Party' which may be the pastel by Draper of a gay scene at Belle Vue, illustrated in this book. Another was described as 'Portrait of King Charles I in his studio'. This is referred to elsewhere in the diaries as being by Peters, and a small discoloured label in Sir John's

---

1. Now at the Museum of La Société Jersiaise.

R

handwriting, perhaps meant to go with the exhibit, says: 'Portrait of King Charles the Martyr presented to a loyal family of Jersey by the Prince of Wales, proclaimed King Charles II in Jersey, 17th February 1648-1649. The shot holes are from French musketry in the Royal Square 6 January 1781". Nothing more is known to explain this highly intriguing item.

On June 28th he recorded; "Channel Islands Exhibition at 12. The inauguration went off admirably notwithstanding the high wind. A very bright and beautiful scene. No contretemps. Music admirable". The next evening he dined with Colonel Le Cornu, then living at Trinity Manor, while he rebuilt his house La Hague Manor, and the following day; "First shilling day, an immense crowd, very orderly up to when I left,": and that evening, despite his age, he attended a ball of about two hundred persons, receiving the Governor, General Guy, and getting home at 3 a.m. There were entertainments for the crowds too, for a few days later, his grandchildren having come on a visit, he said: "Took the two girls to visit the exhibition to witness Herr Dobler's clever conjuring tricks, the cards raised out from the bottle the cleverest. Mr. Moss sang some comic songs, all very amusing, to 200 persons. I fancy that the chicks liked the conjuring best. Blanchie is very inquisitive". The Exhibition closed after a week of considerable success.

CHAPTER NINETEEN

GRAMPY

When something good, and of abundant vitality, is seen to lose its early momentum, to falter and finally to cease, the bystander is bound to feel sad: and this chapter, the last in the book and in the life of Sir John Le Couteur, cannot escape this element of sadness. He had had a long and eventful life, and lived it to the full, but as the years went by and he grew tired and old, he could no longer put into it and derive from it as much as he liked and, what was worse, the people of whom he was fondest slipped away one by one, to make the final journey ahead of him, and he was left almost alone. His wife Harriet, his only son Johnny, his daughter Mary, a grand-daughter, and two life-long friends, his nurse and housekeeper Ann Luce, and the Bishop of Winchester, all died during his closing years. We shall have to come to that later on. But let us first pause at a moment when his little regiment was still at full muster, and they enjoyed together something which formed a bond of union between them, the beautiful gardens of Belle Vue. They were something out of the ordinary.

Throughout his life Sir John visited every public garden and botanical or horticultural exhibition within reach, and on his visits to London his daughter-in-law Mai often accompanied him to pursue an interest they had in common. He was a keen exhibitor, and often a prizewinner in the flower, fruit and vegetable classes in shows in Jersey, noting about one of them: "a very good show of flowers and ladies". In 1868 his record read: "a remarkably good fruit show: superb pears: got 16 prizes, Cheal[1] nine of them for vegetables". He then "presided at a dinner given to General Guy and Baron Chazal at which forty gentlemen attended". In those days private houses grew more vegetables, and far more fruit than they do now. Belle Vue had prodigious crops of fruit, enough to supply not only the family and its expansive dinner-parties, but to send to friends, and even monarchs. In 1834 some Belle de Jersey pears were sent to William IV, who declared them to be the finest he had ever tasted, and choice specimens of La Duchesse d'Angoulême from the same garden were set on Queen Victoria's table in 1841. Nor, as Harriet's album of paintings shows, did they confine themselves to a few varieties. There are a bewildering number of species of pears and apples. Exotic fruits were raised as well. In 1871 there was a "heavy crop of oranges as large as fowls' eggs": and when the Duke of Cambridge was in Jersey "he tasted and much liked some strawberry grapes grown at Belle Vue, as the flavour was very peculiar, much admired by many persons . . . . I have taken the liberty to address a basket of them to the Queen".

It was the hey-day of Jersey nurserymen, and their nurseries were among the many Island attractions to which visitors were always taken. There was Langellier of Upper Clarendon Road, who in 1850 had "30,000 camellia stocks": and Saunders, already established and supplying trees in 1826, important enough to be pointed out to the Queen twenty years later, and fifteen years after that he provided a Miss Lane with 75 camellias

---

1. His gardener.

at 2s. each. Fennimore's Greenhouses at Bel Royal, shown as Graperies or Vineries on the old maps, were famous, and after examining the vines at Hampton Court Sir John wrote: "I wonder if mine is not more forward. The house is too lofty. They must come to Jersey to see Fennimore's vines in order to learn how to grow grapes, the finest in the world". It was said that Fennimore employed 35 men daily for 18 months in levelling and forming his terraces. "He has sent off many cwts of Black Ham and Muscat of Alix grapes: 12 dozen apricots yesterday and the day before. The plums, apples and pears, in addition to the superb show of grapes now there, were perfectly astonishing: a lovely alley of black jet fruit, and rich yellow muscats as a bower. Fennimore told us he pruned all his vines and thinned most of them. Darwin[1] agreed that he had never seen such a garden". This remarkable establishment seems to have changed hands by 1862 and become Pond's Greenhouses, and when Sir John took Emily Sumner to see them, Mr. Pond gave her "two cuttings from his 'Grand Master', for which seedling he got fifteen pounds". The garden at La Chaire, Rozel, was well known and justly admired. When Sir John took visitors to see it in 1853, he called it "Italy in Jersey". Its occupants were "Mr. Curtis, the author of the Botanical Magazine[2], and Mrs. Fothergill his daughter". Mr. Curtis had been "many years steward to the Duke of Newcastle, and had twenty-six thousand acres of arable land under his care; about £4000 a year in wages to pay. The Duke's income might be £30,000 a year clear". A friendship sprang up between Curtis and the Le Couteurs. Curtis was "surprised at the number of rare plants growing at Belle Vue, which he thinks the prettiest spot in the Island": and there were many visits to Rozel to see "his pretty rock garden". "Harriet and I drove to La Chaire to lunch with Mr. Curtis and Mrs. Fothergill. We were there till 5 looking at his lovely and rare plants, several of which he gave us". One day "he loaded our gig with pretty plants for the wilderness. A fine old patriarch of 83. Gave my wife his blessing and good wishes for the New Year, *and a kiss*".

Wherever he went, Sir John noticed gardens, and had in mind the re-stocking of his own. Even in high society he could draw conversation into this favourite channel. "Count Munster came in soon afterwards, with whom I had a conversation about gardening. They lose their laurels and laurestinuses in the winter, but save their dahlias, though left in the ground. How comes that?" How indeed, unless the Count was not very knowledgeable about his garden. Then we find a note: "To bring Evie the Cloth of Gold rose which she remembered I promised her. N.B. the mice do not attack snowdrops. Crocus in the centre of them might be safe?" One list, taken at random, of plants to be ordered from Chiswick and Kew, shows the extent of his knowledge, and the sort of garden he was aiming at; and how very early some of his introductions were.

Magnolia obovata
M. auriculata (Introduced from south-east United States in 1786)
M. tripetula (Introduced from east of United States in 1782)
M. fuscata (Introduced from China in 1789)
Lasippetalum solanum
Berberis coriacea (or coriarea?) (Introduced from Nepal in 1818)
Halesia parviflora

1. Not Charles Darwin.
2. This was Samuel Curtis, (1779-1860), Cousin of William Curtis (1746-1799), founder of Curtis' Botanical Magazine.

Terenia asiatica
Musada frondosa

There is a list of 73 types of geranium. A consignment of roses from a nurseryman in Caen included 60 varieties, none of which is well known now, such as Prince Albert, the Duchess of Kent and Elizabeth Fry. Seeds were received from India, Australia and "the penal settlement, Norfolk Islands", and raised with care at Belle Vue. Many actual bills survive, with the contemporary letter-heads of the nurserymen. A mole-catcher was employed at 19s. per annum. Sir John's rules, written in 1851, for taking camellia cuttings may be of interest to modern horticulturists: "Place a box or pot 8″ deep and water tight near the glass of a greenhouse. Bore 6 holes 4″ from the bottom. Fill bottom with 4″ of rough drainage, on which lay turf upside down. Firm. Lay on sifted soil. Plant cuttings. Fill the bottom up to the holes every morning with boiling water. No top water". In 1855 he wrote: "Made six layers of camellias. I peeled off the bark and rolled strips of spunge round the wound to absorb moisture. Fastened with lead wire": and in 1856: "I am almost convinced that camellias, oranges and lemons should not be repotted above once in two or three years; then only lifted and placed in additional fresh earth, and not shaken or disturbed: one part leaf soil from the valley, one garden soil and one old horse dung".

On 24th March 1842 he and Harriet celebrated their silver wedding with a family dinner. Her name, of course, appears throughout his diaries. She often went to England to stay with her daughter Mary, either on holiday, or to help with nursing in case of illness. She enjoyed normal health, often suffering from colds, as they all did, but nothing more serious than that. On the morning of 2nd February 1865 she was quite well, but news came in of the death of her brother's wife Jane. Though not at first appearing abnormally distressed, she must have had a stroke, for by the afternoon she was paralysed down the right side and could not speak. She never spoke again. She lived for eleven days, during which time her husband and daughter nursed her devotedly, and he kept an hour to hour account of her condition. Next day he handed in a telegram to Mr. Charles Gerhardi, Superintendent of the Telegraph Office in Church Street, sending for his son. Leeches were applied to the patient, gave relief and "tended to restore consciousness". She could recognise Sir John, and when Johnny wrote up his father's diary, as he sometimes did then, he said: "Sent for father, who soon got her quiet again. She knows him at once and seems to cling to her first love". John and Mary Sumner and Mai all came over. On 8th February the diary reads: "My beloved Harriet expired at a quarter past three, surrounded by her weeping children". For the next few days there are no entries, but on the 11th Harry Sumner arrived to attend his grandmother's funeral. "I thought it a great pity to bring him from his studies; however as his father especially wished it, I did not object. As he has spun once, it was running a risk of unsettlement from study to bring him all the way from Colchester for a form. I hope he may not be plucked in consequence. He is grown a fine youth. I hear there are thirteen inches of water in the vault intended for my dear wife's remains. I am going to see to its remedy myself". On the 13th February: "My beloved Harriet was attended to the grave by the Bailiff, Mr. Hammond; Mr. Bertram; Col. Le Couteur of St. John's; Cap. Anley; Col. Malet de Carteret and Col. Hemery as pall bearers. My three daughters and Ann Luce . . . ., and my nephews Dan Janvrin and George Charleton as mourners. All my cousins and relations, with a large concourse of the parishioners; Capt. Brayn and the Police officers; the schoolchildren, and many of the Principaux' ladies, old friends of my dear wife. The shops in St. Aubin were closed and the vessels in the harbour had their flags at half mast . . . . Now I am left, not quite desolate, but with dear unmarried Harriet. The universal respect which was shown to my dear wife's remains tells that her many virtues were fully appreciated. It was really a public display of regard". He gave a paten to St. Aubin's Chapel in her memory. Shortly after her death he wrote to the Queen, telling her how his wife had died and that during her illness, wishing to discover if she were conscious, he had taken to her two bright camellias. She had at once shown pleasure, smiled and pressed his hand. After her death he applied for leave of absence from Court duty, and went abroad with his daughter.

Poor Harriet the daughter had no real life of her own, being always a companion and almost a shadow of her parents. After her mother's death she developed more self-reliance, acting as hostess and housekeeper for her father, and coping with the large household and the entertaining. As a girl she had led quite a gay life, but with advancing years she devoted herself entirely to her father, and the Chapel and schools of St. Aubin's. The present Chapel was built only just before her death, and she had worked untiringly in its interests, as her father's diary of 1861 testifies: "My dear child's reward. She has been for many years the organist at St. Aubin's Chapel, very kindly, patiently and punctually attending, both to teach and to play. Our excellent friend the Rev. Samuel King, F.R.S., had given her a beautiful testimonial of his own appreciation of her services, by an exquisitely carved or turned light-house in ivory, executed by himself, which certainly could not be bought for ten guineas; from him far more precious. Now the congregation have subscribed, and this day the Rev. George Le Maistre, M.A., Minister at St. Aubin's Chapel, with a deputation of nearly fifty gentlemen and ladies, came at half past one o'clock to present to her a magnificent bible; one of the edition of twenty-five presented, or rather printed, for King William the 4th at an original cost of £35 each. It is superbly bound, of the most perfect type; altogether a glorious and worthy and holy testimonial! May God bless her with many years of improving piety, meekness and health, to meditate on its most sacred and righteous precepts. The company, after Mr. Le Maistre's address and Harriet's reply, which I hope to write here[1], partook of cake and wine, and departed much gratified on either part with the touching ceremony". The Rev. King's lighthouse now belongs to the daughter of Harriet's niece Evie.

There are still those who remember Sir John's daughter Harriet, among them Mrs. Webley, who was Mary Grier, and attended the St. Aubin's school. She remembers the Master, Mr. Paul, as being very strict with the children, and the Mistress, Mrs. Paul as "a sweet old lady who taught us needlework". She remembers Harriet Le Couteur in her latter years as a sweet old lady also, "very small, wearing a bonnet and using a stick . . . .; as she passed we would all curtsey to her, and she would smile and say: 'Thank you, children' ". They all loved her at the school, which she often visited and where a huge portrait of Sir John hung in the school room. She used to invite the children up to Belle Vue, where they were allowed to roam the gardens and pick up fir cones. When Harriet died she says "we all cried, and you could not see her coffin for violets". Her funeral was carried out with full Victorian pomp and circumstance, and my father used to tell me this tale about it. The cortège was very long and was proceeding at an excessively slow pace. It had a long way to go to St. Brelade's Church, and Colonel Philip Gosset Pipon, fearing it would be too

1. He did not do so.

much of a strain on all concerned, himself included, leaned out of his carriage window, and gave the cavalry command of: "Trrrot", whereupon all the horses, having Militia training, broke into a smart trot, and the procession reached the church in reasonable time.

Sir John's second daughter, Mary, with her growing family of three girls and four boys, came over to Belle Vue regularly and every visit gave him pleasure. One such time was in June 1875, but in the following September Mary died. Her daughter-in-law Rhoda Sumner, née Utterton, wrote a detailed account of her death, which does not reveal its cause, but shows, which is far more important now, how devoted her family were to her. Her father, with only two months of life left himself, was bowed down by the news, and as Harriet had gone over to help her brother in law, he was alone at the time. But many friends visited and comforted him. Mary's tomb is in Buriton churchyard, to the right of the entrance, under great beech trees, and within sound of her home, the old rectory. The inscription reads. "In memory of Mary Sumner, the beloved wife of Rev. J. M. Sumner, Rector of this parish, second daughter of Sir John Le Couteur, Viscount of Jersey". This remark may mystify those who do not know Jersey. On the other side is the inscription to her husband, saying that he was Rector of Buriton cum Petersfield for forty one years and died ten years after his wife.

On his only son, Halkett, or Johnny, Sir John pinned all his hopes. He once or twice lamented that Halkett and Mai took insufficient interest in Belle Vue, and he threatened to sell it, saying that there was little point in trying to keep the place up if they never came to live in it and had no children. He did not, at that time, know of the cruel diabetes, then incurable, which carried off his son at the early age of forty six. Halkett was still well and on service in 1863 when, at the wedding of the Prince of Wales, "Heath the photographer told me . . . . that the Prince of Wales told him that he would stop the carriage as they left after the wedding, so as to enable him to take a good photograph of the guard of honour, in the quadrangle, commanded by Halkett; which the Prince did, quite having his cool wit about him. Heath said that Halkett's sword came out bright and sharp at the salute, and the Prince and Princess elegant and quite clear and distinct. It was then that the Princess caught Halkett's eye and bowed a gracious smile to him". Not long after that he was considering selling out, to which his father was averse, although he had been offered £8400 for his Colonelcy. He did not in fact sell out, but went to Dublin with his regiment in 1866. By 1868 his health was deteriorating and he was advised to retire, to his father's mortification: "Colonel Low is to arrange with Dolly", he wrote, "about Hal's retirement. His fall from a pinnacle on which no Jerseyman had ever, that I know of, been perched; commanding the first battalion of the finest infantry in the world, which he was doing with credit to himself, so as to have got the sobriquet of Wellington[1]; to fall into the herd of miserable idlers about London, by medical advice! He may repent this step, if he recovers health, all the days of his life". A few days later, "Halkett planted a *Wellingtonia*[2] in the corner of the mound Vallette, where my old charger and Mimi were buried, a tree 5 feet high". Two days after that Halkett and Mai left for London. "The steamer had been neaped and did not pass Elizabeth Castle till 20 min. past seven. Hal is certainly better from his stay here. 1 did not consult 'Domestic Medicine' till he was gone. I now see that his disorder

1. He also resembled the Iron Duke, especially in profile, as a silhouette in the family shows.
2. Added later to the diary were the words: "It died".

is of a very alarming nature. Nothing but *care* of himself may prolong his life above three
or four years. Under such conditions he is justified in quitting the high position he has gained
as a competent Colonel of the Coldstream Guards, by selling out, to my infinite regret".
In 1870 a Dr. Donken in Sunderland was consulted, and Halkett went there for treatment
with his father. It is not clear why Sir John, already 76 years old, accompanied him rather
than Mai. Donken put him on a diet of three quarts of skimmed milk daily, with nothing
else at all. To pass the time they both fished, sketched and walked. It is not surprising to
hear that the patient, who was leading an energetic life, sometimes felt so hungry that he
disobeyed the doctor's orders, for which he was severely scolded. His father kept meticulous
details of his case and diet, and at first there was improvement and Donken was optimistic.

seen at Sunderland, 1870.

The diary is peppered with neat little sketches of the many rigs of sailing vessel, and some
steamers, which they saw in this busy port. After a few weeks in Sunderland they returned
to London, where Dr. Pavey was recommended to them as "being immensely skilled in
diabetes". Pavey declared that "skim milk alone will not support life for any length of time",
and Mai had her doubts about it. After Sir John returned to Jersey, she wrote to tell him
that Halkett was "giving up his treatment and returning to ordinary diet", which distressed Sir John very much. Poor Halkett struggled on against his infirmity, an invalid,
but well enough one day in 1871 to "dine with Mr. Roberts to meet Garibaldi's son".
After his next visit to Belle Vue, the diary makes sad reading: "The poor fellow was moved,
and is doubtful of ever seeing me again. Very miserable when he laments over his state.
Dear Mai tries her best to keep up his spirits". In January 1873 the diary records: "My
beloved only son . . . . died peacefully this morning at 11.55". There was a quiet family
funeral in Jersey, but poor Sir John could not face it. He designed a memorial window
for St. Brelade's Church. Too blind to see it, he was delighted when it was described for
him. The diaries do not tell us much about Mai, but Sir John much admired her good looks
and competence. Apparently she always arrived in Jersey accompanied by a parrot. In 1874
old Ann Luce died also, sorely missed by "the children she had so tenderly reared".

Sir John was devoted to his daughter Mary's seven children. The eldest was Harry
Le Couteur Sumner, and his career was followed with interest, especially when it seemed

that he would eventually inherit Belle Vue. Every detail of his childhood, his time at Eton and Cambridge and his ordination into the church were recorded by his doting grandfather. Soon after ordination, in 1869, he went to see Sir John: "looking very nicely and suitably dressed as a young clergyman, Curate to the Rev. Mr. Hoare at Godstone. He is busy with his Auntie Mai getting up his stores to supply his house, for which he is to pay £20 a year". Next year, "Harry was on the platform at Caterham . . . . to receive me . . . . Drove me to his snug home, a new house, one of a row recently built, kept as clean as a new pin by Mrs. Ball his housekeeper. A sitting room, two bedrooms, a dressing room to mine, snug little kitchen and outhouses. A bachelor's perfect quarter". Harry visited Belle Vue that year and preached in St. Aubin's Chapel. He also caught "eight mullet and whiting, which we had for dinner. Gave them cider cup, which they liked vastly . . . . Harry will be a fine preacher if he takes pains with his elocution. He has a noble voice, and sings and plays finely; a good hearted fellow, honest. Charley is a sweet boy, very intelligent and loves reading". Before long a letter arrived announcing Harry's engagement "to Rhoda Utterton, 21 in November. She is said to be a very amiable girl, and that they are the most united family in Surrey. If so, good stock!" In 1872 they were married in Winchester Cathedral, the bridegroom's father conducting part of the service. The bride wore a white corded silk dress trimmed with white satin, and a tulle veil. There were twelve bridesmaids, and the bouquets were supplied by Hilliers of Winchester. Sir John gave them a breakfast set and a silver tea service. The following year they had a daughter, the first of seven children, and came over to Jersey with the baby, "to my great delight". During their stay they went "to Elizabeth Castle to view the new harbour works there", paid visits, went for picnics and took a hand in hay-making. During this time Rhoda kept a diary for her infant in arms, who was not then old enough to write one herself. It reads: "Arrived in Jersey. Aunt Harriet met us in the carriage and we drove to Belle Vue, where we found great-grandpapa Le Couteur and the old family nurse, Mrs. Luce, at the door. Mrs. Luce took me in her arms and gave me to grandpapa to kiss, for he is very blind . . . . (He) gave me a beautiful present, a gold rattle with bells and whistle and a coral end. It is to be mine unless a little brother puts my nose out of joint. He gave it to me tied with a broad piece of blue ribbon, to be tied round my waist. It was given to his brother, who died, by his godfather Sir Sidney Gordon[1]. Then it was given to uncle Halkett Le Couteur, who died, and so it came to me . . . . Aunt Harriet's levée day: I was exhibited to Mrs. de Lisle[2], Miss Le Jette[3], Mrs. Houghton[4] and Mrs. G. Dumaresq[5] . . . . Mrs. Luce took nurse and me to Bocage, a little house close to Belle Vue which great-grandpapa Le Couteur built and lived in when he married. We saw the room in which Grandmama Sumner was born, and her nurseries . . . . I was exhibited after lunch to Sir Philip and Lady Guy (Governor of Jersey) . . . . In the evening I was taken down in my nightgown to see my great-great-great-aunt Mrs. Dumaresq[6], a dear old lady of 88 who says she has seen six generations of the family . . . . Went one day to see the Attorney General's wife[7] and baby, only a fortnight old. Every day I go downstairs with my rattle to see Grandpapa. I am very much amused with his white beard, and smile and talk to him; and sometimes he takes me in his arms, and is very pleased when he can just see my eyes a little. Today he gave Mamma a lovely ring with a diamond sur-

---

1. Sir Andrew Gordon. 2. Clara de Lisle, from Le Coin. 3. Le Geyt. 4. Née Margaret Le Geyt. 5. Née Rachel Le Geyt.
6. Aunt Sophia, widow of Thomas Dumaresq. 7. Julia Marett and her infant daughter.

rounded with rubies, and Papa £5. Aunt Harriet has given me a short braided frock . . . . When we reached the end of the pier we found there was no boat sailing until late in the afternoon, on account of Waverley having struck on a rock the morning before, in a fog 5 miles off Guernsey on its way from Southampton".

Two years later Harry became Rector of Yateley, and we read in the same diary: "Papa and Mamma have gone to London today from Yateley to stay with Auntie Mai Le Couteur at 85 Eccleston Square, to buy all the furniture for our house; and great-grand-papa Le Couteur has promised them £50 for a turkey carpet, and other things". In December 1875 a son, Bernard, was born, who eventually inherited the Jersey estate, and if Sir John knew of this, as seems possible, it would have been a solace to him in the closing days of his life. The diary goes on to record the baptism of Bernard John Le Couteur Sumner, and that "dear great-grandpapa Le Couteur, who is very ill just now, is one godfather, at his own wish . . . . He gives a salver worth £20". On the 24th December comes the inevitable: "Dear great-grandpapa Le Couteur passed away to his rest early this morning, a blessed change for him especially, 82 years of age and growing gradually blind for many years". Poor Harry died at the age of forty, and never inherited Belle Vue. On Harriet's death in 1895 his widow and children came to live there, and entered into the religious and educational life of the village of St. Aubin, in the true Le Couteur tradition.

Devoted as he was to all his grandchildren, there is little doubt that "darling Evie" was Sir John's favourite. In her he saw a reincarnation of his wife and his daughter, and her quiet, gentle and entirely feminine nature appealed to his chivalrous heart. She was christened Eveline Sophy Jane, and as a baby was "as plump as a partridge, nice blue eyes, a high forehead and pretty little mouth". Her immediate recognition of her grandfather always delighted him, and he never failed to take "sugar plums for Evie" when he went to Buriton. He once wrote of her: "as fair as a lily, with fair auburn curls. She is all life and animation, yet very docile and tractable". On one of her visits to Jersey, he said: "We all went to a picnic in Portelet Bay, where the children were greatly delighted, shrimping and sliding down the grassy slope. Evie seemed never to tire, and followed me over the rocks. When the little dear saw me coming in for dinner, she ran down the hill and to the shore to help me thro' the soft sand".

At about that time her grandfather wrote her a charming letter, telling her about the

The EXPRESS at Corbière, 22. Sep. 1859.

wreck of the Express off Corbière rocks[1] in September 1859, and giving a sketch to explain it, very similar in composition to Ouless' well known engraving of the catastrophe. He says; "I must thank you for your pretty letter before I tell you a very sad story, told me by a sweet little girl about your age. She was a passenger with the Express steamer, which left Victoria Harbour last Tuesday at seven in the morning; it was bright, calm and beautiful. Her Mamma had gone below, and her little sister was with her, sitting close to the steersman. The Captain, to show his skill, had gone close to the rocks by Elizabeth Castle and off Noirmont point . . . . She heard a sailor come up to the steersman and say: 'You are going too near the rocks'. 'I know what I am about', he replied. Another sailor came and said the same. They were just then passing by the Corbière rocks, where you and Harry and all of us had a pic Nic. Still the helmsman stood on, closing to the land, when little Miss Marechaux felt the vessel bump, and graze along the rocks; then she gave another bump, then went on. Her Mamma rushed up and told them to keep close to her. A gentleman who had been asleep in the fore cabin rushed up on deck, calling: 'The vessel is sinking; my berth is under water'. The Commander, for he was not the proper Captain, would have steered on for Guernsey. If he had been allowed to do so, every soul would have been drowned in half an hour. A brave little Captain, our Harbour Master, however, took command of the vessel, made the steersman put the vessel about and ran her on shore, just below the big rock where we dined. Little Miss Marechaux told me she saw one boat with five or six men, go off, cowards leaving all the women behind. Two others, by jumping into another boat too suddenly, were thrown out and drowned. A Mr. Godfray, who lives on the hill[2], came down and helped them to land, going up to his shoulders in the waves, and carried the little girls ashore. When the harbour Master saw men trying to get into the boats, he siezed a pistol and said that he would shoot any man who attempted to get in, till all the women and children had been saved; half the ship being then under water, and the Rev. Mr. Penny perched up in the fore shrouds. He was supposed to have been drowned, but was the first to bring the bad news to St. Aubins. Everybody except the runaways behaved well, not a cry. We all drove to see the wreck on Thursday mng. before breakfast; there she lay, sad to see. I must now answer your questions. Don José and Mrs. White had their cup of oats this morning; Mrs. Grey has a very pretty daughter as grey as herself. Beau is in disgrace, tied up for having deserted. Flora has one pretty little black and white boy. I think I told Harry how Pussy killed the snake. Punch is fat and lazy". A letter full of incident, and with news of familiar horses, cows, dogs, cats and hens, which must have delighted the little girl.

At the age of ten she accompanied him to Jersey alone: "When we got to Portsmouth the train for Southampton had just left, so we had to wait two hours. I took Evie to the dockyard . . . . . showed her the Britannia and Victory, the former commanded in bygone days by her great uncle Philip Pipon, and the latter by her great-uncle Philip Dumaresq. She was greatly delighted with the visit". They had a smooth passage as far as Guernsey, but then a gale blew up: " . . . . I opened the bull's eye in her berth, when a sea broke in and splashed us both; at which she merely laughed and said: 'Oh, Grampy'; when I screwed it down securely. The wind blew so violently after we entered the Albert Pier that the steamer could not be backed to her station by Victoria Pier, and we were nearly two hours in the

1. Corbière lighthouse was not built until 1874.
2. By the quarry, site of the desalination plant now being erected.

harbour before we could land. The waves were beaten down and blown away like dust, as I have seen in an Atlantic storm". During her stay she was given French and English lessons, and piano lessons from Mr. de Vos. When in London he took her to all the sights, famous buildings, art exhibitions, botanical gardens and the zoo: remarking, after two hours at the Kensington Museum, that the child did not seem to be very strong as she had become wearied: his own age then being 75.

In 1870, when Evie was nineteen, Ernest Utterton came into her life. He was the son of the Bishop of Guildford, and brother of Rhoda, who was soon to marry Evie's brother Harry. On his next visit to England, Sir John wrote: "Ernest Utterton came to dinner to make my acquaintance: a very pleasing, pleasant young man, I hope to become an ernest (sic) loving husband to my darling Evie". Next day at a picnic, "Ernest and Evie were gone 'solus cum sola' for a stroll along a meandering stream". In January 1871 they were married and lived at Frensham Rectory, where Sir John soon went to visit them. In October Evie had a daughter, and "I wrote a few lines of congratulation to Ernest on *my* being a great-grandpapa, patriarchal honour. We drank to the health of Miss Utterton in her great-great-grandpapa Sir John Dumaresq's Old Sherry of 1802". Next spring Evie and Ernest brought the baby over to Belle Vue[1], in time for Evie's twenty-first birthday, which was celebrated by a large family party. There were twenty-six members present, and it was lamented that six others had been unable to come. They had asparagus soup; salmon; lamb; chicken; ham; mutton; vol au vent; calf's head; curry; ducklings; crab; chantilly cake; velvet cream and jelly. The last reference to Evie in the diaries is in 1874, when Sir John sent her the cow Polly: "Archdeacon Utterton consecrated Bishop of Lichfield at Lambeth. All our young people there . . . . Polly to the steamer Brittany at 5.50 a.m., for Evie, at Frensham Rectory, Farnham, a beautiful cow, to calve May 25th".

Charles Maunoir Sumner was born in 1856, and a year later Sir John described him as "a cherub, just like what his mamma was at a month old". At his christening his elder brother, then twelve, proposed his health, wishing him to grow up like "those two jolly fellows" his uncles, Charles Sumner and Halkett Le Couteur: "which set us all in a roar. He is a very sharp boy, though a little idle". Young Charles inherited his grandmother's stammer, but as it is only once mentioned we may hope he outgrew it. By 1869, when he was thirteen, he and his sister could beat grandpapa at billiards. In 1866 he was at Mr. Stowe's Academy at Petersfield, collected stamps, had a good school report, and had "given up smoking". He went on to Haileybury, and in 1874 said he wanted to go into the army; and his grandfather wrote to the Duke of Cambridge to obtain him a commision in the 60th Rifles[2].

Mary Sumner had four more children, the youngest of whom, Campbell was only ten when she died. In 1857 Emily Maude was born, and in 1859 Mary Blanche. At the age of seven Emily Maude received her grand-father when he came on a visit and her parents were out for the day. "Maudie did the honours and got me a cold dinner, as I would have nothing cooked, and made me take wine 'as it would be good for me'. We all had a merry, hungry tea". At eight, he said, she had a very intelligent mind, and he gave her lessons in French and Arithmetic. A little later, "she can play duets with her governess", and "when Maudie played her pieces to me I was struck with her fine touch and the feeling with which she

---

1. A photograph of the patriarch was taken with his first great-grandchildren.
2. King's Royal Rifle Corps.

plays". He gave her "one of her grand-mamma's lockets, which she preferred to a cameo brooch, or to one of amethyst set with small pearls". A little later: "Maudie beat W. H. Ridley, M.A. at billiards, 100-90. It is bad for her to play so well". In 1875, when she was eighteen, and on a visit to Belle Vue, he wrote: "Maudie has little appetite. Is she in love?" After his death, in 1882, she married Lothian Bonham Carter, whose family lived in the big house adjoining Buriton Church. At the wedding the village was richly decorated with floral arches. The parishioners of Petersfield gave her a locket with pearls, and those of Buriton a gold bracelet set with sapphires and diamonds. For her wedding she wore a white satin dress with ruching and pearl embroidery, and the ceremony was performed by her brother and brother-in-law, the incumbents of Yateley and Leatherhead. The generous gifts she received from the joint parishes seem to show that after her mother's death and her elder sister's marriage she acted as hostess to her father, and carried on her mother's work in the parishes.

Blanche, two years younger than Maude, was fair. Grandfather was staying with the family on her seventh birthday, and wrote: "Parents as well as the children gave her presents which she received quite prettily before breakfast, giving a kiss to each donor. Mine, two sixpences. She wore a wreath of roses and spring flowers .... She reads admirably". Then later: "Blanche is very industrious and painstaking. Whether she has the gift of soul-stirring, she is yet too young too show". Soon after that the two children came over to stay at Belle Vue, and Grampy arranged music lessons for them with de Vos, and "took Maudie and Blanchie to de Gruchys for dresses and gloves". But in 1875 poor Blanchie died, aged only sixteen, perhaps from tuberculosis, though no cause is given.

Robert Algernon was born in 1860, and was said to be "pale, but very good". A note in a letter-book reads: "To Mary Sumner, on the unexpected birth of a boy", but it does not explain in what way the birth was unexpected.

George Julian Campbell was born in 1866, and first appears when his grandfather went to the Savings Bank to open an account in his name, a commendable habit of grand-fathers. At the age of two he received a menagerie from Grampy. Like all the others, he paid many visits to Belle Vue, and enjoyed all that it had to offer.

Sir John's activities continued up to a very short time before his death. Increasing blindness had limited his scope for some years, and towards the end his diaries are difficult to decipher, except when he asked members of the family, principally Harriet, to make the entries for him. In 1872 he underwent an operation for glaucoma, by Dr. Critchett of 21 Harley Street. He made the journey to London alone, one wonders how, and stayed with his son and daughter-in-law. He was told that he "must submit to chloroform, and have his chest sounded". Next day, after starvation but for a spoonful of brandy, "a couch was prepared for me in Mai and Hal's bedroom, on which I was laid. Both the doctors found my pulse in a quiescent state. Mr. Clover said: 'Would I object to having my hands tied, as jerking motions of the arms might disturb the operator' .... He then put a slip knot of a powerful bandage round the iron of the bedstead, took a double turn round my right wrist, passed it under my right thigh, took a double turn and knot over my left wrist, passed it over my left thigh, and fastened it to the iron of the bedstead. Mr. Clover then applied the chloroform to my nose, which I inhaled freely. In about seven minutes I was insensible. Mr. C. performed the operation on both eyes in about the same time, of which I was wholly un-conscious .... My eyes were immediately bandaged with wet plegets of cold water and lint.

The after sensation was what I experienced when a boy . . . . after a fight, with a pair of black eyes". How like the old warrior, at his advanced age and in circumstances of unavoidable anxiety, to take mental notes of all that happened and chronicle them afterwards in his diary. Two days later the doctor pronounced him cured. He was up and about, and in ten days was back in Jersey. How much benefit he had from this operation is doubtful. He continued to write his diaries at intervals, but the handwriting is erratic, varying between good and almost illegible.

By 1872 he had held the position of A.D.C. to the Sovereign for no less than fifty-two years, becoming the senior member of that corps in 1860, and the post of Adjutant General to the Jersey Militia for nineteen years. He knew the time had come to give them both up, and sent in his resignations, wondering as he did so who would succeed him in each capacity. Soon afterwards, on the 25th July 1872, the honour of Knighthood was conferred upon him, but he had less than four years in which to enjoy it, and one could wish that it had come earlier. He was, pathetically, too far on his way to comprehend it fully, and the old fires which glowed through his autobiography, for that is what his diaries are, would have fanned to a triumphant flame if he had been ten years younger. As it was, he says very little about it. Friends called in dozens, but their congratulations were accepted apathetically. His household were equally dumbfounded. Norris, the coachman, "congratulated me on being Sir John. All the other servants seem wonderstruck". It was too late for all of them. The Colonel was the Colonel. They did not want anything different.

His last illness was mercifully short, lasting a fortnight only. Three doctors were in constant attendance, his friend and godson Dick de Lisle, Dr. Smith and Dr. Godfray, nevertheless he suffered much pain in the closing days of 1875, and of his life. He died on Christmas Eve. By his own wish, his funeral was simple, but a great concourse attended it.

The wheel had come full circle. The span of this eventful life had closed. The voices of Queen Victoria's reign, which have echoed down the varied corridors of these archives, are still, and we can no longer hear their intonation, their laughter, their message, except by reading through the endless, closely-written pages. But there is one small voice which, to me at any rate, has broken through the sound barrier separating the worried world of today from those golden years of long ago, and if you listen carefully you can hear it also. It is the voice of a child, at Buriton. Grampy had been telling him stories, and the voice asked: "Grampy are you going to talk any more?" He was told one more tale, a story to end stories, and then he said to his Mamma:

"How nicely Grampy tells stories".

GENEALOGY OF THE ROYAL FAMILY
to illustrate the Le Couteur papers.

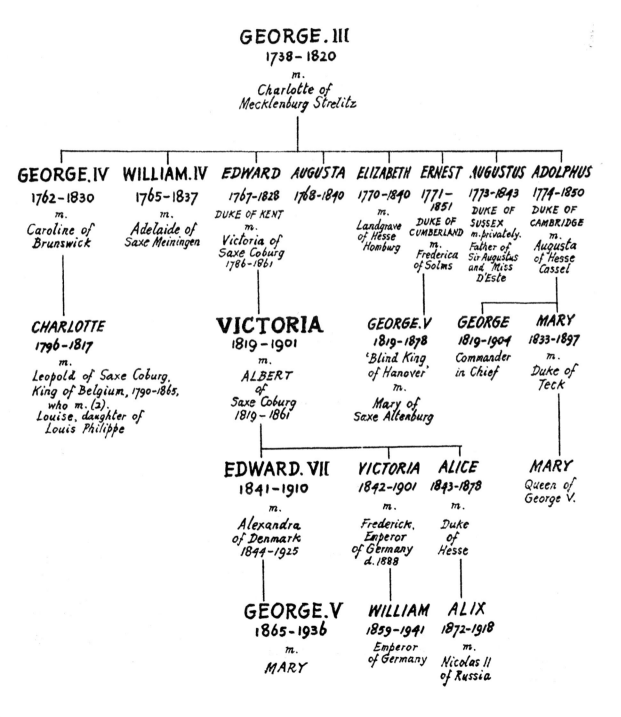

GEORGE. III
1738 - 1820
m.
Charlotte of
Mecklenburg Strelitz

GEORGE. IV	WILLIAM. IV	EDWARD	AUGUSTA	ELIZABETH	ERNEST	AUGUSTUS	ADOLPHUS
1762-1830	1765-1837	1767-1828	1768-1840	1770-1840	1771-1851	1773-1843	1774-1850
m.	m.	DUKE OF KENT			DUKE OF CUMBERLAND	DUKE OF SUSSEX	DUKE OF CAMBRIDGE
Caroline of Brunswick	Adelaide of Saxe Meiningen	m. Victoria of Saxe Coburg 1786-1861		Landgrave of Hesse Homburg	m. Frederica of Solms	m. privately. Father of Sir Augustus and Miss D'Este	m. Augusta of Hesse Cassel

CHARLOTTE
1796 - 1817
m.
Leopold of Saxe Coburg,
King of Belgium, 1790-1865,
who m. (2).
Louise, daughter of
Louis Philippe

VICTORIA
1819 - 1901
m.
ALBERT
of
Saxe Coburg
1819 - 1861

GEORGE.V
1819-1878
'Blind King
of Hanover'
m.
Mary of
Saxe Altenburg

GEORGE
1819-1904
Commander
in Chief

MARY
1833-1897
m.
Duke of
Teck

EDWARD. VII	VICTORIA	ALICE
1841-1910	1842-1901	1843-1878
m.	m.	m.
Alexandra of Denmark 1844-1925	Frederick, Emperor of Germany d. 1888	Duke of Hesse

MARY
Queen of
George V.

GEORGE. V	WILLIAM	ALIX
1865-1936	1859-1941	1872-1918
m.	Emperor of Germany	m.
MARY		Nicolas II of Russia

GENEALOGY OF FRENCH ROYALTY
mentioned in Chapter 10.

LOUIS XIII
m. Anne of Austria

LOUIS XIV
1638 – 1715
m. Marie Thérèse
of Spain

PHILIPPE
DUC D'ORLÉANS. "Monsieur".
1640 – 1701
m.(2) Charlotte of Bavaria, grand-
daughter of the Winter Queen, sister of
Charles I.

PHILIPPE
REGENT
1674 – 1723
m. Françoise Marie, his cousin

LOUIS
1703 – 1752
m. Auguste Marie of Baden

LOUIS PHILIPPE
1725 – 1785

LOUIS PHILIPPE
"ÉGALITÉ"
1747 – 1793

LOUIS PHILIPPE
1773 – 1850
KING OF FRANCE 1830 – 1848
m. Marie Amélie of Naples

FERDINAND
DUC D'ORLÉANS
1810 – 1842
m. Hélène of Meck-
lenburg Schwerin

LOUISE
second wife
of Leopold I of
Belgium, uncle
of Queen Victoria

LOUIS
DUC DE NEMOURS
1814 – 1896
m. Victoria of
Saxe Coburg Gotha

FRANÇOIS
PRINCE DE JOINVILLE
1818 – 1900
m. Françoise
of Braganza

HENRI
DUC D'AUMALE
1822 – 1897
m. Caroline
of Bourbon

ANTHOINE
DUC DE MONTPENSIER
1824 – 1890
m. Louise,
Infanta of Spain

PHILIPPE
COMTE DE PARIS
1838 – 1894
m. Isabelle, d. of
Duc de Montpensier

GASTON
COMTE D'EU

FERDINAND
DUC D'ALENÇON

ISABELLE
m.
Comte de Paris

ANTHOINE

GENEALOGY OF THE LE COUTEUR and JANVRIN FAMILIES.

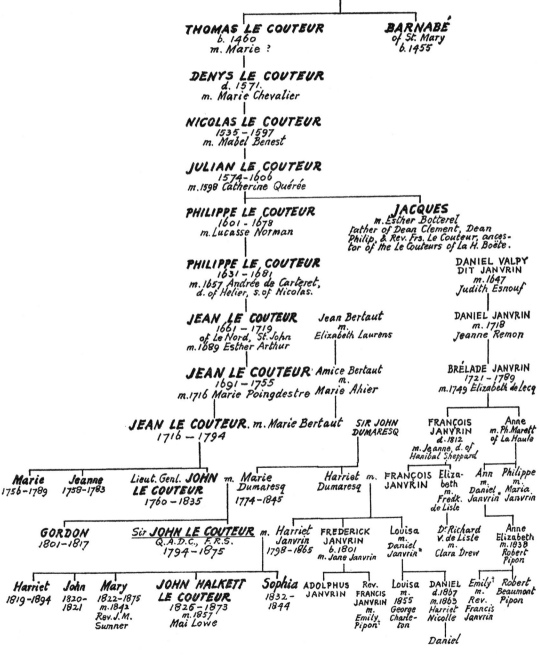

GENEALOGY OF THE DUMARESQ FAMILY
to illustrate the Le Couteur papers

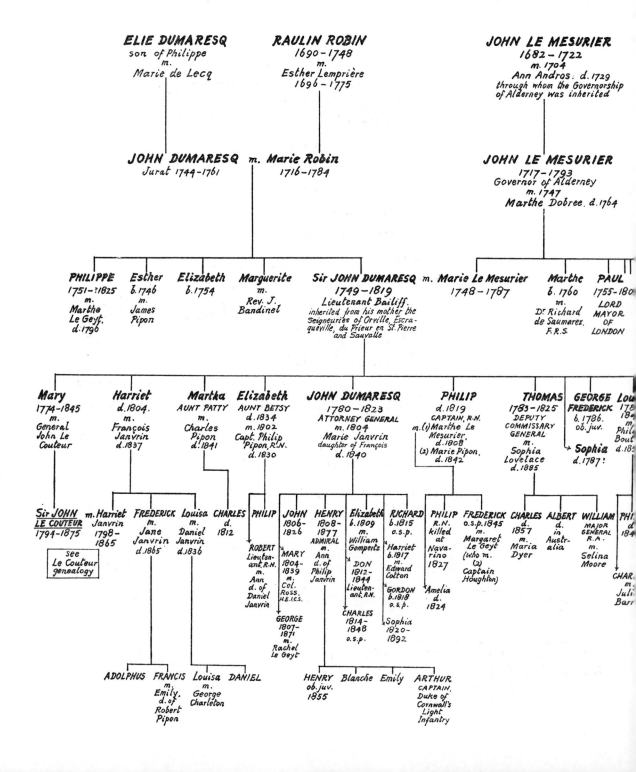

GENEALOGY OF THE SUMNER and UTTERTON FAMILIES

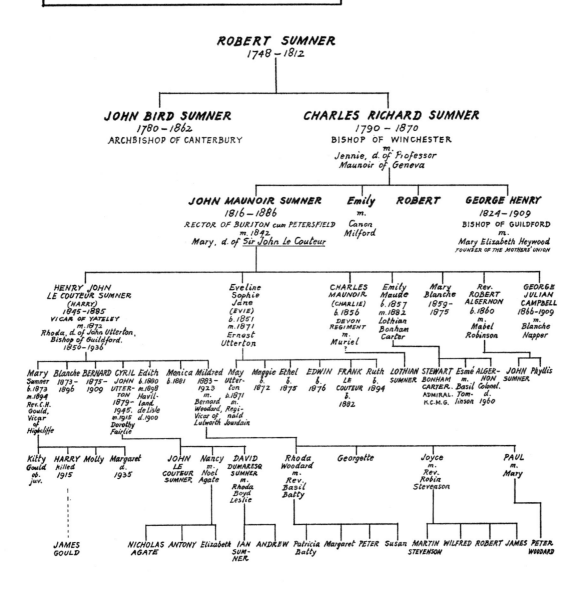

APPENDIX. B.

HERALDRY

For those readers who are interested in heraldry, a short note on the arms used by the families in question may be of value.

In 1859 J. B. Payne produced his Armorial of Jersey which first appeared in instalments, in paper covers, and on rather inferior paper. These early copies are even more rare now than the finished product, printed in two volumes. The families of Le Couteur, Dumaresq and Janvrin all appear in the Armorial, and there was a certain amount of correspondence with J. B. Payne, whom Sir John found "a very pleasant and intelligent young man". He ordered the Armorial from F. G. Collas, of St. Martin's House, who acted as Payne's agent and prepared many of the illustrations for the work. Like so many heads of local families he offered to "give my plate", that is to pay the cost of an engraving of his arms for inclusion in the book. He said in a note, referring to a letter to J. B. Payne "Le Couteur arms may be quartered with Bisson and those of Andrée de Carteret". The next year he wrote: "I have received the proof of the coat of arms with scallop shell; will subscribe to the printing of MS of King Charles II's proclamation[1], signed by Jean Le Couteur[2], if he will let me know the probable cost". He offered to send Payne an article on agriculture and militia in Jersey. However, by 1860, the correspondence had taken on a sterner note. Payne wrote and accused Sir John of having failed to pay the 3 guineas for two parts each of nos. 5 and 6, and asked for payment "as a personal favour". This stung the meticulous Sir John into replying "No applications have been made to me, instead of the many you speak of . . . . I have never paid a debt due by me as a personal favour to any man, ... If you will direct your agent to let me know on what dates the first and the last of the many applications for payment were made, I shall immediately look through . . . . my annual receipts . . . . ".

Some years later, on a visit to Rouen, Sir John went to the Bibliothèque, and reported, " . . . . there are Le Cousturier, Le Coustre, Cousturier, all of the same origin[3], only the first have the doves, which are our old crest. There are Dumarests and a host of good Jersey names to be seen". The plate in the Armorial indeed shows three crests, the dove and olive branch, called "Le Couteur, ancient"; a sword and a sprig of laurel for Le Couteur, the crest used on the signet ring, note paper, book plates, etc; and thirdly "a blackbird proper for Bisson". This intrusion of the Bisson family is curious. Payne gives the wife of Philip Le Couteur, born 1601, as Lucasse Bisson, whereas manuscripts in the collection make it certain that her name was Lucasse Norman, and no Bisson alliance appears at all. Other insular families have been known to claim Bisson ancestry on the flimsiest pretext. As a result of this the plate given in the Armorial shows a quartering of Bisson and de Carteret. with a shield of argent, three bends azure, impaled with the arms of Janvrin, but with no representation of Dumaresq at all. When cut in stone, (that is without colour), these arms appear to be the same as those of the Deanery. But these are red on silver and those of Le Couteur blue on silver.

---

1. See Payne's Armorial, p.176.   2. Unidentified. He signed Jean Le Cousteur but the 's' has been omitted in all subsequent texts.
3. This may be mistaken, v, Chapter 1, page 1.

The arms of Dumaresq are three escallop shells, and they appear on a signet ring, impaling Le Couteur, which belonged to General Le Couteur. The same combination was used on the clasp of the bible, referred to elsewhere, which Sir John had rebound in 1857. The arms of Janvrin were seen on a splendid Jersey silver coffee pot which belonged to the family. The initials ISP scratched on the base identified it as having belonged to Jeanne (not Elizabeth as stated in the Armorial) daughter of Hannibal Sheppard, who married François Janvrin; they were the grandparents of Harriet, Sir John's wife. This gives the coffee pot a date of 1770-80. A clear impression of a seal entitled "from an old family seal which I believe belonged to my father before he went to India" shows three owls quartered with the trefoils of Payn, as used by the Le Couteurs of La Hougue Boëte, distant collaterals.

It would seem that heraldry was not one of the subjects to which Sir John turned his meticulously accurate mind.

APPENDIX. C.

LAND TRANSACTIONS

A very large number of family documents have survived, but the earliest concerning family property is dated 1679, and records the sale of a field, Le Clos de St. Jean et Ste. Marie. (J.301).

This was when the Le Couteur family was still rooted in St. John's parish. As already stated, General Le Couteur sold Les Buttes in St. John, and bought Belle Vue in St. Brelade, from his future father in law, at the time of his marriage to Marie Dumaresq in 1793, which included two houses, presumably Belle Vue and the old house at Le Bocage just to the west, with the surrounding lands, the whole costing 64 quarters of wheat rente.

The earliest reference to the property of which one can be reasonably sure, is in 1734, when Jean Valpy dit Janvrin fils Jean fils Jacques sold it to Thomas Le Vesconte and Sara Esnouf his wife; fourteen years later they sold it to Philip Le Vesconte and in 1775 he in turn sold it to Philip Dumaresq fils Jean. Philip Le Vesconte had a right to the property by *retrait lignager* (ancient claim due to relationship) from Philip Le Sueur fils Philip, who had acquired it from Pierre Le Vesconte fils Pierre.

At Belle Vue Dumaresq involved himself in party politics, being his brother's supporter as leader of the Magot party. He printed newspapers with strong party bias, and left Belle Vue in 1790, going to St. John's parish. In 1792 he sold the property to his elder brother Jean.

Philippe Dumaresq had added Le Bocage (old house) by buying it from Elizabeth Le Bas, daughter of Elie Le Bas and Elizabeth Alexandre in 1787.

The Le Vesconte ownership is recorded for all time in Le Clos d'Esnouf (named after the wife of Thomas Le Vesconte) of two vergées. The total land measurement in 1870 was about 45 vergées, which would have ranked as quite a big farm at the time. More land was added gradually, including Dell Farm, west of Le Bocage, and Allencot, opposite on the north of the road.

Sir John's wife inherited property in St. Aubin. In 1839 she sold to Richard Satchwell a garden bordering La Rue du Moestre (Market Hill) on the understanding that the pump and well on the side road were not included. The purchaser had the right to use the pump but had to contribute to its upkeep. However six years later Satchwell was declared bankrupt and the property reverted to Harriet, who was *tenant après décret* (holder after foreclosure). She sold it to William Dart a builder, frequently employed at Belle Vue.

After Sir John's death the estate passed to his daughter and, at her death, to her various nephews and nieces, of whom the eldest, Harry, had pre-deceased her. Thus naturally the large farm which he had built up became fragmented, and the surrounding houses all now have different owners.

During the German Occupation the house was for a second time occupied by foreign troops, and a contemporary diary[1] records, "1941. Oct. Dossie and Cyril Sumner have fifteen soldiers billeted on them. . . . . November. The troops in the Sumners' house are quite calmly taking his precious wood (stored for this winter) to build up huge fires in the rooms they occupy". Soon after this the owners, Mr. and Mrs. C. Sumner, moved to another house. Hence the miracle of the survival of these papers.

---

1. Kept by the author's mother, Mrs. J. J. Collas.

APPENDIX. D.

DISTINCTIONS GAINED BY
COLONEL JOHN LE COUTEUR AFTER THE APPEARANCE
OF THE FIRST EDITION OF HIS BOOK ON WHEAT.

Membre Honoraire de la Société d'Agriculture de l'Arrondissement d'Avranches, France, 1838.

Diplôme de Membre Correspondant de la Société Nantaise d'Horticulture, France, 1838.

Member of the Society of Arts, 1838.

Médaille d'Honneur, Académie de l'Industrie Agricole, Manufacturière et Commerciale, Paris, 1838.

Diplôme de Membre Titulaire, Société Française de Statistique Universelle, 1838.

Diplôme de Vice-Président de l'Institut d'Afrique à Paris, 1840.

Silver Medal of the Highland and Agricultural Society of Scotland, 1840.

Fellow of the Royal Society, 1843.

Honorary member of the Philadelphia Society for Promoting Agriculture, United States of America, 1844.

Honorary and Corresponding Member of the New York State Agricultural Society, U.S.N.A., 1850.

Prize Medal, Grand Bronze, Class 3, International Exhibition, 1851.

(Details taken from the second edition of the book).

	LIEUTENANT GOUVERNEUR *Lieutenant Governor*	BAILLI *Bailiff*	PROCUREUR GÉNÉRAL *Attorney General*	AVOCAT GÉNÉRAL *Solicitor General*	DOYEN *Dean*
1802	Maj. Gen. **ANDREW GORDON** *1797–1806*	**HENRY FREDERICK** Lord Carteret 1776–1826 Sir **JOHN DUMARESQ** *Lieutenant Bailiff* *1802–1816*	Thomas Le Breton to 1816	Josué Pipon 1800–1810	Edouard Dupré D.C.L. to 1823
1806	Lieut. Gen. **GEORGE DON** to 1809				
1810	Lieut. Gen. **GEORGE DON** to 1814			John Dumaresq to 1817	
1814	Lieut. Gen. Sir **TOMKYNS HILGROVE TURNER** to 1816				
1816	Lieut. Gen. **H.M. GORDON** to 1821	**THOMAS LE BRETON** Lieutenant Bailiff to 1826			
1817			John Dumaresq to 1823	François Jean Le Couteur (of La Hougue Boëte) to 1824	
1821	Sir **COLIN HALKETT**, K.C.B. to 1830				
1823					Corbet Hue, D.D. to 1837
1824			Thomas Le Breton, jr. to 1848	J. W. Dupré to 1848	
1826		Sir **THOMAS LE BRETON** to 1831			
1830	Maj. Gen. **W. THORNTON** to 1835				
1831		Sir **JOHN DE VEULLE** to 1848			
1835	Maj. Gen. **A. CAMPBELL**, C.B. d. 1838				
1838	Maj. Gen. Sir **E. GIBBS**, K.C.B. d. 1847				François Jeune D.C.L. to 1844
1847	Maj. Gen. Sir **J. REYNETT** to 1852				
1848		Sir **THOMAS LE BRETON**, jr. to 1857	Jean Dupré to 1866	Jean Hammond to 1858	
1850					William Corbet Le Breton, M.A. to 1888
1852	Maj. Gen. **F. LOVE**, C.B. to 1857				
1857	Maj. Gen. **G. MUNDY** d. 1860				
1858		**JEAN HAMMOND** to 1880		Robert Pipon Marett, to 1866	
1860	Maj. Gen. **P. DOUGLAS** to 1863				
1863	Maj. Gen. **BURKE CUPPAGE**, R.A. to 1868				
1866			Robert Pipon Marett to 1880	Geo. Helier Horman to 1879	
1868	Maj. Gen. **P. GUY**, C.B. to 1873				
1873	Maj. Gen. **W. NORCOTT**, C.B. to 1878				
1878	Maj. Gen. **LOTHIAN NICHOLSON**, C.B., R.E. to 1883				
1880		Sir **ROBERT P. MARETT** to 1884			

GLOSSARY

TERMS WHICH MAY BE UNFAMILIAR TO READERS.

ASSISE D'HERITAGE. Bi-annual sitting of the heritage division of the Royal Court, at which Seigneurs owing suit of court attend and answer when called. Advocates also renew their oaths.

ASSISE D'HERITAGE DINNER. Dinner given after the Assise d'Heritage to members of the Court and Seigneurs at the expense of the Crown. Now abolished.

BAILIFF, (Bailli). Chief Magistrate of the Royal Court and President of the States Assembly. For a long period non-resident Bailiffs left most of their duties to their Lieutenant Bailiffs.

BAILIWICK. Territory under the jurisdiction of the Bailiff. That of Jersey comprises the Island and its outlying reefs. That of Guernsey includes Alderney, Sark and the smaller islands.

BANON. The period from September to May approximately, during which land was fallow, and animals were permitted to roam on commons and unenclosed fields, is referred to as Banon.

BRANCHAGE, VISITE DU. Annual parochial inspection of roads to see that they are kept clear of encroachments, or of overhanging branches below a stipulated height. The Royal Court makes a Visite Royale, on the same lines, to two parishes annually.

CAMPAGNE. Open unenclosed land.

CHARITE, LA. Funds administered by the parish church authorities for the relief of the poor.

CHARLOT. One of the two political parties in Jersey in the eighteenth century, also called the Laurel Party. They were the Conservatives.

CLAMEUR DE HARO. A legal remedy designed to stop unlawful interference with, or damage to, property, without the delay that would be involved in applying for an order of the Court. The reciting of a set formula by the complainant on the scene of the infringement in the presence of witnesses acts as an immediate injuction to the alleged wrongdoer to stop what he is doing until the grievance has been referred to the Court.

COMITE DES CHAUSSEES. States Committee for the upkeep of harbours. Now altered in scope.

COMMUNE. Part of a fief over which certain owners of properties situated on that fief, had the right of pasturage, and of cutting turf, fern and other vegetation.

CONSTABLE. (Connétable). Civic head and police chief of each parish, elected by his parishioners, and having a seat in the States.

CORVEE. Duty of able men to work on the roads for several days annually. Now abolished.

DENONCIATEUR. Vicomte's assistant in executing the orders of the Court.

DEPUTY. (Député). Representative in the States of a parish, or division thereof.

ELIZABETH CASTLE. Fortress in St. Aubin's Bay, mainly built 1590-1600, with subsequent additions.

EXTENTE. List of Crown revenues, produced at irregular intervals. Those known and published range from 1274 to 1749.

FIEF. Mediaeval term for land granted, by king or overlord, over which the recipient had certain rights as well as obligations. These varied greatly.

GAVELKIND. Form of land tenure controlling division of property. The term is not known in Jersey, but was used by Sir John when commenting on the division of land amongst heirs.

GOVERNOR. The Sovereign's representative in Jersey from 1471-1851, since when a Lieutenant Governor only has been appointed. His main duty was as commander in chief of the troops stationed in the Island, and the Militia.

GREFFIER. Clerk of the Royal Court. There is now a Greffiier for the States Assembly also.

GROSNEZ. A castle in the N.W. of Jersey, already in ruins in the mid fifteenth century.

JURAT. (Juré Justicier). One of twelve honorary judges of the Royal Court, formerly elected for life, and now subject to an age limit. They also had seats in the States until the Reform of 1948.

LOGE AU GREFFE. Any member of the States may require a matter to be 'logé au Greffe' so that a delay occurs before it comes up for discussion, during which time members may give the subject more mature consideration.

MAGOT. The progressive political party in Jersey in the eighteenth century, also called the Rose party. v. Charlot.

MARTELLO. Defensive towers built round the south, west and east of Jersey, between 1780-1800, on a Mediterranean pattern.

MILITIA. Compulsory unpaid service, starting in the early fourteenth century and ceasing to exist only after World War II.

MONT ORGUEIL. A mediaeval fortress on the east coast of Jersey, begun in the reign of King John, and superseded by Elizabeth Castle in the seventeenth century.

PARISH. One of twelve municipal and ecclesiastical divisions of Jersey, of unknown but very ancient origin. They are, St. Brelade, St. Clement, St. Helier, St. John, St. Lawrence, St. Martin de Grouville, St. Martin le vieux, St. Mary, St. Ouen, St. Peter, St. Saviour, and Trinity.

POT. A liquid measure of four pints.

PRINCIPAL. Landowner in a parish paying more than a certain amount of parish rate.

RENTE. An annual charge due on a property, similar to a mortgage originally payable in kind, usually in the form of wheat, but later with the option of paying in cash. This was assessed on the market price of wheat each year, but eventually a fixed monetary equivalent was introduced.

ROYAL COURT. Court of Justice, composed of Bailiff and twelve Jurats. In certain criminal cases a jury may be empanelled.

ST. AUBIN'S FORT. Fortress in St. Aubin's Bay of seventeenth century origin.

SEIGNEUR. Lord or holder of a fief. They were sometimes referred to by the name of their fiefs, such as 'Monsieur de Rozel', or colloquially just 'Rozel'.

STATES. Local Parliament, consisting of twelve Jurats, twelve Rectors, twelve Constables, with the addition in 1856 of twelve Deputies. Alterations in its composition have since been made.

TRESOR, LE. Parish fund for the upkeep of the Church.

VENDUE DES FROMENTS. Sale of wheat rentes due to parish funds.

VERGEE. Local land measurement. $2\frac{1}{4}$ vergées=1 acre.

VICOMTE. (Viscount). Executive officer of the Royal Court, and Coroner.

VRAIC. Seaweed, used as a fertiliser, either fresh, or burnt and applied in the form of ash.

VUE DES CHEMINS. v. Branchage.

VUE DE VICOMTE. The inspection of a site, conducted by the Vicomte by direction of the Court, in the course of legal proceedings concerning the site. After the 'Visite' the Vicomte reported his findings to the Court.

INDEX

T